Everyday Writing

Gregory R. Glau
Northern Arizona University

Chitralekha De Duttagupta
Utah Valley University

PEARSON

Boston   Columbus   Indianapolis   New York   San Francisco   Upper Saddle River
Amsterdam   Cape Town   Dubai   London   Madrid   Milan   Munich   Paris   Montréal   Toronto
Delhi   Mexico City   São Paulo   Sydney   Hong Kong   Seoul   Singapore   Taipei   Tokyo

Editor in Chief: Eric Stano
Senior Acquisitions Editor: Matthew Wright
Assistant Editor: Amanda Dykstra
Senior Development Editor: Marion B. Castellucci
Director of Marketing: Megan Galvin-Fak
Marketing Manager: Kurt Massey
Senior Supplements Editor: Donna Campion
Executive Digital Producer: Stefanie Snajder
Digital Editor: Robert St. Laurent
Production/Project Manager: Barbara Mack

Project Coordination, Text Design, and Electronic Page
    Makeup: Integra
Cover Design Manager: John Callahan
Cover Designer: Base Art Co.
Cover Photo: Steven Chiang/Shutterstock
Manufacturing Manager: Mary Fischer
Senior Manufacturing Buyer: Mary Ann Gloriande
Printer/Binder: QuAD/Graphics Taunton
Cover Printer: Lehigh-Phoenix/Hagerstown

Credits and acknowledgments borrowed from other sources and reproduced, with permission, in this textbook appear on the appropriate page within text or on pages 513–514.

Library of Congress Cataloging-in-Publication Data
Glau, Gregory R.
  Everyday writing / Gregory R. Glau, Chitralekha De Duttagupta.—1st ed.
    p. cm.
  Includes bibliographical references and index.
  ISBN 978-0-205-73659-1 (alk. paper)
  1. English language—Rhetoric.   2. Report writing.   I. Duttagupta, Chitralekha De.   II. Title.
  PE1408.G5587 2011
  808'.042—dc23

                                                    2011036215

10 9 8 7 6 5 4 3 2 1—QGT—14 13 12 11

PEARSON

ISBN-10:   0-205-73659-9
ISBN-13: 978-0-205-73659-1

To my late parents, Narayan Chandra De and Gayatri De (nee Bhoumick),
who were with me throughout in spirit
as I worked on this book.
—Chitralekha De Duttagupta

To my brother Gordon, his wife Pat, and their family,
and to my sister Gretchen, her husband Pete, and their family,
with love.
—Gregory R. Glau

Contents

Note to Students   xxv

Preface   xxx

About the Authors   lii

PART 1 Building Your Reading and Writing Skills   1

Chapter 1 College Reading and Writing   2

What Is College Reading and Writing?   4

Keeping a Journal   4

Critical Thinking   5

   Questions for Critical Thinking   6

Critical Reading   7

   Questions for Critical Reading   7

"How to Excel in Your College Classes" by Raychelle Fox   9

Critical Writing   11

   Questions for Critical Writing   11

Critical Thinking, Reading, and Writing: Visual Texts   13

   Questions for Critical Thinking, Reading, and Writing
   about Visuals   13

MyWritingLab™   15

Chapter 2 Strategies for Reading   16

Pre-reading Strategies   17

Main Idea Strategies   18

   Read the Introduction and Conclusion First   19

   Skim the Passage or Visual   20

*"The Melting Pot Continues: International Students in America" by John
Carter   21*

"What Is Yoga?"   22

   Focus on Headings and Subheadings   24

"The Basics of Global Warming"   24

   Read and Understand Individual Paragraphs   25

   Make a Simple Outline   27

"How Much Do Ski Helmets Help?" by Denis Cummings   27

Supporting Details Strategies   28

Higher-Level Reading Strategies   29

Annotate the Text   30

"Acai Berries and Acai Berry Juice—What Are the Health Benefits?"
by WebMD   30

"Special Olympics: Who We Are"   32

Analyze the Text   33

Post-reading Strategies   34

Responding to the Text   34

Dealing with Difficult Vocabulary   34

MyWritingLab™   35

Chapter 3   **The Reading–Writing Connection: Summary and Response   36**

Introducing Summary   38

Introducing Response   38

Using a Summary   41

Effective Summaries   42

Summary of Qualifications for a Job Application   42

Job Description Summary   43

MyWritingLab™   44

Chapter 4   **The Writer's Situation: Purpose, Audience, and Context   45**

Purpose: Why Am I Writing?   46

Critical Thinking Activity: Questions to Determine Purpose   47

Writing to Inform   47

Writing to Evaluate   48

Writing to Persuade   48

Writing for Other Purposes   49

Audience: For Whom Am I Writing?   50

Critical Thinking Activity: Ask Yourself Questions about
Your Audience   51

Context: What Is the Background for My Writing?   53

Critical Thinking Activity: Ask Yourself Questions about the Reader's
Context   53

The Writer's Rhetorical Situation: A Summary   54

MyWritingLab™   55

Chapter 5 **Using Writing Strategies and Appeals   56**

Strategies for Effective Writing   57
  Description   58
  Narration   59
  Informing   60

  "MP3 Players"   61

  Classification   62
  Definition   63
  Argument   64

  "Give a Cheer to the Experimental AIDS Vaccine and Then Get Back to Work—An Editorial" by The Plain Dealer Editorial Board   65

  Cause and Effect   66

  "Professor Gives Reasons Why Students Fail" by Shamekila Quarles   67

  Comparison and Contrast   68

  "Why British Students Are Opting for American Universities" by Karen Gold and Sarah Cassidy   69

  Writing Strategies at a Glance   70
Persuasion Strategies: Ethical, Emotional, and Logical Appeals   72
  Ethical Appeal: The Appeal to Credibility   73
  Emotional Appeal: The Appeal to Feelings   74
  Logical Appeal: The Appeal to Reason   75
  Persuasion Strategies at a Glance   76
MyWritingLab™   77

Chapter 6 **Getting Started with Your Writing   78**

The Writing Process   80
Invention or Discovery Strategies   80
  Listing   81

  Student Writing: Kim Lee's Listing   82

  Freewriting   83

  Student Writing: Kim Lee's Freewriting   83

  Clustering   84

  Student Writing: Kim Lee's Clustering   84

  Cubing   86

  Student Writing: Kim Lee's Cubing   86

Using Several Invention Strategies 87

MyWritingLab™ 88

Chapter 7 **Drafting Your Paper 89**

What Is the Best Genre for Your Audience and Purpose? 90

Do You Need Research? 91

   ❓ Critical Thinking Activity: Ask Yourself Questions about
Research 91

Outlining Your Paper 92

Student Writing: Kim Lee's Outlining 93

Drafting 94

Drafting Your Thesis Statement 95

Student Writing: Kim Lee's Thesis Statement 97

Drafting Effective Paragraphs 98

Student Writing: Kim Lee's Draft Paragraph 99

Drafting Topic Sentences in Your Paragraphs 99

Student Writing: Kim Lee's Draft of Two Paragraphs 100

Using Transitions in Writing 101

Transitions at a Glance 102

Student Writing: Kim Lee's Transitions 103

Parts of an Essay 104

Introduction 104

Body 104

Conclusion 105

MyWritingLab™ 107

Chapter 8 **Revising Your Writing 108**

Why Is Revision Important? 109

Strategies for Revising 111

Peer Review 111

Effective Revision 112

   ❓ Critical Thinking Activity: Ask Yourself Questions for Peer Review 114

   ❓ Critical Thinking Activity: Ask Yourself Questions for Revision 116

Student Writing: Kim Lee's Revision 116

Editing Your Work 117

Student Writing: Kim Lee's Editing 117

Proofreading Your Work   118

Student Writing: Kim Lee's Proofreading   118

Publishing Your Work   119

Student Writing: Kim Lee's Final Draft   119

MyWritingLab™   122

PART 2 Writing for a Purpose   123

Chapter 9 Writing to Share Experiences: Using Description and Narration   124

The Writer's Situation   125

Sharing an Experience through Description and Narration   126

"7 Ways to Be Worth Following on Twitter" by JoLynne   126

"Graffiti Wall" by Rick Steves' Europe   128

WRITING ASSIGNMENTS   130

Writing Assignment One: Share a Positive Learning Experience   130

Writing Assignment Two: Share a Work Experience   130

Writing Assignment Three: Share a Cultural Experience   131

Optional Multi-Modal Assignment: Tweeting   131

Critical Thinking Activity: Ask Yourself Questions before You Write   131

Invention and Discovery Activities   132

Student Writing: John Wick's Freewriting   132

Writing a Thesis Statement for Your Shared Experience   132

Organizing and Writing Your First Draft   133

Student Writing: John Wick's Draft Introduction   134

Revising: The Key to Effective Papers   135

Student Writing: John Wick's Peer Reviewed Draft   135

Writing Style Tip: Addressing Readers   136

Critical Thinking Activity: Ask Yourself Questions before You Revise   137

Revision Checklist for Your Shared Experience Paper   138

Student Writing: John Wick's Final Draft   138

Critical Thinking Activity: Ask Yourself Questions for Reflection   140

Readings That Share Experiences   141

"Don't Call Me a Hot Tamale" by Judith Ortiz Cofer   141

"My Global Study Experience in Dubai: Strong Self-Image Key to Negotiating in Distant Cultures" by Brittney L. Huntley   143

"The Good Immigrant Student" by Bich Minh Nguyen   147

MyWritingLab™   149

Chapter 10   **Writing to Inform: Using Examples and Process Explanation   150**

The Writer's Situation   152

Informing through Example and Process Explanation   152

"Privacy Mode Helps Secure Android Smartphones" by Science Daily   153

WRITING ASSIGNMENTS   155

Writing Assignment One: Provide Information on Campus Resources   155

Writing Assignment Two: Your College Classes and Your Career   155

Writing Assignment Three: Report on Local or Campus Cultural Events   156

Optional Multi-Modal Assignment: Construct a Brochure for an Art Exhibit or Museum   156

Critical Thinking Activity: Ask Yourself Questions before Writing   157

Invention and Discovery Activities   157

Student Writing: Christie Rosenblatt's Brainstorming   158

Writing a Thesis Statement for Your Informative Text   159

Organizing and Writing Your First Draft   159

Student Writing: Christie Rosenblatt's Introduction   161

Revising: The Key to Effective Papers   161

Student Writing: Christie Rosenblatt's Peer-Reviewed Draft   161

Writing Tip: Quoting a Source   163

Critical Thinking Activity: Ask Yourself Questions before You Revise   163

Revision Checklist for Your Informational Paper   164

Student Writing: Christine Rosenblatt's Final Draft   165

Critical Thinking Activity: Ask Yourself Questions for Reflection   167

Readings That Inform   168

"Cultural Differences? Or, Are We Really That Different?" by Gregorio Billikopf   168

"Developing Global Skills for an International Career" by Debra Peters-Behrens   170

"What's Next for NASA?" by Charles Frank Bolden Jr.   173

MyWritingLab™ 175

Chapter 11 **Writing to Analyze: Using Division and Classification   176**

The Writer's Situation   178

Analyzing through Division and Classification   179

"Climate Change Impact" by the Environmental Protection Agency   179

WRITING ASSIGNMENTS   181
  Writing Assignment One: Analyze Local Opportunities to Volunteer   181
  Writing Assignment Two: Analyze the Requirements of Your College Major   181
  Writing Assignment Three: Analyze Local Attractions   183
  Optional Multi-Modal Assignment: E-mail   183
    Critical Thinking Activity: Questions to Ask before You Start   183

Invention and Discovery Activities   184

Student Writing: Rebecca Tremble's Listing   184

Writing a Thesis Statement for Your Analysis   185

Organizing and Writing Your First Draft   185

Student Writing: Rebecca Tremble's Introduction   187

Revising: The Key to Effective Papers   188

Student Writing: Rebecca Tremble's Peer-Reviewed Draft   188
    Writing Style Tip: Using Bullet Points   189
    Critical Thinking Activity: Questions to Ask before You Revise   190

Revision Checklist for Your Analysis   191

Student Writing: Rebecca Tremble's Final Draft   192
    Critical Thinking Activity: Questions to Ask as You Reflect on Your Writing   194

Readings That Analyze   196

"Women Less Likely Than Men to Fake Soccer Injuries, Study Finds" by Thomas H. Maugh II   196

"Language Change" by National Science Foundation   198

"The Truth About Lying" by Judith Viorst   200

MyWritingLab™ 205

Chapter 12   **Writing to Explain Why: Using Cause and Effect   206**

The Writer's Situation   208

Explaining Why Using Cause and Effect   209

"Five Surprising Reasons You're Gaining Weight" by Kathleen Zelman MPH, RD, LD   211

WRITING ASSIGNMENTS   214
   Writing Assignment One: Explaining Why a Relationship "Works"   214
   Writing Assignment Two: Explaining What Makes a Good Employee   214
   Writing Assignment Three: Explaining Good School Performance   215
   Optional Multi-Modal Assignment: Blogging   215
      Critical Thinking: Questions to Ask before You Start   216

Invention and Discovery Activities   216

Student Writing: Shannon Owens' Cluster Diagram   216

Writing a Thesis for Your Cause and Effect Paper   217

Organizing and Writing Your First Draft   218

Student Example: Shannon Owens' Introduction   219

Revising: The Key to Effective Papers   220

Student Writing: Peer-Reviewed Draft   220
      Writing Style Tip: Awkward Sentence Construction   221
      Critical Thinking: Questions to Ask before You Revise   222

Revision Checklist for Your Cause and Effect Paper   223

Student Writing: Shannon Owens' Final Draft   223
      Critical Thinking Activity: Questions to Ask as You Reflect on Your Writing   226

Readings That Explain Why   227

"The Surprising Causes of Those College Tuition Hikes" by Kim Clark   227

"What Is Keeping Italian Men at Home?" by Claudio Lavanga   229

"Illegal Immigration to the United States" by Udall Center for Studies in Public Policy   231

MyWritingLab™   235

Chapter 13   **Writing to Evaluate: Using Comparison and Contrast   236**

The Writer's Situation   238

Evaluating Using Comparing and Contrasting   239

"Shutter Island" by Roger Ebert   239

WRITING ASSIGNMENTS 243

Writing Assignment One: Evaluating a Web Site 243

Writing Assignment Two: Evaluating a Local Art Exhibit or Live Performance 244

Writing Assignment Three: Evaluating a Friend's Work Ability in a Reference Letter 244

Optional Multi-Modal Assignment: Tweeting 244

Critical Thinking Activity: Questions To Ask before You Start 245

Invention and Discovery Activities 245

Student Writing: Ken Bishop's Freewriting 246

Writing a Thesis for Your Evaluation 247

Organizing and Writing Your First Draft 247

Student Writing: Ken Bishop's Introduction 250

Revising: The Key to Effective Papers 250

Student Writing: Ken Bishop's Peer-Reviewed Draft 250

Writing Style Tip: Sentence Combining 252

Critical Thinking Activity: Questions to Ask before You Revise 252

Revision Checklist for Your Evaluation 253

Student Writing: Ken Bishop's Final Draft 253

Critical Thinking Activity: Questions to Ask as You Reflect on Your Writing 256

Readings That Evaluate 258

"Best Places to Work 2010" by Christina Breda Antoniades 258

"Travel for Distinction: UGA Study Abroad Offers Many Options" by Eva Vasquez 261

"Community College vs. University" by Jeren W. Canning 265

MyWritingLab™ 267

Chapter 14 **Writing to Persuade: Using Multiple Strategies 268**

The Writer's Situation 269

Persuading through Multiple Strategies 271

"In Praise of the F Word," by Mary Sherry 271

WRITING ASSIGNMENTS 274

Writing Assignment One: Solving a Problem at Your School 274

Writing Assignment Two: Solving a Consumer Problem 275

Writing Assignment Three: Solving a Community Problem   275

Optional Multi-Modal Assignment: E-mail   275

　☒ Critical Thinking Activity: Questions to Ask before You Start   275

Invention and Discovery Activities   276

Student Writing: Marcie Willen's Brainstorming   277

Writing a Thesis Statement for Your Persuasive Text   277

Organizing and Writing Your First Draft   279

Student Writing: Marcie Willen's Introduction   282

Revising: The Key to Effective Papers   282

Student Writing: Marcie Willen's Peer-Reviewed Draft   282

　☑ Writing Style Tip: Making Sure Pronouns Have a Clear Reference   283

　☒ Critical Thinking Activity: Questions to Ask before You Revise   284

Revision Checklist for Your Persuasive Paper   284

Student Writing: Marcie Willen's Final Draft   285

　☒ Critical Thinking Activity: Questions to Ask as You Reflect on Your Writing   287

Readings That Persuade   288

"Early Education Pays Off: High-quality Programs Are Good for Kids, for Society and for Business" by James Fish   288

"Your Brain on Languages" by Chris Livaccari   291

"Parent's Guide to Childhood Immunization" by the Centers for Disease Control   293

MyWritingLab™   296

PART 3 Special Writing Situations   297

Chapter 15   **Conducting Effective Research   298**

Developing a Research Topic   299

Choosing Your Own Topic   299

Narrowing Your Research Topic   300

Finding and Evaluating Sources   302

Library Research   302

Consult Your Librarian   302 ● Visit Your Library's Web Site   303
● Familiarize Yourself with the Library Database   303 ● Locate a Book   303
● Locate Periodicals and Specialized Indexes   305 ● Locate Encyclopedias and Dictionaries   308

Internet Research   311

Use Web Search Engines   311 ● Use Keyword Searches   312 ● Evaluate Web Sites   314

Guide to Evaluating Web Sites by Domain 315

Conducting Field Research 316

Observation 316 • Interviewing 317 • Conducting Surveys 317

Planning Your Research 319

Taking Notes 319

Incorporating Sources in Your Writing 321

Quotation 321

Summary 322

Paraphrase 322

Integrating Sources in Your Research Paper: Strategies at a Glance 324

MyWritingLab™ 324

Chapter 16 **Documenting Your Sources 325**

Avoiding Plagiarism 326

Examples of Plagiarism 326

Tips for Using Sources Properly 327

What Is Documentation? 327

MLA Documentation Format 328

MLA In-Text Citation Examples 329

MLA Works Cited Examples 333

Student Writing: Research Paper Formatted in MLA Style 338

APA Documentation Format 346

APA In-Text Citation Examples 346

APA References Examples 347

Student Writing: Research Paper Formatted in APA Style 351

MyWritingLab™ 360

Chapter 17 **Writing Timed Essay Examinations and Making Oral Presentations 361**

Writing Timed or In-Class Essay Examinations 362

Step 1: Determine What the Examination Asks You to Do 363

Examination Planning Checklist 363

Step 2: Plan Your Time 364

Time Planning Checklist 364

Student Writing: Debbie Larsen's Timed Writing Examination 365

Brainstorming and Planning 365 • Writing a Draft 366 • Final Revising and Editing 367

Making an Effective Oral Presentation 368

MyWritingLab™ 370

Chapter 18 **Writing E-mail, Job Application Letters, and Résumés 371**

Writing Effective E-mail 372

E-mail Etiquette in College 372

E-mail in the Workplace 372

Writing an Effective Job Application Letter 373

🗹 Critical Thinking Activity: Questions to Ask before Writing a Job
Application Letter 374

Writing an Effective Résumé 378

Using a Working Résumé 378

Creating a Résumé for a Job Application 379

What to Include 379 • *How to Format a Résumé 380*

MyWritingLab™ 383

PART 4 Handbook of Grammar and Style 385

Chapter 19 **Nouns 387**

Proper Nouns 388

Common Nouns 388

Grammar Spotlight: Countable and Uncountable Nouns 389

MyWritingLab™ 390

Chapter 20 **Verbs 391**

Verb Tenses 391

Verb Forms 392

At a Glance: Verb Tenses and Verb Forms 393

Grammar Spotlight: Irregular Verbs 394

Split Infinitives 395

MyWritingLab™ 396

Chapter 21 **Pronouns 397**

Types of Pronouns 398

At a Glance: Pronouns 399

Grammar Spotlight: Subject and Object Pronouns; Singular and Plural
Pronouns 400

MyWritingLab™ 401

Chapter 22 **Adjectives, Adverbs, Prepositions, Conjunctions, and Interjections 402**

Adjectives 402
At a Glance: Adjectives 403
Adverbs 403
At a Glance: Adverbs 404
Prepositions 405
At a Glance: Prepositions 405
Grammar Spotlight: One Preposition, Several Functions 405
Conjunctions 408
At a Glance: Conjunctions 409
Interjections 409
MyWritingLab™ 410

Chapter 23 **Articles 411**

Definite Article 411
Indefinite Articles 411
A or An? 412
Grammar Spotlight: Using Articles Correctly 412
MyWritingLab™ 417

Chapter 24 **Sentence Elements 418**

Subjects and Predicates 418
Grammar Spotlight: Identifying the Subject 419
Direct and Indirect Objects 419
Transitive and Intransitive Verbs 420
Sentence Complements 421
Dependent and Independent Clauses 422
Passive and Active Voice 424
Active Voice or Passive Voice? 424
Active Voice 424 • Passive Voice 425
Changing from the Active Voice to the Passive Voice
and Vice Versa 425
Active to Passive 425 • Passive to Active 425
MyWritingLab™ 426

Chapter 25 **Types of Sentences 427**

Simple, Compound, and Complex Sentences 427

Declarative, Exclamatory, Imperative, and Interrogative
Sentences   429
MyWritingLab™   430

Chapter 26   **Sentence Agreement   431**

Subject–Verb Agreement   431
Singular Subject–Singular Verb   431
Plural Subject–Plural Verb   432
Grammar Spotlight: Special Types of Subjects   432
Pronoun–Antecedent Agreement   433
Grammar Spotlight: Pronoun Problems   434
MyWritingLab™   437

Chapter 27   **Improving Your Sentences   438**

Comma Splice   438
Run-on Sentence   440
Sentence Fragment   441
Dangling Modifier   441
Revising Dangling Modifiers   442
Misplaced Modifiers   443
Revising Misplaced Modifiers   443
Double Negatives   444
At a Glance: Words Indicating Negation   444
Transitions   445
Transitions between Sentences   445
Transitions between Paragraphs   445
Transitional Expressions   446
At a Glance: Transitions   446
MyWritingLab™   448

Chapter 28   **Periods, Question Marks, and Exclamation Points   449**

Period   450
Question Mark   452
Exclamation Point   455
MyWritingLab™   456

Chapter 29 **Commas   457**

MyWritingLab™ 459

Chapter 30 **Other Punctuation Marks   460**

Semicolon 460
Colon 462
Apostrophe 464
Hyphen and Dash 465
Quotation Marks 468
Parentheses 470
Ellipsis 472
MyWritingLab™ 473

Chapter 31 **Abbreviations and Numbers   474**

Abbreviations 474
Grammar Spotlight: Abbreviations in College Writing 476
Numbers 476
MyWritingLab™ 478

Chapter 32 **Spelling   479**

Homonyms 479
Confusing Word Pairs 481
Capitalization 483
MyWritingLab™ 487

Chapter 33 **Word Choice   488**

Synonyms 489
Antonyms 490
Prefixes and Suffixes 492
    At a Glance: Prefixes 492
    At a Glance: Suffixes 494
Contractions 495
    At a Glance: Contractions 495
Colloquialisms 497

Sexist Language   497

Solving the Problem of Sexism in Language   498

At a Glance: Avoiding Sexist Terms   499

Wordiness   500

MyWritingLab™   504

Chapter 34   **English Idioms   505**

At a Glance: Idioms in English   505

MyWritingLab™   512

Credits   513

Index   515

Readings: Rhetorical Strategies Contents

Narration

"Gandhi" (Paragraph)   59

JoLynne, "7 Ways to Be Worth Following on Twitter"   126

Rick Steves, Graffiti Wall, "New Years in Germany" and "Christmas in Paris"   128

Judith Ortiz Cofer, "Don't Call Me a Hot Tamale"   141

Brittney L. Huntley, "My Global Study Experience in Dubai: Strong Self-Image Key to Negotiating in Distant Cultures"   143

Bich Minh Nguyen, "The Good Immigrant Student"   147

John Wick, "The Day the Can Exploded"   134

Description

"Bushman Rabbit" (paragraph)   58

JoLynne, "7 Ways to Be Worth Following on Twitter"   126

Rick Steves, Graffiti Wall, "New Years in Germany" and "Christmas in Paris"   128

Judith Ortiz Cofer, "Don't Call Me a Hot Tamale"   141

Brittney L. Huntley, "My Global Study Experience in Dubai: Strong Self-Image Key to Negotiating in Distant Cultures"   143

Exemplification

"Original Text"   39

"MP3 Players" (Paragraph)   61

Rebecca Tremble, "Advertising Analysis: Working Together" (Student Essay)   192

Kim Clark, "The Surprising Causes of Those College Tuition Hikes"   227

Eva Vasquez, "Travel for Distinction: UGA Study Abroad Offers Many Options"   261

Ken Bishop, "A Career Taking Pictures?" (Student Essay)   254

Centers for Disease Control, "Parent's Guide to Childhood Immunization"   293

Informing/Process Explanation

Raychelle Fox, "How to Excel in Your College Classes"   9

Gregorio Billikopf, "Cultural Differences? Or, Are We Really That Different?"   168

Debra Peters-Behrens, "Developing Global Skills for an International Career"   170

Charles Frank Bolden Jr., "What's Next for NASA?"   173

Christie Rosenblatt, "Moving from High School into College" (Student Essay)   165

Udall Center for Studies in Public Policy, "Illegal Immigration to the United States"   231

Centers for Disease Control, "Parent's Guide to Childhood Immunization"   293

Cause and Effect

Shamekila Quarles, "Professor Gives Reasons Why Students Fail"   67

Environmental Protection Agency, "Climate Change Impact"   179

Kathleen M. Zelman, MPH, RD, LD, "Five Surprising Reasons You're Gaining Weight"   211

Kim Clark, "The Surprising Causes of Those College Tuition Hikes"   227

Claudio Lavanga, "What Is Keeping Italian Men at Home?"   229

Udall Center for Studies in Public Policy, "Illegal Immigration to the United States"   231

Division and Classification

"Shoppers" (Paragraph)   62

Environmental Protection Agency, "Climate Change Impact"   179

Thomas H. Maugh II, "Women Less Likely Than Men to Fake Soccer Injuries, Study Finds"   196

National Science Foundation, "Language Change"   198

Judith Viorst, "The Truth About Lying"   200

Rebecca Tremble, "Advertising Analysis: Working Together" (Student Essay)   192

Comparing and Contrasting

Karen Gold and Sarah Cassidy, "Why British Students Are Opting for American Universities"   69

"Online Classes: Should College Students Take Them?" (Student Essay)   119

Gregorio Billikopf, "Cultural Differences? Or, Are We Really That Different?"   168

Roger Ebert, "*Shutter Island*"   239

Christina Breda Antoniades, "Best Places to Work 2010"   258

Eva Vasquez, "Travel for Distinction: UGA Study Abroad Offers Many Options"   261

Jeren W. Canning, "Community College vs. University"   265

Ken Bishop, "A Career Taking Pictures?" (Student Essay)   254

Bich Minh Nguyen, "The Good Immigrant Student"   147

Charles Frank Bolden Jr., "What's Next for NASA?"   173

Definition

"Non-Traditional College Student" (Paragraph)   64

Judith Ortiz Cofer, "Don't Call Me a Hot Tamale"   141

Judith Viorst, "The Truth About Lying"   200

Argument

The Plain Dealer Editorial Board, "Give a Cheer to the Experimental AIDS Vaccine and Then Get Back to Work—An Editorial" (Paragraph)   65

Mary Sherry, "In Praise of the F Word"   271

Marcie Willen, "Child Care for Our Student-Parents" (Student Essay)   285

James Fish, "Early Education Pays Off: High-quality Programs Are Good for Kids, for Society and for Business"   288

Chris Livaccari, "Your Brain on Languages"   291

Centers for Disease Control, "Parent's Guide to Childhood Immunization"   293

Readings: Thematic Contents

Education

Raychelle Fox, "How to Excel in Your College Classes"   9

Summary of Educational Qualifications (Student Writing)   42

Shamekila Quarles, "Professor Gives Reasons Why Students Fail"   67

Brittney L. Huntley, "My Global Study Experience in Dubai: Strong Self-Image Key to Negotiating in Distant Cultures"   143

Bich Minh Nguyen, "The Good Immigrant Student"   147

Christie Rosenblatt, "Moving from High School into College" (Student Essay)   165

Debra Peters-Behrens, "Developing Global Skills for an International Career"   170

Thomas H. Maugh II, "Women Less Likely Than Men to Fake Soccer Injuries, Study Finds"   196

Kim Clark, "The Surprising Causes of Those College Tuition Hikes"   227

Eva Vasquez, "Travel for Distinction: UGA Study Abroad Offers Many Options"   261

Jeren W. Canning, "Community College vs. University"   265

Marcie Willen, "Child Care for Our Student-Parents" (Student Essay)   285

James Fish, "Early Education Pays Off: High-quality Programs Are Good for Kids, for Society and for Business"   288

Mary Sherry, "In Praise of the F Word"   271

Chris Livaccari, "Your Brain on Languages"   291

Shannon Owens, "Female Students Are Better Than Male Students: Why?" (Student Essay)   224

Jobs and Careers

Bureau of Labor Statistics, Physicians Assistant Position   43

Debra Peters-Behrens, "Developing Global Skills for an International Career"   170

Thomas H. Maugh II, "Women Less Likely Than Men to Fake Soccer Injuries, Study Finds"   196

Rebecca Tremble, "Advertising Analysis: Working Together" (Student Essay)   192

Christina Breda Antoniades, "Best Places to Work 2010"   258

Ken Bishop, "A Career Taking Pictures?" (Student Essay)   254

James Fish, "Early Education Pays Off: High-quality Programs Are Good for Kids, for Society and for Business"   288

Sample Job Application Letter   377

Sample Résumé   382

Cross-Cultural Experiences

Karen Gold and Sarah Cassidy, "Why British Students Are Opting for American Universities"   69

Rick Steves, Graffiti Wall, "New Years in Germany" and "Christmas in Paris"   128

Brittney L. Huntley, "My Global Study Experience in Dubai: Strong Self-Image Key to Negotiating in Distant Cultures"   143

Bich Minh Nguyen, "The Good Immigrant Student"   147

Judith Ortiz Cofer, "Don't Call Me a Hot Tamale"   141

Gregorio Billikopf, "Cultural Differences? Or, Are We Really That Different?"   168

Thomas H. Maugh II, "Women Less Likely Than Men to Fake Soccer Injuries, Study Finds"   196

National Science Foundation, "Language Change"   198

Claudio Lavanga, "What Is Keeping Italian Men at Home?"   229

Udall Center for Studies in Public Policy, "Illegal Immigration to the United States"   231

Eva Vasquez, "Travel for Distinction: UGA Study Abroad Offers Many Options"   261

Chris Livaccari, "Your Brain on Languages"   291

Lauren Vanier, "Analysis of a Photograph: Women's Progression" (Student Essay)   338

Health

The Plain Dealer Editorial Board, "Give a Cheer to the Experimental AIDS Vaccine and Then Get Back to Work—An Editorial" (Paragraph)   65

Kathleen M. Zelman MPH, RD, LD, "Five Surprising Reasons You're Gaining Weight"   211

Marcie Willen, "Child Care for Our Student-Parents" (Student Essay)   285

Chris Livaccari, "Your Brain on Languages"   291

Centers for Disease Control, "Parent's Guide to Childhood Immunization"   293

Lauren Vanier, "Prevalence of Drug Use on College Campuses" (Student Essay)   352

Relating to and Understanding Others

JoLynne, "7 Ways to Be Worth Following on Twitter"   126

Judith Ortiz Cofer, "Don't Call Me a Hot Tamale"   141

Judith Viorst, "The Truth About Lying"   200

Eva Vasquez, "Travel for Distinction: UGA Study Abroad Offers Many Options"   261

Chris Livaccari, "Your Brain on Languages"   291

Shannon Owens, "Female Students Are Better Than Male Students: Why?" (Student Essay)   224

New Knowledge, New Information

The Plain Dealer Editorial Board, "Give a Cheer to the Experimental AIDS Vaccine and Then Get Back to Work—An Editorial" (Paragraph)   65

Charles Frank Bolden Jr., "What's Next for NASA?"   173

National Science Foundation, "Language Change"   198

Kathleen M. Zelman MPH, RD, LD, "Five Surprising Reasons You're Gaining Weight"   211

Kim Clark, "The Surprising Causes of Those College Tuition Hikes"   227

Eva Vasquez, "Travel for Distinction: UGA Study Abroad Offers Many Options"   261

Note to Students

Before they actually start to write, writers first decide what they want to accomplish. For example, a writer might decide, "I want to convince my audience that one product is superior to another." Only then does the writer figure out *how* he or she might best accomplish this. For instance, this writer may decide to compare and contrast the two products. Each writing task in *Everyday Writing*, therefore, begins with this question: What do I want to accomplish with my writing?

Our purpose for writing this text was to help you improve your writing. Good writing skills will help you succeed in this class, as well as in each of your other college classes and in your everyday personal and professional lives. The text will not teach you one way of writing; rather, we hope it will provide you with a "toolbox" of techniques to use on any piece of writing.

Everyday Writing is divided into four parts:

- Part 1 provides instruction on critical thinking, college reading, and writing. It asks you to think about the central question for all writing: what am I, as a writer, trying to accomplish? Part 1 also provides detailed instruction for each aspect of the *writing process*.
- Part 2 will give you practice in college-level writing:
  - Chapter 9: Writing to Share Experiences: Using Description and Narration
  - Chapter 10: Writing to Inform: Using Examples and Process Explanation
  - Chapter 11: Writing to Analyze: Using Division and Classification
  - Chapter 12: Writing to Explain Why: Using Cause and Effect
  - Chapter 13: Writing to Evaluate: Using Comparison and Contrast
  - Chapter 14: Writing to Persuade: Using Multiple Strategies
- Part 3 of *Everyday Writing* includes chapters on effective research, documenting sources, reports and timed writing, and workplace writing.
- Part 4 is a handy separate reference section that gives an overview of English grammar, lots of practice exercises, and specific connections to additional resources and practice on Pearson's online MyWritingLab.

We believe that *Everyday Writing* will help you improve your writing—which is, after all, the reason you are taking this class.

CHITRALEKHA DE DUTTAGUPTA
GREGORY R. GLAU

MyWritingLab and Your *Everyday Writing* eText!

Technology has changed the way you live your life. Now you can better prepare for class with Pearson's online MyWritingLab (www.mywritinglab .com) and the *Everyday Writing* eText.

Everyday Writing was written to help you improve your writing and succeed with written communication throughout your lifetime. Good writing skills will help you succeed in your college classes and in your everyday personal and professional lives. The *Everyday Writing* eText has many features that will facilitate your learning.

▼ You can take notes and save them in your **Everyday Writing** eText

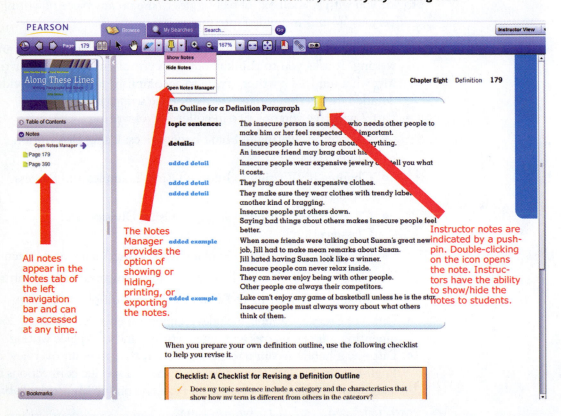

The Notes Manager provides the option of showing or hiding, printing, or exporting the notes.

All notes appear in the Notes tab of the left navigation bar and can be accessed at any time.

Instructor notes are indicated by a push-pin. Double-clicking on the icon opens the note. Instructors have the ability to show/hide the notes to students.

▼ You can search your *Everyday Writing* eText for key terms

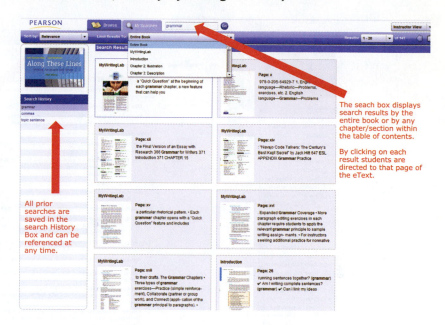

The seach box displays search results by the entire book or by any chapter/section within the table of contents.

By clicking on each result students are directed to that page of the eText.

All prior searches are saved in the search History Box and can be referenced at any time.

▼ You can bookmark pages in your *Everyday Writing* eText

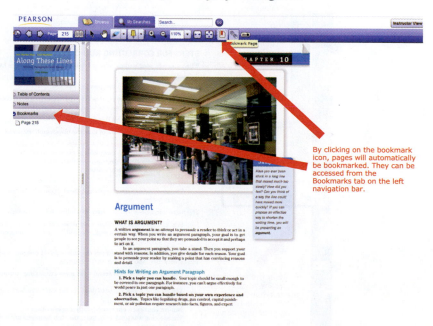

By clicking on the bookmark icon, pages will automatically be bookmarked. They can be accessed from the Bookmarks tab on the left navigation bar.

▼ You can utilize whiteboard capabilities in your *Everyday Writing* eText

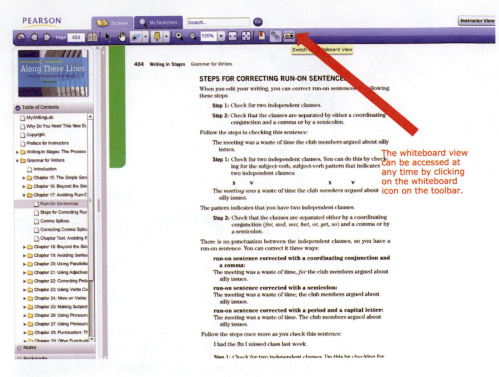

The whiteboard view can be accessed at any time by clicking on the whiteboard icon on the toolbar.

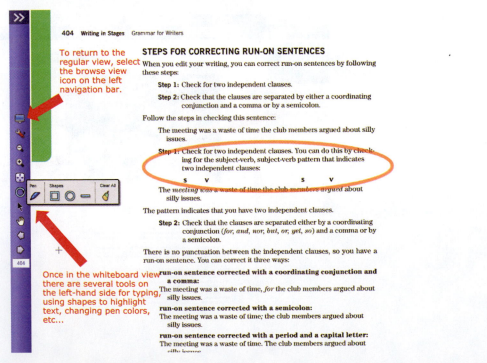

To return to the regular view, select the browse view icon on the left navigation bar.

Once in the whiteboard view, there are several tools on the left-hand side for typing, using shapes to highlight text, changing pen colors, etc...

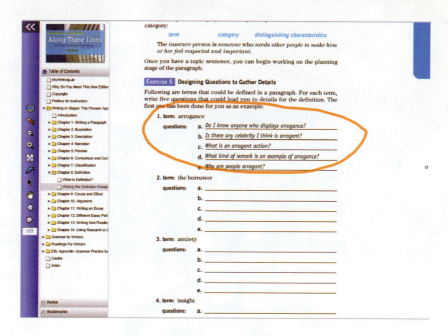

▼ You can highlight in your *Everyday Writing* eText

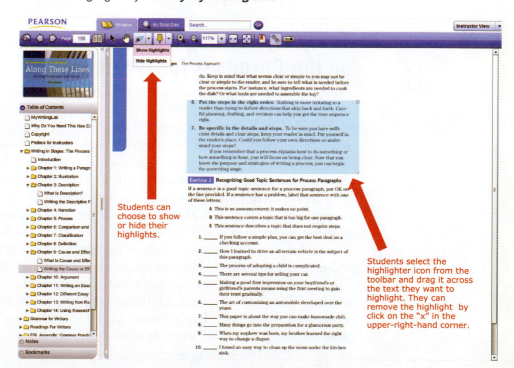

Students can choose to show or hide their highlights.

Students select the highlighter icon from the toolbar and drag it across the text they want to highlight. They can remove the highlight by click on the "x" in the upper-right-hand corner.

Preface

Everyday Writing focuses on the rhetorical considerations that ground any piece of writing ("Why am I writing this? What do I want to achieve? Who is my audience?"). By emphasizing a writer's purpose for writing, *Everyday Writing* teaches students a rhetorical approach that they can apply every day in their writing—to college assignments as well as to writing in the community and in the workplace. Furthermore, where we teach—and we suspect nationwide—basic writers and English language learners form a large and growing proportion of the student population. *Everyday Writing* meets, in one package, the rhetorical needs of these two groups of students who are often institutionally marginalized—and who are, these days, often in the same classes.

Features of

EVERYDAY WRITING

GREGORY R. GLAU
CHITRALEKHA DE DUTTAGUPTA

Everyday Writing Focuses on the Purposes for Writing

Everyday Writing is designed to teach students a conceptual and practical framework for all their writing—a way to approach a writing task, no matter what it is, from a rhetorical perspective: what do I want to accomplish with my writing? Each writing task in *Everyday Writing* begins with that rhetorical focus because we do not believe that anyone starts a piece of writing by first deciding on a mode to use or a genre to employ. Therefore, our instruction is organized by the purposes of writing, with rhetorical modes used as *strategies* for accomplishing those purposes. This approach is effective for both basic and second-language students because it focuses on writing fundamentals rather than surface features of language. To support this rhetorical approach, we provide ample opportunity for students to write in the informal Everyday Writing Activities and the more formal chapter Writing Assignments. Furthermore, we provide images and readings that appeal to students' interest in multicultural, international, and education-related topics, constantly drawing on the thinking skills they have developed in their everyday lives.

Everyday Writing Connects Writing, Reading, and Thinking

We believe that we can help students develop their writing skills with useful reading instruction (many of our students have never used reading strategies for college-level textbooks and, in fact, read only minimally) along with theoretically grounded writing instruction in language that students can understand and internalize. So, after an introductory chapter on the connections among reading, thinking, and writing, *Everyday Writing* starts with reading strategies and activities in Chapter 2 and moves to the reading–writing connection in Chapter 3, which centers on summary and response: how students will use what they read in their own writing. The basic rhetorical approach to writing, which can be used every day a student writes, is the focus of Chapter 4. Students are taught to consider their purpose, audience, and context before starting to write. Chapter 5 introduces the modes as strategies for accomplishing a writer's purpose, and Chapters 6, 7, and 8 provide instruction in the writing process.

The heart of the text, Chapters 9 through 14, consists of six major purpose-based Writing Assignments, where students will learn to share experiences, to inform, to analyze, to explain, to evaluate, and to persuade. In these chapters, students are encouraged to think before they write—to consider first their purpose and audience and then the strategies they will use to accomplish their purposes. Research, documentation, and other special writing situations are presented in Chapters 15 through 18. Finally, Chapters 19 through 34 provide a handy resource for students to check grammar, punctuation, mechanics, and style basics as they edit and proofread their writing.

Everyday Writing Provides a Framework for Learning

Everyday Writing provides instruction along with activities as well as samples from professional and student essays. This integrated approach is designed to provide support and help to students at every stage of their writing—always with an eye to the final, polished essay—so students see how all parts of the process work together to produce the best possible product.

Throughout the text, we emphasize the need for critical thinking and learning through reading and writing. To guide students and help them develop these skills, we provide several features.

- **Learning Objectives.** Each chapter starts with a list of learning objectives that helps frame the chapter's contents for students and guides their learning.

Sample of
Learning Objectives

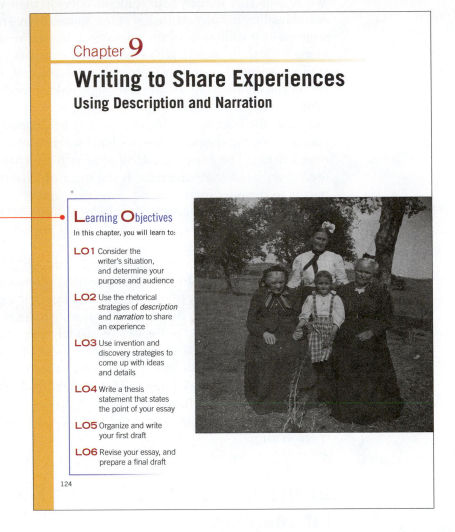

Chapter **9**

Writing to Share Experiences
Using Description and Narration

Learning **O**bjectives

In this chapter, you will learn to:

LO1 Consider the writer's situation, and determine your purpose and audience

LO2 Use the rhetorical strategies of *description* and *narration* to share an experience

LO3 Use invention and discovery strategies to come up with ideas and details

LO4 Write a thesis statement that states the point of your essay

LO5 Organize and write your first draft

LO6 Revise your essay, and prepare a final draft

124

- **Critical Thinking Activities.** Throughout the text, sets of questions to ask before beginning a writing task help students think about what they want to say before they draft or revise. We hope students who use *Everyday Writing* will learn that revision is the key to all good writing, and our critical thinking questions and activities are designed to help them internalize the concept of real revision. These questions remind students that good writing develops from sound thinking; by answering them before writing, students will improve the quality of their work.

(as one of Wick's classmates noted). While it is acceptable to directly address readers in a *letter*, it usually is not a good idea in an academic paper.

John thought about what his classmate suggested and so changed his text to provide the necessary description, without directly addressing his readers:

Original:

The stuff we used to seal the bottoms was called "CoolSeal," and it was a black, tar-like material, and gooey. I don't know how else to describe it to you but to say gooey. Liquid, like motor oil but thicker. And it was black and smelled like gasoline.

Revised:

The stuff we used to seal the bottoms was called "CoolSeal," and it was a black, tar-like material, and gooey. I don't know how else to describe it ~~to you~~ but to say gooey. Liquid, like motor oil but thicker. And it was black and smelled like gasoline.

Sample of Critical Thinking Activity

? Critical Thinking Activity: Ask Yourself Questions before You Revise

Now you have a first draft and have reread it several times, and most likely you also have received suggestions from your classmates (and perhaps from your teacher, family members, or friends). You will recall from Chapter 8 that *revision* means to reconsider and to reenvision your text—not to just fix surface errors. So consider the following:

1. Did I achieve my *purpose*? Did I provide the information and details my *audience* needed to really "share" my experience? Can I think of anything else to add?
2. How effective is my *organizational approach*? Is there another that might be more effective? (For more on organizational approaches,

tatement? Can anyone easily understand my

s and details I might add to help readers see places in the paper where I can "show" what "tell" about it?

Sample of MyWritingLab prompt

Improve Your Vocabulary

Use the highlighted and defined words from "The Good Immigrant Student" in a sentence or in a paragraph.

MyWritingLab For support in meeting this chapter's objectives, log in to www.mywritinglab.com, and select **Essay Development-Describing** and **Essay Development-Narrating**.

- **Chapter Reflections.** We ask students to reflect on what they have done and learned, because we believe that such reflection is a key not just to understanding but to improving, the next time they face a similar writing situation.
- **MyWritingLab.** At the end of each chapter, we give directions for accessing additional online resources and practice to help students achieve the learning objectives of the chapter and demonstrate mastery of the concepts and skills they have learned.

Everyday Writing Provides Many Opportunities to Write

We believe that people learn to improve their writing by drafting, receiving helpful and thoughtful feedback, then revising that writing, receiving more feedback, revising again, and so on—not by doing grammar exercises. We also believe that student writers need to write a lot, so frequent and varied writing prompts and activities give students many writing tasks, from informal to formal, that help them develop their writing skill through practice.

Everyday Writing Activities

Short, informal journal-writing tasks throughout the text give students frequent practice in writing and help them learn how to effectively use a writing journal. These activities extend the everyday writing focus of the text by asking students to think about and share their own writing, workplace, community, or cultural experiences with their classmates.

Sample of
Everyday Writing Activity

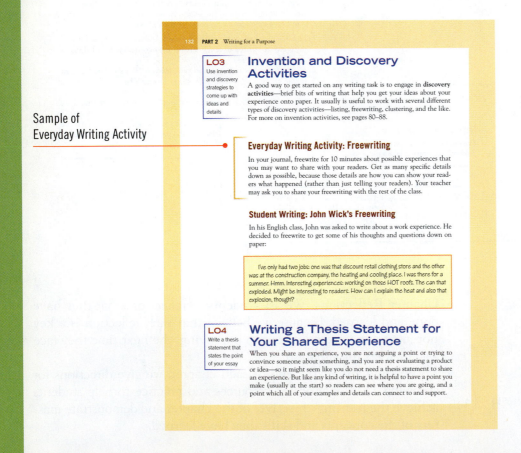

Writing Assignments

In Chapters 9 through 14, major writing assignments (including a multi-modal option) give students an opportunity to write longer texts. These writing assignments are organized by purpose: to share experiences, to inform, to analyze, and explain, to evaluate, and to persuade. Rhetorical modes are presented as strategies students can use to accomplish their purpose for writing. Each Writing Assignment section guides students in the writing process.

- **Invention.** We present a wealth of activities to help students get started with topic selection (difficult for many writers).
- **Thesis statement.** Instruction on constructing a thesis statement helps students develop effective thesis statements for their essays.
- **Organizational diagrams.** These graphics show students how they can structure their first drafts.
- **Peer review.** Suggestions for working with (and providing) feedback help students collaborate on their writing and revise with their readers in mind.

- **Revision checklists.** Items to check before revising help students evaluate the readiness of their drafts for final submission.

Sample of Organizational Diagram

Sample of Revision Checklist

134   PART 2   Writing for a Purpose

does, you select specific parts of the experience and what you learned from it to share with readers:

An Organizational Plan for a Reflective Essay

Why this experience was important to me (or how it affected me)

One part of the experience that was important

Another part of the experience that was important

A third part of the experience that was important

- **Comparative approach.** You would not only *narrate* your experience and provide *descriptions* of what happened, but also *compare* and *contrast* it to other experiences. You most likely would start by noting that you are going to compare and contrast experiences.

An Organizational Plan for a Comparison of Experiences

One experience compared to ⟷ Other experiences

Student Writing: John Wick's Draft Introduction

Here is the introduction to student writer John Wick's first paper that shares his summer working experience:

The Day the Can Exploded

In June, the can exploded, and I found myself covered w
oily goop that smelled like gasoline. My skin started to ting
it was evaporated and I was cool for a time. But then my

138   PART 2   Writing for a Purpose

Use this checklist to see whether your revised paper is finally done, or whether you need to make further changes before printing a final draft.

Revision Checklist for Your Shared Experience Paper

Part of your paper	Check √
Title for your shared experience that gets your readers' attention	
Introduction with a clear thesis statement	
Supporting paragraphs, each with a topic sentence, supporting evidence or examples, and a transition to the next paragraph (all information must relate to your thesis statement)	
Visual aids if they will help the purpose of your shared experience (charts, graphs, tables, etc.)	
Conclusion that summarizes your main points and restates your thesis about your shared experience	

Student Writing: John Wick's Final Draft

Here is student writer John Wick's final draft of his shared experience paper. Notice Wick's use of the rhetorical strategies of description and narration to help readers share his experience.

John Wick
Dr. Zach Waggonner
ENG 090
Mar. 3, 2011   Wick 1

The Day the Can Exploded

This is the story of that ninety degree and cloudless June day when the can exploded, and I found myself covered with thick and oily goop that smelled like gasoline. My skin started to tingle—whatever it was evaporated and I was cool for a time. But then my skin started to burn and I got scared, as I got hotter and hotter. I wondered if I should go see a doctor.

Everyday Writing Provides Many Models of Writing

Early in *Everyday Writing*, we suggest to students that reading and writing go hand in hand and that good readers are better writers. We exemplify this reading–writing connection throughout the text by providing many samples of professional and student writing. Students benefit from reading the work of other writers. By seeing how writers make claims, present evidence, and use language to accomplish their purposes, students can apply these techniques to their own writing.

- **Student writing examples.** Throughout the text, we interweave sample student invention activities, thesis statements, drafts, peer reviews,

Sample of
Student Writing

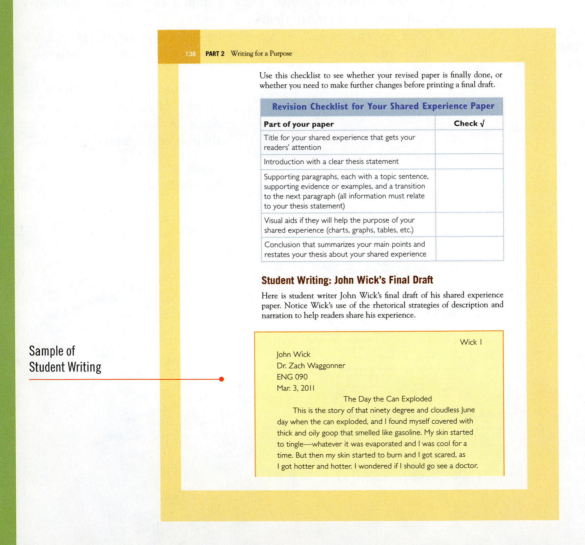

138   **PART 2**   Writing for a Purpose

Use this checklist to see whether your revised paper is finally done, or whether you need to make further changes before printing a final draft.

Revision Checklist for Your Shared Experience Paper	
Part of your paper	**Check √**
Title for your shared experience that gets your readers' attention	
Introduction with a clear thesis statement	
Supporting paragraphs, each with a topic sentence, supporting evidence or examples, and a transition to the next paragraph (all information must relate to your thesis statement)	
Visual aids if they will help the purpose of your shared experience (charts, graphs, tables, etc.)	
Conclusion that summarizes your main points and restates your thesis about your shared experience	

Student Writing: John Wick's Final Draft

Here is student writer John Wick's final draft of his shared experience paper. Notice Wick's use of the rhetorical strategies of description and narration to help readers share his experience.

Wick 1

John Wick
Dr. Zach Waggonner
ENG 090
Mar. 3, 2011

The Day the Can Exploded

This is the story of that ninety degree and cloudless June day when the can exploded, and I found myself covered with thick and oily goop that smelled like gasoline. My skin started to tingle—whatever it was evaporated and I was cool for a time. But then my skin started to burn and I got scared, as I got hotter and hotter. I wondered if I should go see a doctor.

revision changes, final drafts, and so on, so student writers can see how other students worked at constructing effective texts.

- **Professional writing examples.** Professional essays show students how "real" writers accomplish their purposes every day and provide a springboard for in-class discussions. The professional readings often focus on multicultural, international, and education-related topics and exemplify the rhetorical advice on which we focus. In the writing assignment chapters (Chapters 9 through 14), discussion questions and a vocabulary-building activity appear after these professional readings.

Sample of Professional Writing

3. Do you think that the process outlined by writer Peters-Behrens will help someone who wants to work internationally?
4. What is Peters-Behrens' most important piece of advice? Why?
5. Have you ever spoken with a career counselor, as Peters-Behrens suggests in paragraph 11? (For more on résumé writing, see Chapter 18).

Improve Your Vocabulary

Use the highlighted and defined words from Peter-Behrens's essay in a sentence or in a paragraph.

What's Next for NASA?

Charles Frank Bolden Jr.

Charles Frank Bolden Jr. has been the administrator of the National Aeronautics and Space Administration since 2009. He manages NASA's resources to advance the agency's missions and goals. Before joining NASA, he worked for 34 years with the Marine Corps, including 14 years as a member of NASA's Astronaut Office. He has traveled aboard the space shuttle four times between1986 and 1994, commanding two of the missions. This speech was given to the National Press Club in July 2011.

robust: strong; vigorous; healthy

solar system: the sun and the group of celestial bodies that revolve around it

propulsion: to drive forward

depots: a place for storing goods

radiation: the emission of energy in the form of waves and particles

1 As a former astronaut and the current NASA Administrator, I'm here to tell you that American leadership in space will continue for at least the next half-century because we have laid the foundation for success—and failure is not an option.

2 The end of the space shuttle program does not mean the end of NASA, or even of NASA sending humans into space. NASA has a **robust** program of exploration, technology development and scientific research that will last for years to come. Here is what's next for NASA:

Exploration

3 NASA is designing and building the capabilities to send humans to explore the **solar system**, working toward a goal of landing humans on Mars. We will build the Multi-Purpose Crew Vehicle, based on the design for the Orion capsule, with a capacity to take four astronauts on 21-day missions.

4 We will soon announce the design for the heavy-lift Space Launch System that will carry us out of low Earth orbit. We are developing the technologies we will need for human exploration of the solar system, including solar electric **propulsion**, refueling **depots** in orbit, **radiation** protection and high-reliability life support systems.

(continued)

Everyday Writing Provides a Resource for Grammar and Mechanical Issues

While we want students to focus on the content of their writing, correct grammar is crucial, so *Everyday Writing* provides a complete grammar handbook, filled with specific examples to help students see and understand the concepts. All students—native speakers and English learners alike—can benefit from a handy reference to check grammar, punctuation, and mechanics issues that arise in their writing.

- **Handbook of Grammar and Style.** Chapters 19 through 34 provide a brief handbook of grammar, punctuation, mechanics, style, and usage, with exercises to help students apply the correct rules.

- **Grammar Spotlights.** The Grammar Spotlights highlight a topic that basic writers and English language learners (ELLs) often find troublesome. Examples and exercises help students master the correct grammar and style.

PART 4 Handbook of Grammar and Style

400

LO2
Use subject and object pronouns and singular and plural pronouns properly

Grammar Spotlight: Subject and Object Pronouns; Singular and Plural Pronouns

Remember to distinguish between subject pronouns and object pronouns; even though both are personal pronouns, they can be confusing. I, *you*, *he*, *she*, *it*, *we*, and *they* are subject pronouns.

A **subject pronoun** functions as the subject of a sentence.

> <u>We</u> will go on an African safari next year. (You cannot say Us will go on an African safari next year.)
> <u>She</u> should save some money out of every paycheck. (You cannot say Her should save money out of every paycheck.)

An **object pronoun** serves as the object of a verb. Me, *you*, *him*, *her*, *it*, *us*, *you*, and *them* are object pronouns.

> He asked <u>me</u> to help him. (You cannot say He asked I to help him.)
> I invited <u>him</u> to speak at the reception. (You cannot say I invited he to speak at the reception.)

The pronouns *which* and *that* refer to things, while *who* and *whom* refer to humans.

> That computer, <u>which</u> costs $1,000, is the one I like. (You cannot say That computer, *who* costs $1,000, is the one I like.)
> My friend Gary, <u>whom</u> you met last night, is moving to Germany. (You cannot say My friend Gary, *that* you met last night, is moving to Germany.)

Singular and plural pronouns can often be very different:

Singular	Plural	Singular	Plural
I	we	myself	ourselves
me	us	yourself	yourselves
my	our	himself/herself/itself	themselves
mine	ours	his/her/its	their
this	these	that	those

Sample of
Grammar Spotlight

Everyday Writing Meets the Needs of Native and Nonnative Speakers Alike

Basic writers and English language learners form a large and growing proportion of the student population. *Everyday Writing* meets, in one package, the rhetorical needs of these two groups of students who are often institutionally marginalized—and who are, these days, often in the same classroom.

---

170   **PART 2**   Writing for a Purpose

Questions for Discussion and Writing

1. What is your initial reaction to this information?
2. What did you learn from this text? What is the most interesting thing you learned?
3. What was the most unusual thing you learned?
4. Can you point to any generalizations you can make about your own cultural background?
5. Does this excerpt from Billikopf's essay make you want to read the rest of it? You can, at the College of Natural Resources Web site.

Improve Your Vocabulary

Use the highlighted and defined words from Billikopf's essay in a sentence or in a paragraph.

Readings with global and educational themes appeal to a wide range of students

Developing Global Skills for an International Career

Debra Peters-Behrens

Dr. Debra Behrens is a PhD Career Counselor at the University of California, Berkeley, specializing in services to graduate and international students. As you read her advice on how to prepare for an international career, consider: Where do you want to work? What kind of work do you hope to do? Note that this is a process essay in the sense that Behrens is informing her readers of "how" to do something—in this case, how to get ready to work internationally. Process essays are essentially sets of instructions on how to do something.

1   As an international careers counselor, I receive questions daily from people of varied backgrounds who hope to try their luck in the global marketplace. Many job seekers mistakenly believe that they can't begin an international career until their feet are on foreign soil. They overlook their own backyard for resources and training opportunities.

sought-after: desired

The Most **Sought-After** Skills

2   What do international employers really look for in employees and what skills will be needed by professionals to perform successfully in the global marketplace?

3   A study commissioned by the College Placement Council Foundation

surveyed: looked at

surveyed 32 international employers and colleges to determine what international employers seek in prospective employees. They identified the following areas of required knowledge and skills:

Structure of *Everyday Writing*

Part 1: Building Your Reading and Writing Skills

We believe that college students succeed (or fail) based on their ability to think, read, and write, so Part 1 begins with academic reading and writing instruction. The first two chapters center on thinking and reading critically because that is where we believe writing instruction needs to start: helping students become effective at the reading their instructors ask them to do (including correct reading of the writing assignments instructors ask them to construct).

Chapter 1 focuses on the broad concepts of **critical thinking, reading, and writing.** It starts by asking students to consider a key question: why are college reading and writing important? This chapter centers on critical thinking (a concept that may be new to many basic and ELL writers) with a number of activities to help students understand and use the concepts we present. This chapter includes a professional reading (on succeeding in college), advice on working with visual texts, and a section on journal writing. It ends—as all our chapters do—with a chapter reflection.

Chapter 2 centers on specific strategies for **college reading**—something basic and ELL writers often struggle with—and includes a number of reading strategies and activities for students, as well as several brief professional texts. Students learn how to use pre-reading strategies, how to skim texts effectively, how headings can help readers understand a text, and ways to identify thesis and topic sentences and supporting details. The chapter then moves to how to use reading techniques such as annotating and outlining and touches on ways to deal with difficult vocabulary. (This aspect of reading—working with and understanding unfamiliar vocabulary—continues through Part 2 of *Everyday Writing*, where all chapters include vocabulary-building activities for each professional reading.)

Chapter 3 continues our focus on the reading–writing connection by offering instruction and activities on **summaries and response**—basic elements of many college writing assignments. Knowing how to write and use summary and response is critical to academic writing of any kind, in any discipline, as well as to everyday writing in the community and workplace.

Chapter 4 asks students to start every writing task with one central question: why am I writing? It begins our rhetorical instruction and centers on a **writer's purpose** in writing, who his or her **audience** is, the **context** for the piece of writing, and so on. These considerations are central to any writing task, whether the text is for a writing class or is written in someone's everyday life and work. The chapter also includes many visuals and Everyday Writing Activities to help ensure that students are active participants in the learning process.

That leads naturally to a discussion of how to accomplish a writer's rhetorical purpose, so Chapter 5 centers on the **writing strategies (modes) and appeals** that students can employ to achieve their writing purpose. We provide instruction and student activities so students learn to work with and use **description, narration, definition, comparison and contrast**, and other ways to accomplish their writing goals. Here, students also learn how to understand and use ethical, emotional, and logical appeals to persuade readers—always with writing activities, so students stay involved and actively participate as they work through the chapter.

Chapter 6 centers on **invention and discovery** (listing, freewriting, clustering, brainstorming, etc.), always with student activities. Chapter 7 covers writing a **thesis statement** and **organizing** and **drafting** effective paragraphs. This chapter also includes a sample student text that illustrates various concepts and helps students determine the most effective **genre** for their text.

Chapter 8 concludes Part 1 where students end their writing: with **revising, editing, polishing, and publishing** their final text. This chapter continues the sample student paper from Chapters 6 and 7 to illustrate what *real revision* consists of, checklists of questions peer reviewers need to ask (and answer about their own texts), and instruction in and examples of editing, proofreading, and final publishing. A complete, final student paper is included to provide insight on the various aspects of that student's writing and revision process.

Part 2: Writing Assignments

Part 2 of *Everyday Writing* provides six *assignment chapters*, which maintain the rhetorical focus and give students the opportunity to write extended essays. Each chapter centers on a **purpose** along with a focus on the **rhetorical modes** that often best serve that purpose:

Chapter 9: Writing to Share Experiences: Using Description and Narration

Chapter 10: Writing to Inform: Using Examples and Process Explanation

Chapter 11: Writing to Analyze: Using Division and Classification

Chapter 12: Writing to Explain: Using Cause and Effect

Chapter 13: Writing to Evaluate: Using Comparison and Contrast

Chapter 14: Writing to Persuade: Using Multiple Strategies

Each chapter begins with an illustration focusing on the rhetorical purpose of that chapter's writing, as well as a list of learning objectives—so students can immediately understand how the chapter will help them. We follow with rhetorical instruction on how to effectively construct a text that informs, persuades, and so on, along with examples of the most useful writing strategies for a particular aim: **narration, description, comparison and contrast,** and so on. Annotated writing samples and student writing activities help students grasp those modes or strategies.

Three major writing assignments from which instructors can select are provided, plus a "multimodal" option (blogging, tweeting, etc.). Instructors can ask students to write with an academic focus, a cultural/ community focus, or a workplace focus. We provide such a range of writing assignments in the Part 2 chapters because students have interests and lives outside the classroom, and some of the most effective writing can stem from focusing on such interests. Once students have a writing assignment, we ask them to step back and consider Critical Thinking Activity questions *before* they begin their writing assignment— questions that help students consider and articulate their purpose, audience, and so on.

We then ask students to work through a range of invention activities, with student examples to help guide them through each. Once they have a sense of what they intend to focus on for their assignment, we provide instruction on constructing an effective **thesis statement,** diagrams of possible organizational approaches, and brief instruction on revision (with a reference to Chapter 8, which focuses on revision). Annotated peer-revised drafts of student writing follow to help students see what kinds of comments and suggestions they might receive on their own work, as well as what a student writer did in response to those peer-review suggestions.

Often there is a grammatical, mechanical, or style issue that comes along with a particular kind of writing (quoting evidence accurately and properly, for example, in a persuasive text), so we provide a brief example and activity at this point in the chapter.

We provide a second opportunity for students to think critically about how they should proceed with a writing project. The first Critical Thinking question set was early in the process, after they understand the assignment, and the second is when students have a first draft and some feedback. So, we ask students to step back and consider their writing again and how they should plan to revise their text (again considering their purpose, audience, etc.). By asking students to pause and think before they draft and *again* before they revise, we make students more aware of their own writing: what is working and what is not so effective. This critical, rhetorical thinking will help them not only with this particular writing assignment, but with other writing tasks in the future.

Students then receive a revision checklist to guide their revision, along with a complete final version of a student paper to serve as a model of writing. Finally, students are asked to reflect on this writing assignment.

Each chapter ends with three professional texts that illustrate the kind of writing the chapter focuses on, each with discussion questions and a vocabulary activity. Instructors can, of course, pick and choose any or all of these readings and activities to use in their own classrooms.

Part 3: Special Writing Situations

Part 3 of *Everyday Writing* includes chapters on effective research, a guide to documentation, reports and timed writing, and workplace writing. It gives students an introduction to finding and evaluating sources, taking notes, integrating sources into a piece of writing, and citing and documenting sources. Both Modern Language Association and American Psychological Association example citations and model research papers are provided.

Part 4: Handbook of Grammar and Style

The handbook section of *Everyday Writing* is a separate reference/resource. It provides an overview of English grammar, ample practice exercises, and specific connections to additional resources and practice on Pearson's online *MyWritingLab*.

Writing Resources and Supplements

Student Supplements

Your Everyday Writing Journal
ISBN 020519320X

There are a myriad of brief writing activities in *Everyday Writing* designed to help students learn the rhetorical concepts in each chapter, as well as to help students get started on and draft their writing assignments. To facilitate these activities, instructors can ask their students to use *Your Everyday Writing Journal*. This writer's journal gives students even more context and writing advice for each activity, and it provides space for them to get their thoughts and ideas onto paper. Many instructors find that such journals facilitate student writing—and because all activities are in one place this gives students a central location for their invention/discovery activities, reflections, etc. The *Journal* is available separately for purchase or at no additional charge when bundled with the text. The journal is also available as an e-Journal within the *Everyday Writing* eText (accessed through MyWritingLab).

Instructor Supplements

Instructor's Exam Copy for Everyday Writing
ISBN 0205737455

Instructor's Resource Manual for Everyday Writing
ISBN 0205736602

A detailed instructor's manual, written by the authors and Rachel Koch of Coconino Community College, provides teaching suggestions and more activities that instructors can use with each chapter of the text. In addition, the manual also provides a unique **Quick Start** section, designed especially for new instructors, to help them get started using the text effectively and efficiently in their writing classrooms.

PowerPoint Presentation for Everyday Writing
ISBN 0205211003

This PowerPoint presentation, written by Lance Orr of St. Petersburg College, consists of chapter-by-chapter classroom-ready lecture outline slides, lecture tips and classroom activities, and review questions. It is available for download from the Instructor Resource Center at www.pearsonhighered.com/irc.

MyTest Test Bank for Everyday Writing
ISBN 0205115926

Pearson MyTest is a powerful assessment generation program that helps instructors easily create and print quizzes, study guides, and exams. Questions designed to accompany *Everyday Writing* and from other writing test banks are included. You can also create and add your own questions. Save the finished test as a Word document or PDF or export it to WebCT, Blackboard, or other CMS course. Available at www.pearsonmytest.com.

Alternative Versions of *Everyday Writing*

A-La-Carte Version of Everyday Writing
ISBN 020511380X

An unbound, 3-hole punched version of *Everyday Writing* is available for the bookstore to order at a substantial savings to students.

CourseSmart E-book Version for Everyday Writing 1/e
ISBN 0205117600

CourseSmart is one of the world's largest providers of digital course materials. Students can subscribe to *Everyday Writing* as a CourseSmart eText (at CourseSmart.com). The site includes all of the text's content in a format that enables students to search the text, bookmark passages, integrate their notes, and print reading assignments that incorporate lecture notes.

Pearson Custom Library
For class sizes of 25 students or more, Pearson Custom Library enables you to mix and match relevant course materials to create custom books that will not only perfectly fit your course, but will also pass on substantial cost savings to your students. You can add your own content, such as a syllabus, remove chapters you don't plan to use, add content from other textbooks in the library, add readings from *The Mercury Reader*, arrange everything in the sequence that suits your course, and even opt for a black and white or spiral bound textbook to help keep costs down.

Additional Resources for Instructors and Students

The Pearson Writing Package
Pearson is pleased to offer a variety of support materials to help make teaching writing skills easier for instructors and to help students excel in their coursework. Many of our student supplements are available at no additional charge or at a greatly reduced price when packaged with *Everyday Writing*. Visit www.pearsonhighereducation.com, contact your local Pearson sales representative, or review a detailed listing of the full supplements package in the *Instructor's Resource Manual* for more information.

| If practice makes perfect, imagine what *better* practice can do . . .

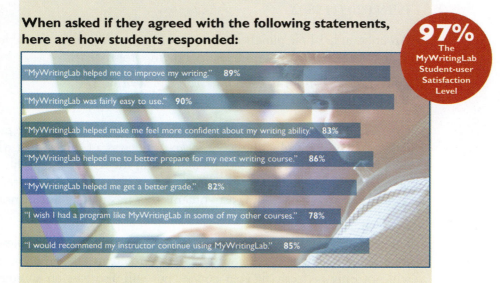

MyWritingLab™

MyWritingLab is an online learning system that provides better writing practice through progressive exercises. These exercises move students from literal comprehension to critical application to demonstration of their ability to write properly. With this better practice model, students develop the skills needed to become better writers!

When asked if they agreed with the following statements, here are how students responded:

97%
The MyWritingLab Student-user Satisfaction Level

"MyWritingLab helped me to improve my writing." **89%**

"MyWritingLab was fairly easy to use." **90%**

"MyWritingLab helped make me feel more confident about my writing ability." **83%**

"MyWritingLab helped me to better prepare for my next writing course." **86%**

"MyWritingLab helped me get a better grade." **82%**

"I wish I had a program like MyWritingLab in some of my other courses." **78%**

"I would recommend my instructor continue using MyWritingLab." **85%**

Student Success Story

"The first few weeks of my English class, my grades were at approximately 78%. Then I was introduced to MyWritingLab. I couldn't believe the increase in my test scores. My test scores had jumped from that low score of 78 all the way up to 100% (and every now and then a 99)."
—Exetta Windfield, *College of the Sequoias* (MyWritingLab student user)

TO PURCHASE AN ACCESS CODE, GO TO
WWW.MYWRITINGLAB.COM

MyWritingLab™

MyWritingLab, a complete online learning program, provides additional resources and better practice exercises for developing writers.

What makes the practice in MyWritingLab so effective?

- **Diagnostic Testing.** MyWritingLab's diagnostic test comprehensively assesses students' skills in grammar. Students are given an individualized learning path based on the diagnostic's results, identifying the areas where they most need help.

- **Progressive Learning.** The heart of MyWritingLab is the progressive learning that takes place as students review media and complete the various exercises within each topic. Students move from literal comprehension, to critical understanding, to the ability to demonstrate a skill in their own writing. This progression of critical thinking, not available in any other online resource, enables students to truly master the skills and concepts they need to become successful writers.

- **Online Gradebook.** All student work in MyWritingLab is captured in the Online Gradebook. Students can monitor their own progress through reports explaining their scores on the exercises in the course. Instructors can see which topics their students have mastered and access other detailed reports, such as class summaries, that track the development of their entire class and display useful details on each student's progress.

- **eText.** The *Everyday Writing* eText is accessed through MyWritingLab. Students now have the eText at their fingertips while completing the various exercises and activities within MyWritingLab. Students can highlight important material, bookmark areas of importance, and add notes to any page for reflection and/or further study throughout the semester. Students also have access to the *Everyday Writing* e-Journal and can print pages and write responses for submission.

Acknowledgments

It takes a community to write and publish a textbook, and we have received support, guidance, and encouragement from a great number of people. In particular, we would like to thank the Dean's Office, University College, Utah Valley University, for supporting this project by awarding Chitra the Scholarly Activities Award three semesters in a row. Also at Utah Valley University, we wish to thank Dr. Forrest Williams, ex-Chair, and Dr. Deborah Marrott, current Chair, Department of Basic Composition and English as a Second Language, for their support and encouragement during the process of writing this book. Thanks are also due to Dr. Thomas Henry, also of the Department of Basic Composition and English as a Second Language, Utah Valley University, for his support and help. At Northern Arizona University, we especially wish to thank Nancy Barron, Giovanina Bucci, Beverly Cleland, Bill Crawford, Laura Gray-Rosendale, Sibylle Gruber, Janice "Cindy" Knoll, Greg Larkin, John Rothfork, Mary Strong, and Allen Woodman for their continual help and support.

We also appreciate the guidance and advice we received from writing instructors all over the country:

Ellen Autenzio, Spartanburg Community College
Unoma Azuah, Lane College
Elizabeth Barnes, Daytona State College
Elaine Bassett, Troy University
Rochelle Bernstein, Seminole State
Susan Naomi Bernstein
Joan Blaih, Kent State University at Trumbull
Christina Blount, Lewis & Clark Community College
Deborah Boudreau, Northeast Texas Community College
Kevin Boyle, College of Southern Nevada
Karen Brown, Wallace Community College Selma
David Bruno, Camden County College
David Charlson, Tulsa Community College
Susan Chenard, Gateway Community College
Joy Clark, Yakima Valley Community College
Carol Copenhefer, Central Ohio Technical College
Cheryl Cornelsen, Oklahoma Panhandle State University
Karen Cox, City College of San Francisco
Virginia Crank, University of Wisconsin, La Crosse
Susan Dalton, Alamance Community College
Suanna Davis, Houston Baptist University
Sheilah Dobyns, Fullerton College
Chris Doyen, Bakersfield College
Javier Duenas, Miami-Dade College

Patricia Dungan, Austin Community College

Kevin Dyer, North Carolina Central University

Margaret Easterlin, Macon State College

William Elgersma, Dordt College

Lowrie Fawley, Keiser University

Dan Foltz-Gray, Roane State Community College

Leanne Frost, Montana State University–Billings

Cyndy Gribas, Hennepin Technical College

Wendy Goodwin, Miami Dade College

Bill Hall, St. Petersburg College

William Hall, Miami-Jacobs Career College

Beth Hammett, College of the Mainland

Leean Hawkins, Onondaga Community College

Zachery Hickman, University of Miami

Calley Hornbuckle, Columbia College

Laura Jeffries, Florida Community College at Jacksonville

Linda Joffe, Excelsior College

Stanley Johnson, Southside Virginia Community College

Billy Jones, Miami Dade College

Gerald Kenney, Keiser University

Terri Kilmartin, Middlesex Community College

William B. Lalicker, West Chester University

Kenneth Levinson, Borough of Manhattan Community College, CUNY

Lindsay Lewan, Arapahoe Community College

Beth Lewis, Moberly Area Community College

James May, Valencia Community College

Ann McNair, University of Southern Mississippi

Susan McNaught, Chesapeake College

Robert Miller Community College of Baltimore County

Sherilyn Moore, Westwood College–South Bay

Ashley Moorshead, Community College of Aurora

Bev Neiderman, Kent State University

David Nelson, Maricopa Community College

Virginia Nugent, Miami Dade College

Sheila Otto, Middle Tennessee State University

Mitzi Ramos, University of Illinois at Chicago

Scott Reichel, Community College of Aurora

Stephanie Sabourin, Montgomery College

Deborah M. Sanchez, North Carolina Central University

Terry Scott Douglass, Chattanooga State Community College

Patricia J. Sehulster, SUNY Westchester Community College

Marcea Seible, Hawkeye Community College

Mary Shannon, California State University, Northridge
Kathleen Smith, Middlesex Community College
Stacy Steinberg, San Diego Miramar College
Riba Taylor, Mendocino College
Elizabeth Thornton, Georgia Perimeter College
Heidi Todd, Athens Technical College
Kendra Vaglienti, Brookhaven College
Stephanie Vie, Fort Lewis College
Maria Villar-Smith, Miami Dade College
Kimberly Weaver, Atlanta Technical College
Concetta Williams, Chicago State University
Elizabeth Wurz, Coastal College of Georgia

The students of Chitra's basic writing course, who tested our materials and provided feedback, also merit our appreciation. We both wish to thank the following students:

Daniel Adams
Yazmin Aleman
Alicia Beck
Kenneth Boggs
Jordann Bradfield
Amando Carrillo
David Cavanaugh
Elizabeth Cruz
Michael De la Barra Chacon
Jonathan Farias
Kevin Fernsten
Mercedes Gamboa
Carrie Hartman
Jeremy Johnson
Atuzembi Kauejao
Natalia Koshkina
Kanokphol Limpanasriphong
Christopher McKenzie
Bryan Mecham
Nachelle Moore
Paulina Ochoa
Paola Ortiz
Mark Orvell Peck
Rosario Pena
Alexandro Pereira da Silva
Debora Rodriguez Fuentes
Roman Sanchez Acost

Jagyeong Seong
Autumn Skaggs
Alex Smith
Callie Smith
Laura Stewart
Amber Tippetts
Katheryn Webb
Thomas Wilson
Jake Wright
Jordan Wright
HyoJeong Yoon

At Pearson, we'd like especially to thank Matt Wright, our editor, who helped us develop the concept of *Everyday Writing* from day one (dating back to a lunch in 2005!). Marion Castellucci, our development editor, did a superb job of conceptualizing and guiding this text, and it is as much hers as it is ours. Joe Opiela provided encouragement and support and guidance all through the project. Eric Stano had thoughtful questions and truly useful advice. At Integra, Debbie Meyer and Jessica Werley expertly guided the production process from start to finish.

Finally, this book would not have been possible without the support of our families. Chitra would like to thank her husband, Abhijit Duttagupta, for being so patient and for spending so many lonely hours uncomplainingly while she was working on this book. Greg especially would like to thank his wife, Courtney, for her love and support and faith in his writing—for more than 45 years now.

CHITRALEKHA DE DUTTAGUPTA
GREGORY R. GLAU

About the Authors

Gregory R. Glau is Associate Professor and Director of the University Writing Program at Northern Arizona University, where he has taught since 2008. From 1994 to 2000, he directed Arizona State University's basic writing *Stretch Program*, and in 2000, he assumed the position of Director of Writing Programs at Arizona State.

Greg received his master's degree in Rhetoric and Composition from Northern Arizona University, and his PhD in Rhetoric, Composition, and the Teaching of English from the University of Arizona.

With Linda Adler-Kassner of Eastern Michigan University, Greg was co-editor of the *Bedford Bibliography for Teachers of Basic Writing* (2001, 2005); for the third edition (2010), he was co-editor with Chitralekha Duttagupta. Greg also is co-author of *Scenarios for Writing* (Mayfield/McGraw-Hill, 2001) and *The McGraw-Hill Guide: Writing for College, Writing for Life* with Duane Roen and Barry Maid (McGraw-Hill, 2011).

Greg has published in the *Journal of Basic Writing, WPA: Writing Program Administration, Rhetoric Review, English Journal, The Writing Instructor, IDEAS Plus,* and *Arizona English Bulletin.* He is co-author of a chapter in *The Writing Program Administrator as Theorist* (Rose and Weiser; Heineman), and author of a chapter in *The Writing Program Administrator's Resource: A Guide to Reflective Institutional Practice* (Enos and Brown; Erlbaum). Greg regularly presents at the Conference on College Composition and Communication and has presented at WPA, MLA, RMMLA, the Western States Composition Conference, NCTE, and other conferences.

Chitralekha De Duttagupta is Assistant Professor of Basic Composition in the department of Basic Composition and English as a Second Language at Utah Valley University in Orem, Utah. From 2001 to 2008, she was a Lecturer and then Senior Lecturer in the Writing Programs at Arizona State University.

Chitralekha received her master's degree in Teaching English as a Second Language from Arizona State University in 1996, and her PhD in Rhetoric/Composition and Linguistics from Arizona State University in 2001.

Chitralekha is co-editor (with Gregory Glau) of the third edition of *The Bedford Bibliography for Teachers of Basic Writing* (2010). She is also on the editorial board of the *Journal of Basic Writing* and is currently a member of the College Section Steering Committee of the National Council of Teachers of English. Chitralekha has presented at the Conference on College Composition and Communication and in several local and regional conferences.

PART 1

Building Your Reading and Writing Skills

Chapter 1 College Reading and Writing

Chapter 2 Strategies for Reading

Chapter 3 The Reading–Writing Connection: Summary and Response

Chapter 4 The Writer's Situation: Purpose, Audience, and Context

Chapter 5 Using Writing Strategies and Appeals

Chapter 6 Getting Started with Your Writing

Chapter 7 Drafting Your Paper

Chapter 8 Revising Your Writing

College Reading and Writing

Learning **O**bjectives

In this chapter, you will learn to:

LO1 Use a journal effectively

LO2 Use critical thinking skills for college-level work

LO3 Use critical thinking skills when reading

LO4 Use critical thinking skills when writing

LO5 Apply critical thinking, reading, and writing skills to visual texts

You are probably looking forward to the day when, like the student in the photograph, you will be in your graduation gown, proudly holding your degree. Think ahead to that day, as well as to the path that lies ahead of you in college:

- How important is graduating from college to you? Why?
- Why do you think a college degree is something special?
- College is about critical thinking, critical reading, and critical writing. What do you think these terms mean?
- What kinds of reading and writing are you expecting to do in college?

Welcome to college and to a whole new world of reading and writing. Of course, you have been reading and writing for a long time, so you may be wondering, "What is different about reading and writing in college?" You may be thinking of the reading and writing you have done since you learned to read and write in elementary school:

- You read books, letters, comic strips, and so on, as you were growing up.
- You may read the news to catch up on events in your city, the nation, or around the world, or to follow sports.
- You may read a grocery list so you can get the items your family needs.
- You wrote essays, exams, and papers in high school.
- You may have written a few text messages or e-mails to your friends this morning.
- You may keep a diary or journal, or perhaps you write poetry and short stories in your free time.
- You may have posted comments online or written letters to the editor of a newspaper when you felt strongly about an issue.
- You have filled out college application forms (and perhaps financial aid forms) that required a lot of writing and reading.
- You may do different kinds of reading and writing at work.

Therefore, you have already learned that it is important to read closely so you don't miss any details. You have also probably learned that most writing needs to be broken down into introductory, body, and concluding paragraphs that are easy for readers to follow. However, writing in college is a little different from the reading and writing you have done so far. The next section of this chapter discusses this in greater depth.

What Is College Reading and Writing?

Reading and writing in college build on the reading and writing strengths you already possess, but extend them even further. In college, you must engage in **academic reading and writing.** What this means is that because you are now part of the academic community of your college or university, you will be reading and writing to meet its expectations—standards that are usually set by college professors. In many of your college classes, you will have to respond critically to assigned readings or conduct library and/or Internet research requiring a lot of reading. This reading will enable you to complete writing assignments using sophisticated prose and different kinds of writing strategies. For instance, you may have to write:

- Essays for your writing classes.
- A research paper for your history class.
- A scientific report for your biology class.
- A marketing proposal for your business class.

Each of these assignments requires a different kind of writing using a different kind of approach based on your **purpose, audience,** and **context** (for a discussion of these terms, see Chapter 4). Each also requires you to use different kinds of writing strategies (such as a summary, analysis, or evaluation) so that you may achieve your purpose in writing. You may also be required to make an argument about an issue. This argument will have to be supported with evidence. At the same time, you will have to take into account opposing points of view. This course and this text will teach you to navigate these features of college writing very successfully.

Keeping a Journal

LO1
Use a journal effectively

Writers often keep a **journal,** or diary, in which they record thoughts, events, impressions, and reflections. Journaling has also been popular with people from other walks of life, and they have kept their journals for different reasons. Perhaps the most famous diary is the one kept by Anne Frank (*The Diary of Anne Frank*) in which she recorded her family's days hiding from the Nazis in the early 1940s.

Your writing instructor may require that you keep a journal as part of the work you do for the class. This journal can be a lined notebook in which you take notes, freewrite on a given topic, record your responses to what you are reading, or reflect on your reading and writing experiences. You can also maintain your journal on your computer, though you may need to bring a notebook to class for journal-writing purposes. Of course, if your teacher allows it, you may bring your laptop to class with your electronic journal on it.

Keeping a journal in a college reading and writing course has several benefits:

- It allows you to write down your impressions about the reading and writing activities you are engaged in.
- It can help you clarify your thoughts through writing and may assist you in discovering new ideas.
- It can help you write a better organized and more detailed paper because you can see your thoughts recorded.
- It can strengthen your writing skills; the more you write, the better you become at it.
- It allows you to go back and read what you have written and maybe use that for later writing.
- It requires little time, because it is mainly a quick record of your thoughts.

Everyday Writing Activity: Keeping a Journal

Set up a writing journal. Then, in your journal, respond to the following questions. Your instructor may ask you to share your responses with the rest of the class.

1. Have you kept a journal or notebook in the past, for schoolwork or outside of school? What was your experience maintaining that journal?
2. If you have not kept a journal in the past, how and where did you record your reactions to what you were reading and writing and observing?

LO2
Use critical thinking skills for college-level work

Critical Thinking

While a journal is very useful during the reading and writing process, you must also develop a set of **critical thinking skills** before you can successfully read and write for college. College reading and writing are heavily based on this skill set. Do not confuse the term "critical" with "criticizing"; they are two different things. Critical thinking involves mental skills and forms of questioning such as those given here:

Questions for Critical Thinking

- **Comprehending:** What is the text about?
- **Evaluating:** What are the strengths and weaknesses of the topic and of the text?
- **Reasoning:** Why are things the way they are? What should be the logical order of things?
- **Problem-solving:** Is there really a problem? Who does it affect? How can the problem be solved?
- **Analyzing:** When examining all angles and supporting evidence, what becomes clear? Also, what are the different parts that make up the whole?
- **Synthesizing:** What is the best way to combine various ideas to form something new?
- **Making distinctions:** Is it fact or opinion, and how can I distinguish between the two?

In other words, critical thinking means trying to discover the truth through active thought processes instead of simply by accepting what is presented to you. The ability to think actively and critically is the sign of a well-educated person, and it is what professors expect from students in college. As you engage in the critical thinking process, jot down your thoughts in your journal so that you have a record for later reference.

Critical thinking will enable you to **read critically** and **write critically.** These sets of skills are linked and interdependent, and they work together to help you in all of your college classes. As you go through college, you will find yourself using these skills more and more frequently as you read, write, and grapple with complex ideas and subject matter in your courses.

Everyday Writing Activity: Critical Thinking

Think of times in your academic career when you had to use all or some of the critical thinking skills discussed above and listed here. What were the circumstances? Record your responses in your journal. Your instructor may ask you to share your responses with the rest of the class.

Comprehending	Problem-solving	Evaluating
Reasoning	Analyzing	Synthesizing
Making distinctions		

LO3

Use critical thinking skills when reading

Critical Reading

Critical reading is as important to good college writing as critical thinking is. Even though you are enrolled in a writing class, it is important to remember that reading and writing are interdependent activities. This means that reading and writing work hand in hand with one another. A good reader is a good writer and vice versa. Seventeenth-century English essayist, poet, and dramatist Joseph Addison reminded us many years ago that "Reading is to the mind what exercise is to the body." So the more you read, the more active your brain is, and the better you are able to think and to write, just as the more you exercise, the more flexible and strong your muscles are, and the better physical shape you are in.

Your writing professor will probably assign a great deal of reading, and your writing assignments may be based on the assigned readings. You will also use writing to analyze and respond to readings in class or for homework. In addition, you will have to read your assignment requirements very carefully to make sure you understand exactly what you have to do to do well on the assignment. Therefore, it is important for you to be an active reader who uses critical thinking skills during the reading process (see Chapter 2 for more on reading strategies). Learning to read critically will help you develop a healthy, questioning attitude and enable you to do well in all your college courses.

When you start to read a piece of text, your goal should be to read it objectively and ask probing questions (using critical thinking) about the text. Your aim is to go beyond the surface facts and make a judgment of the text based on reading between the lines. The following is a list of questions that may be helpful to ask while you are engaged in reading:

 ## Questions for Critical Reading

- What is the **topic?** Are there any subtopics?
- What is the writer's **main point?** Does it come across clearly?
- What is the writer's **purpose** in writing? Is the writer making an argument about something? Is the writer trying to inform the reader? Explain a process? Evaluate something? Analyze something?
- What **writing strategies** has the writer used to develop his/her ideas? *Narration? Description? Argumentation? Comparison/Contrast?* Something else? A combination of strategies? (For a discussion of these writing strategies, see Chapter 5.)
- Who is the writer's **audience?** How well does the writer meet the audience's needs? How could the writer have better met the audience's needs?

(continued)

- How has the writer **organized** the reading? From general (beginning broadly) to specific? From specific to general? Chronologically, based on a timeline? Would a different organizational pattern have been more suitable? Why?
- What is the **introduction** like? Does it capture the reader's attention? What could be added to better gain reader attention?
- Has the writer effectively **concluded** the text? If not, how should the writer have concluded?
- What is the writer's **tone?** Formal? Informal? Business-like? Sarcastic? Humorous? Angry? Would a different kind of tone have been more suitable? Why?
- What kind of **vocabulary** has the writer used? Easy-to-understand words? Difficult words? Vocabulary that is specific to particular disciplines?
- Has the writer used **dialogue?** Has the writer used **quotes** by others?
- What is the **sentence structure** of the text? Short sentences? Long sentences? Wordy, convoluted sentences?
- Has the writer used **visual aids** such as photographs or charts? If yes, how do those visuals help the text?

While this looks like a long list, you will not have to apply these questions to every piece of text that you read; these are suggestions only. Also, you are not limited to this list of questions. The questions you should ask while reading will vary with the text you are reading. But remember to ask questions; that way you will be a critical reader and an *engaged* reader—that is, a reader who is involved in the reading, thinking about it and beyond it, to make connections with what is already known. As in critical thinking, we strongly recommend that you jot down your thoughts in your journal as you are reading so that you can refer to them later.

Everyday Writing Activity: Critical Reading

Think back on your past reading activities using the following prompts. Record your thoughts in your journal. Your instructor may ask you to share your responses with the rest of the class.

1. What kinds of things do you like to read?
2. What kinds of out-of-school reading have you done in the past?

3. Which of the critical reading questions mentioned earlier have you used before?
4. Have you used these critical reading questions primarily for school reading or when you have read for pleasure?
5. Which of the critical reading questions mentioned earlier have you never used before? Why do you think you did not use them?

Everyday Reading Activity: Critical Reading

Read the following essay, asking the critical reading questions listed on pages 7–8. Write down your responses in your journal. Your instructor may ask you to share your responses with the rest of the class.

How to Excel in Your College Classes
Raychelle Fox

excel: to do something really well

1 Every college and university wants its students not just to pass their courses but to **excel** in them, and they provide lots of resources to help their students. Unlike high school, your college will not force you to study in a certain way or to take advantage of the resources they offer—you have to do that for yourself. Here are some ideas for you to consider.

Get to Class, and Get There on Time

attributed: indicated as the author of a saying

ensure: to make sure something happens

2 While this quotation has been **attributed** to people ranging from Homer Simpson to Albert Einstein, the comedian and film director Woody Allen is the person who said "90 percent of life is just showing up." While "just showing up" will not **ensure** that you succeed in college, it is an important first step. If you don't go to your classes, you miss all sorts of useful information: changes of dates when assignments are due or tests will be given, new information that is not in the textbook, the chance to discuss important concepts and ideas with classmates, and so on.

3 Our first piece of advice, then, is to attend class, and get there on time (late-arriving students disrupt their classmates, the instructor's lecture, etc.). Another piece of advice: Use technology wisely, which means shut off your cell phone during class. You can survive for a class period without seeing every text message that you might receive! Remember, attending college is your "job" right now, and you are paying for your classes; it makes little sense to pay for something that you do not take advantage of.

(continued)

Meet With Your Instructors

4   Each of your instructors holds weekly office hours, which are open times for students to visit with them to ask questions, clarify assignments or concepts, discuss papers, and so on. Your instructor's office hours are listed on your course **syllabus**. Take advantage of this opportunity. Meeting your instructors gives them the chance to get to know you, too, since in large classes instructors cannot learn every student's name or get to know everyone.

Take Advantage of Your College's Resources

5   Most colleges have writing centers where students can get free extra help with their writing. The tutors ("writing coaches" is what they really are) who staff these centers are very well trained. They can help you with papers for any of your classes, whether you are just getting started, trying to do research on your subject, having trouble organizing your thoughts, or looking for feedback on a draft. Most colleges also offer tutoring in other areas, including those often-difficult math and science classes. Your college may also provide other forms of help, from organized study groups to what is called supplemental instruction, where you can get extra help for a specific class. Take the time to talk with your advisor about the resources on your campus...and take advantage of them.

Pay Attention to Your Own Ways of Learning

6   Think of how you learn most effectively and attend your classes with your own learning style in mind. For example, if seeing information helps you understand it better, be sure to sit where you can clearly see the video screen or chalkboard. If you learn by doing, then actively participate in all in-class activities. If you are easily distracted, sit in the front where your instructors can see you, and you will be less distracted. If you actively pay attention and participate in class discussions and ask questions, you will be less likely to daydream. If you find yourself sitting next to another student who distracts you by talking, move to different seat for future classes.

7   Finally, plan your semester: make a calendar noting when tests and papers are due. Then plan for daily study time as well as recreational time; when you have study time on your schedule, you are more likely to do it.

syllabus: an outline of a course, listing books, test dates, and so on

Improve Your Vocabulary

Use the highlighted and defined words from "How to Excel in Your College Classes" in sentences or in a paragraph.

Everyday Writing Activity: Critical Reading Reflection

In your journal, write your responses to the following questions. Your instructor may ask you to share your responses with the rest of the class.

1. Reflect on your experience using the critical reading process for "How to Excel in Your College Classes." What worked well for you? Why? What did not work so well for you? Why?
2. How would your reading experience have been different had you not used critical reading questions?
3. What is the most useful or interesting piece of advice you got from this essay? How might you use that advice?

LO4

Use critical thinking skills when writing

Critical Writing

Critical thinking and critical reading pave the way for successful critical writing. When you are writing for college, you must be careful that you don't just write to complete an assignment. If you do, then the writing may end up not meeting the academic standards of your professors. To write successfully for college, you must be a critical writer who thinks critically and reads critically. Critical writing requires that you ask yourself some probing questions (critical thinking) before you write and as you write. Some of the questions you need to ask yourself during this process are listed here:

 ## Questions for Critical Writing

- Why am I writing? What is my purpose?
- Who is my audience? What might my audience already know about my subject? What would my audience be interested in learning about the subject?
- How can I best meet my audience's needs?
- What is my main point? What are my supporting points? How many supporting points should I include in my paper?
- What writing strategies should I use to convey my point to my readers? *Summary? Narration? Description? Argumentation? Comparison/Contrast? Analysis?* A combination of strategies? Why?
- What kinds of information will help me get my point across to my readers? Examples? Facts? Charts and graphs? Tables? Photographs?
- What should be the tone of my writing? Formal? Informal? Business-like? Humorous? Why?

(continued)

- What should be my vocabulary choice? General? Specialized? Why?
- What is the best way to begin my essay? Why?
- How should I conclude my essay? Why?
- What is the best way to organize my essay? Why?
- How can I make my paragraphs more coherent, that is, more understandable and easy to follow?
- What kind of support does my essay need? Are personal examples good enough? Should I research for facts? Why or why not? If I need to do research, where should I begin? At the library? On the Internet?

This is a list of suggestions only. Depending on the kind of writing assignment you need to complete, you may have to add to (or cut from) this list. However, if you remember to ask yourself questions along these lines *before* you write and *while* you are writing, you will have taken some big steps toward writing a strong academic essay. As with critical thinking and critical reading, when you work on a writing assignment, we strongly recommend that you jot down your responses to these critical writing questions in your journal so that you do not forget them and can refer to them later. Keeping track of your thoughts in your journal about your writing process—how you went about writing a particular piece of text—will also guide you the next time you write something because you will have a record of your writing process to which you can refer as necessary.

Everyday Writing Activity: You as a Writer

In your journal, describe yourself as a writer. Think back to the writing you have done over the years, for school or outside of school, in English or in another language. Your audience is your classmates and your writing professor. Use the following prompts to help you write:

- What do you like to write? What don't you like to write? Why?
- What kinds of writing do you do on a daily basis?
- What are your strengths in writing? Your weaknesses?
- How careful are you to think about audience needs when writing?
- Do you usually consider your purpose in writing?
- How much time do you spend revising your writing?

Your instructor may ask you to share your responses with the rest of the class.

LO5
Apply critical thinking, reading, and writing skills to visual texts

Critical Thinking, Reading, and Writing: Visual Texts

Critical thinking, critical reading, and critical writing activities are not limited to printed text. All of these skills can successfully be applied to visual texts as well, using many of the same strategies. Visuals—whether they are simple photographs or paintings, television images or other forms of media images such as newspaper/magazine advertisements, advertisements on the Internet, billboards, or animations—are an important part of communication, and they often shape social and cultural values and beliefs. Therefore, it is important to apply critical thinking and then, by extension, critical reading and writing skills to them so that we understand them better. Some of the questions you may want to ask when thinking critically, reading critically, and writing critically about visuals (in addition to the ones already suggested in the previous pages) may include the following:

 ## Questions for Critical Thinking, Reading, and Writing about Visuals

- What is the image about? Is there a title that tells readers this?
- What is to be noted about its
  - size?
  - shape?
  - color?
  - background imagery?
  - How do they contribute to the overall message of the image?
- How do the different parts of the image work together to convey a point or create an effect?
- Are there any captions (texts accompanying the image) in the image? If so, how effective are they?
- Have any special effects (shading, borders, patterns) been used in the image? To what effect?
- What is missing in the image?

Everyday Writing Activity: Critical Thinking, Reading, and Writing about Visual Texts

In your journal, respond to the following questions. Your instructor may ask you to share your responses with the rest of the class.

1. Reflect on the photos using the critical thinking questions on page 13. How is doing this different from/similar to using the critical thinking questions for a written text? Make a list of similarities and differences.

2. Reflect on whether you had to apply any critical reading skills to the visuals. Why or why not?

3. Reflect on your experience using the critical writing questions for both visuals. How is it different from/similar to using the critical writing questions for a printed text? Make a list of similarities and differences.

4. Reflect on your overall experience using critical thinking, critical reading, and critical writing strategies for the visuals. Was your experience the same for both visuals? If not, why do you think you had different experience(s) for the two images?

Everyday Writing Activity: Chapter Reflection

In your journal, respond to the following prompts. Your instructor may ask you to share your responses with the rest of the class.

1. List the five most important things you learned from this chapter.
2. In what ways do you think this chapter will influence the reading and writing you do for college?
3. Think about the everyday reading you do outside your college classes. Where do you suppose you will you use the critical reading skills you learned in this chapter?
4. Think about the everyday writing you do outside your college classes. Where do you suppose you will you use the critical writing skills you learned in this chapter?

MyWritingLab™ For support in meeting this chapter's objectives, log in to **www.mywritinglab.com** and select **Getting Started** and **Critical Thinking: Responding to Text and Visuals**.

Chapter 2

Strategies for Reading

Learning Objectives

In this chapter, you will learn to:

LO1 Use critical reading strategies to improve your college reading

LO2 Respond to what you are reading, and develop your vocabulary

Chapter 1 introduced you to, among other things, the concept of reading critically for college. Think back to your reading habits in the past and look forward to the reading you anticipate having to do in college:

- How important is being a good reader in college to you? Why?
- What kinds of reading do you expect to do beyond college?
- What kinds of reading for pleasure do you do?

Reading should be fun and interesting and useful—and reading is how you will learn most of what you learn in college. There will be much more to read than in high school, and some of the reading material will be more complex than you may be used to. However, the strategies in this chapter will help you become a successful reader for college by helping you to:

- Comprehend what you read.
- Retain key ideas and concepts from your textbooks and other reading.
- Become a critical thinker who is fully engaged in the academic reading process.

Once you have grasped the main idea of the text, you can then proceed to analyze it as a critical reader, asking questions and trying to make a judgment about the reading as you engage with it more thoroughly. Reading strategies can be categorized as pre-reading strategies, reading strategies, and post-reading strategies.

LO1

Use critical reading strategies to improve your college reading

Pre-reading Strategies

While it is important to read as comprehensively as possible, there are some reading strategies that can be successfully employed *before beginning to read* and *during the reading process* to make reading more efficient and fast, and that will help you grasp and retain the main idea of the passage better. The first group of strategies is collectively known as **pre-reading strategies.** These are the strategies that we recommend you use *before* beginning to read. They are based on the prior knowledge that you, as a reader, bring to the reading. You may use all, or as many, of them that apply to the passage you intend to read. Using them will help you make sense of the text early on by building up some expectation and understanding of the text through what you recall about the topic. This will help you connect with the text better and make you more ready to interact with the new material. Pre-reading strategies can include the following:

- Think about the title, and the subtitles, if any, of the reading:

   What do you already know about the topic indicated by the title and the subtitle(s)? For instance, if the topic of the reading is cultural differences, ask yourself what you know about cultural differences in general or differences between specific cultures (e.g., U.S. culture and Mexican culture; U.S. culture and Japanese culture; Chinese culture and Korean culture).

Do you have any direct experience with the topic?

What feelings, if any, do you have about the topic?

- Look at any available visuals:

    What do these visuals remind you of, if anything?

    What might these visuals indicate about the content of the reading?

- Determine the purpose for your reading:

    Why are you reading this passage? To be informed? To evaluate? To understand an argument? To compare/contrast between two or more things/ideas/issues?

- Consider the author of the reading:

    What do you know about the author, specifically his/her life and his/her background?

    What might be the writer's purpose in writing this passage?

    Are the writer's views/outlook likely to influence what he/she says in the reading?

Record your pre-reading observations in your journal. You may want to create a table in your journal, as in the following example, to help you:

What I Already Know about the Reading	
Title/Subtitle	
Visuals	
Purpose	
Author	

Main Idea Strategies

After you have completed engaging with the pre-reading strategies, the next step is to employ some **main idea strategies** as you begin reading. Each reading has a main idea. Here, we provide you with five different main idea strategies that will help you pinpoint the main ideas of a reading. This will help you improve your reading comprehension and make you more successful in your college courses. You may use one or several of the strategies outlined here, depending on your preferences and the type of passage you intend to read.

Read the Introduction and Conclusion First

The first strategy that will help you get the main idea of the text is to *read the introduction and the conclusion before reading anything else*. The introduction previews the text; that is, it tells readers what the chapter, passage, article, or even the entire book *is* about, while the conclusion summarizes what the chapter, passage, article, or even the entire book *was* about. If you arm yourself with this information before reading the rest of the material, you will find it much easier to read and understand the rest of the text. Look at the following example:

> Jade—a gemstone of unique symbolic energy, and unique in the myths that surround it. With its beauty and wide-ranging expressiveness, jade has held a special attraction for mankind for thousands of years.

This passage is the introductory paragraph of an article published by the International Colored Gemstone Association on the gemstone jade. It tells readers right away that the rest of the article is going to focus on the uniqueness of jade and its special attraction for humans.

Now look at the concluding paragraph from the same article:

> Symbolic energy and beauty, the traditional and the modern are combined in jade in a particularly harmonious way. And in gemstone therapy it is said that jade "stimulates creativity and mental agility on the one hand, while also having a balancing and harmonising effect." So this beautiful gemstone brings us joy, vivacity and happiness all at the same time—and what, in our times, could we possibly need more?

Reading the conclusion, you can safely assume that at least part of the article elaborated on the impact of the gem on human lives. Armed with this knowledge, it will be much easier for you as a reader to go back and read through the entire article—and understand its message.

Everyday Writing Activity: Reading Introductions and Conclusions

Read the following paragraph from the National Post Web site. In your journal, write what you think is the main idea of the passage for which it serves as the introduction. Your instructor may ask you to share your responses with the rest of the class:

> It wasn't that many decades ago that man risked life and limb to hunt whales, the mightiest denizens of the deep. Today, armed with digicams and zoom lenses instead of harpoons, we voyage to the ends of the Earth for a chance to view whales in their natural habitat.

Now read the following concluding paragraph from Businessinsider.com; in your journal, write what you think is the main idea of the reading. Your instructor may ask you to share your response with the rest of the class:

> Facebook's strong network effects, low cost of goods sold, strong growth rate, and dominance of social networking should command a hefty revenue multiple—say 25X. Applying this multiple to our 2008E revenue of $350 million, we estimate a current value of $9 billion.

Skim the Passage or Visual

Another main idea strategy that you can use to help you comprehend a text better is to *skim the passage* very quickly before beginning to read in-depth. To *skim* means to examine rapidly, or glance through very quickly, a piece of text. While reading as thoroughly as possible is very important, many students try to read every word that is in the text. After all, if the words are part of the sentence, they should be critical to understanding the text, right? Wrong. It is unnecessary to read and understand every word. Many words are grammatical parts of speech that are necessary to construct a correct sentence, but are not necessary for comprehension.

Therefore, we recommend that you should skim the text first to grasp the main idea of the text. What is its focus? What is its message? Locating keywords (main words) or key phrases (main phrases) will help you answer these questions and will help you remember the main idea of the text much better than if you try to understand each and every word in the passage during the first reading. It will also increase your reading speed. If the reading passage is supplemented by visual aids such as tables, graphs, and/or charts, simply skim them because they highlight the information that is also presented in text form. Once you have a grasp of the main idea in the text, you can then go back and read the text for the more detailed information.

The Melting Pot Continues: International Students in America

John Carter

The following is an example of a passage that you may be asked to read in college. It shows how to skim for the main idea by identifying important words, phrases, and data.

Key phrase: nation of immigrants

Important data: 582,984 students

Key words: business, engineering, and sciences

Important data: 3.9 percent

Important words: leading nations (India, China, Korea)

1   America is often characterized as a **nation of immigrants.** And nowhere is our melting pot identity more evident than on U.S. college and university campuses.

2   In 2006–2007, according to data compiled by the Institute of International Education, **582,984 students** from all over the world were enrolled in American colleges and universities in a wide range of fields, but centered mainly on **business, engineering, and the sciences.**

Numbers on the Rise

3   In the aftermath of September 11, 2001, the number of international students in America showed either a much lower rate of growth or an actual decrease until 2006–2007. But last year, as U.S. college total enrollment topped 15 million for the first time, international student enrollment nearly matched its all-time high of 586,323, set in 2002–2003. That means that **3.9 percent** of all college students in the United States are from other countries.

Where Do They Come From?

4   The **leading nations** of origin for international students are **India** (83,833 students), **China** (67,723), and **Korea** (62,392). Among the top 20, the percentage of change compared to the previous year—in terms of sending more or fewer students to study in America—was fairly small. But No. 12 Saudi Arabia, No. 13 Nepal, and No. 20 Vietnam each registered major increases: Saudi Arabia, 128.7 percent; Nepal, 27.9 percent; and Vietnam, 31.3 percent.

Where Do They Go?

5   Coming as no surprise, the most populous state in the nation attracts more international students than any other state. In this latest year for which

(continued)

Important data:
77,987 international
students in
California, etc.

Key phrase: economic
impact

data are available, **77,987 international students** were enrolled in colleges
and universities in **California**, followed by New York (65,884), Texas (49,081),
Massachusetts (28,680), Florida (26,875), and Pennsylvania (23,182).

Economic Impact

6   All told, their **economic impact**—tuition and fees, living expenses for
themselves and their dependents, and U.S. support mainly from the schools
they attend—totaled nearly $14.5 billion. As it has been year after year, more than
60 percent of their funding comes from their personal and family financial assets.
The next largest funding source is the college or university they are attending.

Once the key words and phrases have been identified, it is relatively easy
to identify the main idea of the passage, as seen here:

The number of international students coming to the United States from all over
the world, mainly to study business, engineering, and the sciences, continues to
rise, with the majority coming from India, China, and Korea. Most of them are
attracted to populous states like California, New York, and Texas. They pay for
most of their own education and living expenses and have a positive financial
impact on the U.S. economy.

Everyday Writing Activity: Skimming a Text

Skim the following text from the American Yoga Association Web site,
locating words and phrases, and then write the main idea in your journal.
Your instructor may ask you to share your response with the class.

What Is Yoga?

1   The classical techniques of Yoga date back more than 5,000 years. In ancient
times, the desire for greater personal freedom, health and long life, and heightened self-understanding gave birth to this system of physical and mental exercise,
which has since spread throughout the world. The word *Yoga* means "to join or
yoke together," and it brings the body and mind together into one harmonious
experience.

2   The whole system of Yoga is built on three main structures: exercise,
breathing, and meditation. The exercises of Yoga are designed to put pressure
on the glandular systems of the body, thereby increasing its efficiency and total
health. The body is looked upon as the primary instrument that enables us to

work and evolve in the world, and so a Yoga student treats it with great care and respect. Breathing techniques are based on the concept that breath is the source of life in the body. The Yoga student gently increases breath control to improve the health and function of both body and mind. These two systems of exercise and breathing then prepare the body and mind for meditation, and the student finds an easy approach to a quiet mind that allows silence and healing from everyday stress. Regular daily practice of all three parts of this structure of Yoga produce a clear, bright mind and a strong, capable body.

If the text you are reading includes a visual like a pie chart, graph, or table, you can quickly skim it to see what the idea being highlighted is, or what the details included are, without necessarily having to read the accompanying text, especially in the initial stages of reading.

In the case of the pie charts below, for example, readers can skim the first pie chart to see the numbers of different mobile handset brands sold

Mobile handsets sold January to June 2010

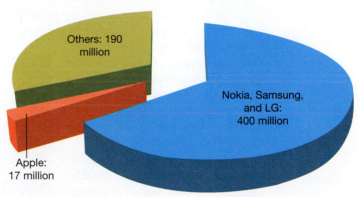

Share of industry profits January to June 2010

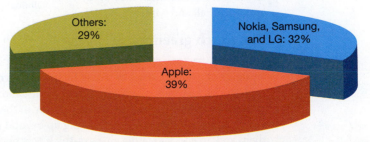

Source: http://tech.fortune.cnn.com/2010/09/21/pie-chart-apples-outrageous-share-of-the-mobile-industrys-profits/

from January to June 2010. A quick skim shows, for instance, that Nokia, Samsung, and LG brands sold the most handsets combined. The second pie chart shows which brand has what share of the mobile handset industry profits in the same year. It is clear from that chart that Apple had the greatest share of industry profits.

Focus on Headings and Subheadings

Very often, the main points of a reading are summarized in the heading and the subheading(s). Thus, another very effective way to identify the main idea of a text is to *focus on the main heading and the subheading(s) to see what ideas and thoughts are being emphasized.* Once you get the main point of the text, it will be much easier to read and grasp what the individual paragraphs, and consequently, the entire text, is trying to communicate. Look at the following passage from the Web site Fightglobalwarming.com:

The Basics of Global Warming

The greenhouse effect

1   The atmosphere has a natural supply of "greenhouse gases." They capture heat and keep the surface of the Earth warm enough for us to live on. Without the greenhouse effect, the planet would be an uninhabitable, frozen wasteland.

2   Before the Industrial Revolution, the amount of carbon dioxide (CO_2) and other greenhouse gases released into the atmosphere was in a rough balance with what could be stored on Earth. Natural emissions of heat-trapping gases matched what could be absorbed in natural sinks. For example, plants take in CO_2 when they grow in spring and summer, and release it back to the atmosphere when they decay and die in fall and winter.

Take action to cap global warming pollution now

Too much greenhouse effect

3   Industry took off in the mid-1700s, and people started emitting large amounts of greenhouse gases. Fossil fuels were burned more and more to run our cars, trucks, factories, planes and power plants, adding to the natural supply of greenhouse gases. The gases—which can stay in the atmosphere for at least fifty years and up to centuries—are building up beyond the Earth's capacity to remove them and, in effect, creating an extra-thick heat blanket around the Earth.

. . .

How much is too much?

4   Already, people have increased the amount of CO_2, the chief global warming pollutant, in the atmosphere to 31 percent above pre-industrial levels. There is more CO_2 in the atmosphere now than at any time in the last 650,000 years. Studies of the Earth's climate history show that even small changes in CO_2 levels generally have come with significant shifts in the global average temperature.

. . .

The science is clear

5   Scientists are no longer debating the basic facts of climate change. In February 2007, the thousands of scientific experts collectively known as the Intergovernmental Panel on Climate Change (IPCC) concluded that there is greater than 90 percent likelihood that people are causing global warming.

As you can tell by looking at the title, the article is about the basics of global warming, so you can expect that discussion in the reading. The caption under the photograph tells readers that global warming should be reduced as soon as possible. Each of the subheadings also makes a point. The first subheading is "The greenhouse effect." That tells readers right away that the paragraphs under the subheading will explain what the greenhouse effect is. The second subheading is "Too much greenhouse effect." Now readers know that the paragraphs included in this subheading will discuss the excessive amounts of greenhouse gases being released into the atmosphere. The third and fourth subheadings are "How much is too much?" and "The science is clear." They tell readers that the paragraphs in the third section will discuss what amounts of temperature change are acceptable, while the last section deals with the thought that scientists are agreed that climate change is a fact and that people are responsible for the phenomenon known as global warming.

Read and Understand Individual Paragraphs

Focusing on the meaning of individual paragraphs is also a way to read more effectively. This breaks up the reading into smaller sections and makes it easier to manage. In reading individual paragraphs, the key is to read and understand the **topic sentence** in each paragraph. The topic sentence is the sentence that sums up the main point of each paragraph, and it is usually the first sentence of a paragraph, though it can also be the last sentence of a paragraph or be somewhere in between. Once you locate it and understand it, you have probably understood the main idea of that paragraph. As you will see when we discuss topic sentences in your own papers (Chapter 7), understanding how they function in a text is important in both reading and writing.

Consider the following example from Articleinsider.com:

> **Middle Eastern cuisine is one of the best reasons to visit the countries of the Middle East.** The sights, smells, and flavors of this unique food will open you up to a whole new experience. Though some of the foods and ways of preparing them are foreign to the average Westerner, the richness and exotic flavors of these local specialties often find their way into menus around the world, where they become familiar favorites.

The topic sentence is the first sentence of the paragraph, in bold. Reading it, we know that the rest of the paragraph is probably going to be about the unique foods of the Middle East. Look for such clues as you are reading; they will help you understand the main idea of the paragraph and, by extension, the main idea of the text better. Repeat this process with each paragraph.

Everyday Writing Activity: Topic Sentence

Underline the topic sentence in the following paragraph from the Animal Diversity section of the University of Michigan Web site. Then write down in your journal what you think the main idea of the paragraph is, based on the topic sentence. Your instructor may ask you to share your responses with the rest of the class.

> Although mammals share several features in common, Mammalia contains a vast diversity of forms. The smallest mammals are found among the shrews and bats, and can weigh as little as 3 grams. The largest mammal, and indeed the largest animal to ever inhabit the planet, is the blue whale, which can weigh 160 metric tons (160,000 kg). Thus, there is a 53 million-fold difference in mass between the largest and smallest mammals! Mammals have evolved to exploit a large variety of ecological niches and life history strategies and, in concert, have evolved numerous adaptations to take advantage of different lifestyles. For example, mammals that fly, glide, swim, run, burrow, or jump have evolved morphologies that allow them to locomote efficiently; mammals have evolved a wide variety of forms to perform a wide variety of functions.

Make a Simple Outline

Creating a simple outline of a reading can be helpful in getting a sense of its main idea and the supporting details (for more on supporting details, see page 28). This outline can simply take the form of a list that highlights the contents of the reading. Look at the following example from Virtualoceania.net on New Zealand cities:

New Zealand cities are small by international standards regarding population, but they do contain all the amenities that cities should have. The plus side to New Zealand cities is the lack of pollution and crime that plagues big international cities. By comparison, New Zealand cities are safe and friendly places, yet the night life, restaurants, theatre, and art are lively and varied. In addition to this, New Zealand cities are usually located within spectacular natural settings such as the coast, hills, and mountains, and even volcanoes.

The biggest city in New Zealand is Auckland, and the capital city of New Zealand is Wellington, the third biggest city. Both these cities are situated on the more populous North Island. The biggest city in the South Island and second biggest in New Zealand is Christchurch.

There are about 600 towns in New Zealand that service New Zealand's rural industry.

- Simple outline:
  - New Zealand cities small but modern
  - No pollution or crime
  - Lively cultural/social scene
  - Close to natural settings
  - Auckland largest city
  - Wellington capital city
  - Christchurch biggest city in the South Island
  - 600 rural towns

Everyday Writing Activity: Outlining

Read the following passage, and write a simple outline for it in your journal. Your instructor may ask you to share your responses with the rest of the class.

How Much Do Ski Helmets Help?
Denis Cummings

1   The death of actress Natasha Richardson, who died Wednesday from bleeding in her skull caused by a skiing accident, has rekindled a debate

(continued)

over the use of helmets on the ski slope. Richardson was not wearing a helmet when she fell during a beginner's lesson Monday at Quebec's Mont Tremblant ski resort.

2   "It's sad, it's really sad," said Canadian Member of Parliament Hedy Fry, a doctor who introduced a bill in 2007 requiring all ski and snowboard helmets meet federal guidelines. "So many Canadian youths, so many Canadians, get (brain injuries) and it could be prevented… It has to take a celebrity to bring this to the fore."

3   Her death may inspire Quebec Sports Minister Michelle Courchesne to require all skiers and snowboarders to wear helmets. An organization of emergency room doctors has been pushing for a mandatory helmet rule, citing a 2006 Norwegian study that found "60 per cent of head trauma could be avoided by wearing a helmet."

4   The use of helmets by skiers has increased over the past decade due in large part to the high-profile skiing deaths of Michael Kennedy and Sonny Bono in 1997 and 1998, respectively. According to the National Ski Areas Association, 43 percent of skiers and snowboarders wore helmets in 2008, up from 25 percent in 2003.

5   Though the number of serious injuries has declined as helmet use increases, the number of deaths has not been affected, and more than half of the deaths on the slope last year involved skiers wearing helmets.

6   Dave Byrd, director of education and risk for the NSAA, explained to CNN that helmets often cannot prevent serious head injuries in violent crashes. Most helmets are designed for speeds of 14 mph or less, but skiers tend to travel between 25 and 40 mph.

7   Byrd believes that skiing responsibly is the best way to prevent injury. "Our position is the skier's behavior has as much or more to do with the safety of the sport as does any piece of equipment," he said.

Supporting Details Strategies

The main idea of a text, which is its most important point, is usually backed up by details, examples, evidence, facts, and ideas that support and elaborate on the main idea. These are known as supporting details. Understanding the main idea and the supporting points enables readers to comprehend the reading passage properly. As you will learn in Chapter 7, supporting details are vital to your own writing as well, so knowing how they work in a text is important.

Perhaps the best way to identify the supporting details is to keep in mind what the writer's point is and then locate the details that elaborate on the main idea. The following paragraph from Essortment.com clearly shows the details that support the main idea of the text:

Masks have been used by the world's diverse cultures for centuries. The ancient Greek actors used masks for special theatrical representations. Eighteenth century Europeans frequented masked balls where the masks were elaborately decorated with beads and feathers. The Chinese still use masks in their traditional dances. African cultures have perhaps the richest mask traditions. In African societies masks are used for funeral ceremonies and harvest dances. They figure prominently in the rite of passages for young men, and have become a source of pride in modern-day celebrations. Masks are unique to each specific African society and their shape and accessories have special meanings for the different cultures.

The writer's main idea, expressed in the topic sentence, is that masks have been used over time by many different cultures. The details that support this idea are examples referring to the use of masks in ancient Greek culture, in 18th-century European culture, in past and present Chinese culture and to the rich African culture of using masks.

Everyday Writing Activity: Identifying Supporting Details

Read the following passage from Helium.com and, in your journal, write down the main idea and the supporting details. Your instructor may ask you to share your responses with the rest of the class.

Learning a foreign language benefits a person in several ways. It allows you to communicate when traveling, have a better understanding of a foreign culture, improve foreign business relations, and expand the capabilities of the mind. Learning a foreign language will help you to appropriately interact with other cultures and avoid the many faux pas made by many foreigners, sometimes causing embarrassing or insulting situations. Learning a second language will make your travel more enjoyable, and you more employable.

Higher-Level Reading Strategies

Identifying the main idea and the supporting ideas will enhance comprehension of college-level reading material. However, college requires more than just comprehending the material; as we pointed out in

Chapter 1, college is also about critical thinking. As college students, you need to go beyond comprehension to higher-level thinking skills where you engage and interact with the text more actively. In this section, we discuss two reading strategies that are useful for greater engagement with the text:

- Annotation.
- Analysis.

Annotate the Text

To *annotate* is to make written notes in the margins to yourself about the text as you are reading it. This will help you to identify the main idea, the secondary idea(s), the supporting examples, and so on. It will also enable you to identify opposite points of view, as well as ask questions where you don't understand or don't agree with the writer. Because annotations are notes to yourself, they do not need to be fully written out. And you can write abbreviated notes, or mark and comment on things in the text that will help you understand the reading better. Here is an example.

Acai Berries and Acai Berry Juice—What Are the Health Benefits?
WebMD

How is acai pronounced? What does its juice taste like?

Touted means sold: marketers sell the benefits of acai berries.

Good question.

1   Have you heard about the acai berry? Do you want to know more about the health benefits of acai berries and berry juice? Acai berries are highly <u>touted</u> by marketers who say it's one of the elite superfoods with anti-aging and weight loss properties. Some manufacturers use acai berries in cosmetics and beauty products. But do scientific studies support these claims of acai benefits?

What is the acai berry?

2   The acai berry is an inch-long reddish, purple fruit. It comes from the acai palm tree (Euterpe oleracea), which is native to Central and South America.

Antioxidant means: helps prevent heart disease and cancer.

3   Research on the acai berry has focused on its possible <u>antioxidant</u> activity. Theoretically, that activity may help prevent diseases caused by oxidative stress such as heart disease and cancer.

Is the acai berry healthy?

Sounds like everyone should eat more purple and blue foods.

4   Acai contains several substances called anthocyanins and flavonoids.

5   The word anthocyanin comes from two Greek words meaning "plant" and "blue." Anthocyanins are responsible for the red, purple, and blue hues in many fruits, vegetables, and flowers. Foods that are richest in anthocyanins -- such as blueberries, red grapes, red wine, and acai -- are very strongly colored, ranging from deep purple to black.

6   Anthocyanins and flavonoids are powerful antioxidants that help defend the body against life's stressors. They also play a role in the body's cell protection system. Free radicals are harmful byproducts produced by the body. Eating a diet rich in antioxidants may interfere with aging and the disease process by neutralizing free radicals.

7   By lessening the destructive power of free radicals, antioxidants may help reduce the risk of some diseases, such as heart disease and cancer.

Are there known health benefits of acai berries?

I wonder if anyone I know eats these?

8   Some studies show that acai fruit pulp has a very high antioxidant capacity with even more antioxidant content than cranberry, raspberry, blackberry, strawberry, or blueberry. Studies are ongoing, though, and the jury is still out.

9   People eat acai berries to address various health conditions. But so far, acai berries have no known health benefit that's any different than that of other similar fruits.

Can acai berries boost weight loss?

Again, that "superfood" word—look that up.

10   Scientists are learning more about the functional power of <u>superfoods</u>, such as the acai berry. Although acai is touted in some weight loss products, few studies have tested the benefit of acai in promoting weight loss.

11   For now, plenty of research supports eating a diet rich in antioxidants. There's no doubt that berries and other fruits are a key part of any healthy diet promoting weight loss. The jury's still out on whether there is something special about acai's ability to shed excess pounds.

Why are acai berries used in beauty products?

12   Some cosmetics and beauty products contain acai oil in the ingredient list. That's because acai oil is a powerhouse of antioxidants.

Interesting. I'll have to check my shampoo.

13   Studies show that acai oil may be a safe alternative to other tropical oils used in beauty products such as facial and body creams, anti-aging skin therapies, shampoos and conditioners, and other products. When acai oil is processed and stored long-term, the antioxidant levels remain high.

Do acai berries and acai juice have any side effects?

14   If you have pollen allergies or have a known hypersensitivity to acai or similar berries, you may want to avoid this fruit. When eaten in moderate amounts, though, acai is likely safe.

Everyday Writing Activity: Annotation

Annotate the following passage from the Special Olympics Web site, marking/commenting on it as needed. Then write a short paragraph in your journal describing your annotations and why you made them. Your instructor may ask you to share your response with the rest of the class.

Special Olympics: Who We Are

1   Special Olympics is composed of passionate, committed individuals from every walk of life, who recognize the value and unique gifts of people with intellectual disabilities. And, who together share the common belief of dignity, equality and opportunity for ALL people.

2   Special Olympics is a global nonprofit organization serving the nearly 200 million people with intellectual disabilities, with a presence in nearly 200 countries worldwide. With seven regional offices, we are constantly expanding to add new Programs in every part of the world—which is why we can say with all truth that "the sun never sets on the Special Olympics movement."

Special Olympics founder Eunice Kennedy Shriver with a Special Olympics China athlete.

3   Every day, 365 days a year, our Board members, global leadership, staff, and volunteers work to bring Special Olympics to as many communities as possible. Speaking hundreds of languages and coming from diverse cultures and backgrounds, the common thread tying us together is our belief in people with intellectual disabilities and in Special Olympics: its unique ability to envision and create a world where every person is celebrated and accepted—all through the simple platform of sport.

4   In the decades since Eunice Kennedy Shriver founded Special Olympics in 1968, Special Olympics has been supported by a who's who of outstanding leaders in the fields of sports, education, business, government, and disability advocacy. They serve on the International Board of Directors, give financial and political support, act as spokespeople, help build awareness, and establish connections with important organizations and reluctant governments. International Board members include President of Iceland Olafur Grimmson; Olympic Romanian gymnast Nadia Comaneci; pop singer and actress Vanessa Williams; Coca-Cola CEO Muhtar Kent; and First Lady of Panama Vivian Fernández de Torrijos.

5   Under the Board's guidance and the guidance of Special Olympics leaders, our global family of grass-roots volunteers, athletes, family and staff work tirelessly to ensure a quality sports experience for Special Olympics athletes and an accepting community for their families. Every day, talented individuals in offices around the world work to bring our sports, education, and health

programs to as many places as possible. We work so that we may realize founder Eunice Kennedy Shriver's vision: to improve the lives of people with intellectual disabilities everywhere, and, in turn, transform the lives of everyone they touch—building a better, more accepting world for all of us.

Analyze the Text

A very effective way of reading to engage with the text is to analyze it. To analyze a text means to break it down into its component parts in order to be able to critique it. Usually, when analyzing a reading, readers analyze the following:

- **The assumptions made by the writer:** When a writer makes assumptions, it means the writer believes something is true, when it may or may not be so. For instance, when a writer writes that young drivers are risky drivers, he/she is assuming that all young drivers are unsafe drivers, when that may not be the case. It is important for readers to be alert to such assumptions.
- **The evidence used by the writer:** As readers, you should look carefully at the evidence presented by the writer to support his/her points. Has the writer used evidence effectively, or is the evidence used weak and unrelated to the writer's claim?
  - **Weak and unrelated use of evidence:** *In some places of the world, winter can be harsh. However, a lot of people don't like to buy too many winter clothes.* (Clothing preferences have nothing to do with the harshness of the season.)
  - **Strong use of evidence:** *In some places of the world, winter can be harsh. For instance, winter brings bitter cold and heavy snow to parts of Afghanistan.* (Here, the writer gives a specific example of a particular place where winter is often harsh.)
- **The sources, if any, used by the writer:** As a critical reader, you should look carefully at the sources (if any) used by the writer to support his/her idea:
  - How relevant are the sources? Are they directly related to the topic?
  - How current are they? Are they more than three to five years old?
  - How objective, and therefore, how reliable, are the sources? Do they promote one point of view over the other? Are they fact-based rather than opinion-based?
- **The biases of the writer:** As readers, be aware that writers often bring their own biases and values to their writing, which affects the

reliability and objectivity of their work. As you read, therefore, ask yourself the following questions:

- What is the writer's background?
- What are his/her political and/or religious views? How might they have influenced his/her writing?
- Does the passage reveal any other kind of author bias?

<table>
<tr><td>

LO2

Respond to what you are reading, and develop your vocabulary

</td><td>

Post-reading Strategies

You can improve your critical reading skills by using two post-reading strategies: responding to the reading and learning new vocabulary.

</td></tr>
</table>

Responding to the Text

A *written response to what you have read after you have finished reading* is an excellent strategy that ensures you have understood what you read. You can also view it as a conversation between you and the writer about the reading. Use your journal to write your responses so that you will have a record of your thoughts and can refer to them as necessary. There are several ways you can respond to the reading:

- Write a summary of the reading in your journal to ensure that you understand it well (see Chapter 3 on writing a summary).
- Write a letter to the author in your journal, agreeing or disagreeing with him/her, asking questions about the reading, and/or seeking clarifications. It is important to speak your thoughts freely, expressing appreciation for the reading (or disappointment) or confusion or frustration (or disagreement).
- Relate the reading to your own life. What connections can you make? Where do you see a disconnect? Why?
- You and a classmate can discuss the reading to see how each of you reacted to the reading. Do you agree with each other in your opinion of the reading? Do you disagree about anything?

Dealing with Difficult Vocabulary

As you read, you may come across unfamiliar words that will disturb the flow of your reading and your ability to fully comprehend it. Throughout this book, we have provided you with the meanings of some of the difficult vocabulary in the readings. On pages 21–22, we also discussed the importance of identifying key words and inferring meaning from them. This strategy may bypass the need to understand each and every word. However, if you encounter difficult vocabulary whose meaning needs to be clarified, you can follow a few simple strategies to help you understand what the word means:

1. **Look at the word in the context in which it is used.** For instance, if the sentence reads, "The musician enthralled his readers with his beautiful music," you can safely assume that "enthralled" means something similar to "to charm" or "to captivate," because the music is beautiful. Similarly, in the sentence, "The patient came to the rehabilitation center for physical therapy," you can infer from the phrase "physical therapy" that rehabilitation probably means a place where one comes for exercise that will restore good health.

2. **Look at prefixes and suffixes.** Together, they are the building blocks of many words in English. A prefix is a linguistic element that is attached to the *beginning* of a word to indicate its meaning. Thus, if you know the meaning of the prefix, you can figure out what the word means. For instance, "re" means "again," so the word "revision" means "to see again." Similarly, the prefix "un" means "not"; thus, "unable" means "not able." A suffix, on the other hand, is a linguistic element that is attached *after* the main word. If you know the meaning of the suffix, you can often decipher what the whole word means. For instance, the suffix "ful" means "filled with." Thus, "joyful" means "filled with joy." Similarly "ist" means "one who does something"; thus, "pianist" means "one who plays the piano." See pages 492–494 for a list of some of the most common prefixes and suffixes.

3. **Look up unfamiliar words in any standard dictionary.** It will give you the meaning of the word, and often also its part of speech, its origin, and sometimes its synonym, too. Depending on the dictionary, it may also include examples of how the word may be used in a sentence. You can also consult online dictionaries.

Everyday Writing Activity: Chapter Reflection

Please respond to the following questions in your journal. Your instructor may ask you to share your responses with the rest of the class.

1. What are the main points about reading effectively that you learned from this chapter?
2. Which of the pre-reading strategies do you think you may find most useful as you continue to read for your college courses? Why?
3. Which of the post-reading strategies do you think you may find most useful as you continue to read for your college courses? Why?

MyWritingLab™ For support in meeting this chapter's objectives, log in to **www.mywritinglab.com** and select **Reading Skills** and **Vocabulary Development**.

Chapter 3

The Reading–Writing Connection: Summary and Response

Learning Objectives

In this chapter, you will learn how to:

LO1 Identify ways summaries are used in writing

LO2 Organize, write, and use a summary

f you were involved in a car accident, you would accurately **summarize** what took place in an accident report. Anyone else involved in the accident would also file a summary report—and a police officer will summarize the information from those texts into his or her own report.

You might also **respond** to that auto accident by being really mad (if someone ran into you) or apologetic (if the accident was your fault) or ashamed (if you did something really stupid that caused the accident). You also might respond to the police officer's report if you were listed at fault for the accident and you do not think it was your fault.

We summarize and respond to all sorts of things:

- Doctors take notes and summarize their visits with patients. Those summaries are critical to effective patient care.
- Credit reports summarize a person's credit history, and based on such a summary, the person will or will not be approved for a mortgage or other loan: loan officers respond to what is, in effect, a summary through the decision they make about the loan.
- You may have a detailed résumé listing all of your work experience. But when you apply for a job, you probably will summarize that résumé in your job application letter. Potential employers will respond to your job application.
- Workplace evaluations often include a summary of a person's job description, along with summaries of what the person accomplished. Supervisors respond to those evaluations by making raise decisions and the like.
- Your teachers may sit down with you and summarize your work for the semester. Your academic advisor will summarize collected information from all of your teachers and respond by helping guide your future coursework.

In high school, you probably wrote book reports that contained a summary of the book. You may also have responded to the book by arguing that it used narrative effectively or had a great story line. You also may have written reports that critiqued a text or a character or explained how a text, film, or cultural event created an emotional *response* in the audience.

Now, in your college writing class you might be asked to summarize and also respond to an essay or other text. And in many of those classes you will be asked to *use* those summaries in your own papers. Summarizing what someone else wrote about your topic often provides evidence to support your own claims and assertions.

We have paired *summary* and *response* in this chapter because they are useful connections between reading and writing. As you know, Chapter 2 centered on college-level reading. The next few chapters will focus on college-level writing. One "bridge" between the two includes summarizing the things you read and responding to them.

Introducing Summary

The purpose of a **summary** is to provide the most important details of something. When writing a summary, you must consider (1) your audience (and what they already may know about your subject), (2) how much information (and what kind of information) they will need to understand what you are summarizing, and (3) what kind of format that information should be in. A summary includes what is called the "gist" of the text: the most important points a text makes. *Gist* means the essentials, the most important parts of something. When you summarize, your summary should be just that: the most important parts of the text you read.

Everyday Writing Activity: Summarizing Part of a Your Day

In a brief paragraph in your journal, summarize what you did during a one-hour period today. You select the time you want to summarize. Your instructor may want you to share your responses with the rest of the class.

Introducing Response

Response can take a number of forms. Often we think of an emotional response, but there are many other ways to respond to something. You might respond to something by making logical connections to other events or texts; you might respond by arguing that something is incorrect or misguided; you might compare what you read about to something else.

For example, once you summarized an hour of your day (in the preceding activity), you might respond to that summary by thinking, "I wasted that whole hour playing video games. I could have been studying. Now I worry that I won't pass the test." Or, you might respond by writing, "It really helped clear my mind to get away for a while and not think about that test I have tomorrow. Now I can study more effectively."

Everyday Writing Activity: Responding to Your Own Summary

In a brief paragraph in your journal, respond to your own summary of part of your day. Your instructor may want you to share your response with the rest of the class.

Student Writing: Summarizing a Text

The everyday writing activities have given you the chance to practice a little. Now, here is a longer text and a brief student summary of that text.

Original Text

U.S. Fish and Wildlife Service Releases Annual List of Foreign Candidates under Endangered Species Act

1   The U.S. Fish and Wildlife Service today released its Annual Notice of Review of Foreign Species, a yearly appraisal of the current status of foreign plants and animals that are considered candidates for protection under the Endangered Species Act (ESA). Currently, there are 594 foreign species listed under the ESA, compared to about 1,371 species native to the United States.

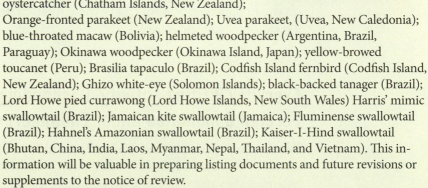

2   The Service designated 20 foreign species as candidates for ESA protection. Candidate species are those for which the Service has enough information on their status and threats to propose them as threatened or endangered, but developing a proposed rule to add them to the federal lists of threatened and endangered wildlife and plants is precluded by higher priority listing actions.

3   As part of this review, the Service is soliciting additional information on these 20 candidate species, which include the southern helmeted curassow (Bolivia, Peru); Bogota rail (Colombia); Takahe (New Zealand); Chatham oystercatcher (Chatham Islands, New Zealand); Orange-fronted parakeet (New Zealand); Uvea parakeet, (Uvea, New Caledonia); blue-throated macaw (Bolivia); helmeted woodpecker (Argentina, Brazil, Paraguay); Okinawa woodpecker (Okinawa Island, Japan); yellow-browed toucanet (Peru); Brasilia tapaculo (Brazil); Codfish Island fernbird (Codfish Island, New Zealand); Ghizo white-eye (Solomon Islands); black-backed tanager (Brazil); Lord Howe pied currawong (Lord Howe Islands, New South Wales) Harris' mimic swallowtail (Brazil); Jamaican kite swallowtail (Jamaica); Fluminense swallowtail (Brazil); Hahnel's Amazonian swallowtail (Brazil); Kaiser-I-Hind swallowtail (Bhutan, China, India, Laos, Myanmar, Nepal, Thailand, and Vietnam). This information will be valuable in preparing listing documents and future revisions or supplements to the notice of review.

4   All candidates are assigned a listing priority number based on the magnitude and imminence of the threats they face. In many cases, habitat loss and degradation is the most significant threat to these species. The complete notice

(continued)

and list of proposed and candidate species that appears in the Federal Register and can be found online at http://www.fws.gov/endangered/what-we-do/international-activities.html.

5   Listing foreign species under the ESA can generate conservation benefits such as increased awareness of listed species, research efforts to address conservation needs or funding for in-situ conservation of the species in its range countries. The ESA provides for limited financial assistance to develop and manage programs to conserve listed species in foreign countries, encourages conservation programs for such species, and allows for assistance for programs, such as personnel and training.

Summary of "List of Foreign Candidates Under Endangered Species Act"

There are about half as many foreign species as there are American species listed as endangered under the U.S. Endangered Species Act (ESA) (594 foreign as compared to 1371 native species).

The U.S. Fish & Wildlife Service recently added 20 foreign species to the list, most of them birds from the Pacific, Asia, and South America. Species are listed when the Service has sufficient information on threats to them. In many cases, the loss or decline of their habitat, or where the species lives, is the biggest threat.

Once a species is listed by the Service, there is more awareness of the dangers it faces, which can improve research and conservation efforts. The Fish & Wildlife Service also has some funding available to help with local research and programs.

How do you, as a reader, respond to this text about foreign species placed on the Endangered Species List of the United States? Do you think this is a good or a bad idea? Why?

Everyday Writing Activity: Responding to "List of Foreign Candidates Under Endangered Species Act"

When your instructors ask you to respond to a text, they will give you guidance on *how* to respond—what they would like you to focus on. For example, they may ask you to respond by focusing on:

- What new information you learned from the text.
- Whether you agree (or not) with the text, and why.
- How the text relates to other texts you read for the class.
- Your initial reactions to the text: surprise, interest, etc.

In no more than two paragraphs, in your journal respond to "List of Foreign Candidates Under Endangered Species Act" by writing about what surprised you when you read this text—and why you were surprised. Your teacher may ask you to share your response with several of your classmates.

LO1

Identify ways summaries are used in writing

Using a Summary

As we mentioned earlier, one way to use a summary is to learn from it as you write it: the act of putting down on paper the most important parts of any text you read will help you understand and remember it. And, of course, you will use that summarized information in the papers you write.

Here is an example: student writer Lea Charles was asked to research what was being done in various countries to help their wild animal populations not just to survive, but to flourish. As part of her research, she wrote a brief summary of the "List of Foreign Candidates Under Endangered Species Act." How can student writer Lea use her summary in her own paper? Possibilities include:

Ways Lea Can Use Her Summary	Example
Mentioning the focus of the information in her own title	**Title:** *How Foreign Species Can Be Listed as Endangered, Which Helps to Save Wild Animals*
Using her summary as part of her introduction	**Start of Lea's introduction:** *Many people would be surprised to learn that there are about half as many foreign species as there are American species listed as endangered under the U.S. Endangered Species Act (ESA) (594 foreign as compared to 1371 native species).*
Using part of her notes to summarize one aspect of the essay	**Lea can summarize something from the essay in the body of her text:** In many cases, the loss or decline of their habitat, or where the species lives, is the biggest threat.
Using part of her summary in her own conclusion	**Part of Lea's conclusion:** *Just by listing them, the Fish & Wildlife Service creates more awareness of the dangers those species face, which can improve research and conservation efforts around the world.*

Note that all of Lea's uses of the "List of Foreign Candidates" text came directly from her own summary notes of that text. Once she read and annotated that text, and then turned her annotations into a summary, Lea found that summary useful when she wrote her own paper.

LO2

Organize, write, and use a summary

Effective Summaries

There are many possible ways that you might be asked to construct a summary; here are a few examples.

Summary of Qualifications for a Job Application

When you apply for a job, you usually provide a résumé—a list of your past education, work experience, references, and so on. Many job applications ask for a letter to accompany your résumé. Such a letter often includes the reasons you want the position and a summary of your past experience and education—a summary that will help readers of that letter see how you "fit" the job requirements. To construct such a summary as part of your letter, you would go over your own experience and educational background, *summarizing* the most important and relevant details. That section of your application letter might look like these examples from student Harry Moore's application for a medical assistant's position:

This summary hits the highlights of Moore's education, and how, specifically, it relates to the position he is applying for.

This summary outlines Moore's past background and his experience with computer software.

Summary of Educational Qualifications

The job advertisement asks for an Associate's Degree in Medical Technology. As listed on my résumé, my recent AA degree included an extra twelve hours of coursework in medical imaging. In addition, my three classes in medical databases give me a background in how the imaging results are stored, accessed, and used by medical professionals.

Summary of Technical Qualifications

My college classes included Microsoft Excel (Advanced) and Entourage (Advanced). In addition, I have used all Microsoft Office products in a fast-paced office environment for six years. My database experience includes advanced work with Access. I am familiar with all office machines, including FAX machines and high-speed copiers.

Everyday Writing Activity: Summarize Your Educational Background

In your journal, briefly summarize your own high school experience and educational background. That could include a high school diploma, a GED, or perhaps another test that you took and passed. In a résumé, you would list the classes you took, sports or other activities were you involved in, and so on. But for a summary, you put that information into narrative form. Your instructor may ask you to share your writing with the rest of the class.

Job Description Summary

Job descriptions are summaries that form the basis of any employee evaluation—positive or negative. After all, how could a supervisor explain how well (or poorly) an employee is doing his/her work without first outlining what those duties involve?

Here is a job description from the Bureau of Labor that summarizes the duties of physician assistants. It could be used as the basis for a workplace evaluation that would compare and contrast how well the employee performed these job duties:

Bureau of Labor Statistics

Physician assistants (PAs) practice medicine under the supervision of physicians and surgeons. They should not be confused with medical assistants, who perform routine clinical and clerical tasks. (Medical assistants are discussed elsewhere in the Handbook.) PAs are formally trained to provide diagnostic, therapeutic, and preventive healthcare services, as delegated by a physician. Working as members of a healthcare team, they take medical histories, examine and treat patients, order and interpret laboratory tests and x rays, and make diagnoses. They also treat minor injuries by suturing, splinting, and casting. PAs record progress notes, instruct and counsel patients, and order or carry out therapy. Physician assistants also may prescribe certain medications. In some establishments, a PA is responsible for managerial duties, such as ordering medical supplies or equipment and supervising medical technicians and assistants.

Everyday Writing Activity: Summarize Your Work Experience

In your journal, and in no more than one page, summarize your own work background and experience. If you have not yet had what might be called

(continued)

a "formal" job, perhaps you mowed lawns, or shoveled snow, or did work around your own home: those are all work experiences for you to summarize. Your instructor may ask you to share your summary with the rest of the class.

Everyday Writing Activity: Responding to a Physician's Assistant Job

In your journal, and in no more than two paragraphs, respond to the type of work a Physician's Assistant does, as outlined in the preceding job description. Would you like to do this kind of work? Why or why not? Your instructor may ask you to share your response with the rest of the class.

Everyday Writing Activity: Writing to Reflect on This Chapter

In your journal, answer these questions to reflect on what you have learned in this chapter.

1. One important thing to remember when I summarize is to _____.
2. I can use the summaries I write when _____.
3. One time I summarized a text was when I _____.
4. One time when I summarized a situation was when I _____.
5. I would summarize the "List of Foreign Candidates Under Endangered Species Act" by writing: _____.
6. I might respond to Lea Charles's summary of the "List of Foreign Candidates Under Endangered Species Act" by writing: _____.

MyWritingLab™ For support in meeting this chapter's objectives, log in to **www.mywritinglab.com** and select **Summary Writing**.

Chapter 4

The Writer's Situation: Purpose, Audience, and Context

Learning **O**bjectives

In this chapter, you will learn to:

LO1 Determine the writer's purpose in writing

LO2 Analyze the writer's audience

LO3 Identify the writer's context—that is, the environment in which the writing will be written and read

As the photograph on the previous page reminds us, languages are different; the same meaning can be expressed in many different ways. Think of your familiarity with other languages:

- Have you ever had the opportunity to learn to read and write in a different language?
- If yes, which one(s)?
- If no, would you be interested in learning a different language? If yes, say why, and which one(s) you would be interested in learning. If not, say why not.
- Do any of your family members or your friends know how to read and write in a foreign language? If yes, which one(s) are they familiar with?

No matter what language you use, you must construct a piece of writing in that language. Like all things that people make, writing has to be "built." This building process starts with first thinking about the writing. Just as an architect draws up a blueprint of the building he/she is going to build, based on the purposes to which it will be put, similarly the writer begins with thoughts on what he/she may write based on purpose, audience, and context before actually starting to write. Just as building a house is time-consuming and hard work, writing is also a process that takes time and effort. In this chapter you will learn to think about your purpose, audience, and context before starting to write.

LO1

Determine the writer's purpose in writing

Purpose: Why Am I Writing?

The first step in thinking about writing is to ask yourself the following questions:

Why am I writing? What is my purpose?

These questions are important because writing does not happen in a vacuum; all good writing has one, or several, reasons for writing behind it because almost all writers want to *do* something with their writing. These reasons are known as your **purpose** in writing. Therefore, before you begin to write, ask yourself why you are writing, what your purpose is. Different kinds of writing have different purposes, and good writers stay focused on their purpose in writing. For instance:

- If you are writing a college textbook or a newspaper article, your purpose is to provide information about the subject or topic you are writing about.
- If you are writing a newspaper editorial, or an opinion piece, your purpose is to persuade your readers about something.

- If you are writing for a popular magazine, your purpose could be either to inform readers about a topic or to entertain them.
- If you are writing a review of a movie or a book, your purpose is to evaluate.
- If you are writing a how-to manual, your purpose is to inform readers how to, for example, assemble a piece of furniture or hook up the DVD/Blu-ray player to the TV.
- If you are writing a comic strip, your purpose is to entertain.
- If you are writing an advertisement, your purpose is to sell something or attempt to influence readers' mind about something.
- If you are writing a letter to your grandmother or to your friend Sam, your purpose is to find out how they are doing, and you write accordingly.
- If you are writing to fulfill a college assignment, your instructor will most likely tell you your purpose for writing, and you need to keep that in mind as you are writing.

 ## Critical Thinking Activity: Questions to Determine Purpose

Before you get started on your writing, ask yourself the following questions:

1. Why am I writing?
   - Am I writing to inform?
   - Am I writing to evaluate?
   - Am I writing to persuade?
   - Am I writing to entertain?
   - Am I writing to explain?
2. Or am I writing with some other purpose in mind?

The following sections describe what characterizes some of these different kinds of writing. Once you have your purpose for writing clearly thought out, then you are closer to actually starting to write.

Writing to Inform

To *inform* is to let somebody know something or bring them up to date about something, or to make something clearer to the reader. Writers often write to inform readers about matters that are important to them. For instance:

- You could write to your favorite aunt informing her about your performance in a recent play.
- You could explain in an e-mail to your pen pal in Germany the significance of the American holiday of Thanksgiving.

- You could write to inform your local city council that the street lights near your house have not been lighting up at night and they need to be checked out.
- You could write a report to your college president informing her about the recent student government elections.
- You could inform your English teacher in an e-mail why you were not in class last Tuesday.
- You could write an essay in your college magazine informing your fellow students, faculty and staff members of the consequences of environmental pollution on campus.

Because this kind of writing provides information to the reader, it often includes facts, statistics, and relevant background information (social, political, historical, religious, financial, etc.)

Writing to Evaluate

To *evaluate* means to assess something—to appraise its value or its worth, its strength(s), and its weakness(es)—based on specific criteria. Writers frequently write with the goal of evaluating something in order to make a judgment about it, and pass that judgment on to readers. For instance:

- You could write an evaluation of your current or previous English class, or your math class, or any other class, for future students.
- You could write an evaluation of student dining facilities for the campus newspaper.
- You could write an evaluation of a recent movie, concert, or football game for your college student magazine.
- You could write an evaluation of available housing around your campus for students looking for cheap, affordable apartments.

Usually, evaluation essays require constructing a list of specific **criteria**—those things on which you will base your evaluation and that will help you come to a conclusion about the topic. For example, when evaluating apartments, you may use the criteria of location and rent and judge each apartment accordingly. Because an evaluation is judgmental in tone, it uses a lot of evaluative words like *good*, *well done*, *poorly presented*, *brilliant*, *organized*, and the like.

Writing to Persuade

Often in academic writing, your goal is to argue effectively, which means that your readers understand your position, your argument. They may not *agree* with you, but they can, at least, see where you are coming from and what your points and evidence are. To **persuade** someone, though, you want that person to be convinced by your argument and, most often, to act because of your argument (e.g., to vote for a certain candidate).

Often, you will try to persuade someone to act, or to do something, so if he/she does what you suggest, he/she clearly has been persuaded. For example, if your best friend suggested that a new exhibit at your college art museum was one that you should see, and if you were persuaded by her, then you would *believe* it was an interesting exhibit and you would take the time to see it.

In an argument, therefore, your writing needs to be clear and thoughtful, it must make a point (your **thesis**), and it must provide evidence to support that point (for a discussion of thesis statements, see Chapter 7) always with the goal of getting your readers to do something.

Writing for Other Purposes

Please remember that informing, evaluating, and persuading are not the only purposes in writing. These purposes are simply the more common ones. Writers may also write to share an experience, analyze an event, or explain the effects of something new. There can be many other additional purposes for writing, depending on what the writer wants the writing to do, as well as who the writer is writing for (the audience) and the context in which the writing is going to be written and read. Audience and context will be discussed in the next two sections of this chapter.

Everyday Writing Activity: Writing about Purpose

In your journal, please provide one example *of your own* for each the different kinds of purposes in writing discussed in the previous pages. For example, explain a situation (in no more than one paragraph) where you wrote to

- Inform.
- Evaluate.
- Persuade.

Who was your audience? What was your topic? If you can remember your point (your thesis), also list it. Why did you construct this piece of writing (for a classroom assignment, for some personal reason, etc.)? Your instructor may ask you to share your responses with the rest of the class.

Audience: For Whom Am I Writing?

Audience, in the context of writing, refers to the reader. Writers have readers, just as speakers have listeners and performers have an audience of spectators. Your teacher has you, his/her students, listening to him/her. The difference between a speaker and a writer's audience is that often a speaker's audience is physically present, while the writer's audience is usually not present physically. However, readers *are* there, even if invisible, and the writer's task is to keep them and their needs in mind throughout the entire writing process. Good writing is always **reader centered** (meets readers' needs) rather than **writer centered** (written more for the writer and not for the readers).

Everyday Writing Activity: When You Are the Audience

This image shows readers—everyday people like you and us—who are the writer's audience. Look at the image, and respond to the following questions in your journal. Your instructor may ask you to share your responses with the rest of the class.

- How often do you visit a bookstore?
- What kinds of books do you like to browse through when you are at a bookstore? Please make a list of such books in order of preference.
- How often do you buy books from a bookstore? Once a month? Once in three or six months? Once a year or less?
- What kinds of books do you buy when you visit a bookstore?

- Do you prefer to buy books from an online bookstore, like Amazon .com or BarnesandNoble.com, or would you rather buy from an actual bookstore like the one in the image? Why?
- How often have you thought of yourself as a reader whose needs and interests the writer is trying to satisfy?

Because audience is such a critical element of writing, you need to *think* about your audience and ask yourself the following questions about your audience *before* you begin writing, as well as during the writing and revising process:

Critical Thinking Activity: Ask Yourself Questions about Your Audience

1. Who are my readers?
2. What might my audience already know about my topic?
3. What does my audience need to know that I should include in my writing?
4. Do I know enough about my subject, or do I need to conduct research about it?
5. Will visual aids of some kind help my audience see and understand what I mean?
6. What is the most effective way to organize and present my information to my audience?

Everyday Writing Activity: Writing about Details for Your Audience

Imagine this scenario. You are attending school, far away from home, and this weekend you have decided to inform your parents, your cousin Anne, and your pen pal Rashid, who lives in Morocco, how college life is working out for you. In your journal, write out what you think each of them would like to know. Then, consider these questions:

- What similarities and differences do you notice in what your different readers would like to know?
- How do you account for these differences, and what does this tell you about meeting audience needs?

Record your responses in your journal. Your instructor may ask you to share your responses with the rest of the class.

Everyday Writing Activity: Writing about Purpose and Audience

In Chapter 1, we discussed how important visual texts were and that, even though they are different in kind than written texts, they have messages to communicate to their viewers.

In the following photographs, determine what the purpose is—that is, what message each photograph is trying to communicate—and who you think the audience of each photograph is. Note your observations in your journal. Your instructor may ask you to share your responses with the rest of the class.

LO3

Identify the writer's context—that is, the environment in which the writing will be written and read

Context: What Is the Background for My Writing?

Context refers to the situation that generates the need for writing. There are two different kinds of context in writing: the writer's context and the reader's context.

The **writer's context** is the setting in which the writing is created. For instance:

- Students such as yourselves write in an academic context; your teacher has given you an assignment with specific criteria, and now you need to write to complete the assignment.
- Your classmate Ya Feng, who recently dropped out of school, may need to write a letter to the Registrar's Office asking for a refund of his tuition.
- Your supervisor at work may need to write an e-mail to all customer service representatives regarding improvement in phone etiquette.
- Your uncle may need to write to his health insurance company regarding nonpayment for a medical procedure he recently underwent.

The **reader's context** is the setting in which your writing is to be read. It requires thinking of the following questions before you begin writing:

Critical Thinking Activity: Ask Yourself Questions about the Reader's Context

1. Where are your readers likely to be when they are reading your writing? At home? At work? On the train/bus to work or returning home?
2. What is the world around them like? For instance, hybrid cars are being promoted for environmental reasons. If you are writing to your brother to encourage him to buy a hybrid car, what is his "world" like in terms of gasoline prices, his level of environmental awareness, and so on?
3. Are there any major political, social, and/or cultural upheavals, controversies, or excitements around your audience that might affect how they approach your writing? In this context, what should you include that might affect how readers approach what you write?
4. If you are writing to promote a product through an advertisement, the general public will be exposed to it along with many other ads on their way to work, or as they are flipping through magazines or television channels. In this context, what words, colors, and images will make your advertisement stand out from all the other advertisements that are available to the general public?

It is often easy to overlook the context in which the writing is received, but as a writer you should keep context in mind *before* you start to write and *as* you shape your writing. Doing so (along with thinking about purpose and audience) will help you decide how to shape your writing, how formal it should be in tone, and what you should include (evidence, facts, expert commentary, photographs). It will also help you decide what is not likely to be effective for your purpose in writing and for the audience you are writing to.

Everyday Writing Activity: Writing about Context

In your journal, list three writing situations in which you have found yourself in the past that generated the need for writing. Then, in no more than one paragraph for each, describe the context in which you were writing. Your instructor may ask you to share your responses with the rest of the class.

The Writer's Rhetorical Situation: A Summary

This chapter has focused on three elements writers should think about *before* beginning to write: (1) purpose, (2) audience, and (3) context. They are the foundations of all good writing, and along with the **writer** (the writer's age, gender, educational, social and cultural background, and so on, are all important) and the **topic,** they make up the writer's **rhetorical situation,** or the circumstances under which the writer writes. A rhetorical situation exists whenever a writer writes. Understanding these elements will help you write a focused, well-organized, and meaningful essay.

Everyday Writing Activity: Chapter Reflection

In your journal, please respond to the following prompts:

1. I learned that purpose in writing is _____.
2. I learned that audience in writing is _____.
3. I learned that context in writing is _____.

4. I learned that thinking about purpose, audience, and context *before* writing is necessary because _____.

5. I learned that what makes a writer's rhetorical situation is _____.

MyWritingLab™ For support in meeting this chapter's objectives, log in to www.mywritinglab.com and select **The Writing Process**.

Chapter 5

Using Writing Strategies and Appeals

Think about your writing habits as you prepare yourself for intensive writing in college, both in your writing courses and in other college classes you will be taking:

- Do you sometimes have multiple ideas for writing that you often write down here and there, as in the accompanying photo?
- If you do not write your ideas down in haphazard fashion, where do you write them?
- Do you feel stressed if you have too many ideas, or do you feel relieved that you have so many ideas for writing?
- How easy or difficult is it for you to structure your ideas into a piece of writing?

In Chapter 4, you learned about the importance of purpose, audience, and context—the rhetorical situation—in writing. These elements involve *why* you write, *to whom* you are writing, and *what* moves you to write. Chapters 5 through 8 will emphasize strategies involving *how* you write.

Sometimes, writers have trouble deciding how to come up with things to write about, how to present ideas to the reader, or how to make their purpose for writing clear to the audience. Experienced writers overcome these problems by using certain writing strategies that help them shape their writing for their intended audience and purpose. These strategies include *description, narration, informing, classification, definition, argument, cause and effect,* and *comparison and contrast*. Experienced writers also use their own credibility, emotional appeals, and logic to strengthen their writing. Called *ethos, pathos,* and *logos*, these strategies help writers persuade their audiences. The writing strategies and the appeals are discussed in this chapter. Once you learn to use them, you will be more prepared to write for college because:

- Your writing will meet the needs of your audience and your purpose in writing.
- You will be a more credible writer—someone who can be trusted and believed.

Strategies for Effective Writing

LO1

Use common writing strategies to help achieve your purpose in writing

One way to view the writing strategies is to see them as **modes** of writing or as writing patterns that help a writer develop and organize ideas to achieve his/her purpose. You can also view these strategies as tools that can help a writer better plan the writing. Just as a carpenter needs certain tools in order to do a job well, a writer also needs certain tools in order to write well.

The writing strategies can be used to write an entire essay, such as an analysis essay, an argument essay, or an evaluation essay, and so on, or they may be used as a method of development of a particular paragraph or paragraphs within an essay. For instance, you can write an argument essay in which the first few paragraphs *describe* the topic, and then the remaining paragraphs *argue* for or against it.

The following sections of this chapter explain and give examples of these writing strategies.

Description

The goal of descriptive writing is to **describe** a thing, person, place, or idea to readers in a way that they can understand and visualize what is being described without being physically present. Descriptions are often called paintings in words; just as an artist uses paint, so the descriptive writer "paints" a picture for readers through words.

Description uses of a lot of specific details, such as size, color, age, condition, weight, height, and so on, depending on the subject being described. **Sensory details** (using the five senses of sight, smell, taste, touch, and hearing) are also used, as is figurative language, such as similes and metaphors. Similes and metaphors are figures of speech that compare two often unlike things. A **simile** uses the word "like" or "as" to compare, as in the phrase "Her teeth are white as milk," while a **metaphor** compares without using "like" or "as." An example of a metaphor is "The inside of the house is a furnace" (meaning that it is very hot inside the house).

In college, your writing instructor may ask you to write an essay describing the most beautiful sunset you have ever seen. Your education professor may ask you to write a description of the services provided by a local daycare. Your culinary arts instructor may ask you to describe the meal prepared by a prominent chef who did a demonstration for your class.

The following passage from Experiencefestival.com describes the Bushman rabbit, a species of rabbit that is one of the rarest in the world.

The species typically has a black stripe running from the corner of the mouth over the cheek. It has a brown woolly tail, cream-colored fur on its belly and throat, and a broad, club-like hind foot. Its tail is pale brown with a tinge of black toward the tip.

This passage is focused on a single subject—the Bushman rabbit—and there are very vivid and specific details (adjectives) used to describe the animal, such as "brown woolly," "cream-colored," "broad club-like," and "pale." The writer has also used a simile: "club-like hind foot." Readers can easily "see" the bushman rabbit through the writer's description.

Everyday Writing Activity: Descriptive Paragraph

Using the strategy of description, write a paragraph on one of the following in your journal. Your instructor may ask you to share your paragraph with the rest of the class.

- A stormy day.
- My ideal vacation place.
- My favorite item of clothing.

Narration

To **narrate** means to tell something. A narration is often a detailed story, sometimes written chronologically, and often from the writer's point of view. When a writer uses the narrative strategy, he/she is telling the reader a story because it is a good way to get the writer's point across.

In college, you may have to use narration in your psychology class where you have to narrate the details of a case study. For your women's studies class, you may have to write a narrative essay on the life of one or more women's rights activists. Your writing teacher may ask you to write a personal narrative of a significant childhood event.

The following paragraph from the autobiography of Mahatma Gandhi, the political and spiritual leader of India during that country's independence movement, is an example of narrative writing:

There is an incident which occurred at the examination during my first year at the high school and which is worth recording. Mr. Giles, the Educational Inspector, had come on a visit of inspection. He had set us five words to write as a spelling exercise. One of the words was "kettle." I had misspelled it. The teacher tried to prompt me with the point of his boot, but I would not  be prompted. It was beyond me to see that he wanted me to copy the spelling from my neighbor's slate, for I had thought that the teacher was there to supervise us against copying. The result was that all the boys, except myself, were found to have spelled every word correctly. Only I had been stupid. The teacher tried later to bring this stupidity home to me, but without effect. I could never learn the art of "copying."

This paragraph exhibits all the characteristics of writing in the narrative mode:

- It provides details of one specific incident in Gandhi's life (the visit by a school inspector).
- It is told from the point of view of the writer.
- It is well organized, telling the events in the sequence in which they unfolded.

Everyday Writing Activity: Narrative Paragraph

Using the strategy of narration, write a paragraph about one of the following in your journal. Your instructor may ask you to share your paragraph with the rest of the class.

- A significant life experience.
- My first day in college.
- A memorable holiday.

Informing

To **inform** means to provide readers with knowledge. The goal of many college essays is to provide information or explain something to the reader (which are usually the goals of the textbooks you read in college, too). Thus, informative writing often includes a lot of facts, statistics, and examples in order to explain how something is done, how something works, how something is made, or how something happened.

In college, you may be asked to write an informative essay for your religious studies class, where you explain the principles underlying a major world religion. Your biology professor may ask your class to write an informative report on the life cycle of the frog. In a chemistry class, you may have to write a report explaining how to produce oxygen in a test tube.

The following text is about something you may already be familiar with: an MP3 player. As you read this brief text from Explainthatstuff .com, consider these questions:

- What did you learn that was new information to you?
- Is this an effective informative text? In what ways?
- How effectively does this text explain how MP3 technology works? What can you point to in the essay as an example?

MP3 Players

1   Technology can be absolutely astounding! MP3 players, such as iPods, are a great example. Smaller than a pack of cards and only a little heavier, they can store thousands of music tracks, photos, or videos so you can take them with you wherever you go. A typical

Quite possibly the best thing I have ever bought in my life: my 20GB Apple iPod. I still can't quite believe that this tiny little beauty holds (at the last count) 3,717 tracks on 401 albums by 250 artists—and yet fits in my pocket!

20GB (gigabyte) iPod has enough memory to store about 500 CDs—rather more than you can fit in your pocket! So what exactly is "MP3" and how does it work?

What is MP3 technology?

2   An MP3 player gets it name from the MP3 files that you store on it. Just as DOC is a type of computer file used by the Microsoft Word word-processing program, and PDF is another type of file for storing documents, so MP3 is a particular file type used for storing music. Think of MP3 as another type of computer file and an MP3 player as a special type of computer, dedicated to playing back sounds, and you're halfway to understanding how it all works.

3   It takes space to store information. If you've got some encyclopedias on CD-ROMs or DVDs, you'll know that computers are particularly good at cramming large amounts of information into pretty tiny spaces. The *Encyclopedia Britannica*, whose 20-odd volumes fill a whole shelf in your local public library, fits comfortably onto a couple of CDs or a single DVD. Tricks like this are possible because computers use a technique called compression—a way of squeezing information so it takes up much less room.

This passage is a good example of writing to inform: it informs readers about what MP3 technology is and how it is based on file compression.

Everyday Writing Activity: Informative Paragraph

Using the strategy of informing, write a paragraph on one of the following in your journal. Your instructor may ask you to share your paragraph with the rest of the class.

- Tourist sites in country X.
- How to bake a cake (or cook some other food item of your choice).
- The process of registering for classes on your campus.

Classification

To **classify** is to organize things into categories according to some basic similar characteristics. It is a useful writing skill, especially if your purpose in writing is to analyze something. Just as things have to be sorted and grouped in a logical way, ideas are often categorized so they can be presented to the reader in a more organized and analytical way.

Classification requires the use of a single organizing principle. For instance, if your topic is exercising, exercising equipment could be your organizing principle. In that case, do not use another organizing principle such as attitudes toward exercising.

In college, you may be asked to write an essay for your sociology class classifying your friends by the majors they have chosen. Your economics professor may ask you to write an essay classifying countries according to their economic power (economically prosperous to economically stable to economically weak and unstable). For your first-year composition class, you may be asked to write a research paper categorizing colleges in the United States by the degrees they offer.

The following paragraph on shoppers and their shopping techniques from PBWorks.com is a good illustration of the use of classification as a writing strategy, and its role in analyzing a topic.

Shoppers can be classified according to their shopping techniques, as necessity shoppers, over spenders, and impulsive shoppers. Necessity shoppers have an uncomplicated and normal shopping technique. They purchase only the items that are necessary, such as food and toiletries, and they only get these items when they need them. The over spenders purchase too many items and they spend too much money on them. They buy unnecessary products, such as clothes and accessories. They can turn a simple trip to the store into a wallet draining extravaganza. Finally, there are impulsive shoppers. They are a combination between necessity shoppers and over spenders. They intend to be necessity shoppers by buying items that they need, but they turn into over spenders  by buying unnecessary clothes and useless items. Even though there are millions of shoppers worldwide, they can easily be classified by their techniques as necessity shoppers, over spenders, or impulsive shoppers.

The paragraph is focused on the central topic of shopping, and the organizing principle is the shopping technique of shoppers. The categories are necessity shoppers, overspenders, and impulsive shoppers. The shopping techniques of each category is analyzed through classification of categories.

Everyday Writing Activity: Classification Paragraph

Using the strategy of classification, write a paragraph on one of the following in your journal. Make sure to determine your organizing principle first. Your instructor may ask you to share your paragraph with the rest of the class.

- Television shows.
- Cars.
- Magazines.

Definition

To **define** is to explain to readers what a term means by providing basic information about the topic and supporting that information with facts and examples for better understanding. Like classification, definition is a helpful writing strategy when writers want to analyze something. It is also useful when writers want to explain something to readers or inform them about something. There are various ways of defining a term:

- **Defining by analysis:** relating the term to be defined with others in the same category and highlighting the similarities and differences. For instance, you could define a migraine by comparing it to a sinus headache or a tension headache.
- **Defining by function:** explaining what something does or how it works. For instance, you could define a digital clock by explaining how it works.
- **Defining by structure:** explaining how something is organized or is put together. For instance, you could define organized tours by explaining how tour companies set up different kinds of tours such as bus tours, walking tours, hiking tours etc.
- **Defining by what a term is not:** explaining a term by showing how it is different from something else. For instance, you could define socialism by stating that it is not communism, and then pointing out the dissimilarities between the two political philosophies.

In college, you may be asked to write an essay defining a specific learning theory for your education class. Time management may be the topic of a definition essay you have to write for your college success course. For your nursing class, you may have to write a definition essay on the topic of chronic illness.

The following paragraph defining a nontraditional college student appeared on the University of Idaho Web site. It is a good illustration of the use of definition as a writing strategy:

> To understand what a "nontraditional student" is, we should first define "traditional student." A traditional college student is between the ages of eighteen and twenty-two, attends school full time, is single, and does not work full time. In contrast to this, a nontraditional student is over the age of twenty-two, usually attends school less then full time, often has a family, and may work full time. Cross defines the nontraditional student as "an adult who returns to school full or part time while maintaining responsibilities such as employment, family, and other responsibilities of adult life. These students also may be referred to as adult students, re-entry students, returning students and adult learners." The major difference between the two student groups is the number of responsibilities outside of the classroom.

In this paragraph, there is a central topic—the nontraditional college student—that is being defined, there is a clear definition, and the definition is achieved by defining the nontraditional student by what he/she is not—a traditional student.

Everyday Writing Activity: Definition Paragraph

Using the strategy of definition, write a paragraph on one of the following in your journal. Your instructor may ask you to share your paragraph with the rest of the class.

- Fast food.
- Globalization.
- Higher education.

Argument

In writing, argument does not mean a fight or dispute. Rather, **argument** is writing that presents a point of view based on logical reasoning, not personal opinion. The goal is most often **persuasion,** to persuade readers to do something (like vote for a specific candidate) or to persuade readers to change their minds on a controversial/debatable topic and agree with the writer. The writer's point of view is presented in the form of a **thesis statement** (for more on thesis statements, see pages 95–97). The writer also often uses facts, statistics, and data (obtained through research) to make the argument more convincing. Good argument writing also discusses the opposite point of view so that the argument does not appear one-sided. Some argument writing may not persuade readers enough to make them act differently or to change their mind, but if it is successful, readers will at least understand the writer's point of view.

In college, your writing teacher may ask you to write an argument essay on a controversial topic such as whether all college graduates should be required to learn a foreign language. Your economics professor may ask you to write an essay arguing that capitalism is the best economic choice for countries in the 21st century. Your political science professor may ask you to write an argument essay supporting one-party democracy versus multiparty democracy (or vice versa).

The following paragraphs on the AIDS vaccine from a newspaper editorial are a good example of the use of argument in writing:

Give a Cheer to the Experimental AIDS Vaccine and Then Get Back to Work—An Editorial
By The Plain Dealer Editorial Board

1   It's too soon to call the experimental AIDS vaccine a major breakthrough.

2   In trials, it's only had a 30 percent success rate—a vaccine is considered successful when it protects 70 percent to 80 percent of the people who use it.

3   And scientists still aren't sure why they've achieved even those limited successes with the treatment, which combines two older vaccines that did not work on their own and which, in combination, still do not appear to slow down the AIDS advance in most infected patients.

4   Yet despite its limitations, researchers are pretty excited—for understandable reasons. After years of "groping down an unlit path…a door has opened," as Dr. Anthony S. Fauci, director of the National Institute of Allergy and Infectious Diseases, puts it.

5   Still, it's best to remember that that door is merely ajar.

6   "No one should stop taking steps to protect themselves against [AIDS]," says Earl Pike, executive director of the AIDS Taskforce of Greater Cleveland. That's good advice.

(continued)

7   AIDS continues its stealthy advance, including among senior citizens and the African-American community, and among gay men and other groups who neglect prevention at their peril. Whether through monogamy, condoms or abstinence, prevention remains critical. So does getting tested for the disease and talking to partners.

8   Those with the disease—20,000 in Ohio, 33 million throughout the world—must also continue to take the medicines that keep them healthy and slow the spread of the disease.

9   Even a 30 percent success rate for a vaccine is something to celebrate. But the key word is *experimental*, and that word won't change until researchers improve on these promising findings.

10   Right now, they have more questions than answers.

11   While researchers search for a medical silver bullet, low-tech AIDS prevention has to remain a priority.

The editorial demonstrates all the characteristics of good persuasive writing: the topic is controversial (some will agree that the tested AIDS vaccine will prevent the disease, while others may not believe the claim), there is a clear position (thesis) adopted on the topic (that the results should be treated with cautious optimism), the reasons why it is important to be cautious are clearly laid out (that two older vaccines did not work on their own, and even in combination the older vaccines did not slow down the progress of AIDS among most infected patients), and the views of those who think the results are significant are acknowledged.

Everyday Writing Activity: A Persuasive Paragraph

Using the strategy of argument, write a paragraph on one of the following in your journal. Your instructor may ask you to share your paragraph with the rest of the class.

- Everyone should go to college.
- Animal research should be banned.
- Computers are not always good for humans.

Cause and Effect

Cause and effect essays focus on *why* things happen (the causes) and *what* happens as a result (the effects). If you do well in school, the cause is that you studied hard, and the effect can be that you get a scholarship for the next academic year. Sometimes, many causes can create one effect, or one cause can create many effects. For instance, talking on the cell phone, bad weather, and drinking while driving (many causes) can result in a traffic accident (one effect). Exercising regularly (one cause) can build muscle mass, promote better health and reduce medical costs (many effects). Cause and effect is a useful writing strategy because it helps to organize ideas in writing. Transition words (see pages 445–447) are useful in writing cause and effect essays.

In college, your history professor may ask you to write an essay on the causes and effects of World War I. Your life science professor may ask you to write a research paper exploring the causes for vanishing plant and animal species and the subsequent effects on the environment. In your education class, you may be assigned to write a paper exploring the causes and effects of illiteracy in a certain part of the world.

The following paragraphs from the Grambling University newspaper use the cause and effect writing strategy:

Professor Gives Reasons Why Students Fail

Shamekila Quarles

1   "Why Students Fail" was the title of the seminar that the Department of English sponsored on Thursday, March 23. The event featured Dr. Ray Foster, a current GSU faculty member.

2   Dr. Foster has been teaching and researching at GSU for 21 years. He began the seminar by informing the audience of questions he has posed to past and present administrators about why students do not perform well. He said that the two most common answers were "They [students] are not serious" and "College isn't for everybody."

3   Foster enlightened the audience with over 15 variables that help to determine success or failure. The list included: attendance, punctuality, poor writing, problem solving, notebook organization, and lack of persistence.

4   According to Foster, "Students may lack one or more of these variables. Knowledge becomes a part of you."

This passage demonstrates the characteristics of a cause and effect essay: the writer reports on the causes a professor provides for the given effect, which is student failure. These causes include, among others, not taking college seriously, college isn't for everybody, not attending classes, and being late for class.

Everyday Writing Activity: Cause and Effect Paragraph

Using the strategy of cause and effect, write a paragraph on one of the following in your journal. Your instructor may ask you to share your paragraph with the rest of the class.

- Causes and effects of plagiarizing in college.
- Causes and effects of dropping out of college.
- Causes and effects of stress in humans.

Comparison and Contrast

Comparison and contrast is a writing strategy that **compares** (shows how two or more things are similar) or **contrasts** (shows how two or more things are different). This means that there are at least two topics that the writer is focused on when writing a comparison and contrast essay. Usually the subjects for comparison and contrast are related to each other in some fashion, because the goal of comparison and contrast as a writing strategy is to make connections between texts or ideas, which leads to greater understanding and better evaluation of the topics at hand. You could compare and contrast certain **characteristics** of two composers (e.g., Beethoven and Mozart), two seasons (summer and winter; fall and spring) or two cuisines (Italian cuisine and French cuisine). However, you could not realistically compare and contrast playing a sport like basketball, for instance, with choosing a cell phone, because they are very unrelated topics.

Comparison and contrast uses one of two clear writing patterns. The writer may focus on characteristics of one topic first, then focus on the same characteristics of the other topic. The writer may also compare and contrast one characteristic of the two topics e.g. price, then compare and contrast the second characteristic e.g. location, then compare and contrast the third characteristic e.g. ease of access, and so on. The characteristics will vary, depending on the topics.

In college, your economics professor may ask you to write an evaluation of the economic policies of two U.S. presidents using the writing strategy of comparison and contrast. For your psychology course, you may be asked to evaluate Freudian theories as compared to Jungian theories. Your sociology course may require you to compare and contrast the study habits of high school students with those of junior high school students.

The following excerpt from the Independent Web site outlines some of the similarities and differences between college in Britain and college in the United States and is a good example of the use of comparison and contrast as a writing strategy:

Why British Students Are Opting for American Universities

Harvard? Princeton? Yale? More and more British students are choosing to study in the US—and for some the cost can be minimal. Karen Gold and Sarah Cassidy report.

1   The news that more students from the United Kingdom are applying to study at top American universities surprises Brits who think that British education is superior and less costly than that in the US.

2   Sydney Engle, 18, chose to study at the Ivy League Princeton University in New Jersey because she wanted to keep her options open. She couldn't decide what to study, chemistry or classics. In the UK, she had to choose. In the US she could delay her choice.

3   "The advantage of the US system is that you don't declare your major until the end of the second year and even then you can take additional subjects," she says. "I am enrolled in honours chemistry, as well as in a maths, philosophy and Latin course—about invective, slander and insult in Latin literature. It's fantastic."

4   However, for Sydney, studying at Princeton has proved much more expensive than the UK—her first year has cost $48,000 for room, board and tuition. That is because her parents are deemed well off enough to afford it.

5   But a little known fact is that many British families would qualify for help from American universities because relatively the British are less well off than Americans. If the family income—after assessment for tax, medical expenses, the cost of elderly dependent relatives—is below $60,000 (£32,000), the student's contribution to fees and accommodation, including an annual flight back home, will be precisely zero....

This passage is a good example of comparison/contrast writing. It compares two characteristics: the timing required to declare a major and also the financial aspects of attending college in the UK and in the United States. This comparison leads to a better understanding of the similarities and differences between the British and American college systems.

Everyday Writing Activity: Comparison and Contrast Paragraph

Using the strategies of comparison/contrast, write a paragraph on one of the following in your journal. Your instructor may ask you to share your paragraph with the rest of the class.

- Two hobbies.
- Two social networking sites.
- Two writers.

Writing Strategies at a Glance		
Writing Strategy	**Characteristics**	**Examples**
Description	Uses a lot of details, including sensory details. Uses vivid vocabulary. May use figurative language (similes and metaphors). Leaves readers with a clear picture of what is being described.	Describe a place such as the Grand Canyon, the Great Wall of China, the Swiss Alps. Describe a person. Describe a thing, such as the new laptop you recently bought.
Narration	Tells a story clearly and sometimes chronologically. Often, though not always, uses writer's point of view. Detailed.	Narrate the details of a significant event in your life, such as –your high school graduation. –your first job. –your first fight (with a sibling, friend etc.).
Informing	Provides usually unknown information for the reader. Uses facts, statistics, examples etc.	Inform readers how to program a cell phone. Inform your classmates about the town in which you grew up. Inform your pen pal of the significance of a particular holiday in your country/culture.

Writing Strategy	Characteristics	Examples
Classification	Classifies according to categories. Uses a single organizing principle to classify.	Classify athletes by the sports they play, such as those who play basketball, those who play football, those who are gymnasts, and those who are swimmers. Classify computers by type (laptop, desktop, netbook etc.). Classify automobiles by price (luxury, mid-priced, economy, etc.).
Definition	Explains what a term means. Uses basic information and examples to define. Defines by function, by structure, by analysis, by what a term is not.	Define wireless networking (by function). Define molecule (by structure). Define snowboarding (by analysis). Define alcoholism (by what it is not).
Argument	Focuses on controversial topic. Based on logical reasoning. Adopts clear position on topic. Often uses research to support claim. Considers other viewpoints.	Argue that all college students should be required to perform community service (or not). Argue that it is more important to solve local problems than global problems (or not). Argue that any reading is better than no reading (or not).
Cause and effect	Explains why something happens [cause(s)] and what the result is [effect(s)]. Uses transition words to express cause and effect.	Explain cause(s) and effect(s) of lack of sleep. Explain cause(s) and effect(s) of the growth of technology. Explain cause(s) and effects of smoking.
Comparison and contrast	Compares (shows similarity) and contrasts (shows differences between two or more things, ideas, people, places etc.). Compares/contrasts by subject and by characteristic.	Compare and contrast two popular digital cameras. Compare and contrast two popular movies. Compare and contrast two music albums.

Everyday Writing Activity: Writing Strategies

Step 1

In your journal, indicate the appropriate writing strategy for each writing situation:

- Writing an article for your college magazine about your trip to a foreign country this summer.
- Writing a letter of disagreement to the mayor of your city who wants to close down some of the community's homeless shelters.
- Writing in your personal diary about the beautiful sunset you watched from your apartment window yesterday evening.
- Writing in your college newspaper about how to participate in elections for your campus student government.
- Writing an assignment for your writing class where you discuss the advantages and disadvantages of print books and e-books.
- Writing a letter to your friend who wants to know what your plans are this holiday season.
- Writing a letter to your school president giving reasons your school should move from the quarter system to the semester system (or vice versa).
- Writing an essay for your nutrition class discussing the value of organic and nonorganic foods.

Step 2

After you have completed the preceding activity, pick one of these topics, and write a paragraph on it in your journal, using at least one of the writing strategies you have learned about in this chapter. Your instructor may ask you to share your paragraph with the rest of the class.

LO2

Use rhetorical appeals to help achieve your purpose in writing

Persuasion Strategies: Ethical, Emotional, and Logical Appeals

There are three *means* by which the writer persuades the audience when using the strategy of argumentation. These means are known as appeals. The three appeals are ethical appeals, emotional appeals, and logical appeals. They are often called *ethos, pathos, logos*—the Greek terms that Aristotle originally used. Good speakers, Aristotle said, use these three appeals in different ways, depending on their purpose and audience. You don't necessarily have to remember the Greek words, but we find it helpful to keep them in mind, especially in relation to writing:

- The ethical appeal (*ethos*) refers to the character of the speaker or writer—his/her credibility. Your rabbi, minister, priest, or imam is believable when speaking or writing on religious matters because of his/her background, education, experience, and so forth.
- The emotional appeal (*pathos*) refers to how an audience is affected by a writing or a speech. It is easy to think of this as "pathetic," but that is not correct: an emotional appeal can be sad, of course, but also can be happy, or patriotic, and so on.
- The logical appeal (*logos*) refers to the use of facts, data, a logical organization, and so on, by the writer or the speaker, which makes the text credible.

You already know the appeals and use them all the time. For example, if you wanted to borrow the family car to take friends to a party on Saturday night, what kind of appeal are you making when you ask:

- Dad, can I borrow the car Saturday night? I promised I'd drive the gang to Matt's party. Every time I've borrowed the car I've brought it home safely.

This is an *ethical* appeal: your father will believe you because you've done well in the past.

Now, what if you ask:

- Dad, can I borrow the car Saturday night? I promised I'd drive the gang to Matt's party. And if I can't drive, that new girl won't go out with me. I may never have a girlfriend.

This is an *emotional* appeal: you are appealing to your father's emotions.

Now, what if you ask

- Dad, can I borrow the car Saturday night? I promised I'd drive the gang to Matt's party. I'll make sure I bring it home with a full tank of gas, and on Sunday, I'll wash it.

This is a *logical* appeal: you are giving reasons why you should be allowed to borrow the car.

Let us look at these appeals one by one.

Ethical Appeal: The Appeal to Credibility

The **ethical appeal** refers to the *credibility* or the *trust* that readers place in the writer. If readers do not trust or believe a writer, then they will not be persuaded by what the writer has to say. If readers feel that the writer is to be trusted, then they will be more inclined to understand and accept his/her point of view. Usually, if the writer is well known or an authority on the topic being discussed, that writer will be much more credible than someone who is unknown to readers. For example, if a movie reviewer writes that a new film is terrific, why would you believe that person? One reason may be that this reviewer's judgment about movies has been accurate in the past. Another reason that you may believe the reviewer is because he/she works for a respected newspaper. This makes the reviewer's recommendation believable and credible.

The following examples highlight the role played by a writer's ethical appeal:

- If boxing champion George Foreman were to write an article on boxing, he would have much more ethical appeal for readers than your next-door neighbor who was on his high school boxing team before giving up the sport. This is because Foreman has much more experience with boxing than your neighbor and is also well known in the field of boxing.
- An article published by a respected news outlet (*The New York Times*, *The Washington Post*, CNN.com, BBC.com, or any well-established international, national, or local newspaper) carries more *credibility* than a news report published in a tabloid.
- Statistics on world illiteracy published by an organization such as UNESCO (United Nations Educational, Scientific and Cultural Organization) will be seen by readers as more credible than statistics published by a local organization.

Emotional Appeal: The Appeal to Feelings

The **emotional appeal** refers to the appeal made to the audience's imagination or emotions. It is a common rhetorical appeal used by writers to sway the audience's emotions; once readers identify with what the writer thinks and feels, they may be more easily persuaded to side with the writer. A common way of appealing to readers' emotions is through the use of a narrative or story that highlights the values and beliefs of the writer. In most academic writing, the emotional appeal is used *less often* than the other appeals, simply because it is less effective.

The following examples highlight how the emotional appeal can be used in writing:

- You want your school to increase the blood donations that are made each year by students, staff, and faculty. You write an article for your campus newspaper urging more blood donations, including a story about how a blood transfusion saved someone's life. Language such as

"Think of how *your* blood saved a young child's life" or "The satisfaction you will feel at the good deed will be immeasurable" will play on readers' emotions and may make them volunteer to be a blood donor.

- You are concerned at the lack of homeless shelters in your city, and you are especially concerned because another winter is just around the corner. Therefore, you write a letter to your city council members, urging that the city open more shelters before winter sets in. To appeal to the council members' emotions, you use emotional appeals such as "Imagine sleeping on a park bench night after night in sub-zero temperatures," or "Imagine standing outside in a blizzard, unable to go inside." Such use of language will probably evoke sympathy in the readers because they may instinctively put themselves in those positions and realize the grimness of the situation for the homeless. They may then be persuaded to release funds necessary to open more shelters.

- Writers arguing for controlling industrial pollution may try to make their point stronger by pointing out the illnesses caused by the emissions of harmful chemicals into the atmosphere. Language such as "Imagine getting lung cancer, not because you smoked, but because the giant corporation in your neighborhood spewed fumes from its factories without caring about your health," or "Your child has asthma, not because it runs in your family, but because the local factory has regularly been releasing toxic gases into the air which affected his lungs," will appeal to readers' emotions, make them more receptive to the writer's ideas, and move them to action, to petition the concerned people, which is the writer's goal.

Logical Appeal: The Appeal to Reason

The **logical appeal** refers to persuading readers through the use of logic and reason in writing. This is perhaps the most important of all the appeals because a good argument is based primarily on good reasons, backed by solid evidence. Data often help with logical appeals, because they are based on facts and/or research. Logical appeals also help a writer's ethical appeal, because readers realize that the writer is arguing from a solid base.

The following examples highlight the use of logical appeals in writing an argument:

- Writers who wish to argue that cell phones should be banned while driving could refer to studies like the 2003 study from the Harvard Center of Risk Analysis that estimates that cell phone use while driving contributes each year to 6 percent of crashes, resulting in 330,000 injuries, 12,000 of them serious and 2,600 of them fatal.

Writers could also point to a University of Utah study that says that hands-free devices do not make it safe to talk while driving.

- Opponents of boxing as a sport could support their argument by referring to the fact that 11 medical associations around the world have said that chronic brain damage is caused by repeated blows to the head, such as those experienced by all boxers, and that having head guards and shorter rounds have a minimal effect on the potential damage.

- Those who favor a vegetarian diet could argue, based on a report published by the American Dietetic Association, that appropriately planned vegetarian diets, including total vegetarian or vegan diets, are healthful, nutritionally adequate, and may provide health benefits in the prevention and treatment of certain diseases, such as heart disease, blood pressure, diabetes, and cancer for individuals of all ages.

Persuasion Strategies at a Glance		
Appeals	**Characteristics**	**Purpose**
Ethical appeal	Based on writer's credibility. Well-known experts, writers, and reliable sources have credibility.	To persuade audience by emphasizing writer's credibility.
Emotional appeal	Based on emotions (pity, sympathy, love, anger, etc.). Use of emotional and imaginative language.	To persuade audience by evoking relevant feelings.
Logical appeal	Based on logical reasons and solid evidence.	To persuade audience by showing the logic behind the writer's thoughts.

Everyday Writing Activity: Persuasive Appeals

In the following writing situations, determine the kind of appeal most suitable to making an effective argument. Write your answer in your journal, along with a one-paragraph explanation of why you chose that particular appeal as the most suitable. Your instructor may ask you to share your responses with the rest of the class.

- A text message to your girlfriend/boyfriend, with whom you have recently broken up, intimating that you would like to be together again.
- A note written by a physician to a health insurance company requesting approval of a particular medical procedure for a patient.
- An editorial in the local newspaper pointing out that the town's roads need repair before winter sets in.
- An advertisement for a particular brand of orange juice in a popular magazine, pointing out that the juice is rich in Vitamin C and is calcium-fortified.
- An e-mail sent by your school's president to all members of the campus community requesting donations for a new science building on campus.

Everyday Writing Activity: Chapter Reflection

In your journal, please respond to the following prompts. Your instructor may ask you to share your responses with the rest of the class.

1. I learned that the writing strategies introduced in this chapter are _____.

2. Some of the characteristics of each of the writing strategies are _____.

3. The writing strategies I have mainly used in my writing so far are _____.

4. I learned that appeals used in persuasive writing are _____.

MyWritingLab™ For support in meeting this chapter's objectives, log in to www.mywritinglab.com and select **Essay Development-Describing, Narrating, Illustrating, Division/Classification, Process, Definition, Argument, Cause and Effect,** and **Comparison and Contrast.**

Chapter 6

Getting Started with Your Writing

Learning Objectives

In this chapter, you will learn to:

LO1 Describe the stages of the writing process

LO2 Use strategies to discover what to write about, including listing, freewriting, clustering, and cubing

For many writers, it can be difficult to come up with ideas to write about, and it also is hard to get those ideas onto paper. Writers often look like the student on page 78, who is thinking and writing, and it is sometimes hard work.

In Chapter 5, you learned about using writing strategies and appeals in your paper. But before you can decide on what strategies to use, you must have something to write about. That is, you need to have ideas that you can develop into a complete paper using the writing strategies of your choice.

Everyday Writing Activity: How to Decide What to Write About

In your journal, answer these questions. Your instructor may ask you to share your responses with the rest of the class.

1. Do you often find yourself staring out of the window, like the student in the photograph, wondering what you should write about?
2. If you do, how do you solve the problem of finding ideas for your paper?
3. Do you have a favorite place (e.g., in your bedroom, at the kitchen table, near a window, or curled up on a couch) where you sit and think about ideas for your paper?
4. Do you discuss ideas for your paper with your friends, roommates, or family members (or anybody else)?
5. Do you jot down ideas on notepads or make a computer file where you type in your ideas as they come to you?

You may sometimes experience "writer's block"; that is, you may have trouble coming up with ideas for your paper. This can cause anxiety and stress, and you may feel that you can never be a good writer. That is an incorrect assumption; many experienced writers also face trouble from time to time in coming up with ideas about writing. However, they overcome these difficulties by employing **invention strategies** that help them generate ideas for their writing. We see such strategies as ways to discover things to focus on: to help you decide on a **topic,** what to write about that topic, and so on.

You may also feel unsure about what **genre,** or *kind* of writing will be suitable for expressing your ideas and how you can organize and draft an essay that flows nicely for the reader. This chapter, and the next two, will help you with these writing tasks—and make you more prepared to write for college—by introducing you to the writing process.

The Writing Process

The writing process has six major steps, each one as important as the others. These steps are:

1. **Invention:** discovering/finding ideas and getting started.
2. **Drafting:** organizing and getting those ideas onto paper.
3. **Revising:** making sure you say what you want to say; often, you'll get suggestions from others on how to improve your work.
4. **Editing:** final word choice, style, and polishing your work.
5. **Proofreading:** final checking for spelling errors, fragments, and the like.
6. **Publishing:** final printing and turning in your work.

Often there is another step: **reflecting** on your work. Here is where you look back and think about what you did that was effective, what you might do differently next time, and so on. Such reflection makes it easier the next time you face a similar writing assignment.

In this chapter, we will discuss the first step, discovering what to write about. In Chapter 7 we will focus on drafting, and in Chapter 8 we will introduce you to revising, editing, proofreading, and publishing your work.

Invention or Discovery Strategies

Canadian writer Stephen Leacock once wrote, "Writing is no trouble: you just jot down ideas as they occur to you. The jotting is simplicity itself—it is the occurring which is difficult." Do you find that to be true for you, too?

Invention work or **discovery** activities, also known as **prewriting** ("pre" means "before"), begins when you start thinking about a writing task. It refers to the activities you engage in *before* you actually begin writing. Because of this, it is also known as **brainstorming,** which means that you use your brain to think about the ideas to write about. Whichever term you prefer to use, invention basically involves coming up with a topic, thinking about the topic, generating ideas to write about, and planning for the writing. Just as athletes engage in warm-up activities before a game actually starts, writers use invention activities to warm up.

Invention activities are very useful if you are suffering from writer's block and feel like the student in the accompanying photo. To overcome writer's block, you can use several discovery activities. You will find that some work better for you than others—so try a couple each time you have a writing assignment. The most common invention strategies are:

- Listing.
- Freewriting.
- Clustering.
- Cubing.

We will now discuss these one by one.

Listing

Listing means simply to write down a group of items. Just as when you go to the grocery store, you make a list of items to buy (bread, eggs, milk, apples, etc.), similarly, when you write, you make a list of all the possible ideas you may want to include in your writing. Without a list you may forget the ideas that come to your mind, just as you may forget what to get from the grocery store without a list.

If you had to write an essay on possible career choices after graduation, you could make a list that looks like this:

- Professor.
- High school teacher.
- Journalist.
- Computer programmer.
- Nurse.

In the body of your essay, you may want to take up one or more of these career choices and discuss what you like about them. But before you can do that, you need to make a list of what about the profession appeals to you the most. For example, suppose you decide to focus on becoming a professor or a journalist. Your list of why you may want to become a professor might look like this:

- Interaction with students.
- Work involves doing research.
- Option to teach or not teach during the summers.
- Social respect.

If you are considering becoming a journalist, your list might look like this:

- Ability to work for a major media outlet and probably to live in a big city.
- Chance to report on major news events.
- Opportunity to interview well-known personalities.
- Chance to travel.

Because it is a list, it may look like a simple "to do" list or a grocery list. Of course, you want to keep on adding to the list as you are writing and as more ideas cross your mind; listing is not confined only to the initial stages of writing. Once you have as complete a list as you can think of, then you can begin drafting.

Student Writing: Kim Lee's Listing

Student writer Kim Lee has been asked to write an essay for her composition class that focuses on the advantages and disadvantages of online classes. Kim has not taken one of these classes, so she will have to do some research—but she also has some initial ideas, so she makes a list:

Advantages:
- I can take online classes on "my time."
- I can take them from home since I have cable and Internet access.
- No gas or time spent getting to class.
- NOT having to find a parking spot would be wonderful!!

Disadvantages:
- May be hard to get answers to questions.
- I'd miss the face-to-face contact, I think.
- How would they know it was me taking the class? Would some students cheat?
- I might procrastinate.

Everyday Writing Activity: Listing

In your journal, make a list of possible ideas you may include for an essay on one of the following topics:

- The challenges of being a first-year college student.
- Reasons for the popularity of fast food.

- Electric cars.
- Why dogs make good pets.

After you have finished listing, reflect on and respond to the following questions in your journal:

1. What aspects of listing worked well for you?
2. What aspects of listing did not work well for you?
3. What do you think of listing as an invention activity? Would you recommend it to other student writers?

Freewriting

Freewriting is exactly what the term implies: writers write down their thoughts freely, without worrying about grammar, spelling, punctuation, and so on. Sometimes when writers are engaged in freewriting, they write nonstop, without stopping their typing or lifting their pens from paper. This can go on for 5 to 10 minutes. At the end of the freewriting process, there will be some material that you can use for your essay, and there will be some material that you probably will have to discard. However, freewriting helps get your ideas flowing and will give you a starting point for your essay.

Student Writing: Kim Lee's Freewriting

To help her start on her assignment to write a paper about online classes, student writer Kim did some freewriting. Note that if she can't think of what to write, she continues to write something (even if it is "I can't think of what else to say"). Here is Kim's freewriting:

I don't know where to start but I sure like the idea of online classes, so I wouldn't have to drive to campus. That's such a hassle with parking and all, and I'm often late to class. I wonder how hard it would be to get answers to questions, though? I ask a lot of questions and would hate to have to wait for an answer until the teacher read her e-mail. I can't think of what else to say! And I like meeting other people, which I couldn't do online. I don't think we could meet, anyway. But gas is getting more expensive so it'd sure save some money to have online classes . . .

Everyday Writing Activity: Freewriting

In your journal, freewrite on the following topics for 5 to 10 minutes each:

- A favorite sport.
- The Internet.
- Volunteering.
- Robots.

After you have finished freewriting, reflect on and respond to the following questions in your journal:

1. What about freewriting seems useful?
2. What is not particularly helpful?
3. Do you need to do some more freewriting in order to write a complete essay? Do you have something to start with, at least?
4. What do you think of freewriting as an invention activity? Would you recommend it to other student writers?

Clustering

Another invention activity that can help you develop ideas for writing is known as clustering (it is also known as spider webbing or mind mapping). Generally speaking, a cluster, spider web, or mind map is several things or ideas grouped together. For our purposes, **clustering** means grouping ideas to see how an essay might be developed and organized. This activity is particularly suited for visual learners because the whole essay can be laid out in visual form. Follow these steps to create your own cluster:

- In the center of a plain sheet of paper, write down your essay topic and circle it.
- Draw smaller circles radiating from the circle in the center.
- In the smaller circles, write down your main ideas for the topic.
- Draw smaller circles radiating from the secondary circles, and inside them write down the secondary ideas related to each main idea.
- Add more circles as necessary in order to develop your essay.
- When your cluster is complete, you are ready to draft. During the writing process, if you need more clusters, keep adding them and filling them with ideas. If you need to delete any clusters, you can do that, too.

Student Writing: Kim Lee's Clustering

A cluster diagram on the topic of online college classes may look like this one, constructed by student Kim Lee:

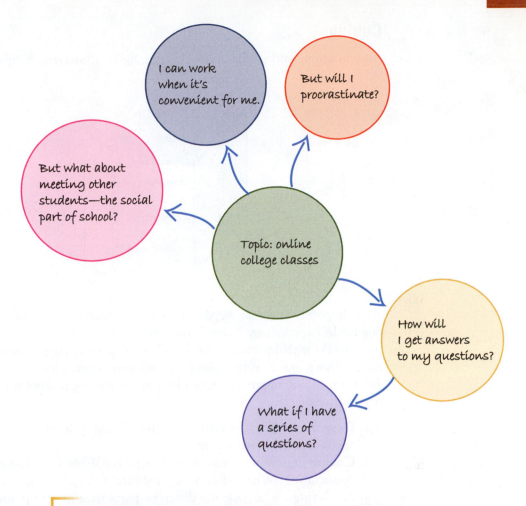

Everyday Writing Activity: Clustering

Choose one of the following topics, and create a cluster diagram in your journal that will help you eventually write an essay from the ideas developed:

- Why smart phones are popular.
- Using e-books for all of your college courses.
- Advantages and disadvantages of cosmetic surgery.
- Solar energy: how to use it.

After you have finished clustering, reflect on and respond to the following questions in your journal:

1. What aspects of clustering worked well for you?
2. What aspects of clustering did not work well for you?
3. What do you think of clustering as an invention activity? Would you recommend it to other student writers?

Cubing

As you know, and as the accompanying figure illustrates, a cube has six sides.

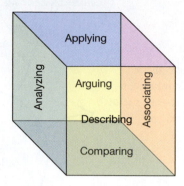

At this point, you may be thinking of the Sudoku cube or the older, but no less intriguing, Rubik's cube, and wondering: What does a cube have to do with brainstorming for ideas? Actually, **cubing** is an invention activity that is very useful for developing some ideas about a topic. Taking a cubing approach means looking at the topic from six different perspectives:

1. **Describing:** What is your topic like? What is its size, shape, color, texture, smell, taste, sound?
2. **Comparing:** What is your topic similar to? What is it different from?
3. **Associating:** What other topic(s) is (are) related to your topic?
4. **Analyzing:** What are the different parts that make up your topic? How are these parts similar? How are they dissimilar? How do they "work together" to make up the whole of the topic?
5. **Applying:** What applications does your topic have? Where and how can it be used?
6. **Arguing:** What arguments can be made for or against your topic? How strong are these arguments?

Cubing is probably not used as widely as the other invention strategies, but it can be very effective. It may require you to devote more time in the initial stages, but in the long run it can give you multiple perspectives on your topic. We encourage you to try it.

Student Writing: Kim Lee's Cubing

Student writer Kim Lee decided to try cubing to help her get started and came up with these comments:

1. Describing: Online classes are held online, which means you need Internet access that is reliable. There is no talking—only e-mail or online chat. No classrooms needed, no teacher or classmates physically present.
2. Comparing: Are online classes better or worse, harder or easier, than traditional classes? How can anyone tell? Are they cheaper than regular classes?
3. Associating: Other related topics might include books for online classes (I don't think there are a lot of e-books, but I might be wrong) and maybe hybrid classes, where you meet online only part of the time.
4. Analyzing: Do online classes count the same when students graduate or transfer? Do teachers teaching online courses have the same credentials as those teaching traditional courses?
5. Applying: How does taking online classes help a student in his/her education? Will taking such classes help later in finding a job and in the workplace?
6. Arguing: Advantages: Online classes save commuting time, saves gas, no parking issues, can work at my own pace. Disadvantages: no social interaction, there may be technology issues, classes may not transfer.

Everyday Writing Activity: Cubing

Choose one of the following topics, and use cubing to develop as much material as you can for an essay:

- Skateboards.
- A popular rap artist.
- Alternative therapies such as homeopathy or naturopathy.
- GPS systems.

After you have finished cubing, reflect on and respond to the following questions in your journal:

1. What aspects of cubing worked well for you?
2. What aspects of cubing did not work well for you?
3. Do you need to do some more cubing in order to write a complete essay? Do you have something to start with, at least?
4. What do you think of cubing as an invention strategy compared to the other invention activities you have learned about so far? Would you recommend it to other student writers?

Using Several Invention Strategies

Even though the invention strategies have been discussed separately, several strategies can be used for the same writing assignment. That is, you don't have to stick to only one strategy at a time; for a single piece of writing, you can use any combination of these strategies depending on your needs, your audience's needs, and your purpose for writing. You may also find that some strategies work better for you, personally.

Everyday Writing Activity: Chapter Reflection

In your journal, please respond to the following prompts. Your instructor may ask you to share your responses with the rest of the class.

1. Invention/discovery strategies are important because _____.
2. One invention/discovery strategy that seems to work effectively for me is _____.

MyWritingLab™ For support in meeting this chapter's objectives, log in to **www.mywritinglab.com** and select **Prewriting** and **The Writing Process.**

Chapter 7

Drafting Your Paper

Learning Objectives

In this chapter, you will learn to:

LO1 Choose the best genre, or format, for your writing

LO2 Decide whether you need to do research

LO3 Outline your paper

LO4 Draft thesis statements, paragraphs, topic sentences, and transitions

LO5 Identify the parts of an essay: introduction, body, and conclusion

O nce you have done some invention work and have some ideas about your topic, you are almost ready to begin drafting. However, there are still some things to consider: the genre of your writing, whether you need to do any research (and if so, what types of research will help the most), whether or not to construct an outline, and so on.

<table>
<tr>
<td>

LO1

Choose the best genre, or format, for your writing

</td>
<td>

What Is the Best Genre for Your Audience and Purpose?

</td>
</tr>
</table>

Genre refers to the type or the category of text—for example, a letter, an essay, a book review, a research report, or a proposal, to name just a few. Once you know your audience and purpose, consider what genre would work best. Would it be:

- An academic paper?
- A memo?
- An e-mail?
- A formal report?
- A combination (for example, a cover letter followed by a report)?

A writer's decision about the form of the writing is influenced by who the writer is writing for and what he/she is trying to accomplish. For example, you would not write a handwritten letter using a pencil to the president of your college to complain about rising tuition costs. But you might use that pencil and handwritten note for a family member. You probably would not send an informal note to a company to complain about a product you bought; rather, you would write a formal letter, asking for a refund. Often your instructor or the assignment itself will specify the genre of your writing task, but if not, then you need to determine the best genre depending on your audience and purpose.

The writing strategies discussed in Chapter 5 will also influence your writing. For instance:

- If you decide to write a descriptive text, you would use the rhetorical strategy of description in your paper (or letter or memo or report).
- If your purpose is to write a narrative, then you would use the rhetorical strategy of narration in your paper (or in a letter or a memo, etc.).
- If you decide that your purpose is to write an argument, you would use the rhetorical strategy of argumentation in your paper (or in a letter or a memo etc.).

Sometimes multiple writing strategies can be used in the same piece of writing, but there will be only one genre of writing. Thus, if you were comparing and contrasting two paintings by the same artist, you could begin by describing the impact the paintings by this artist had, before comparing and contrasting two of his works. Your writing would use two strategies—description and comparison and contrast—but it would be in only one genre: it might be an academic paper (for a class), a letter (for a comparison you are writing for family members), or a review of an art exhibit (for a local paper).

Do You Need Research?

LO2

Decide whether you need to do research

In at least some of the writing you do for college classes, you will need to conduct research so that you have information, data, facts, examples, and so on, to help achieve your purpose. Research can include many activities. When you take notes about a place or activity that you are observing, that is research. When you interview a friend about the subject for your paper, that is research. When you go to the library and read books or articles on your topic, that is research.

What research you might need to conduct depends on your topic, your audience, and your writing purpose. In the chapters in Part 2, we provide specific examples of research you might conduct for the kind of writing assignment you are asked to do. In Chapters 15 and 16, we explain how to conduct research and document your sources. At the beginning of a writing project, though, you want to consider these questions:

 ## Critical Thinking Activity: Ask Yourself Questions about Research

1. What information (data, facts, examples, statistics, quotations, etc.) will help me achieve my writing purpose?
2. What might my audience already know about my topic? What else might they need to know so they will understand and perhaps even agree with my point?
3. Are there visual aids that might help me show what I mean, so my readers can see the same things that I see?
4. What questions do I have about my topic, and where might I find answers to those questions?

Once you have thought about those questions, you can plan what kind of research will help you. In some cases, talking to people (interviewing them, even if informally) will be useful. Often, books and articles from your campus library will be useful.

Outlining Your Paper

Once you have generated ideas from your invention work (see Chapter 6), have decided what genre your paper should be, and have done any necessary research, how do you turn all of that into a first draft? One way is to write an outline.

An **outline** is a list that shows the important parts of your essay, identifying the primary topic, the main ideas and the secondary ideas, along with examples, details, and so on. While outlining is more time-consuming than listing, it can be a useful activity before you write a first draft.

Note that making *too detailed* an outline might actually inhibit your writing. Writing is a way to discover and learn about your topic, and whenever you write about something, you will learn more about it. Constructing a detailed outline assumes that you know what you wish to say about your topic, *before* you write about it, which may stop you from actually learning about your topic as you write on it. However, there is nothing wrong with constructing an outline in very broad terms—the major things you want to focus on.

Outlines can be simple or detailed. A simple outline (also known as a scratch outline) on the topic of "Family" would include the following major headings. If you wanted to get more detailed, you could include the names and more information [shown in brackets]:

Scratch Outline: Family

- **Immediate family**
  - **Parents**
    - **Mom, Dad**
      [Mom, 48, an aeronautical engineer with Info Tech; Dad, 50, history professor at Best University, San Diego. Both very busy and spend long days at work]
  - **Siblings**
    - **Sally, Mary, Nick**
      [Sally, 20, college student at Boston College; Mary 16, City High School sophomore; Nick, 12, City Middle School student, San Diego. All three like to play softball and basketball]
- **Extended family**
  - **Grandparents**
    - **Grandpa Jim and Grandma Elizabeth**
    - **Grandpa Henry and Grandma Rebecca**
      [Extended family consists of paternal grandparents living in Seattle, Grandpa Jim (75, retired) and Grandma Elizabeth (76, homemaker) and maternal grandparents Grandpa Henry

(68, avid gardener) and Grandma Rebecca (68, church choir singer), also living in Seattle. See them every Christmas]

- **Aunts**
  - Kim, Holly, Jane, Alicia
    [Kim (40, elementary school teacher in Philadelphia), Holly (38, violinist, lives in Colorado Springs, Colorado), Jane, 35 (television news anchor in Tucson, Arizona), Alicia (33, homemaker, lives with her family in Seoul, South Korea)]
- **Uncles**
  - **Mike, Jim**
    [Mike (42, university professor in Osaka, Japan), Jim (28, insurance adjuster, lives in Butte, Montana)]

Student Writing: Kim Lee's Outlining

Student writer Kim Lee constructed this outline of what she had in mind for her paper about online classes:

I. There are advantages and disadvantages
   A. Advantages include
      i. Work at my own pace
      ii. Saves gas
      iii. Saves time
      iv. Saves parking issues
      v. Convenient
   B. Disadvantages include
      i. Not meeting people
      ii. Hard to get questions answered (maybe)
      iii. Technology issues
      iv. No social interaction
      v. I might procrastinate

Everyday Writing Activity: Outlining

Choose one of the following essay topics, and create both a simple outline and a detailed outline in your journal:

- Olympics.
- Choosing a major in college.
- Audio books
- A favorite hobby.

(continued)

After you have finished, reflect on and respond to the following questions in your journal. Your instructor may ask you to share your responses with the rest of the class.

1. What worked well for you as you tried to create an outline for your topic?
2. What did not work well for you?
3. Do you prefer a simple outline or a more detailed outline? Why? What are the advantages and disadvantages of each?

LO4

Draft thesis statements, paragraphs, topic sentences, and transitions

Drafting

To **draft** means to start writing a *version* of your essay. The drafting process comes after invention activities and after you have done some outlining of your topic. You have now generated some ideas that you can work on developing and supporting, and you have also decided (though this may change during the process of drafting) what the genre of your writing is going to be. *Remember:* Writing is a *recursive* or *nonlinear* process, which means that it does not progress in a straight line. It is a back-and-forth process, and invention does not stop when you begin drafting; you can, and should, keep on engaging in invention activities as you are writing. Visually, this is what the writing process may look like once you begin drafting:

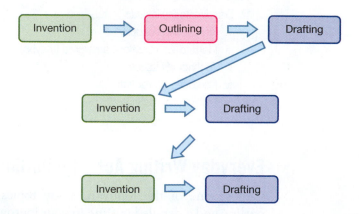

After writing a couple of paragraphs, you may run out of ideas. If that happens, you can use any, or all, of the invention activities mentioned in Chapter 6 to generate *more* ideas. Then you draft some more.

You will probably need to write several drafts, accompanied by several phases of invention, before you have a draft that meets your expectations and assignment criteria.

Don't let the continuous drafting and redrafting worry you; all writers go through this process as they fine-tune their thoughts. It can be a challenging process, but it is also very exhilarating, as you find your ideas gradually taking shape in front of you. The key point is that you can write as many drafts as you need until you have a draft that you are satisfied with.

While drafting, don't worry about mechanics, that is, grammar, spelling, punctuation, and the like. To do so would be a waste of time because your essay will go through more revisions (see Chapter 8), which may mean that some of what you have written down so far may not stay in your paper. You need to keep on moving forward with your ideas, fleshing them out until you have sorted them through.

Drafting can take time, so don't expect to write a draft in one sitting. It can take several hours, or even several days, before you have a rough draft written. As you are writing, stop periodically to read what you have so far. It will help you stay focused on what you are writing so that you do not trail away into writing something that is not linked to your topic.

Drafting is very flexible. If you cannot think of an introduction for your essay, for example, you can start writing the body paragraphs. After you have a body, go back and read it, and perhaps that will help you come up with an introduction for your essay. Or maybe you want to write the conclusion first. Go for it. After that, you can write the introduction and body paragraphs (for a discussion of introduction, body, and conclusion, see pages 104–105).

Drafting is a messy process; there isn't one way to do it, but as you do get your ideas onto paper or onto your computer screen, you will find your ideas falling into place. Before you know it, you will have a draft that is ready for revision. See page 106 for an example of an early student draft.

Drafting Your Thesis Statement

Part of writing a draft is deciding what the thesis statement should be. In college, you will be expected to have a thesis statement in each paper you write. Begin with a *working thesis statement,* one that you can modify as necessary. Some of the main characteristics of a **thesis statement** are:

- It tells readers what the main point of the entire writing is, just as a topic sentence tells readers what the main point of a paragraph is (for more on topic sentences, see pages 99–101). You can view the thesis statement as the topic sentence for the entire essay. The ideas in the paragraphs are connected to the thesis statement, just as the branches of a tree are connected to the trunk of the tree.

- It is typically one sentence long, though it can be longer depending on the needs of your audience and your purpose for writing.
- It is usually placed somewhere in the introductory paragraph, though, again, depending on the needs of your audience and your purpose for writing, it can appear later in the essay.

A thesis statement helps the writer keep the essay organized by emphasizing the main point of the essay. Your thesis statement should be very specific; it should cover only what you are going to discuss. If not, it is a weak thesis statement. Look at the following examples:

> **Weak thesis statement:** In this essay, I will discuss my experiences in college so far.

This is a weak thesis statement because it is vague and too broad. It does not tell the reader which specific college experiences the writer is going to focus on and what the point of the essay is.

> **Strong thesis statement:** Three aspects of my college experience have impressed me so far: my classes, my interaction with my peers, and my participation in student government elections.

This is a strong thesis statement because it tells the reader the importance of the writer's college experiences and which aspects of the college experience the writer is going to focus on: description of classes, interaction with peers, and participation in student government elections.

Here is another example of weak and strong thesis statements:

> **Weak thesis statement:** It is important to have a nutritious diet.

This statement is weak because it does not explain why it is important to have a nutritious diet.

> **Strong thesis statement:** It is important to have a nutritious diet because such a diet can prevent disease and slow the aging process.

This is a strong thesis statement because it tells readers at the outset *why* it is important to have a nutritious diet: it can prevent disease and slow aging. The rest of the essay will discuss *how* a nutritious diet can prevent disease and slow the aging process.

Your purpose in writing will also determine what your thesis statement is going to be like. For example:

- If you are writing an essay where your purpose is to describe your high school graduation, your thesis statement can simply say, "On the day of my graduation from high school, my friends and I were excited to be awarded our diplomas."
- If your purpose is to write a comparison and contrast essay on the study habits of younger college students versus older college students, your thesis statement can read, "It is interesting to compare and contrast the similarities and differences in the study habits of younger college students and older college students."
- If your purpose is to write an argument essay addressed to your school administrators, who are considering raising parking rates on campus, your thesis statement can read: "There are two main reasons rates for parking on campus should not be raised: it will hurt students financially, and it will be the second rate increase in as many years."

Note that your thesis statement may change during the writing process, as you learn more about your topic. That is a good thing— and one of the truly positive aspects of a college education: it is okay to change your mind about something as you learn more about it. Do you agree?

Student Writing: Kim Lee's Thesis Statement

Assume that student writer Kim Lee has been asked to construct an informative paper that outlines the benefits and problems of online classes. Kim might start with this thesis statement:

> There are both advantages and disadvantages to online classes, but the positive aspects outweigh the negative.

However, then she might *change her mind* as she talks to students and conducts other research on online classes. For example, Kim might come to the *opposite* conclusion of what she started with and decide that the disadvantages of online classes outweighed their benefits. Her new thesis statement would be:

> There are both advantages and disadvantages to online classes, but the negative aspects outweigh the positive.

Everyday Writing Activity: Weak and Strong Thesis Statements

Indicate which of the following are weak thesis statements and which are strong thesis statements. Use *W* for weak and *S* for strong thesis statements. Then, in your journal, rewrite the weak thesis statements into strong thesis statements. Your instructor may ask you to share your responses with the rest of the class.

_____ 1. Rich countries should provide more aid to poor countries.

_____ 2. There are two main advantages to online shopping: it can be done from the comfort of home, and some of the best deals are available online.

_____ 3. Because it is fast, safe, and relatively cheap, flying is a popular way to travel.

_____ 4. It is better if a parent can stay home with a child for the first year after it is born.

_____ 5. Fast food diets are not very healthy.

Drafting Effective Paragraphs

Once you have identified your audience and purpose and have come up with a working thesis statement, it is time to begin writing the rest of your draft. As you write, you need to organize your ideas into paragraphs. A **paragraph:**

- Is a self-contained body of writing (often within a larger body) usually made up of three to eight sentences. Generally, the length of a paragraph is flexible and should be determined by the needs of your audience and your purpose in writing.

- Usually deals with *one* particular point or idea. This idea is often referred to as the "controlling idea" of the paragraph. Having one controlling idea ensures the unity and coherence (understandability) of the paragraph. This controlling idea is expressed in the form of a **topic sentence** (see pages 99–101 for a more detailed discussion of the topic sentence). *Note:* Do not confuse the topic sentence of a paragraph with the topic of your writing.

- Includes supporting sentences to develop that one main idea. These sentences can provide examples, illustrations, facts, statistics, and expert testimony and can use the rhetorical strategies of description, narration, comparison and contrast, argument, and the like, as needed, to support or explain the original idea.

- Is indicated by beginning on a new line, which is indented from the left margin. This helps the reader know where a new paragraph begins.

A completed piece of writing is made up of several paragraphs. Breaking up ideas into paragraphs helps writers stay focused on the idea being developed; dealing with too many ideas at a time can make the writing disorganized. Paragraphs also help readers stay focused on the idea being developed without becoming confused by several different ideas at once. They also serve to give readers a break in the reading; just as humans need to stop and take breaths, and underwater swimmers need to come up periodically for air, readers also need pauses in their reading. It recharges them and makes them ready to move on to the next paragraph.

Student Writing: Kim Lee's Draft Paragraph

Student writer Kim's draft paragraph shows the introduction, development, and conclusion of an idea:

> Online classes are convenient for students because students can log onto their computers whenever they want to—they don't have to be "in class" at any specific time. They can do the required class work when they want to. Some students, after all, work better late at night. Also, if the student has a job during the day, then she could not take a class during the day. That not only would be *inconvenient*, but impossible! I asked my friend Jenny, who took two online classes last semester, and Jenny told me that she "loved" being able to work on her papers and do the quizzes any time, day or night.

As you can see, the main focus of the paragraph is that online classes are convenient for students, expressed in the very first sentence of the paragraph. The sentences following the first sentence explain why, and provide an example from Kim's friend.

Note: If your idea has several different points to it (known as an "extended idea"), and/or the paragraph is getting too long, you can present the idea in multiple paragraphs. For instance, if you wish to make the point that it is important to learn a foreign language, and you have several reasons in support of that point, you may wish to present those reasons in different paragraphs, with each reason well-supported with facts, evidence, examples, etc.

Drafting Topic Sentences in Your Paragraphs

Just as an essay makes its main point through the thesis statement, each paragraph also should have a statement indicating its central point. This is known as the *topic sentence* of the paragraph. Topic sentences are sometimes placed in the middle of a paragraph; they can even be the last sentence of a paragraph. However, we recommend placing them at the beginning of a paragraph because that is the easiest way of guiding readers to the point you are making in that paragraph. It will also help keep you, the writer, organized as you draft the paragraph, and prevent you from straying off-topic.

An essay with a thesis statement and paragraphs with topic sentences often follows this format:

- **Main paper point** (first paragraph), expressed through the thesis statement.
- **First supporting point** (second paragraph), expressed through the topic sentence, with examples and details to show the reader what you mean, always connected back to the main point.
- **Second supporting point** (third paragraph), expressed through the topic sentence, with examples and details to show the reader what you mean, always connected back to the main point.
- **Third supporting point** (fourth paragraph), expressed through the topic sentence, with examples and details to show the reader what you mean, always connected back to the main point.
- **Fourth supporting point** (fifth paragraph), expressed through the topic sentence, with examples and details to show the reader what you mean, always connected back to the main point.

This can go on, with as many points, and supporting details for those points, as your audience and purpose require.

Student Writing: Kim Lee's Draft of Two Paragraphs

In the following paragraphs, student writer Kim's first sentence is clearly her thesis statement ("Even though there are some disadvantages, taking online classes gives students three important advantages."). Then note how she transitions to her first supporting paragraph ("This paper will examine all three of these advantages, starting with convenience."). Then also note her topic sentence for the second paragraph and how she provides details and examples to help support the topic sentence in that paragraph.

Thesis statement

Supporting sentences

Transition to the first supporting paragraph

> Even though there are some disadvantages, taking online classes gives students three important advantages. Online classes let students take those classes when it is convenient to them. Online classes can save time and travel costs. And, online classes let students work at their own pace. This paper will examine all three of these advantages, starting with convenience.

Topic sentence of the supporting paragraph

Supporting evidence and examples

Reporting on an interview Kim did with a friend

Transition to the next paragraph

> Online classes are convenient for students because students can log onto their computers when they want to. Put another way, they do not have to "be in class" at a specific class time. They can do the required class work when they want to. Some students, after all, work better late at night. An online class lets that student do her work at midnight or 1:00 a.m. Also, if the student has a job during the day, she could not take a class during the day. That not only would be *inconvenient*, but impossible! I asked my friend Jenny, who took two online classes last semester, and Jenny told me that she "loved" being able to work on her papers and do the quizzes any time, day or night. Jenny also reported that while she did not have to "be at class" at a specific time, there were deadlines for turning papers, etc., in. They just were more flexible deadlines than you have in a normal class. Finally, Jenny said that taking the online classes was not only convenient, they also saved her time (and money) in other ways.

Everyday Writing Activity: Topic Sentences and Supporting Sentences

The following paragraph comprises of a group of sentences that are not in order. Please identify the topic statement of the paragraph as well as the supporting sentences, and, in your journal, rearrange them into a well-constructed paragraph. Your instructor may ask you to share your response with the rest of the class.

> Ben also likes to read horror stories, such as those written by Stephen King. He reads the newspaper daily because he likes to keep up with current events. My neighbor Ben is an avid reader of newspapers, science fiction, and horror stories. He enjoys science fiction writers such as Isaac Asimov and Humayun Ahmed.

Everyday Writing Activity: Drafting a Paragraph

Choose one of the topics you did invention activities for (Chapter 6), and, based on the material you generated, draft a paragraph in your journal. Indicate which one is the topic sentence of the paragraph and which ones are the supporting sentences. Your instructor may ask you to share your response with the rest of the class.

Using Transitions in Writing

What happens when you have said what you want to say in your paragraph and are ready to move on to another idea? New ideas should always be presented in a new paragraph. So that your ideas stay connected and your writing flows smoothly, you need to make a transition from one idea to another.

Transitions are one or more words or sentences used at the end of a paragraph or the beginning of the new paragraph; they often summarize the idea in the previous paragraph and also look forward to the idea in the next paragraph. This helps the movement from one paragraph to the next while maintaining the relationship between ideas. Transitions are the glue that holds your writing together, or the bridge that connects two different parts of a piece of writing. Transitions can also be used *within* paragraphs to help readers anticipate what is coming next in the paragraph.

The following table highlights some common transitions and the relationships between ideas that they indicate:

Transitions at a Glance	
To Show This Relationship...	**...Use These Transitional Words**
Similarity	similarly, likewise, in the same manner, also
Difference	in contrast, on the contrary, however, but, on the other hand, yet, nevertheless, in spite of
Chronological	first, second, third, finally, next, then, following that, after, earlier, later, thereafter, subsequently, immediately, simultaneously, today, tomorrow, afterward, prior to, before
Cause and effect	so, therefore, thus, consequently, hence, as a result
Example	for example, for instance, namely, to illustrate, that is
Emphasis	in fact, of course, indeed, for this reason, to repeat, hence, thus, at the same time
Additional	in addition to, also, moreover, and, besides, furthermore, again
Conclusion	on the whole, finally, to conclude, to summarize, therefore

If you find yourself having trouble linking together your ideas from one paragraph to the next, or even within a single paragraph, use this table for suggestions on transitions.

Student Writing: Kim Lee's Transitions

Here is an example of student writer Kim's use of transitions (the transitions are underlined in this passage from her first draft):

Transition within paragraph

Transition within paragraph
Transition between paragraphs

Transition within paragraphs

Transition within paragraph

There are many advantages to distance learning. Students can take courses from the comfort of their homes, when they have time, and do not have to travel to campus and deal with traffic on the roads, or parking issues. There is <u>also</u> no need to worry about filling up the gas tank, which saves money and helps the environment. Students can work at their own pace, and there is usually a lower instructor to student ratio for online courses as compared to traditional courses. <u>Moreover</u>, such courses are becoming more and more widely recognized by employers.

<u>However, there are several disadvantages to online courses, too</u>. They can be more expensive than taking traditional courses. Students <u>also</u> miss out on face-to face interaction with classmates and the teacher. Many educators argue that the classroom environment is more conducive to learning than learning individually, since learning occurs best in group settings. <u>In addition</u>, there are no labs where students can practice and experiment with what they are learning, so the hands-on aspect of education is missing.

Everyday Writing Activity: Using Transitions

Rewrite the following sentences in your journal, using the most appropriate transitions. Your instructor may ask you to share your responses with the rest of the class.

1. Public transportation is a good way to travel. It can be inconvenient sometimes.
2. Winter is the season for skiing and snowboarding. Winter is the time when most people suffer from coughs and colds.
3. It is past midnight. I am going to bed.
4. John waited all day for his friend Ibrahim. John gave up waiting for Ibrahim and went to the concert by himself.
5. Renee went grocery shopping. She made lunch. She took an afternoon nap. Renee went to see a movie.
6. Seok-Kyo came to America to study. His twin, Jin-Ho, stayed in Korea.
7. Studying in America is expensive. Scholarships and financial aid are available to many students.

(continued)

8. Faisal wants to call his family in Kuwait. He needs to find out what the cost will be.
9. Sheila is planning to travel next summer. She has begun to make plans.
10. Many students read the campus newspaper. Some students prefer getting their news from online newspapers.

LO5

Identify the parts of an essay: introduction, body, and conclusion

Parts of an Essay

Paragraphs are the building blocks of any essay and give the essay its structure. Typically, an essay has three major parts: the **introduction**, the **body**, and the **conclusion**.

Introduction

The introduction introduces the topic of the essay to the reader in broad fashion, and then narrows it down to one specific aspect of the topic. This specific focus is introduced in the thesis statement. The introduction also provides relevant background information on the topic. Here is an example:

Here the writer provides some background information.

Note the strategy of "definition" here, as the writer defines "body language."

This last sentence is the writer's thesis statement.

> Body language is an important form of nonverbal communication that uses various parts of the body to send signals about what a person is feeling or thinking about something. Body posture, hand gestures, feet tapping, eye movements are all considered body language that can be used along with speech, or by themselves as a form of communication. While the use of body language varies greatly between people and cultures, there are some common signs that are easily recognized that indicate, among other messages being sent out, when a person is interested and when a person is being dominating.

Body

The body of the essay develops the topic in several paragraphs, using the appropriate writing strategies. Each of the paragraphs contains a topic statement and uses transitions within and between paragraphs as needed. Here is an example:

The first sentence is the topic sentence of the paragraph.

> When a person is interested in a conversation or an activity, there are various ways of indicating that interest without speaking. The person may move closer to listen and observe, and even incline his/her head closer for better listening or for better viewing. Sometimes the whole body may lean forward. The eyebrows may be furrowed to indicate concentration, and the interested person may ignore other talkers around him or any other activity around him. <u>Also</u>, the person's body may be still, though he/she may nod occasionally to indicate agreement with what the listener is saying or with the activity taking place.

The "also" signals a transition within the paragraph.

Transition to a new paragraph, using the transition word, "too."

> The signs are clear, <u>too</u>, when a person is dominating others. The person may stand upright, with his/her hands on the chest and legs spread wide apart so that the body seems bigger and taller. The dominating person may invade the other person's body space by moving physically closer. He/she may <u>also</u> use facial gestures that indicate disapproval. These gestures include pursed lips, frowns, and staring straight at the person being dominated.

The first sentence is also the topic statement for the new paragraph.

Conclusion

The conclusion brings the essay to a close, usually by reaffirming the point made in the thesis statement and summarizing the main points expressed in the essay. The conclusion should never introduce a new topic or a new idea. Here is an example:

Restates the thesis of the paper.

Reminds readers of the focus of the two body paragraphs.

> Body language is an important part of communication, perhaps more important than many of us realize. It can indicate anything from being interested to being dominating. If we learn more about how body language communicates attitudes, ideas, and emotions, we will be better able to understand each other. It will also help us understand how our own, often unconscious, body language communicates our thoughts and feelings to others.

Everyday Writing Activity: Identify the Parts of Kim Lee's Essay

Here is part of Kim Lee's first draft of her paper about online education. Underline and identify:

- Kim's thesis statement.
- Kim's topic statements for each paragraph.

(continued)

- The transitions Kim uses within each paragraph.
- The transitions Kim uses between paragraphs.

Your instructor may ask you to share your work with the rest of the class.

Even though there are some disadvantages, taking online classes gives students three important advantages. Online classes let students take those classes when it is convenient for them. Online classes can save time and travel costs. And, online classes let students work at their own pace. This paper will examine all three of these advantages, starting with convenience. It will also cover some of the disadvantages of taking online classes.

Online classes are convenient for students because students can log onto their computers when they want to. Put another way, they do not have to "be in class" at a specific class time. They can do the required class work when they want to do that work. Some students, after all, work better late at night or early in the morning. An online class lets that student do her work at midnight or 1:00 a.m. Also, if the student has a job during the day, then she could not take a class during the day. That not only would be *inconvenient*, but impossible. I asked my friend Jenny, who took two online classes last semester, and Jenny told me that she "loved" being able to work on her papers and do the quizzes any time, day or night. Jenny also reported that while she did not have to "be at class" at a specific time, there were deadlines for turning papers, etc., in. They just were more flexible deadlines than you have in a normal class. Finally, Jenny said that taking the online classes was not only convenient; they also saved her time (and money) in other ways.

Not having to get to school (and pay for parking there) is another benefit of online classes. These days, everyone knows how expensive gasoline is, and even bus passes are expensive. In addition, not having to get to campus saves a lot of time. Depending on where a student lives, he or she could save an hour a day just in travel time. And he or she also could save the time and hassle of getting to the bus stop, subway station, etc. All of that adds up to a real time savings for the student—time he or she could be using to work on the class's homework.

With any college class, there is always reading and writing to do, and the problem is finding the time to do it all. Online classes let students work at their own pace, when they want to work (and when it is convenient for them to do that work). When you're in a classroom, you are constrained by the time the class has to work with. Put another way, the class might run out of time before all of your questions get answered, or before you can finish the required work. In an online class, that is not the case, as you can work at your own pace and take as long (or as little) time as you need. This is a big advantage of online classes.

Everyday Writing Activity: Chapter Reflection

In your journal, respond to the following prompts. Your instructor may ask you to share your responses with the rest of the class.

1. A thesis statement is _____.
2. A topic sentence is _____.
3. A paragraph is _____.
4. Transitions are _____.
5. The different parts of an essay are _____.

MyWritingLab™ For support in meeting this chapter's objectives, log in to **www.mywritinglab.com** and select **Thesis Statement, The Topic Sentence, Developing and Organizing a Paragraph, Recognizing the Essay, Essay Introductions, Conclusions, and Titles,** and **Essay Organization**.

Chapter 8

Revising Your Writing

Learning Objectives

In this chapter, you will learn to:

LO1 Explain what revision is and why it is important

LO2 Use different strategies, including peer review, to revise your writing

LO3 Edit your writing

LO4 Proofread your writing

LO5 Publish, or finalize, your writing

Consider the accompanying cartoon. Where do you write? Surely not on your roof, as Snoopy is doing! Do you have a favorite place to write? A favorite time of day or night? Do you keep a cup of coffee or a soft drink at your side? Do you start on paper and then write a draft on a computer? After you have some ideas on paper or in a computer document, how do you go about revising your work?

Why Is Revision Important?

LO1

Explain what revision is and why it is important

According to the Modern Language Association, "Revision is a lifelong writing skill that writers practice in order to develop in their chosen fields. The writer is one who writes, but the real writer is one who re-vises." Thus, a very important part of the writing process is revising, as this quote tells us. It is an activity as important as the actual writing itself.

The word **revision** means to "re-vision," that is, to "re-see." In other words, revision means to take a fresh look at your writing, to "re-think" and "re-consider" what you want to say. In fact, we believe that all writing is "re-writing": while you always start with some ideas on paper, you almost always revise those ideas. Even when you write something as simple as a shopping list, more often than not you will go back and add specifics (like the particular brand of cereal you want to buy), additional items (for example, a pair of pants or a sweater), and so on.

Famous author E. B. White (author of *Charlotte's Web*, among other books) also wrote about writing. One of his most famous works is a book he wrote with William Strunk called *The Elements of Style*. One comment that White made in the book was, "When you say something, make sure you have said it. The chances of your having said it are only fair." We think of revision as helping us to make sure that we say what we want to say in a way that our readers can understand. Unless we revise our work, the chances of saying what we want are, as E. B. White told us, "only fair."

Everyday Writing Activity: How Do You Revise?

In no more than two paragraphs, define "revision" and also describe your own revision process in your journal:

First, define the word "revision." What does this term mean to you?

Second, when you revise a paper for school, what do you do? Describe your revision process in as much detail as you can, so your readers will

(continued)

be able to see and understand how you revise your own work. You might explain if you

- Re-read your paper from the start and then make changes.
- Re-read just sections before changing them.
- Ask others (friends, classmates, parents) to read your work and make suggestions on how to improve it.
  - If you do ask others for advice, how do you decide what "to do" with their suggestions?
  - How do you determine which of their suggestions you will really try to attend to, in your revision?

Your instructor may want you to share your definitions of revision and your revision process with the rest of the class. If you do share your writing, how do your definitions of "revision" compare with your classmates' definitions? How many different "revision processes" are there in your class? When you learned how your classmates go about revising their work, did you learn any new ideas that you might try when you revise your next paper assignment?

Having to rewrite does *not* mean that you are a poor writer. Even the most successful writers have to revise (the famous novelist James A. Michener once said that he was not a very good writer—but that he was a very good *rewriter*). Writing is discovery, and as you were drafting you may not have put down your best thoughts and ideas, or organized them very well, or even got them all down on paper. Therefore, when you have a draft that you are somewhat satisfied with, you need to reread it to see how you can improve it. Revision can help you improve in the following areas:

- You can make your writing more interesting or clearer to the reader.
- You can add examples or details or evidence that you overlooked when you were drafting. Often when we write a first draft, we make a claim and forget that we need evidence to support that claim, so when we revise, we add evidence.
- You can get rid of material that is not really necessary or that you have repeated.
- You can make more effective vocabulary choices if necessary.
- You can reorganize your paper so that it is more effective.
- You can determine if you are meeting assignment requirements.
- You can refocus your text if you have strayed from your original topic.

As you can see from this list, revision does not mean correcting mechanical problems in your writing; that is called *editing* and *proofreading* (which we will cover later in this chapter). *Revision* means working to make the *content* of your essay better: to say exactly what you want to say to your reader. It is, therefore, not a process you can ignore. It may mean you have to go back and rewrite a large portion of your paper, but it will be worthwhile in the long run, because it will ensure a more effective paper (and a better grade) than if you don't revise.

<table>
<tr>
<td>

LO2

Use different strategies, including peer review, to revise your writing

</td>
<td>

Strategies for Revising

Are there any specific methods one can use when revising? We recommend four:

1. **Read your paper out loud to yourself.** Read slowly; it is often easier to catch writing problems that way.
2. **Read your draft several times.** Read at different times of the day; the time of day may make a difference.
3. **Listen to someone else read your paper.** Simply listening, without having to read your work, can help you pinpoint problems in your writing.
4. **Get help from your classmates.** If your instructor organizes a peer review session in which you exchange drafts with one or more of your classmates, they can give you suggestions on what you can do to make your paper stronger. Your instructor also may provide feedback and suggestions on how to write a more effective paper.

</td>
</tr>
</table>

Peer Review

We tell our own students that **peer review**—having classmates read each other's work and comment on it and make suggestions on how to improve it—is the *hardest work* we will ask them to do, all semester. We think that it is difficult to read someone else's text and make suggestions about it, because when you are reading your classmates' papers, you really need to pay attention to what they have to say, always thinking about how they can make the writing more effective. This is hard but important work, and we also tell our students that they want the comments and suggestions they make on their classmate's papers to be *reciprocal*. If you expect to receive useful feedback and suggestions on your own papers, you must provide good and thoughtful and helpful feedback to your classmates on their papers. That is what *reciprocal* means: to give in the same way that you hope to receive. If you don't work hard when you review a classmate's paper, you cannot expect your peers to work hard when they comment on your writing. It does little good to tell a classmate, "I really liked your paper. It's really good." That might be easy to do and to say, but you will probably be embarrassed when you get *your own* paper back with all sorts of good suggestions on how to make it more effective.

Everyday Writing Activity: Practicing Peer Review

Consider for a moment that you have been asked to help a classmate revise the following paragraph, which is her start on describing how she revises her own writing:

> I plop down in front of my computer and I'm not very happy that I have to revise this description of how I revise something, as usually I just write a paper and turn it in. But I guess I start my revision by reading through my paper again just to see if I'm clear and when I find a place where I may not be clear, I reword some of it. I look for commas and other things that aren't right, too.

If your instructor asked you to make suggestions to your classmate on how she might improve this bit of writing, what would you say? What would you focus on? What questions would you ask?

It might be useful, as an example, to ask the writer why she seems to resist revising her writing. If you could ask her some useful questions, she might see the benefit of revising (for example, you could ask, "Do you seem to get better grades when you revise your papers?"). You also might ask her what she means by "clear" when she writes that she reads "through her paper again just to see if I'm clear." And, what does she mean when she says she "rewords" some of her work—what does that mean, exactly?

Asking such questions might help the writer understand her revision process better, which will lead to more effective writing and revising.

Your instructor may ask you to share your questions with the rest of the class.

Effective Revision

In the preceding text and activity, the focus was on making a piece of student writing "more effective." What does it mean to make a text "more effective"?

That depends completely on what the writer is trying to accomplish for his/her audience. Consider something as simple as making a list of needed items for your dorm room (that is your **purpose** in making the list) that you would like your roommate to purchase (your roommate is your **audience**). You might start with a simple list:

- Extension cord.
- Small table.
- Check on (don't buy) the price of a microwave oven.
- Spare light bulbs.

But when you hand your list to your roommate, you get some questions:

- How long an extension cord do you want me to get? Does it need to have three prongs for the socket and the plug-in-end? What are we going to use it for?
- What size should the table be?
- Do you mean a really small microwave? Is there a size or wattage or something specific I should look for?
- What wattage light bulbs, and how many?

Now, you have just gotten some "peer review" feedback on your list: questions your reader needs answered in order to understand what you have in mind so he/she can get the items you need for your room.

How detailed do you have to be when you revise this list? Consider what you want to accomplish: to have your roommate purchase what you need based on the list you create. So, for example, if you wanted to get an extension cord that would blend in with the color of the wall in your dorm room, you might add

- 6' cord, tan (brown if they don't have tan). Be sure it has a 3-pronged plug, or our toaster won't work.

If the small table is meant to hold your laptop, you might add

- at least 20" square. It needs to be about 30" high, too. Wood is better than plastic, but don't spend more than $15 on it, please.

Revision, therefore, is often clarifying what you want to say, to make sure your reader(s) understands what you hope your writing will accomplish.

Everyday Writing Activity: What Would You Like for Your Birthday?

In your journal, write a brief note (no more than one page) to your closest friend describing what you would like as a birthday present for your upcoming birthday.

Then write another note, also in your journal, to a relative who lives in another city, someone you have not seen in a long time, asking for that same present.

You probably will find, when you compare the two notes, that you had to do a significant amount of revision to the note to your friend as you wrote the note to your relative. This is because you had to provide much more information and detail and description when you wrote to that distant relative. After all, your best friend probably already knows pretty much what you would like, even down to the brand and size.

Your instructor may want you to share your notes with the rest of the class.

The key question for any piece of writing and any revision is always this: what does your reader need to know for your writing to accomplish what you hope it will? Later, as you write your assignments, your instructor will provide guidance on reviewing your peers' papers, but here are some examples of the kinds of questions you might ask, as you read your classmates' papers, to help them revise their writing:

 # Critical Thinking Activity: Ask Yourself Questions for Peer Review

1. What is the thesis, the point the writer wants to make? How might he/she make it more clearly? What information do I need, as a reader, to "get the point"?
2. What information is unclear or confusing to me? What suggestions can I make to help the writer clarify that information? What information might be presented more understandably as a graph or chart or table or photograph?
3. What parts need examples to "show" what the writer means? What kinds of examples might I suggest to my classmate, so his/her readers can really see and understand what he/she means?

Questions such as these—that you try to answer as you are reading a paper—are designed to help you help the writer construct a more effective text. Think of peer review as a way for you to communicate with the writer, acting in the role of a real reader. While your instructor will most often provide the class with some questions to consider as you read and make suggestions about your classmates' papers, it also is useful for *you* to think about possible questions, too: what would you like to see in a paper, as a real reader of that paper?

Consider, for example, a paper written about people who send text messages as they drive. That can be dangerous, right? Well, the writer can say so, but might it be more effective to show a table with statistics? Or a photo of a crashed car? You need to think of such questions as you provide feedback. Of course, the questions you ask will depend on the topic.

Everyday Writing Activity: Asking Questions

A writing assignment that instructors sometimes ask their students to do is to tell about an important event—something that has made a difference to that student and the student's life. Students will write about something that happened to them (being elected to the Student Council; moving to a new city; starting at a new school; playing in the winning football game).

If your class was asked to write this kind of a paper and you were reading a classmate's work to help her revise that first draft, what kinds of questions might you ask? Well, think about what you, as a reader, would like to know about the event your classmate was writing about. *Those* are the things you would look for in her paper, right? And if you did not find them, you would then ask her about those details, wouldn't you?

For this activity, consider the questions a reporter usually asks: *who, what, when, why, where,* and *how.* Write a question or two about each one of these "reporter's questions" for a paper about an event that influenced the writer. We'll give you an example for the first one, and then you can do the rest:

- *Who*: Who was involved? Who was there when you (started at the new school; played on that winning team), and in what ways did they influence the event you are writing about? What other people were involved, and how did the event affect them?
- *What:*
- *When:*
- *Why:*
- *Where:*
- *How:*

Your instructor may ask you to share your questions with the rest of the class.

Peer review is, of course, designed to help the writer: readers comment about and make suggestions on how to improve the text. But peer review also helps you in your own writing, because by reading and commenting on texts written by others, you learn to read better and to understand how to make your *own writing* more effective. Put another way, by helping your classmates with their papers, you will learn how to better read and improve your own work. We suggest you ask yourself the following questions while reading or listening to your own draft:

Critical Thinking Activity: Ask Yourself Questions for Revision

1. What needs improvement? Organization? Writing style? Word choice (to make your ideas clearer to your reader)?
2. How can I make those improvements?
3. Is my draft meeting my audience's expectations? (For a discussion of audience, see pages 50–52.)
4. Is the purpose of my writing clear? (For a discussion of purpose, see pages 46–47.)
5. Are my paragraphs well developed and coherent? If not, how can I make them better?
6. Is my word choice appropriate?

Once you have identified what aspects of your paper require revision, work on them, and then repeat the strategies mentioned. Do so as many times as necessary, until you are completely satisfied that you cannot make your paper better than it now is.

Student Writing: Kim Lee's Revision

Here is an example of student Kim Lee's introduction and her revision of her introduction. Kim chose to write about the benefits and problems with online education. Here is Kim's original introduction with her revisions marked in red:

Even though there are some disadvantages ~~taking~~ online classes ~~gives~~ have ~~students~~ three important advantages for students. Online classes let students take those classes when it is convenient for ~~them~~ students. Online classes can save time and travel costs. And online classes let students work at their own pace which can help students succeed. This paper will examine all three of these advantagees, starting with convenience. It will also cover some of the disadvantagees of taking online classes, as students need to consider those, too.

Kim's revised introduction is more detailed in its content, which gives the reader a better sense of what her paper will focus on. Note also that, while revising, Kim has not corrected some of the spelling and punctuation errors that are present in the introduction. That is left for the next stage: editing and proofreading.

LO3
Edit your writing

Editing Your Work

Editing your paper means that you read through your work and consider the words you have used: do they really say what you want to get across to your readers? If not, change them. The editing stage is also your chance to polish your text, to make it as effective and as clear as possible.

There are several ways to edit your paper:

- Read slowly and loudly, trying to "hear" each sentence. A lot of sentence structure and word choice errors can be spotted this way.
- Your instructor may pair you with a classmate who can help you with editing your paper.
- Ask your instructor for help with anything you are uncertain about, and/or seek the help of a tutor at your school's writing center.

Do not turn in your paper without editing it!

Student Writing: Kim Lee's Editing

Note how, in the following example, student writer Kim Lee added some words to her introduction to clarify what she meant. Kim Lee's edited introductory paragraph, with her changes marked in red, looks like this:

Even though there are some disadvantages online college classes have three important advantages for students. Online classes let students take those classes when it is convenient for the students. Online classes can save students time and travel costs. And, online classes let students work at their own pace, which can help students succeed. This paper will examine all three of these advantagees, starting with convenience. ⚬ This paper will also cover some of the disadvantagees of taking online classes, as students need to consider those, too, before they decide to take an online class.

Everyday Writing Activity: Editing

Working with a classmate, edit the following paragraph. Your instructor may ask you to share your edited paragraph with the rest of the class.

> The latest and many important part of knowing weather paterns is weather or not it will snowand maybe then also when it might. And if so how much. It can be dangerous to drive in the snow, so drive slow and watch out for ice especially black ice. Which is dangerous, too. But you cant always see it. And always where your seatbelt and then you will be safer in the snow.

LO4

Proofread your writing

Proofreading Your Work

Proofreading is the final stage in the writing process. It means to revise your paper for grammar, spelling, punctuation, and other mechanical problems that might be present in your writing and that might hinder smooth reading. It takes place after you have gone through the revision process and are satisfied that you have no more changes to make regarding the content of your paper. It should *not* be done while you are drafting your essay or revising it; you will probably be making changes to your essay during those processes, so any proofreading changes you make will be a waste of time and effort, because the changes you make may disappear during the drafting/revising process.

There are a couple of items to watch for as you proofread your paper:

- If you are not sure of how a particular word is spelled, look it up in a dictionary. You may also use the spell-check feature in your computer, but that may be less reliable than using a dictionary.
- If there are punctuation issues (comma splices, run-ons, etc.) or grammar issues (verb tenses, subject–verb agreement, etc.) that you are unsure of, please check the Handbook section of this text for direction.

Student Writing: Kim Lee's Proofreading

Kim Lee's proofread introductory paragraph, with spelling and punctuation errors corrected and her changes marked in red, looks like this:

> Even though there are some disadvantages, online college classes have three important advantages for students. Online classes let students take those classes when it is convenient for the students. Online classes can

> save students time and travel costs. Finally ~~And~~, online classes let students work at their own pace, which can help students succeed. This paper will examine all three of these advantages, starting with convenience. This paper will also cover some of the disadvantages of taking online classes, as students need to consider those, too, before they decide to take an online class.

LO5

Publish, or finalize, your writing

Publishing Your Work

Publishing is the final, and very exciting, stage of the writing process. It means that a piece of writing has gone through the entire writing process and is now ready for readers. Professional writers will submit their writing for publication, whether as a book, a magazine or Web article, a collection of essays, and so forth. For student writers like you, publishing means your paper is ready to submit to your instructor for a final grade. You want to be sure to follow any formatting directions your instructors provide (double spacing, margins, font size, etc.). Your paper reflects your best effort, and you should feel very proud of yourself!

Student Writing: Kim Lee's Final Draft

Lee 1

Kim Lee

Professor Beverly Cleland

ENG 090

24 Jan. 2012

Online Classes: Should College Students Take Them?

Even though there are some disadvantages, online college classes have three important advantages for students. Online classes let students take those classes when it is convenient for the students. Online classes can save students time and travel costs. Finally, online classes let students work at their own pace, which can help students succeed. This paper will examine all three of these advantages, starting with convenience. This paper will also cover some of the disadvantages of taking online classes, as students need to consider those, too, before they decide to take an online class.

(continued)

Online classes are convenient for students because students can log onto their computers when they want to. Put another way, they do not have to "be in class" at a specific class time. Students can do the required class work when they want to do that work. Some students, after all, work better late at night or early in the morning. An online class lets those students do their work at midnight or 1:00 a.m. Also, if a student has a job during the day, then she could not take a class during the day. That not only would be *inconvenient*, but impossible. Jenny Sims, who took two online classes last semester, reports that she "loved" being able to work on her papers and do the quizzes any time, day or night. Jenny also noted that while she did not have to "be at class" at a specific time, there were deadlines for turning papers, etc. in. They just were more flexible deadlines than you have in a normal class. It is important that students realize that online classes are not "correspondence" classes, or "mail in" classes, where students can submit their work at any time. Online classes have specific deadlines. Finally, Jenny noted that taking the online classes was not only convenient; they also saved her time (and money) in other ways.

Not having to get to school (and pay for parking there) is another benefit of online classes. These days, everyone knows how expensive gasoline is, and even bus passes can be expensive. In addition, not having to get to campus saves a lot of time. Depending on where a student lives, he or she could save an hour or more a day just in travel time. He or she also could save the time and hassle of getting to the bus stop, subway station, etc. All of that adds up to a real time savings for the student—time he or she could be using to work on the class's homework.

Also, this homework can be done at the student's own pace. This takes a lot of pressure off the student. As long as the student keeps the posted deadlines in mind, and turns in the work accordingly, the student should succeed in the class. There is also no last minute scrambling to do the daily class work or the daily course readings.

There are some disadvantages to online classes, including that students and teacher may have trouble communicating. The teacher may not be available when the student needs an answer to his or her question. Students also need to be very clear in the questions they ask, and teachers also must be specific and clear in their answers. Otherwise, miscommunication may happen.

Also, students need to be able to work at their own pace in an online class, as the teacher is not there to remind the student about due dates, etc. Jenny Sims reports that in her first online class, she procrastinated a lot, so her work was not as good as it could have been, which hurt her final grade. Students must take responsibility for their own learning, especially in an online class.

One other possible disadvantage to online classes is the technology: it does not always work. Students sometimes do not have the right computer or a fast enough Internet connection, or they do not know how to use the software. As Jenny Sims reports, it is up to the student to be able to do the work required in an online class.

Online classes are beneficial to college students as they are more convenient, can save students time and money, and allow students to work at their own pace. The main disadvantages of online classes are that students and teachers may have trouble communicating, students may procrastinate at getting the work done, and students have to have and understand how to use the technology required. Overall, the advantages of online classes outweigh the disadvantages.

Work Cited

Sims, Jenny. Personal Interview. 20 Jan. 2012.

Everyday Writing Activity: Chapter Reflection

In your journal, respond to the following prompts. Your instructor may ask you to share your responses with the rest of the class.

1. What are the main points about revising that you learned from this chapter?
2. What are the main points about editing and proofreading that you learned from this chapter?
3. Explain how you might go about revising your work differently than you did in the past, based on what you learned in this chapter.

MyWritingLab™ For support in meeting this chapter's objectives, log in to **www.mywritinglab.com** and select **Revising the Essay** and **Editing the Essay**.

PART 2

Writing for a Purpose

Chapter **9** Writing to Share Experiences: Using Description and Narration

Chapter **10** Writing to Inform: Using Examples and Process Explanation

Chapter **11** Writing to Analyze: Using Division and Classification

Chapter **12** Writing to Explain Why: Using Cause and Effect

Chapter **13** Writing to Evaluate: Using Comparison and Contrast

Chapter **14** Writing to Persuade: Using Multiple Strategies

Writing to Share Experiences
Using Description and Narration

Learning **O**bjectives

In this chapter, you will learn to:

LO1 Consider the writer's situation, and determine your purpose and audience

LO2 Use the rhetorical strategies of *description* and *narration* to share an experience

LO3 Use invention and discovery strategies to come up with ideas and details

LO4 Write a thesis statement that states the point of your essay

LO5 Organize and write your first draft

LO6 Revise your essay, and prepare a final draft

The photograph on the opposite page shows four generations of the family of one of the authors. Imagine the experiences these women might have shared with each other, especially what life was like when the older women were as young as the little girl. What was life like as they grew up? Where did they live? What was school like? Who were their friends? What did they eat? What did they worry about?

What experiences do you and your family share (and tell, and often retell)? About moving from a small town to a large city? About grandparents moving from one state or country to another? Of marriages and births (and, sadly, deaths), of streets lived on and homes lived in and cars driven and ridden in, of cousins and birthday parties and holiday celebrations and family disagreements? Of vacations enjoyed and others ruined because of bad weather? Of a special gift you once gave or received or one you are now planning to give?

How do you share those experiences? If you are like most of us, you generally rely on two rhetorical strategies as you share family experiences: *description* and *narration*. Briefly, *description* includes an explanation of things like the weather, the people, the place, the smells around you, the sounds, and so on. *Narration* is the telling of your experience: where you start, the events you tell about, the sequence in which you tell them (your organization), and so on. These rhetorical strategies work together to help your reader understand your story, to "share" your experience with you. (For more on rhetorical strategies, see Chapter 5.)

Everyday Writing Activity: Sharing an Experience

In no more than one page in your journal, share one of your favorite family experiences—perhaps a story you have heard from a parent or grandparent about their youth. Be sure to use both *description* and *narration* as you share this family experience. Your instructor may want you to share your response with the rest of the class.

<table>
<tr><td>

LO1

Consider the writer's situation, and determine your purpose and audience

</td><td>

The Writer's Situation

Was it difficult to use *description* and *narration* to share a family experience? Just as with any writing task, you have to figure out out what to include and what to emphasize. You always start sharing an experience keeping your **purpose** and **audience** in mind.

Your *purpose* in sharing an experience is to provide sufficient details, in an interesting story, so your reader can understand that experience—or

</td></tr>
</table>

better, perhaps so readers can *see* and *experience* it themselves. The American writer Ernest Hemingway once wrote that

> *I'm trying in all my stories to get the feeling of the actual life across—not to just depict life—or criticize it—but actually make it alive. So that when you have read something by me you actually experience the thing.*

Hemingway's goal is a worthwhile one when you write to share experiences, so consider this: what details can you provide to help your own readers see and understand and actually share the experience you are describing and narrating? If your goal is to share the walk from the bus stop to your classroom, you want to focus on details about that walk (the feel of the sidewalk, the weather, who you met along the way, perhaps the sound of traffic rumbling by, etc.). If your goal is to share your experience of getting more and more worried about an upcoming test, as you made that same walk, you will emphasize different details (your queasy stomach, the answers for the test that you were trying to remember, and so on).

As you consider what your purpose is, you also need to think about your *audience*: What might they already know about the experience you want to share with them? What would you like them to know? What information (or pictures, or specific words) will help them see and understand your experience? How much description will they need? How much of the story do you need to narrate, for them to see what you see?

<table>
<tr><td>

LO2

Use the rhetorical strategies of *description* and *narration* to share an experience

</td><td>

Sharing an Experience through Description and Narration

There are many ways and places to share experiences, but two popular ways are on the Web—on Twitter or by writing a blog.

7 Ways to Be Worth Following on Twitter

JoLynne

You may follow a friend on Twitter as he/she shares experiences by posting "tweets," or very brief messages. Notice how this writer, JoLynne (known as @dcrmom on Twitter), outlines her own use of Twitter and then describes some specific ways to improve tweets.

</td></tr>
</table>

Do you know a "Twitteraholic"?

1   Hi. I'm JoLynne and I'm a Twitteraholic. Yes, I'm unashamedly and unapologetically addicted to Twitter. I use Twitter to build relationships, to keep connected to the outside world, to distract me from the housework,

JoLynne describes the ways she uses Twitter.

Note how JoLynne also *narrates* her own story of how she uses Twitter.

and to find articles and information that I wouldn't discover otherwise. I choose carefully whom I follow on Twitter. As with any other social network, there are ways to grow your community. In Twitter-speak, this means to gain followers. I've put together this list based on the characteristics of the people I most enjoy following on Twitter.

1. Be Interesting

JoLynne describes how to be interesting when you tweet.

2   It's fine to announce what you're doing and thinking and what you had for lunch, as long as you do it in a way that is entertaining to your followers. Twitter is micro-blogging, and like on your blog, if all you do is give a play-by-play of your mundane daily happenings, you will lose followers. The people I enjoy following find a way to make me smile with their quips and one-liners, even if they are just informing me what they had for breakfast. Here are a couple of examples from the past few days.

These examples help the reader see what JoLynne is describing.

3   @subdiva could have said, "Packing to go to Disney tonight!" but instead she wrote: "Packing up to ring in the New Year on the happiest place on earth. No, not the wine store…"

4   @rocksinmydryer could have said, "I hate dieting" but instead she wrote: "May I just say, for the record, that PORTION CONTROL STINKS? Thank you, that is all."

5   Of course not everything you post has to be clever, but if you're just sharing your thoughts and happenings, try to make it worth reading.

2. Be Informative

Here JoLynne suggests providing information as a way to help readers see what you mean.

Do you like JoLynne's personal reactions to the examples she provides?

6   Not every tweet should answer the question, "What are you doing right now?" If you are going to participate in the Twitter community, you need to give something back. I love it when people post links to helpful articles or leave bits of advice and information. Post whatever comes naturally to you. @skinnyjeans reminds her followers every day to get up and drink a glass of water and gives us a much-needed pep talk in the middle of the afternoon. I love this! @problogger always links to the articles he is reading, and I have found lots of new bloggers to follow this way. Not all helpful information has to be your own. If you see a good tweet, do a "retweet" so your followers can get the benefit of the information that is being shared.

3. Be Interactive

7   Don't be a "hit and run" tweeter! In other words, don't just log into Twitter to tell people what you are doing or link to your post and then leave. Respond to tweets, ask questions, answer questions. Twitter is a conversation, not a monologue, and the more you participate, the more you will get out of it, and the faster your community will grow.

…

Questions for Discussion and Writing

1. What new things did you learn from this brief Web posting?
2. Did this piece make you want to tweet?
3. How effective is JoLynne's use of description to help you, as a reader, understand what she is trying to show you?

Graffiti Wall

Rick Steves' Europe

The following stories come from travel guru Rick Steves's Web site. In what is normally called a **blog,** *Steves explains the Graffiti Wall:*

> *Our Graffiti Wall is a* **lively community of European travelers** *who generously share their experience and enthusiastically learn from each other. There's probably as much information here as in the rest of this Web site combined. Find the topic of interest and browse or contribute.*

These particular stories are from travelers sharing their holiday experiences in Europe. As you read them, think about anything new you learned (perhaps a travel tip that will help you). Also consider how these folks used both description *and* narration *to share their travel experiences. In longer stories, photographs or maps might have helped readers share these travel experiences.*

The writer gets right to the point.

Note how he narrates the story of that evening sequentially: one thing after another.

The writer adds descriptive details about Bleigießen for readers (like us!) who are unfamiliar with it; still sequential narration.
More details and description.

This writer compliments the advice from Rick Steves as she starts sharing her travel experiences.

New Years in Germany

1   I didn't get to make it for Christmas, but in my most recent trip to Germany, I got to experience New Years with a German family! I never realized how lame USA New Years is. We had a traditional meal cooked on a Raclette grill. We then made a warm punch called Feuerzangenbowle which had wine, gin, fruit juices, cloves, and sugar that you set on fire and melt (search for pictures online). Then we played Bleigießen, which is when you melt lead figures over a candle and throw them in water which hardens them into a shape you interpret to give you your fortune for the next year. After that we set off indoor fireworks on which popped out confetti and streamers. Then at midnight you go outside and set off real fireworks. And everyone in the town is setting theirs off too, so you can see fireworks going off all around you. Amazing experience!

—Ryan, Indiana, PA, USA

Christmas in Paris

2   I just got back from visiting Paris (December 8-20, 2009) for the first time. Rick's 2010 Paris Guide was my Bible! I kept it w/ me at all times. I saw great typical and unusual sites Rick talked about and had just a fabulous time--Paris is

She describes shopping areas and the things she bought.

Weather details help readers share the experience.

Comments on others she saw visiting while narrating her own experiences.

Describes examples of entertainment.

beautiful at Christmas! There are little Christmas markets all over town, especially Montmarte and Champs-Élysées, which sell everything from imported tourist trinkets to homemade jam and handwoven wall hangings/rugs. It was cold but sunny most of the time--I wore my silk long johns out! I got all my Christmas shopping done there--and how special it will be for my family to get presents directly from France?! Interestingly, there were few Americans--most of the tourists seemed to be from Britain or Japan. There were still lines for the major sites--I stood in line at the Louvre for an hour, but it gave me time to people watch.

3   I saw Sting's performance of songs from his new winter cd and saw The Nutcracker Ballet at the Opera Bastille. I even popped in to see a movie (in English w/ French subtitles) one particularly cold afternoon.

4   As an aside, the Pompidou Centre, the modern art museum, is a must-see for artists/art lovers. I'm an artist and was in paradise--There was a special women's art exhibit, which was really powerful.

5   All in all, it was a great trip--I'm already planning my next one--this time to Rome, Venice and Florence in May 2010.

—Jill Henry, Olympia, WA, USA

Questions for Discussion and Writing

1. What new things did you learn from these brief travel postings?
2. Did either of these stories make you want to visit Germany or Paris? Why or why not?
3. What would you tell a reader about your own travel experiences? What details would you be sure to include? What information would you *not* want to tell readers about your experiences?

Everyday Writing Activity: Where Have You Been?

In no more than one page in your journal, share a travel experience of your own, using the strategies of description and narration. Because you only need to write one page, focus on a short trip—perhaps to a nearby relative's home. Your instructor may want you to share your response with the rest of the class.

WRITING ASSIGNMENTS

The writing assignments that follow all ask you to share an experience. But what is an "experience" that you might want to share?

As you will see when you work through some of the discovery activities to help you get started writing, it is important to realize that for an experience to be memorable and interesting to your readers, that experience does *not* have to be a sad or emotional or major experience for you. Often we find that our students, when we ask them to share an experience, think that for an event to have significance and seem important, it has to be sad or life-changing. But that is not the case: if an experience is important to you, then it also will be interesting to your readers—if you provide the right kind of *description* that helps them understand the experience, as well as being an interesting story, and also provide a *narrative* that keeps readers interested.

Writing Assignment One: Share a Positive Learning Experience

By this time of your life, you have learned a lot both inside and outside the classroom. Think back over your classroom experiences as well as other times when you have learned something outside of school. Perhaps you learned how to improve a relationship, or to put something together, or to solve a particular problem. Perhaps you learned how to effectively communicate with someone else, either in speech or in writing. Perhaps you learned how to work together with several others on some project. Perhaps you constructed a paper for a class assignment on a topic that really interested you and that you did especially well on. Perhaps it was learning how to play a position in a little league or other sports team. Whatever experience you decide to share, make sure that you focus on a positive experience.

For this assignment, share that experience. Use the rhetorical strategies of *description* and *narration* to share your experience.

Writing Assignment Two: Share a Work Experience

For this assignment, assume that you have been asked to share a work experience that you have had, either a good or a negative experience. Perhaps it was working with a "tough" boss. Perhaps it was working with others, some of whom you did not get along with, on the job. Perhaps it was doing a task that you did not want to do. Perhaps it was getting your first raise. Perhaps it was overcoming the fear of doing something you were afraid of doing. Perhaps it was just applying for your first job.

For this assignment, share that positive or negative experience. Use the rhetorical strategies of *description* and *narration* to share your experience.

Writing Assignment Three: Share a Cultural Experience

For this assignment, assume that in your Art History class you have been asked to visit a local cultural exhibit and to share your experience of that visit. If the event you attend lends itself to using some visual images in your paper, please include them.

For this assignment, share your experience of visiting the cultural event. Use the rhetorical strategies of *description* and *narration* to share your experience.

Optional Multi-Modal Assignment: Tweeting

If you are given Writing Assignment Three, where you share your visit to a local art museum, concert, exhibit, or the like, use Twitter as you go through the exhibit or display to share your experiences with others. Enjoy your tweeting!

 ## Critical Thinking Activity: Ask Yourself Questions before You Write

Spend a little time now considering the assignment you have been asked to construct, and do some planning for the assignment. Answer these questions:

1. Your purpose in writing is to share an experience with your readers. How do you think you might use *narration* and *description* to "share" an experience?
2. How would you describe the audience for your paper?
3. When someone tells you about an experience he/she has had, what kinds of details and examples and visual aids are the most useful to you?
4. When you share an experience, the details and descriptions you use come from your memory. But are there other sources you might draw on? (People who were involved in your experience? People you talked to about that experience? Notes or letters or e-mails you might have written about it? Photographs?)

LO3

Use invention and discovery strategies to come up with ideas and details

Invention and Discovery Activities

A good way to get started on any writing task is to engage in **discovery activities**—brief bits of writing that help you get your ideas about your experience onto paper. It usually is useful to work with several different types of discovery activities—listing, freewriting, clustering, and the like. For more on invention activities, see pages 80–88.

Everyday Writing Activity: Freewriting

In your journal, freewrite for 10 minutes about possible experiences that you may want to share with your readers. Get as many specific details down as possible, because those details are how you can show your readers what happened (rather than just telling your readers). Your teacher may ask you to share your freewriting with the rest of the class.

Student Writing: John Wick's Freewriting

In his English class, John was asked to write about a work experience. He decided to freewrite to get some of his thoughts and questions down on paper:

> I've only had two jobs: one was that discount retail clothing store and the other was at the construction company, the heating and cooling place. I was there for a summer. Hmm. Interesting experiences: working on those HOT roofs. The can that exploded. Might be interesting to readers. How can I explain the heat and also that explosion, though?

LO4

Write a thesis statement that states the point of your essay

Writing a Thesis Statement for Your Shared Experience

When you share an experience, you are not arguing a point or trying to convince someone about something, and you are not evaluating a product or idea—so it might seem like you do not need a thesis statement to share an experience. But like any kind of writing, it is helpful to have a point you make (usually at the start) so readers can see where you are going, and a point which all of your examples and details can connect to and support.

So, you might want to make a thesis statement that summarizes your experience:

- Working for a really difficult boss turned into a great learning experience for me.
- I learned how to put engines together the summer I worked on my uncle's '57 Chevy.
- I used to build scale models, and that experience really helped me when I took my first architecture class.
- I was afraid to attend the art gallery opening, as I didn't know what to expect, but was pleasantly surprised that I fit right in.
- I was really afraid when I applied for my first job, but the interviewer made me feel comfortable right away.
- My parents were so proud of me when I got my first raise.

Often, students think their **topic** is the same as their **thesis,** but they really are different. Your **topic** is the subject you are focusing on (your experience), while your **thesis** is a general point about that experience ("I had a good experience when I …" or "I learned a lot during my senior year, playing football …").

At this point, you might delay writing a thesis statement until you have all the details on paper. Or, if you do construct a thesis statement now, you may want to revise it once you have a draft completed.

LO5
Organize and write your first draft

Organizing and Writing Your First Draft

To share an experience, you can select from several organizational approaches:

- **Sequential approach.** You tell about your experience in time order: first this happened, and then this happened, and then this other thing happened.

A Time Order Organizational Plan

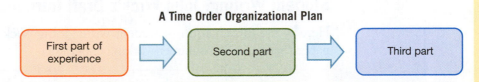

First part of experience → Second part → Third part

- **Reflective approach.** You start where you are now and look back on the experience, explain what you learned, and so on. Rather than discussing the experience step-by-step, as the sequential approach does, you select specific parts of the experience and what you learned from it to share with readers:

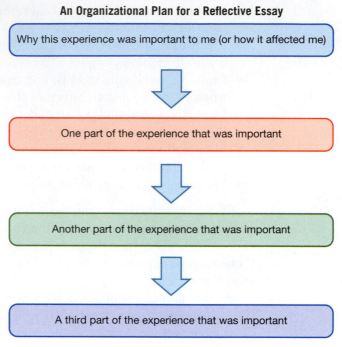

An Organizational Plan for a Reflective Essay

Why this experience was important to me (or how it affected me)

One part of the experience that was important

Another part of the experience that was important

A third part of the experience that was important

- **Comparative approach.** You would not only *narrate* your experience and provide *descriptions* of what happened, but also *compare* and *contrast* it to other experiences. You most likely would start by noting that you are going to compare and contrast experiences.

An Organizational Plan for a Comparison of Experiences

One experience compared to   Other experiences

Student Writing: John Wick's Draft Introduction

Here is the introduction to student writer John Wick's first draft of his paper that shares his summer working experience:

> ### The Day the Can Exploded
>
> In June, the can exploded, and I found myself covered with thick and oily goop that smelled like gasoline. My skin started to tingle—whatever it was evaporated and I was cool for a time. But then my skin started to

> burn and I got scared, as I got hotter and hotter. I wondered if I should go see a doctor.
>
> Matt and I were working at the old fairgrounds on its cooling system, what we called then "swamp coolers," and our job was to clean them with a wire brush, mop them out, and then reseal the bottoms of the coolers. The stuff we used to seal the bottoms was called "CoolSeal," and it was a black, tar-like material, and gooey. I don't know how else to describe it to you but to say it was a gooey liquid, like motor oil but thicker. And it was black and smelled like gasoline.

Note that Wick immediately lets his readers know that his main rhetorical strategies will be *description* and *narration*: to describe what happened and to tell the story of his experience. He also is showing (rather than telling) his experience to his readers by using interesting descriptive words and phrases ("gooey," "like motor oil," "black," "smelled like gasoline").

LO6

Revise your essay, and prepare a final draft

Revising: The Key to Effective Papers

As you will recall from Chapter 8, once you have a first draft of a paper, it almost always is useful to revise that text, because it is next to impossible to say exactly what you want to in any first draft.

If possible, set your draft aside for a day or so, and then reread it. Remember that "revision" means to reconsider your paper, to rethink and perhaps to "reorganize" it. So as you reread your paper, think about the larger issues and how you might make your paper more effective: are there ways to improve your thesis statement, the examples you provide, the details about your experience, and so on, to help readers really share that experience? (There is much more advice on revising your paper in Chapter 8.)

In most writing classes, your teacher will ask you to help each other by providing feedback and suggestions on each other's papers. There are several different approaches to this; your teacher will guide you. (For more on effective responding, see Chapter 8; for more on what *to do* with the comments you receive, see the following sections.)

Student Writing: John Wick's Peer Reviewed Draft

One of student writer Wick's classmates read and responded to his first draft. Here is part of the draft along with his classmates' comments and suggestions. If you were reading and responding to Wick's paper, what comments and suggestions would you make?

Great first line. Made me want to read more. What is your point?

Sounds really uncomfortable.

Good "telling" of what your job was and the material you were working with. I wonder if more details about the weather, etc., would help?

Awkward to address readers directly.

The Day the Can Exploded

In June, the can exploded, and I found myself covered with thick and oily goop that smelled like gasoline. My skin started to tingle—whatever it was evaporated and I was cool for a time. But then my skin started to burn and I got scared, as I got hotter and hotter. I wondered if I should go see a doctor.

Matt and I were working at the old fairgrounds on its cooling system, what we called then "swamp coolers," and our job was to clean them with a wire brush, mop them out, and then reseal the bottoms of the coolers. The stuff we used to seal the bottoms was called "CoolSeal," and it was a black, tar-like material, and gooey. I don't know how else to describe it to you but to say gooey. Liquid, like motor oil but thicker. And it was black and smelled like gasoline.

Here is how student writer Wick responded to this reader's suggestions.

A classmate asked. "What is your point," so student writer Wick added a clear thesis statement.

A reader asked for more description about the weather, which writer Wick added.

This is the story of that ninety degree and cloudless June day when the can exploded, and I found myself covered with thick and oily goop that smelled like gasoline. My skin started to tingle—whatever it was evaporated and I was cool for a time. But then my skin started to burn and I got scared, as I got hotter and hotter. I wondered if I should go see a doctor. I learned right then to be more careful at whatever work I do (including opening cans that have been sitting in the hot sun all day). I remember seeing one of those Time & Temperature signs on the way to work, and it was already 91° that morning.

Matt and I were working at the old fairgrounds on its cooling system, what we called then "swamp coolers," and our job was to clean them with a wire brush, mop them out, and then reseal the bottoms of the coolers. The material we used to seal the bottoms was called "CoolSeal," and it was a black, tar-like material, and gooey. I don't know how else to describe it to you but to say …

Writing Style Tip: Addressing Readers

Student writer Wick made another revision in response to a comment from a classmate that suggested that he not "directly address" his readers. Wick was trying to draw his readers into his paper, to involve them, and one way to do so is to address them as "you." But that can be awkward (as one of Wick's classmates noted). While it is acceptable to directly address readers in a *letter,* it usually is not a good idea in an academic paper.

John thought about what his classmate suggested and so changed his text to provide the necessary description, without directly addressing his readers:

Original:

The stuff we used to seal the bottoms was called "CoolSeal," and it was a black, tar-like material, and gooey. I don't know how else to describe it to you but to say gooey. Liquid, like motor oil but thicker. And it was black and smelled like gasoline.

Revised:

The stuff we used to seal the bottoms was called "CoolSeal," and it was a black, tar-like material, and gooey. I don't know how else to describe it ~~to you~~ but to say gooey. Liquid, like motor oil but thicker. And it was black and smelled like gasoline.

 ## Critical Thinking Activity: Ask Yourself Questions before You Revise

Now you have a first draft and have reread it several times, and most likely you also have received suggestions from your classmates (and perhaps from your teacher, family members, or friends). You will recall from Chapter 8 that *revision* means to reconsider and to reenvision your text—not to just fix surface errors. So consider the following:

1. Did I achieve my *purpose?* Did I provide the information and details my *audience* needed to really "share" my experience? Can I think of anything else to add?
2. How effective is my *organizational approach?* Is there another that might be more effective? (For more on organizational approaches, see pages 133–134.)
3. How clear is my *thesis statement?* Can anyone easily understand my point?
4. Are there other *examples and details* I might add to help readers see what I mean? Are there places in the paper where I can "show" what I mean, rather than just "tell" about it?

Use this checklist to see whether your revised paper is finally done, or whether you need to make further changes before printing a final draft.

Revision Checklist for Your Shared Experience Paper

Part of your paper	Check √
Title for your shared experience that gets your readers' attention	
Introduction with a clear thesis statement	
Supporting paragraphs, each with a topic sentence, supporting evidence or examples, and a transition to the next paragraph (all information must relate to your thesis statement)	
Visual aids if they will help the purpose of your shared experience (charts, graphs, tables, etc.)	
Conclusion that summarizes your main points and restates your thesis about your shared experience	

Student Writing: John Wick's Final Draft

Here is student writer John Wick's final draft of his shared experience paper. Notice Wick's use of the rhetorical strategies of description and narration to help readers share his experience.

Wick 1

John Wick

Dr. Zach Waggonner

ENG 090

Mar. 3, 2011

The Day the Can Exploded

This is the story of that ninety degree and cloudless June day when the can exploded, and I found myself covered with thick and oily goop that smelled like gasoline. My skin started to tingle—whatever it was evaporated and I was cool for a time. But then my skin started to burn and I got scared, as I got hotter and hotter. I wondered if I should go see a doctor.

Wick 2

I learned right then to be more careful at whatever work I do (including opening cans that have been sitting in the sun all day). I remember seeing one of those Time & Temperature signs on the way to work, and it was already 91° that morning.

Matt and I were working at the old fairgrounds on its cooling system, what we called then "swamp coolers," and our job was to clean them with a wire brush, mop them out, and then reseal the bottoms of the coolers. The material we used to seal the bottoms was called "CoolSeal," and it was a black, tar-like material, and gooey. I don't know how else to describe it but to say gooey. Liquid, like motor oil but thicker. And it was black and smelled like gasoline.

"Swamp coolers" use water, and as it evaporates the water leaves calcium behind, and that is what we had to scrape off with the wire brushes. Then we would paint on the CoolSeal. I had opened CoolSeal cans a hundred times before, but this one must have been defective, or had been sitting in the sun and got too hot or something. When I popped it open, there was a lot of pressure and the can just exploded, covering me with the stuff. I remember from Physics class that when things heat up (like the CoolSeal can left in the sun) the material can expand, causing pressure inside the can. I made it worse, as I wanted the CoolSeal to be as liquid as possible, so I *shook* the can, hard. That must have made the pressure inside even higher.

I hollered at Matt and he grabbed some rags and we tried to wash it off, but the CoolSeal was too sticky. I mean, it is designed to stick to the bottom of a rusty cooler, so it's easy for anyone to imagine how it stuck to me. Matt then grabbed the hose supplying water to the coolers and started watering me off. The cold water felt really good. He sprayed me hard. Once I could see, I got some rags and wiped off my face and arms.

That ended our work for that day, as I was soaked and scared and exhausted. Thank goodness there was water there! That night at home when I took a shower, I found CoolSeal in my hair, and it hurt pulling out the little balls of it.

(continued)

Wick 3

I learned some lessons that hot June day: do not leave cans in the sun, and do not shake hot cans, and the next time, I'll be sure to put a rag over the top of any paint or CoolSeal or other can before opening it.

 ## Critical Thinking Activity: Ask Yourself Questions for Reflection

In your journal, please answer the following questions:

1. How did you decide what experience to share?
2. How did you decide what organizational approach to use?
3. How did you decide what details and examples to use, to help readers understand your experience?
4. What could your classmates do next time to make their comments and suggestions more helpful to you?
5. What one revision did you do that was the most useful?
6. What did you learn about your own writing process, through the process of writing this paper?
7. Did writing about this experience make you think about *other* experiences you would like to share?
8. What did you learn from writing this paper that will help you as you write other papers in the future?

Readings That Share Experiences

These texts will help you get some sense of how other writers share their own experiences: what they include, how they *describe* the people involved, how they *narrate* their stories, and so on.

Note: Words highlighted **in blue** are terms used in the "Improve Your Vocabulary" activity after each reading.

Don't Call Me a Hot Tamale

Judith Ortiz Cofer

The first reading, by Judith Ortiz Cofer, describes her experiences growing up in New Jersey—and how she often was stereotyped as a "hot tamale." Cofer was born in 1952 in Puerto Rico and is an acclaimed novelist and poet. Much of her writing explores her experiences as a minority Hispanic woman, as this essay does.

rendition: version; song sung in a certain manner

prime: first; main

microcosm: small piece of; example of something

casas: house

bodega: market

surveillance: watching; spying on

señoritas: unmarried females

Anglo: white; Caucasian

humiliated: embarrassed

semiformal: not quite formal, as in dress or an event

1   On a bus to London from Oxford University, where I was earning some graduate credits one summer, a young man, obviously fresh from a pub, approached my seat. With both hands over his heart, he went down on his knees in the aisle and broke into an Irish tenor's **rendition** of "Maria" from *West Side Story.* I was not amused. "Maria" had followed me to London, reminding me of a **prime** fact of my life: You can leave the island of Puerto Rico, master the English language, and travel as far as you can, but if you're a Latina, especially one who so clearly belongs to Rita Moreno's gene pool, the island travels with you.

2   Growing up in New Jersey and wanting most of all to belong, I lived in two completely different worlds. My parents designed our life as a **microcosm** of their *casas* on the island—we spoke in Spanish, ate Puerto Rican food bought at the *bodega,* and practiced strict Catholicism complete with Sunday mass in Spanish.

3   I was kept under tight **surveillance** by my parents, since my virtue and modesty were, by their cultural equation, the same as their honor. As teenagers, my friends and I were lectured constantly on how to behave as proper **señoritas.** But it was a conflicting message we received, since our Puerto Rican mothers also encouraged us to look and act like women by dressing us in clothes our **Anglo** schoolmates and their mothers found too "mature" and flashy. I often felt **humiliated** when I appeared at an American friend's birthday party wearing a dress more suitable for a **semiformal.** At Puerto Rican festivities, neither the music nor the colors we wore could be too loud.

(continued)

agonized: worried over; anguished

4   I remember Career Day in high school, when our teachers told us to come dressed as if for a job interview. That morning, I **agonized** in front of my closet, trying to figure out what a "career girl" would wear, because the only model I had was Marlo Thomas on TV. To me and my Puerto Rican girlfriends, dressing up meant wearing our mother's ornate jewelry and clothing.

vulgar: inappropriate; disgusting

5   At school that day, the teachers assailed us for wearing "everything at once"—meaning too much jewelry and too many accessories. And it was painfully obvious that the other students in their tailored skirts and silk blouses thought we were hopeless and **vulgar**. The way they looked at us was a taste of the cultural clash that awaited us in the real world, where prospective employers and men on the street would often misinterpret our tight skirts and bright colors as a come-on.

6   It is custom, not chromosomes, that leads us to choose scarlet over pale pink. Our mothers had grown up on a tropical island where the natural environment was a riot of primary colors, where showing your skin was one way to keep cool as well as to look sexy. On the island, women felt freer to dress and move provocatively since they were protected by the traditions and laws of a Spanish/Catholic system of morality and **machismo**, the main rule of which was: *You may look at my sister, but if you touch her I will kill you.* The extended family and church structure provided them with a circle of safety on the island; if a man "wronged" a girl, everyone would close in to save her family honor.

machismo: maleness or masculinity; showing how tough one is

7   Off-island, signals often get mixed. When a Puerto Rican girl who is dressed in her idea of what is attractive meets a man from the mainstream culture who has been trained to react to certain types of clothing as a sexual signal, a clash is likely to take place. She is seen as a Hot Tamale, a sexual **firebrand**. I learned this lesson at my first formal dance when my date leaned over and painfully planted a sloppy, overeager kiss on my mouth. When I didn't respond with sufficient passion, he said in a resentful tone: "I thought you Latin girls were supposed to mature early." It was only the first time I would feel like a fruit or vegetable—I was supposed to *ripen*, not just grow into womanhood like other girls.

firebrand: militant in some way

8   These stereotypes, though rarer, still surface in my life. I recently stayed at a classy metropolitan hotel. After having dinner with a friend, I was returning to my room when a middle-aged man in a tuxedo stepped directly into my path. With his champagne glass extended toward me, he exclaimed, "**Evita**!"

Evita: Eva Peron of Argentina

9   Blocking my way, he bellowed the song "Don't Cry for Me, Argentina." Playing to the gathering crowd, he began to sing loudly a ditty to the tune of "La Bamba"—except the lyrics were about a girl named Maria whose exploits all rhymed with her name and gonorrhea.

10   I knew that this same man—probably a corporate executive, even worldly by most standards—would never have regaled a white woman with a dirty song in public. But to him, I was just a character in his universe of "others," all cartoons.

11   Still, I am one of the lucky ones. There are thousands of Latinas without the privilege of the education that my parents gave me. For them every day is a struggle against the misconceptions perpetuated by the myth of the Latina as whore, domestic worker or criminal.

omnipotent: all-powerful

bilingual: able to talk in more than one language

12   Rather than fight these pervasive stereotypes, I try to replace them with a more interesting set of realities. I travel around the U.S. reading from my books of poetry and my novel. With the stories I tell, the dreams and fears I examine in my work, I try to get my audience past the particulars of my skin color, my accent or my clothes.

13   I once wrote a poem in which I call Latinas "God's brown daughters." It is really a prayer, of sorts, for communication and respect. In it, Latin women pray "in Spanish to an Anglo God / with a Jewish heritage," and they are "fervently hoping / that if not **omnipotent**, / at least He be **bilingual**."

Questions for Discussion and Writing

1. What is your initial reaction to Cofer's experience?
2. Have you ever been stereotyped? Have you ever stereotyped someone else?
3. What in this essay do you find humorous? Why?
4. In paragraphs 4 and 5, Cofer describes how she and her friends dressed to look like "career girls," but then were ridiculed for wearing "everything at once." Have you ever done anything similar?
5. Cofer often uses the rhetorical strategy of *description* in this essay. What can you point to in her essay that helps you really see what she means?

Improve Your Vocabulary

Use the highlighted and defined words from "Just Don't Call Me a Hot Tamale" in a sentence or in a paragraph.

My Global Study Experience in Dubai: Strong Self-Image Key to Negotiating in Distant Cultures

Brittney Huntley

Student Brittney Huntley shares her experiences—good and bad—of living in Dubai. She focuses especially on narrating parts of her own story, while describing some of the people she interacted with. Does Brittney's story make you want to live or study abroad? Why or why not?

(continued)

1 Last year, as a sophomore at the University of Cincinnati, I decided to live and study abroad as part of the university's Global Studies Program. I chose Dubai, United Arab Emirates, which many of my fellow students may have never heard of. Dubai is one of seven emirates (a federation of independent states, ruled by an emir) that make up the United Arab Emirates, located in the southeastern corner of the Arabian Peninsula. The UAE is a desert country about the size of South Carolina and is bordered by the Persian Gulf, Saudi Arabia and the Gulf of Oman. The UAE boasts one of the highest standards of living in the world.

2 Ten years ago, Dubai consisted of sand and very poor Bedouin people who lived **nomadic** lives, and depended mostly on **marine life** to feed their families. Today, Dubai has considerable wealth and economic stability because of its oil and tourism industries, mainly tourism. Some call Dubai the "Las Vegas" of the Middle East because of its extravagant architecture and fabulous lifestyle. Dubai is home to **expatriates** from all over the world. Its diverse population encourages international cooperation on both corporate and cultural levels.

3 As a result of my experience in Dubai, I have a new perspective of the Middle East and Islam. Based on my knowledge and experiences, I challenge other African-American students and people of the world to redirect their attention to the things that matter most in terms of our being respected globally. Most of us are a part of the working class, and may feel that we have little time for politics and traveling abroad. Many of us are uninterested in international affairs. But, what if I told you that as an African-American woman, I was labeled, sexually harassed, and constantly defending myself against negative stereotypes of African Americans in Dubai, due to the negative influence of rap music and U.S. television? Because of the extensive use of the word "nigga" by African-American rap artists, comedians, and TV programs that supposedly characterize the "hood," I found that this word is now a part of the daily conversation of Arabs and Africans in various parts of the globe. Ignorance and stereotypes are inescapable and widely spread, negatively affecting individuals and in some cases entire races. The lack of understanding about African-American people was so great that I created a history project identifying history's most awakening civil rights movements, drawing on similarities between world leaders, while shining light on the history and culture of African Americans.

The "N" Word

4 While in Dubai I met Mohammed, an Ethiopian Muslim, and others who had adopted much of the African-American rap culture. Mohammed's clothing, speech, and **demeanor** all reflected that he admired rap videos. Mohammed, the Emirati (natives of the UAE) and other expatriates regularly greeted themselves and me with the word "nigga," which was very offensive to me. I hated Mohammed's obsession with the word. He used it in his daily conversation, when he would greet me, and especially during basketball games. I understand why he thought the basketball court was the proper setting for its use, but

nomadic: society constantly moving from place to place

marine life: sea life

expatriates: people temporarily living away from their country of birth

demeanor: way of acting

I asked Mohammed where he learned "nigga". He said that when he lived in South Central Los Angeles, the Blacks taught him to differentiate between the words "nigga" and "nigger," which would determine whether or not you offend an African American. "Nigga" is jargon for "nigger," therefore; many Blacks feel that "nigga" is less offensive. How sad that my African brothers would think that calling me such a name would be acceptable to me!

I Love Black People

5   While in Dubai, I also met a young white woman from Brown University. It seems that in all our encounters she could only use rap music to initiate conversation. She explained how she lived in wealthy upper Rhode Island. Her brother lived in the southern area, where he was frequently robbed and now had a racist perspective of Blacks. She said that most of her encounters with Black people were positive and that she "absolutely loved us." While at the computer lab, she opened Windows Media Player and presented her collection of **Biggie Smalls** albums and **Tupac** downloads. I never corrected her for her limited interest in who I was as a person. Truthfully, I was so shocked at how insensitive and limited her interactions were with someone like me, that I forgot to get angry.

Biggie Small: African American rap artist; also known as the Notorious B.I.G.

Tupac: African American rap artist

The History Presentation

6   While in Dubai, I confronted my history professor about her unreasonable grading system and biased perspective of Americans. In addition to her making negative references to the United States, she applied different, higher standards to American students than to those who were local. When I met with her, concerned I not could expect to earn a fair grade, I agreed to write two research papers and create a presentation on Middle Eastern history in order to pass the course. At this point, I had experienced the positive and negative messages music can convey and the stereotypes that are generated, resulting in a real **distortion** of our true image and culture in this part of the world. I felt **compelled** to defend my honor as an African-American woman against the negative images of us in the Middle East, as characterized in the images of rap artists and their degrading lyrics. I am proud to be an African American, but I am very disappointed at how little our people actually know or care about our history, and how little of our true culture is positively depicted in the Middle East. Music is a powerful source of communication, with the power to distort or destroy the reputation of individuals and even an entire race. I felt compelled to speak up about these distortions.

distortion: incorrect way of seeing something

compelled: forced

My Message

7   My presentation was entitled, "Awakening Civil Rights Movements in History." I welcomed this opportunity to shatter stereotypes. I introduced the African-American people as major contributors in the Civil Rights Movement of the 1950s-1960s: We inspired people worldwide to fight for not only civil rights, but human rights. I drew on comparisons between world leaders like Dr. Martin Luther King Jr., the leader of Indian independence Mohandas Gandhi, and

(continued)

Egyptian president and statesman Gamal Abdel Nasser. I wanted the students to know that the Civil Rights Movement began with the African-American people of the South. The students were interested and attentive, as was my professor; they respected me for my knowledge and dignity, and therefore gained respect for my people. I encouraged the students to seek a better understanding of African-American people and our history and who we really are, without relying on negative images depicted in the media. I received an "A" in the course.

My Learning

8   My experiences in Dubai were so challenging that I needed time to process the educational benefit once I returned to the United States. This article gives me a chance for reflection. I feel proud of myself for turning what could have been a negative experience into a positive one. I learned to negotiate and stand up for myself among strangers, alone in another part of the world. I feel empowered by my strength in overcoming adversity through my faith in God and by conveying the dignity of my people that my parents instilled in me. The power to change attitudes and minds is important to me. I have decided to make it my life's work. On reflection, this awareness has finally made my Middle Eastern experience truly worthwhile.

Questions for Discussion and Writing

1. What was your immediate reaction to Huntley's essay?
2. Were you surprised at the racism she ran into?
3. What can you point to in the essay where Huntley uses the rhetorical strategy of *narration?*
4. What in the essay can you point to where Huntley uses the rhetorical strategy of *description?*
5. Huntley mentions the "lack of understanding" of her own culture (paragraph 2) that she encountered in Dubai. Do you have any experiences when someone did not understand your own background and culture?
6. In paragraph 6, Huntley notes the "positive and negative messages music can convey and the stereotypes that are generated." Can you think of some positive and negative examples of stereotypes that music generates?

Improve Your Vocabulary

Use the highlighted and defined words from "My Global Study Experience in Dubai: Strong Self-Image Key to Negotiating in Distant Cultures" in a sentence or in a paragraph.

The Good Immigrant Student

Bich Minh Nguyen

Bich Minh Nguyen and her family fled Saigon on April 29, 1975, when she was eight months old. Nguyen's novel Short Girls *was published by Viking Penguin in 2009 and was named as one of the best books of the year by Library Journal. "The Good Immigrant Student" appears in slightly different form in Nguyen's* Stealing Buddha's Dinner, *which received the PEN/Jerard Award from the PEN American Center, as well as several other major awards. Nguyen's writing has appeared in a number of magazines. She currently teaches at Purdue University.*

tainted: spoiled

stigma: mark of some kind; usually has a negative connotation

imperious: overbearing

striding: walking; moving forward

insufferably: intolerably; unacceptably

Palmer cursive: a method that helps students learn excellent penmanship

pinched: shrunken; squeezed

ilk: kind; same as

infamous: famous in a negative way

1   I transferred to Ken-O-Sha Elementary in time for third grade, after Rosa* finally admitted that taking the bus all the way to Sherwood was pointless. I was glad to transfer, eager to be part of a class that wasn't, in my mind, **tainted** with the knowledge of my bilingual **stigma**. Third grade was led by Mrs. Alexander, an **imperious**, middle-aged woman of many plaid skirts held safe by giant gold safety pins. She had a habit of turning her wedding ring around and around her finger while she stood at the chalkboard. Mrs. Alexander had an intricate system of rewards for good grades and good behavior, denoted by colored star stickers on a piece of poster board that loomed over us all. One glance and you could see who was behind, who was **striding** ahead.

2   I was an **insufferably** good student, with perfect **Palmer cursive** and the highest possible scores in every subject. I had learned this trick at Sherwood. That the quieter you are, the shyer and sweeter and better-at-school you are, the more the teacher will let you alone. Mrs. Alexander should have let me alone. For, in addition to my excellent marks, I was nearly silent, deadly shy, and wholly obedient. My greatest fear was being called on, or in any way standing out more than I already did in the class that was, except for me and one black student, dough-white. I got good grades because I feared the authority of the teacher; I felt that getting in good with Mrs. Alexander would protect me, that she would protect me from the frightful rest of the world. But Mrs. Alexander was not agreeable to this notion. If it was my turn to read aloud during reading circle, she'd interrupt me to snap, "You're reading too fast" or demand, "What does that word mean?" Things she did not do to the other students. Anh†, when I told her about this, suggested that perhaps Mrs. Alexander liked me and wanted to help me get smarter. But neither of us believed it. You know when a teacher likes you and when she doesn't.

3   Secretly, I admired and envied the rebellious kids, like Robbie Andrews who came to school looking bleary-eyed and **pinched**, like a hungover adult; Robbie and his **ilk** snapped back at teachers, were routinely sent to the principal's office, were even spanked a few times with the principal's **infamous** red

*The author's stepmother.
†The author's sister.

(continued)

**corporal
punishment:**
discipline through
pain; often refers to
spanking

Dock-Sides: type of
shoe; boat deck shoe

ensembles:
collections

nubby: bumpy

paddle (apparently no one in Grand Rapids objected to **corporal punishment**). Those kids made noise, possessed something I thought was confidence, self-knowledge, allowing them to marvelously question everything ordered of them. They had the ability to challenge the given world.

4   Toward the middle of third grade, Mrs. Alexander introduced a stuffed lion to the pool of rewards: the best student of the week would earn the privilege of having the lion sit on his or her desk for the entire week. My quantity of gold stars was neck and neck with that of my two competitors, Brenda and Jennifer, both sweet-eyed blond girls with pastel-colored monogrammed sweaters and neatly tied **Dock-Sides**. My family did not have a lot of money and my stepmother had terrible taste. Thus I attended school in such **ensembles** as dark red parachute pants and a **nubby** pink sweater stitched with a picture of a unicorn rearing up. This only propelled me to try harder to be good, to make up for everything I felt was against me: my odd family, my race, my very face. And I craved that stuffed lion. Week after week, the lion perched on Brenda's desk or Jennifer's desk. Meanwhile, the class spelling bee approached. I didn't know I was such a good speller until I won it, earning a scalloped-edged certificate and a candy bar. That afternoon I started toward home, then remembered I'd forgotten my rain boots in my locker. I doubled back to school and overheard Mrs. Alexander in the classroom talking to another teacher. "Can you believe it?" Mrs. Alexander was saying. "A foreigner winning our spelling bee!"

5   I waited for the stuffed lion the rest of that year, with a kind of patience I have no patience for today. To no avail. In June, on the last day of school, Mrs. Alexander gave the stuffed lion to Brenda to keep forever.

Questions for Discussion and Writing

1. Nguyen tells of part of her third-grade experiences. Do you remember your third grade? Can you recall anything that happened to you during that time?
2. What is the most unusual or interesting thing you learned from Nguyen's story?
3. How effectively does Nguyen use *description?* What descriptions can you cite from the essay that really help you see what Nguyen means?
4. Did you ever feel "out of place" at school, as Nguyen did?
5. Nguyen tells of her experiences in third grade using the rhetorical strategy of *narration*. What can you point to in her story where she effectively uses this strategy?

Improve Your Vocabulary

Use the highlighted and defined words from "The Good Immigrant Student" in a sentence or in a paragraph.

MyWritingLab™ For support in meeting this chapter's objectives, log in to **www.mywritinglab.com**, and select **Essay Development-Describing** and **Essay Development-Narrating**.

Chapter **10**

Writing to Inform
Using Examples and Process Explanation

Learning **O**bjectives

In this chapter, you will learn to:

LO1 Consider the writer's situation, and determine your purpose and audience

LO2 Use the rhetorical strategies of *example* and *process explanation* to inform

LO3 Use invention and discovery strategies to come up with ideas and details

LO4 Write a thesis statement that states the point of your essay

LO5 Organize and write your first draft

LO6 Revise your essay, and prepare a final draft

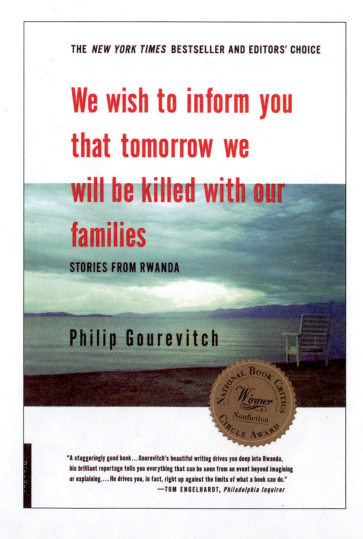

THE *NEW YORK TIMES* BESTSELLER AND EDITORS' CHOICE

We wish to inform you that tomorrow we will be killed with our families

STORIES FROM RWANDA

Philip Gourevitch

NATIONAL BOOK CRITICS
Winner
Nonfiction
CIRCLE AWARD

"A staggeringly good book... Gourevitch's beautiful writing drives you deep into Rwanda, his brilliant reportage tells you everything that can be seen from an event beyond imagining or explaining.... He drives you, in fact, right up against the limits of what a book can do."
—TOM ENGELHARDT, *Philadelphia Inquirer*

This book title is shocking and probably got your attention. Why? Do you *want* to be informed about someone's death in advance of its happening? Do you want to read this book? Why or why not? Here is the first paragraph of Gourevitch's text:

IN THE PROVINCE of Kibungo, in eastern Rwanda, in the swamp- and pasture-land near the Tanzanian border, there's a rocky hill called Nyarubuye with a church where many Tutsis were slaughtered in mid-April of 1994. A year after the killing I went to Nyarubuye with two Canadian military officers. We flew in a United Nations helicopter, traveling low over the hills in the morning mists, with the banana trees like green starbursts dense over the slopes. The uncut grass blew back as we dropped into the center of the parish schoolyard. A lone soldier materialized with his Kalashnikov, and shook our hands with stiff, shy formality. The Canadians presented the paperwork for our visit, and I stepped up into the open doorway of a classroom.

Are you more or less interested in reading this book, now that you know it starts out in a classroom?

We admit we used this book cover and opening passage as a way to get your attention on writing to **inform**. Informative writing may seem boring, but it really does not have to be, as the Gourevitch passage shows. Often it is the kind of writing we can really learn from. Informational texts are designed to provide us with **information,** and to **explain** that information in ways we can understand and sometimes can **use.** And informational writing is a kind of writing you read all the time; your college textbooks, as well as newspaper reports, are a perfect example of informational writing. You also use informational writing all the time. The following writing activity is an example.

Everyday Writing Activity: Giving Directions

One thing everyone does is to give directions to other people.

In your journal, briefly explain in writing how to get from where you are right now—your classroom—to where you sleep at night (your home, apartment, dorm room, etc.). You can also use a drawing or map if you think that would help your readers go from your current location to where you live. Your instructor may want you to share your response with the rest of the class.

Some of you may have found this brief writing activity to be pretty easy. But sometimes it is hard to explain directions, just as it can be difficult to explain measurements when you do not have a tape measure or to accurately describe a color or angle.

LO1

Consider the writer's situation, and determine your purpose and audience

The Writer's Situation

How would you describe your **purpose** if you were asked to write an informational text? You probably would say you want to provide information to your readers, in a way they could understand it. You do not want to argue or to convince someone; you are not evaluating a product or service; you are not analyzing something. That means that informational texts are generally neutral in how they present their information: here is the information, and you the reader, get to decide what to do with it.

Considering your **audience** is critical in informational writing. You do not want to give them information they already know, but you do want to give them enough information so they can understand the subject you are writing about. And, you want to provide your information in the most effective way for your readers to understand it.

LO2

Use the rhetorical strategies of *example* and *process explanation* to inform

Informing through Example and Process Explanation

Consider for a moment all the things you read that are informational and that explain how to do something:

- The assignment for your English class's next writing task, explaining what the instructor expects from you.
- Your college newspaper's article on the campus "Go Green" program to save energy.
- The instructions for using that new smart phone you got for your birthday.
- Online directions about preregistration for next semester.

The fact is, you read and write a lot of texts (and visuals) that are designed to inform and explain—do you agree?

The following reading is an example of informational writing.

Software Creates Privacy Mode to Help Secure Android Smartphones

Matt Shipman

Matt Shipman writes for the North Carolina State University Newsroom. The Newsroom publicizes NCSU research studies, faculty news, and campus events that are of interest to the general public.

A brief summary or "abstract" of the essay

The photograph illustrates various smartphone privacy settings

The quotation provides information to readers about the focus of the essay

Did you know that some phones have privacy settings?

Information about the different kinds of settings

Have you ever heard of a "Bogus setting"?

Information on changing settings for various applications

1   Researchers at North Carolina State University have developed software that helps Android smartphone users prevent their personal information from being stolen by hackers.

2   "There are a lot of concerns about potential leaks of personal information from smartphones," says Dr. Xuxian Jiang, an assistant professor of computer science at NC State and co-author of a paper describing the research. "We have developed software that creates a privacy mode for Android systems, giving users flexible control over what personal information is available to various applications." The privacy software is called Taming Information-Stealing Smartphone Applications (TISSA).

3   TISSA works by creating a privacy setting manager that allows users to customize the level of information each smartphone application can access. Those settings can be adjusted any time that the relevant applications are being run—not just when the applications are installed.

4   The TISSA prototype includes four possible privacy settings for each application. These settings are Trusted, Anonymized, Bogus and Empty. If an application is listed as Trusted, TISSA does not impose additional information access restrictions. If the user selects Anonymized, TISSA provides the application with generalized information that allows the application to run, without providing access to detailed personal information. The Bogus setting provides an application with fake results when it requests personal information. The Empty setting responds to information requests by saying the relevant information does not exist or is unavailable.

5   Jiang says TISSA could be easily modified to incorporate additional settings that would allow more fine-grained control of access to personal information. "These settings may be further specialized for different types of information, such as your contact list or your location," Jiang says. "The settings can also be specialized for different applications."

(continued)

An example helps show what the writer means

6   For example, a user may install a weather application that requires location data in order to provide the user with the local weather forecast. Rather than telling the application exactly where the user is, TISSA could be programmed to give the application generalized location data—such as a random location within a 10-mile radius of the user. This would allow the weather application to provide the local weather forecast information, but would ensure that the application couldn't be used to track the user's movements.

Information on the updating process for the application

7   The researchers are currently exploring how to make this software available to Android users. "The software modification is relatively minor," Jiang says, "and could be incorporated through an over-the-air update."

8   The paper, "Taming Information-Stealing Smartphone Applications (on Android)," was co-authored by Jiang; Yajin Zhou, a Ph.D. student at NC State; Dr. Vincent Freeh, an associate professor of computer science at NC State; and Dr. Xinwen Zhang of Huawei America Research Center.

9   The paper will be presented in June at the 4th International Conference on Trust and Trustworthy Computing, in Pittsburgh, Pa. The research was supported by the National Science Foundation and NC State's Secure Open Systems Initiative, which receives funding from the U.S. Army Research Office.

Questions for Discussion and Writing

1. What new information did you learn from this essay?
2. Were you surprised at any of the information in this essay?
3. If you have a smartphone, did this essay raise some concerns for your privacy?
4. What rhetorical strategies can you point to in the essay?
5. Overall, how effective is this essay as an example of informational writing? Why?

Everyday Writing Activity: Explaining Why a Writing Task "Worked"

In your journal and in no more than one page, share information with your readers about a writing task that "worked" for you. Provide specific examples to show how the piece of writing accomplished what you wanted it to accomplish. For example, perhaps at one time you wrote a letter of complaint to a business, and the letter accomplished what you set out to do: get a refund. Or perhaps you wrote a letter of apology to a good friend that accomplished what you wanted it to: your friend forgave you. Your instructor may want you to share your responses with the class.

WRITING ASSIGNMENTS

The writing assignment your instructor will ask you to do—and there are several options below—all ask you to write to inform: to tell your readers about something. In your informational writing, you may use several rhetorical strategies. For example, the *Science Daily* essay (on page 153) uses the rhetorical strategies of *description* (about privacy settings in some smartphones), *narration* (how TISSA created a solution to the privacy problem), *example* (a specific weather application), and *process* (how the application could be easily updated). (For more on rhetorical strategies, see Chapter 5.)

Writing Assignment One: Provide Information on Campus Resources

For this assignment, assume that for your Transition to College Class you have been asked to write an informational essay that describes the campus resources that are available to students at your college or university. Your main audience will be, of course, other students, so consider:

- What resources might be the most useful for you to inform your classmates about?
  - Tutoring services for help with their writing class?
  - Tutoring services for help with their other classes (math, sciences, etc.)?
  - Supplemental learning help for some of their classes?
  - Health services on campus?
  - Counseling services?
  - Employment services?
  - Dining services?

Writing Assignment Two: Your College Classes and Your Career

For this assignment, assume that in your Life Planning class you have been asked to explain, using specific examples, how the college classes you are now taking (and will take later) will help you *get* and *do* the job you hope to have once you graduate.

First, describe the position you hope to one day have (business owner; doctor; mechanic; programmer; medical technician; attorney; pharmacist; teacher), and outline the kind of work that job entails. What might that job require you to do? How are the classes you are taking right now preparing you for that work?

Then, explain how the classes you currently are taking, or soon will take (you may have to look at your college catalog to see what courses your major requires) will help you learn how to do that work. Provide specific examples from your classes, and explain how they will help you obtain your career goals.

By examining the connections between the classes you are currently taking and where you want to end up, you will inform yourself (and your readers) how those classes directly relate to your hoped-for career path.

Writing Assignment Three: Report on Local or Campus Cultural Events

To provide your classmates with information on what is happening in your community or on campus, write an informational essay on local campus or community cultural events that your classmates might be interested in. These could include art exhibits, speakers, museum exhibits, musical events, films, and so on.

Consider what information your audience will need about these cultural events:

- What is happening?
- Why might it be interesting to your classmates?
- Is there any cost involved?
- What are the details of the event (date and time, etc.)?
- Will visual aids (photographs, illustrations) help your audience as they consider whether or not to attend the events you describe?

Optional Multi-Modal Assignment: Construct a Brochure for an Art Exhibit or Museum

For this assignment, assume that in your art history class you have been asked to construct a brochure for a local art exhibit or for your college art museum. As you know, a brochure is an informative text; in this case, it will provide information about the topic you choose. Consider:

- Who might be interested in reading about the exhibit or museum?
- What might they already know about it? What information would they need to know to make a decision to visit it?
- How might visuals help your brochure? How should they be arranged? What might you say about them?

Critical Thinking Activity: Ask Yourself Questions before Writing

If you spend some time considering your information before you start writing your text, your end result will be more effective. So consider:

1. Your *purpose* in writing is to provide information to your readers. By definition, such a paper should be pretty neutral: you should not try to argue a point, or to evaluate something, or to analyze the subject you are writing about. Instead, your purpose is to provide information to your readers, and then they can make up their own minds about that information.
2. How you would describe the *audience* for your information, for the assignment you have been asked to write about?
3. What *rhetorical strategies* (like *description* or *definition* or *providing examples*) might be most effective for your informational text?
4. When someone provides you with information about a subject, what kinds of *details and examples* and *visual aids* are the most useful to you to understand that subject? How might answering that question help you as you write your own paper?

LO3
Use invention and discovery strategies to come up with ideas and details

Invention and Discovery Activities

We suggest that a good way to get started on any writing assignment, in or out of school, is to engage in **invention/discovery activities**—brief bits of writing that you can do to get your ideas onto paper. There are a number of ways you can help yourself (and your paper) by getting started with activities to help you discover ideas about your possible writing subject. (For more details on invention/discovery activities, see Chapter 6).

Everyday Writing Activity: Brainstorming

Brainstorming, as you know, asks that you get your ideas down on paper. The form and format does not matter—you can write whole sentences or just a word to remind you of something.

In your journal, brainstorm what you think you might like to write about for the assignment you have been asked to complete. Get down on paper as many ideas as you can. Your instructor may want you to share your ideas with the rest of the class.

Student Writing: Christie Rosenblatt's Brainstorming

In her Transition to College class, student writer Christie Rosenblatt was given an assignment to inform her readers of what they might expect their first semester at college. Christie's instructor told the class that while they could share their own first-semester experiences in this paper, they also needed outside sources: others they could talk with as well as information they could locate in their college library.

Christie decided to brainstorm on the subject, to get some ideas onto paper:

> One thing I learned my first semester was how much bigger my college is than my high school was. There are no "home rooms" and classes are sometimes in far-away buildings. I have to really hustle between my math and education classes, or I'd be late. And the professors give you what they call a syllabus, which tells everything required for the class, when papers and test are due, etc. They have office hours so students can come and ask questions, etc. They also expect you to take responsibility for your learning—a little different from high school.
>
> I was pretty homesick and so was my roommate, Jill. I think I want to interview her. We did some things to help that homesick feeling, like we both joined that chess club. And we called home a lot....I could also interview cousin Jeremy, who just finished his first year of college. Wonder what his first semester experience at college was like?
>
> Perhaps I can also look at newspapers in the library—some may have news reports about the first semester experience of college students. The librarians might be able to help me ...
>
> Another thought ... should I write my paper in the 3rd person instead of in the first, since the first person isn't usually used in academic writing? Maybe that's the way to go?

Remember that the idea behind doing invention activity is to help you get started with your writing (for other kinds of invention activities that student writer Rosenblatt could have done, see Chapter 6). Often, it is really hard to just sit down and write, so using several invention activities—listing, free writing, brainstorming, clustering—will help you not only get some ideas onto paper; they also will help you develop a preliminary **thesis statement**.

LO4
Write a thesis statement that states the point of your essay

Writing a Thesis Statement for Your Informative Text

Now, it might seem odd that when you are writing to inform or explain that you would even *need* a thesis statement, but without a main idea to focus on, your writing will be unorganized and scattered. Student writer Rosenblatt's thesis might simply be, "There are a number of things new college students have to deal with, and there are several ways to deal with them." Or it might be something very different. Once you have some ideas on paper, you probably will come to some main point you want to make, what is called your *thesis statement*. (For more on thesis statements, see pages 95–98).

Students sometimes think their topic is the same as their thesis, but they really are different. Your **topic** is the subject you are focusing on (in student writer Christie Rosenblatt's case it is the transition from high school to college), while your **thesis** is what you want to focus on, about your topic.

As we noted earlier, your thesis statement, at this point in your writing process, should not be set in stone. It is a good starting point for your first draft, but assume it might change as you learn more and as you start, and continue writing your informative paper, through the writing itself.

LO5
Organize and write your first draft

Organizing and Writing Your First Draft

Now you have some ideas on paper in the form of lists, or perhaps you constructed a cluster diagram showing how your ideas relate to one another, or perhaps you have a few pages of free writing. You also have a good idea of your thesis statement—the point about your subject that you want to thoroughly explain to your readers. So, where do you go from here? How can you take what you have so far and start to organize it into an effective informative text?

Almost always, you want to put your thesis right at the start of your informative paper, so your reader knows exactly that your subject and focus is ("There are several tips that will help you drive safely in the snow," or "First-semester college students face many hurdles, but there are ways to overcome them."). One organizational approach (and one that student writer Christie Rosenblatt might use) is to explain each problem new students face, and then how they might deal with those problems:

An Organizational Plan for an Informative Essay

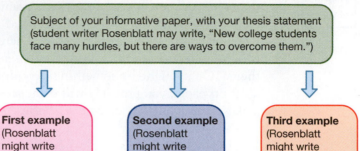

Subject of your informative paper, with your thesis statement (student writer Rosenblatt may write, "New college students face many hurdles, but there are ways to overcome them.")

First example (Rosenblatt might write about homesickness)

First process example (Christie might explain one way to solve homesickness)

Second process example

Second example (Rosenblatt might write about living on campus and roommate issues)

First process example

Second process example

Third process example

Fourth process example

Third example (Rosenblatt might write about working that first semester)

First process example

Second process example

Third process example

We have illustrated only three examples; in your own paper, you probably will have several more. Student writer Rosenblatt, for example, might want to inform her readers about these things new college students have to deal with:

- Homesickness.
- Learning to live with a roommate (who is not a family member).

- Juggling working and school.
- Time management.
- Effective studying of difficult subjects.

Student Writing: Christie Rosenblatt's Introduction

Here is the introduction to student writer Christie Rosenblatt's first draft of her paper that outlines some of her thoughts on moving from high school to college and the problems first-semester students might run into. Note that she has decided to use the third person instead of the first person:

> Every student has his or her own experiences while transitioning from high school to college. Some may experience excitement and fear and wonder and a lot of fun with all the new people and the new experiences. But there may also be unexpected problems that first semester: juggling work and school, roommate issues, and homesickness.

Note that Rosenblatt immediately draws her readers into her text by trying to get her reader's attention by involving that reader:

> ... But there may also be unexpected problems that first semester: juggling work and school, roommate issues, and homesickness.

LO6
Revise your essay, and prepare a final draft

Revising: The Key to Effective Papers

Once you and your classmates have a draft of your informative papers, your instructor may provide feedback on that paper and most likely will ask your class to help each other, by providing feedback and suggestions on each other's papers. There are many ways to do this (your instructor will guide you), and there are some general questions he/she may ask you to respond to as you read your classmates' papers.

Student Writing: Christie Rosenblatt's Peer-Reviewed Draft

Several of student writer Rosenblatt's classmates read and responded to her first draft. Here is part of that draft along with their comments and suggestions. What suggestions would you have made on her paper? What rhetorical strategies can you see at work in her text?

Good to draw the reader into your paper.

What about tuition-related problems? This is your thesis, I believe. Can you make the thesis more direct?

These seem like real problems.

Interesting to know.

Every student has his or her own experiences while transitioning from high school to college. Some may experience excitement and fear and wonder and a lot of fun with all the new people and the new experiences. But there may also be unexpected problems that first semester: juggling work and school, roommate issues, and homesickness. However, there are ways to overcome these hurdles.

Sometimes students are surprised at how big the campus is, with lots of grass and many buildings and many were very big. It can take a long time to walk to each class from the last one with only a ten-minute break between classes. Also, juggling work and school the first semester can be difficult. Many students need to earn money to pay for school, but that work takes away from studying, so some students don't do as well in their classes as they hoped they might. For instance, Mathilda Mannino, who works at a fast food place was so tired when she came home at night that she said, "All I wanted to do was to sleep, not to study." Her grades that first semester were not the best, either.

At the same time, college is also an opportunity to meet a lot of new people. In some classes, students do introductions the first day, so they can know some of the people right away. This can make way for strong friendships or college dorm roommates, such as the friendship between Jill Martin and Jeremy Black.

The important thing about getting suggestions from your classmates on your papers is that they represent *real readers* who are responding to your ideas, so always take their suggestions and comments seriously.

Here is how student writer Rosenblatt responded to a reader's suggestions: about her second paragraph, Christie's classmates wrote

- What about tuition-related problems?
- This is your thesis, I believe. Can you make the thesis more direct?

Here is how Christie revised this paragraph of her informational text:

Christie includes tuition-related problems.

Christie makes the thesis more direct, as requested.

Every student has his or her own experiences while transitioning from high school to college. Some may experience excitement and fear and wonder and a lot of fun with all the new people and the new experiences. But there may also be unexpected problems that first semester: juggling work and school, paying tuition on time, roommate issues, and homesickness. These hurdles can be overcome, as this essay shows, through not working, good time management, forming study groups, compromising with roommates, participating in campus extracurricular activities, and calling home frequently to overcome homesickness.

Writing Tip: Quoting a Source

Student writer Rosenblatt interviewed her roommate, Mathilda, and then quoted her in her paper. Note that Christie introduces the quotation, and puts Mathilda's exact words in quotation marks.

> For instance, Mathilda Mannino, who works at a fast food place, was so tired when she came home at night that she said, "All I wanted to do was to sleep, not to study." Her grades that first semester were not the best, either.

At the end of her paper, Christie wants to make sure her readers know that the quotation from Mathilda came from an interview with Mathilda. Mathilda and Christie probably just talked about their experiences, so Christie did not formally "interview" Mathilda. However, in academic writing, writers must indicate where anything that is not their own words or ideas came from. Put another way, writers must attribute any words or ideas they got from others: they must tell their readers who those words or ideas belonged to. The way to attribute the words or ideas you got from someone you spoke with is to put them at the end of your paper, on your **works cited** or **reference** page (for more on works cited and reference pages, see Chapter 16):

> Mannino, Mathilda. Personal interview. 11 Feb. 2011.

Now, readers know that Christie got that quotation by talking to Mathilda Mannino on February 11, 2011.

Critical Thinking Activity: Ask Yourself Questions before You Revise

Now you have a first draft of your informative paper, have reread it several times, and most likely you also have received comments and suggestions from your classmates (and perhaps from your instructor, family members, or friends). You will recall from Chapter 8 that *revision* means to rethink and to reenvision your text—not to just fix surface errors. So consider:

1. Did any of the suggestions I received say anything about me not achieving my *purpose?* That I perhaps had misunderstood or misrepresented

the information and details my *audience* needed to understand my subject?

2. Did I get any comments about the examples I provided? Does that part of my paper need more examples to help readers see what I mean?

3. Did any of the comments I received indicate that I might want to reorganize my informational text? Did anyone indicate that I did not effectively explain or illustrate any process I outlined? If so, what changes might I make?

4. Did anyone tell me that they did not understand or seem to have misunderstood the *thesis statement* for my informational writing? How can I clarify it?

5. Did anyone suggest a *visual* (chart, graph, table, photograph, etc.) that might help improve my text?

Use this checklist to see whether your revised paper is finally done, or whether you need to make further changes before printing a final draft.

Revision Checklist for Your Informational Paper	
As you think about writing the first draft of your paper, consider the parts of it that you want to make sure to include in your text:	
Part of Your Paper	**Check √**
Title for your paper that gets your readers' attention	
Introduction with a clear thesis statement	
Supporting paragraphs, each with a topic sentence, providing evidence or examples, and a transition to the next paragraph (Each example should illustrate something useful about your subject, to provide information to help readers better understand it.)	
Step-by-step instructions, if you are writing to inform about a process	
Visual aids if they will help readers understand the information you are providing	
Conclusion that summarizes your main points and restates the thesis of your informational text	

Student Writing: Christie Rosenblatt's Final Draft

Here is student writer Christie Rosenblatt's final draft of her informative paper about moving from high school to college:

Rosenblatt 1

Christie Rosenblatt
Dr. Barbara Hanks
English 099
24 Apr. 2011

Moving from High School to College

Every student has his or her own experiences while transitioning from high school to college. Some may experience excitement and fear and wonder and a lot of fun with all the new people and the new experiences. College is truly an opportunity to meet a lot of new people. But there may also be unexpected problems that first semester: juggling work and school, paying tuition on time, roommate issues, and homesickness. These hurdles can be overcome through not working, good time management, forming study groups, compromising with roommates, participating in campus extracurricular activities, and calling home frequently to overcome homesickness.

Sometimes juggling work and school the first semester can be difficult. Many students need to earn money to pay for school, but that work takes away from studying, so some students don't do as well in their classes as they hoped they might. For instance, Mathilda Mannino, who works at a fast food place, was so tired when she came home at night that she said, "All I wanted to do was to sleep, not to study." Her grades that first semester were not the best, either. Mary Ellen Behm, who also worked her first semester, says that "it just about killed me, working and taking 15 hours of classes," and that she had to give up her job her second semester. So, that is one solution to the work/school problem: give up the job.

(continued)

Of course, some students need to keep their jobs and they can do so by making out a detailed time management sheet for every week of the semester, and also noting down important dates such as when tuition is due. Planning a daily schedule involving work, classes, and studying time with study groups can be very helpful, and may even open up times for when students can go to the movies, and so on. As Mathilda says, "Making a time management sheet saved my college life from becoming truly chaotic."

Another problem new college students often face is suddenly finding themselves living with a stranger, in a very small room. Many first-semester college students never lived away from home until they went to college, so living with a new person can be a real culture shock. Roommates often have issues with each other: loud music, piles of clothing, late nights, etc. Switching roommates may not always be the solution; in fact, it might make things worse. The best thing to do is to work through the problems. Form study groups with roommates. Talk. Discuss. Compromise.

Homesickness can also be an issue. One thing that can really help, though, is to participate in campus extracurricular activities (without hampering school work, of course). For example, students can join the chess club and learn how to play chess, and perhaps join the swing dancing club, or the swimming club, depending on their interests. Just getting to know a lot of other students, and doing things together with them, can help get over homesick feelings. Calling home a lot is another option, too.

There are several problems new college students might encounter during their first semester at school. They can include figuring out how to work and go to school at the same time, learning how to live with a new roommate, and

Rosenblatt 3

homesickness. All of these hurdles can be overcome, though, with a few useful techniques.

Rosenblatt 4

Works Cited

Behm, Mary Ellen. Personal interview. 12 Feb. 2011.

Mannino, Mathilda. Personal interview. 11 Feb. 2011.

 ## Critical Thinking Activity: Ask Yourself Questions for Reflection

Please respond to the following questions in your journal. Your instructor may ask you to share your responses with the rest of the class:

1. How did you decide what to focus on? How did you decide on your thesis statement for your informative paper?
2. Did you conduct any research? What would you do differently next time in terms of research?
3. What kinds of invention/discovery activities did you do? What was the most helpful? The least? Why?
4. What could your classmates do next time to make their comments and suggestions more useful to you?
5. What did you learn about your own writing process through the process of writing this paper?
6. Did you use visual aids in your informative paper? If so, what did you learn about using them that will help you in future assignments? If you did not use visual aids, do you think if you had, they may have improved your paper?
7. Did you procrastinate at starting your paper? What might you do differently next time?
8. What did you learn from writing this paper that will help you as you write to inform in the future?

Readings That Inform

Your instructor may ask you to read and perhaps discuss and write about one or more of the texts that follow. We selected these texts to help you get a sense of what effective informative writing looks like and how it functions.

Note: Words highlighted **in blue** are terms used in the "Improve Your Vocabulary" activity after each reading.

Cultural Differences? Or, Are We Really That Different?

Gregorio Billikopf

This section of an essay by Gregorio Billikopf provides some interesting (and, at times, humorous) information on cultural differences and how sometimes they turn into negative stereotypes. As you read it, ask yourself, What new information did I learn from writer Billikopf? In what way did he provide that information to me?

1   In 1993, I had my first opportunity to visit Russia as a representative of the University of California. I was there to provide some technical assistance in the area of agricultural labor management. "Russians are a very polite people," I had been tutored before my arrival. One of my interpreters, once I was there, explained that a gentleman will pour the *limonad* (type of juice) for the ladies and show other courtesies.

2   Toward the end of my three week trip I was invited by my young Russian host and friend Nicolai Vasilevich and his lovely wife Yulya out to dinner. At the end of a wonderful meal Yulya asked if I would like a banana. I politely declined and thanked her, and explained I was most *satisfied* with the meal. But the whole while my mind was racing: "What do I do? Do I offer her a banana even though they are as close to her as they are to me? What is the *polite* thing to do?"

3   "Would *you* like a banana?" I asked Yulya.

4   "Yes," she smiled, but made no attempt to take any of the three bananas in the fruit basket. "What now?" I thought.

5   "Which one would you like?" I fumbled.

6   "That one," she pointed at one of the bananas. So all the while thinking about Russian politeness I picked the banana Yulya had pointed at and peeled it half way and handed it to her. Smiles in Yulya and Nicolai's faces told me I had done the right thing. After this experience I spent much time letting the world know that in Russia, the polite thing is to peel the bananas for the ladies. Sometime during my third trip I was politely **disabused** of my notion.

7   "Oh no, Grigorii Davidovich," a Russian **graciously** corrected me. "In Russia, when a man peels a banana for a lady it means he has a *romantic* interest in her." How embarrassed I felt. And here I had been proudly telling everyone about this tidbit of cultural understanding.

disabused: corrected about something incorrect

graciously: kindly

distorted: deformed

8   Certain lessons have to be learned the hard way. Some well meaning articles and presentations on cultural differences have a potential to do more harm than good and may not be as amusing. They present, like my bananas, too many generalizations or quite a **distorted** view.

9   Some often-heard generalizations about the Hispanic culture include: Hispanics need less personal space, make less eye contact, touch each other more in normal conversation, and are less likely to participate in a meeting. Generalizations are often dangerous, and especially when accompanied by recommendations such as: move closer when talking to Hispanics, make more physical contact, don't expect participation, and so on.

10   Here is an attempt to sort out a couple of thoughts on cultural differences. My perspective is that of a foreign born-and-raised Hispanic who has now lived over two decades in the United States and has had much opportunity for international travel and exchange.

Commonality of humankind

belief structure: what someone believes in

myriad: many; varied

appropriate: correct; fitting

tolerance: the ability to put up with things

gallantry: heroism; chivalry

etiquette: manners

assimilation: becoming part of

ideological: relating to beliefs or world view

correspondent: reporter

11   Differences between people within any given nation or culture are much greater than differences between groups. Education, social standing, religion, personality, **belief structure**, past experience, affection shown in the home, and a **myriad** of other factors will affect human behavior and culture.

12   Sure there are differences in approach as to what is considered polite and **appropriate** behavior both on and off the job. In some cultures "yes" means, "I hear you" more than "I agree." Length of pleasantries and greetings before getting down to business; level of **tolerance** for being around someone speaking a foreign (not-understood) language; politeness measured in terms of **gallantry** or **etiquette** (e.g., standing up for a woman who approaches a table, yielding a seat on the bus to an older person, etc.); and manner of expected dress are all examples of possible cultural differences and traditions.

13   In México it is customary for the *arriving* person to greet the others. For instance, someone who walks into a group of persons eating would say *provecho* (enjoy your meal). In Chile, women often greet both other women and men with a kiss on the cheek. In Russia women often walk arm in arm with their female friends. Paying attention to customs and cultural differences can give someone outside that culture a better chance of **assimilation** or acceptance. Ignoring these can get an unsuspecting person into trouble.

14   There *are* cultural and **ideological** differences and *it is good* to have an understanding about a culture's customs and ways. Aaron Pun, a Canadian ODCnet **correspondent**, wrote: "In studying cross cultural differences, we are not looking at individuals but a comparison of one ethnic group against others. Hence, we are comparing two bell curves and generalization cannot be avoided." Another correspondent explained the human need to categorize. True and true, but the danger comes when we act on some of these generalizations, especially when they are based on faulty observation. Acting on generalizations about such matters as eye contact, personal space, touch, and interest in participation can have serious negative consequences.

Questions for Discussion and Writing

1. What is your initial reaction to this information?
2. What did you learn from this text? What is the most interesting thing you learned?
3. What was the most unusual thing you learned?
4. Can you point to any generalizations you can make about your own cultural background?
5. Does this excerpt from Billikopf's essay make you want to read the rest of it? You can, at the College of Natural Resources Web site.

Improve Your Vocabulary

Use the highlighted and defined words from Billikopf's essay in a sentence or in a paragraph.

Developing Global Skills for an International Career

Debra Peters-Behrens

Dr. Debra Behrens is a PhD Career Counselor at the University of California, Berkeley, specializing in services to graduate and international students. As you read her advice on how to prepare for an international career, consider: Where do you want to work? What kind of work do you hope to do? Note that this is a process essay in the sense that Behrens is informing her readers of "how" to do something—in this case, how to get ready to work internationally. Process essays are essentially sets of instructions on how to do something.

1   As an international careers counselor, I receive questions daily from people of varied backgrounds who hope to try their luck in the global marketplace. Many job seekers mistakenly believe that they can't begin an international career until their feet are on foreign soil. They overlook their own backyard for resources and training opportunities.

sought-after: desired

The Most Sought-After Skills

2   What do international employers really look for in employees and what skills will be needed by professionals to perform successfully in the global marketplace?

surveyed: looked at

3   A study commissioned by the College Placement Council Foundation surveyed 32 international employers and colleges to determine what international employers seek in prospective employees. They identified the following areas of required knowledge and skills:

Domain knowledge

4 Colleges in the U.S. are presently preparing their graduates well in domain knowledge, or knowledge in one's academic discipline, although employers expressed concern that increasingly greater demands and higher standards may soon result in inadequately prepared graduates.

cognitive: related to thinking

5 The three most important skills were **cognitive** skills, social skills, and "personal traits." Problem-solving ability, decision making, and knowing how to learn are highly prized **generic** skills. Social skills were described as the ability to work effectively in group settings, particularly with diverse populations. Personal traits mentioned frequently included flexibility, **adaptability**, and the capacity to be innovative. Employers often mentioned that colleges do not **adequately** address this type of skill development.

generic: same class of something; standard

adaptability: ability to change

adequately: sufficiently

Cross-cultural competence

concerted: sustained

6 Students must make a **concerted** effort to acquire the knowledge, skills, and traits gained through cross-cultural interaction because we are more geographically and linguistically insulated than most other countries.

7 On-the-job training and prior work experience. Employers seek applicants who have been successful in applying their domain knowledge or academic studies and generic skills in the workplace. They say that colleges do not place sufficient emphasis on work experience.

Acquiring the Skills

Get experience

8 An internship or a stint as a volunteer can be invaluable to recent graduates or career changers. Locate organizations at the local level which have similar goals to those of larger international organizations. Service organizations address issues of health, housing, economic development, and employment—all of which are local as well as global concerns.

interagency: working between several groups

9 For example, one client wanted to find a position in development work in the developing world. I suggested that she research local human service organizations to find an internship that would provide her with opportunities to work with on-going projects. She found an internship as an **interagency liaison** with a relief organization that distributed medicine, food, and supplies to countries affected by war or natural disasters.

liaison: connection

10 Many job seekers plan to teach English as a second language with little or no experience beforehand. Even a brief stint as a volunteer language assistant can provide insight into the challenges and rewards of the work. Testing a field in familiar settings can make for a smoother transition abroad.

Build your resume

11 Job seekers often do not have the time or the money to pursue a degree program, but in some instances a few courses may sufficiently augment the

(continued)

optimum: perfect

experience and education you already have. Consult a career counselor to help you assess your skills and identify approaches for strengthening your background. A counselor can also help you determine an **optimum** strategy for meeting your goals. Investigate extension and continuing education programs offered by local colleges and universities for courses in computer science, graphic design, and foreign languages.

Research the job market

12   Gather information by researching a variety of sources: professional association Web sites and journals. The public library is a treasure trove of information. Many university libraries will issue a community user card for a
nominal: inexpensive
nominal annual fee.

13   After you have a grasp of key issues and trends you may want to get the perspective of people who are active in the field. Use your alumni directory and professional associations as resources for networking and information interviewing. Do not set up an information interview and then ask your informant for a
imposition: force something onto someone
job. People generally resent the **imposition**. Instead, use the time to ask questions that are not covered in print material, including "If you were me, what would you do next?," "If you had to do it all over again, is there anything you would do differently?," and "What strategies did you use that were most successful?"

14   With a focused and well-organized approach, you can be on the path to developing skills for a global career.

Go Where the Action Is

15   Many U.S. cities are becoming global in population and perspective as people with diverse linguistic, national, and cultural backgrounds converge to
locales: locations
live and work. Living in these **locales** can help you acquire cross-cultural competence and find work in fields such as business, cultural exchange, and health and human services with a focus on certain regions of the world. All major cities have world trade centers which support international commerce, as do some mid-sized and smaller cities.

16   If you're interested in the Asian Pacific Rim, for example, a job with a multinational organization in Seattle, Portland, or San Francisco may be a good starting point. Miami, Houston, and San Diego hold great potential for international trade between the U.S. and Latin America. New York and Los Angeles are centers of international business, diplomacy, and cultural affairs. Washington, DC provides a strong base for finding international employment, particularly in government and nonprofit organizations.

Questions for Discussion and Writing

1. What is your initial reaction to this information?
2. What did you learn from this text? What is the most interesting thing you learned?

3. Do you think that the process outlined by writer Peters-Behrens will help someone who wants to work internationally?
4. What is Peters-Behrens' most important piece of advice? Why?
5. Have you ever spoken with a career counselor, as Peters-Behrens suggests in paragraph 11? (For more on résumé writing, see Chapter 18).

Improve Your Vocabulary

Use the highlighted and defined words from Peter-Behrens's essay in a sentence or in a paragraph.

What's Next for NASA?

Charles Frank Bolden Jr.

Charles Frank Bolden Jr. has been the administrator of the National Aeronautics and Space Administration since 2009. He manages NASA's resources to advance the agency's missions and goals. Before joining NASA, he worked for 34 years with the Marine Corps, including 14 years as a member of NASA's Astronaut Office. He has traveled aboard the space shuttle four times between 1986 and 1994, commanding two of the missions. This speech was given to the National Press Club in July 2011.

robust: strong; vigorous; healthy

solar system: the sun and the group of celestial bodies that revolve around it

propulsion: to drive forward

depots: a place for storing goods

radiation: the emission of energy in the form of waves and particles

1   As a former astronaut and the current NASA Administrator, I'm here to tell you that American leadership in space will continue for at least the next half-century because we have laid the foundation for success—and failure is not an option.

2   The end of the space shuttle program does not mean the end of NASA, or even of NASA sending humans into space. NASA has a **robust** program of exploration, technology development and scientific research that will last for years to come. Here is what's next for NASA:

Exploration

3   NASA is designing and building the capabilities to send humans to explore the **solar system**, working toward a goal of landing humans on Mars. We will build the Multi-Purpose Crew Vehicle, based on the design for the Orion capsule, with a capacity to take four astronauts on 21-day missions.

4   We will soon announce the design for the heavy-lift Space Launch System that will carry us out of low Earth orbit. We are developing the technologies we will need for human exploration of the solar system, including solar electric **propulsion**, refueling **depots** in orbit, **radiation** protection and high-reliability life support systems.

(continued)

International Space Station

5   The International Space Station is the centerpiece of our human space-flight activities in low Earth orbit. The ISS is fully staffed with a crew of six, and American astronauts will continue to live and work there in space 24 hours a day, 365 days a year. Part of the U.S. portion of the station has been designated as a national laboratory, and NASA is committed to using this unique resource for scientific research.

6   The ISS is a test bed for exploration technologies such as **autonomous** refueling of spacecraft, advanced life support systems and human/robotic **interfaces**. Commercial companies are well on their way to providing cargo and crew flights to the ISS, allowing NASA to focus its attention on the next steps into our solar system.

Aeronautics

7   NASA is researching ways to design and build aircraft that are safer, more fuel-efficient, quieter, and environmentally responsible. We are also working to create traffic management systems that are safer, more efficient and more flexible. We are developing technologies that improve routing during flights and enable aircraft to climb to and descend from their cruising altitude without interruption.

8   We believe it is possible to build an aircraft that uses less fuel, gives off fewer emissions, and is quieter, and we are working on the technologies to create that aircraft. NASA is also part of the government team that is working to develop the Next Generation Air Transportation System, or NextGen, to be in place by the year 2025. We will continue to **validate** new, complex aircraft and air traffic control systems to ensure that they meet extremely high safety levels.

Science

9   NASA is conducting an **unprecedented** array of missions that will seek new knowledge and understanding of Earth, the solar system and the universe. On July 16, the Dawn spacecraft begins a year-long visit to the large **asteroid** Vesta to help us understand the earliest chapter of our solar system's history. In August, the Juno spacecraft will launch to investigate Jupiter's origins, structure, and atmosphere. The September launch of the National Polar-orbiting Operational Environmental Satellite System Preparatory Project is a critical first step in building a **next-generation** Earth-monitoring satellite system.

10   NASA returns to the moon to study the moon's gravity field and determine the structure of the lunar interior with the October launch of GRAIL. In November, we launch the Mars Science Laboratory named Curiosity on its journey to Mars to look for evidence of **microbial** life on the red planet. And in February 2012, we will launch the Nuclear Spectroscopic Telescope Array to search for **black holes**, map **supernova** explosions, and study the most extreme active **galaxies**.

---

autonomous: independent

interfaces: the place at which different and often unrelated systems meet

validate: to support, grant official sanction

unprecedented: something that has not happened before

asteroid: small, rocky celestial body

next-generation: looking towards the future

microbial: microorganism; germ

black holes: celestial objects with a strong gravitational field that do not let light escape

supernova: the explosion of a star

galaxies: large groups of stars and associated matter

Questions for Discussion and Writing

1. What did you know about NASA before you read this passage?
2. What did you learn from this text? What is the most interesting thing you learned?
3. What do you think of NASA's future plans? Which one seems the most interesting or ambitious?
4. How useful do you think it is to send humans to space?
5. Would you like to work for NASA? Why or why not?

Improve Your Vocabulary

Use the highlighted and defined words from "What's Next for NASA?" in a sentence or in a paragraph.

MyWritingLab™ For support in meeting this chapter's objectives, log in to **www.mywritinglab.com** and select **Essay Development—Illustrating** and **Essay Development—Process.**

Chapter 11

Writing to Analyze
Using Division and Classification

Learning Objectives

In this chapter, you will learn to:

LO1 Consider the writer's situation, and determine your purpose and audience

LO2 Use the rhetorical strategies of *division* and *classification* to analyze something

LO3 Use invention and discovery strategies to come up with ideas and details

LO4 Write a thesis statement that states the point of your essay

LO5 Organize and write your first draft

LO6 Revise your essay, and prepare a final draft

onsider the accompanying photograph. To analyze the body language in this photograph, you would first describe what you see:

- The woman is standing with her mouth open, a hand at her throat, and her eyes are wide.
- The young girl on the left is watching something and is holding what appears to be a television remote control. She is pouting.
- The center girl has her mouth open, a hand on her face, and is holding a large box of popcorn.
- Finally, the young girl on the right is also holding something—a video game of some kind?—and she has her head balanced on a hand and is looking at something different than the other people in the picture.

We have just *divided* the body language in this photograph. Now, we could *classify* it, which means to put something into categories. In the example of this photograph, you could classify the body language by body parts (what their hands are doing, eyes are doing, mouths are doing, and so on).

For fun, how would you classify the emotions the people in the picture display, based on what their bodies showed you? You might say that

- The woman who is standing looks surprised or shocked at what she is seeing, based on her mouth, wide eyes, and hand at her throat.
- The girl on the left appears to be looking at the same thing as the woman, but her eyes and mouth indicate that she may be skeptical. She also looks like she's ready to change the TV channel!
- The girl in the center could either be yawning or thinking something like, "Oh, my!" and she appears to be looking at the camera. Or, she could have a toothache!
- Finally, the girl on the right is looking where no one else is, seems happy (smile) and is holding something other than a TV remote. A game controller?

If you were to classify the body language here by emotions, then, you could say the photograph shows people who are shocked, surprised, sleepy, and having fun. Overall, you could say the various parts of this photograph, when you analyze it, shows four different people displaying—based on their body language—four different emotions.

Thus, **division** is the first step in an analysis: what are the parts or aspects or pieces of the subject you are analyzing? **Classifying** is the second part: what are some larger categories you can put the smaller divisions into? Once you have the various parts of your subject classified, you can then draw conclusions on how all of those parts work together.

Everyday Writing Activity: Analyze a Classmate's Body Language

Pair up with a classmate, and talk for five minutes about the classes each of you is taking. As you talk, take notes on your classmate's body language: Does he/she smile or frown? How does he/she hold his/her hands? How does he/she sit? Is he/she leaning toward or away from you? Are his/her legs crossed? Is his/her body language different when he/she talks as compared to when you are talking? Does he/she make eye contact or look away? Does his/her body language change depending on which class he/she is discussing?

In your journal and in no more than one page, describe the various aspect of your classmate's body language (you are using the rhetorical strategy of division to do this). Then, use the rhetorical strategy of classification to characterize how each bit of body language works to illustrate an emotion of some kind—happiness, curiosity, sadness, and so on.

For example, you might note that when your partner talked, he/she smiled and looked directly at you, and his/her hands were moving as she talked. Those are three aspects or divisions of his/her body language. You could classify them as friendly: he/she wanted you to understand and relate to what he/she was saying. Or you might notice that then he/she talks about a class he/she dislikes, the edges of his/her mouth drop, making him/her look sad; his/her forehead might wrinkle, he/she may use more dramatic gestures to indicate his/her displeasure with the class, and so on.

Underline each aspect or component you divided your partner's body language into (hand position, sitting position, etc.). *Circle* each classification you made. Your instructor may want you to share your responses with the rest of the class.

Think about what you just did: you observed a classmate and took notes on his/her body language. You *divided up* what you saw into various parts or aspects of that body language. Then, you *classified* how those parts worked together to show the emotions your friend exhibited. Thus, you analyzed someone's body language.

The Writer's Situation

LO1

Consider the writer's situation, and determine your purpose and audience

When you write to analyze, your **purpose** is to understand the various aspects of your subject and then to explain how they work together. As you consider your purpose, you also need to think about your **audience:** What do they already know about the subject you are analyzing? What aspects of that subject are most important to explain and show and discuss? How do all those pieces function together?

LO2
Use the
rhetorical
strategies of
division and
classification
to analyze
something

Analyzing through Division and Classification

This brief section of an analysis by the Environmental Protection Agency (EPA) focuses on the reader—a strategy that helps draw readers into the essay. As you read this brief analysis, consider how the EPA uses *division* to describe some of the ways, both good and bad, that each of us might be affected by climate change (health, the cost of food, etc.). The agency uses headings for each aspect of climate change that it touches on. These aspects or parts all combine into the general classification of ways that climate change may affect readers. You can read some background on climate change, also from the EPA, on page 24 of this text.

Climate Change Impact
Environmental Protection Agency

Most people are concerned about their health, so this first section will interest readers.

Note the range of detail, from cities to young and as older people.

The second division; as with temperature, the cost of food affects everyone.

Third division, one often in the news.

The writer mentions some positive effects of climate change. That adds to the essay's credibility.

A huge number of people live on the coast.

Scientific results suggest that climate changes may affect you in the following ways:

1 **Health.** Longer, more intense and frequent heat waves may cause more heat-related death and illness. There is virtual certainty of declining air quality in cities since greater heat can also worsen air pollution such as ozone, or smog. Insect-borne illnesses are also likely to increase as many insect ranges expand. Climate change health effects are especially serious for the very young, very old, or for those with heart and respiratory problems. Conversely, warmer winter temperatures may reduce the negative health impacts from cold weather.

2 **Agriculture and Forestry.** The supply and cost of food may change as farmers and the food industry adapt to new climate patterns. A small amount of warming coupled with increasing CO_2 may benefit certain crops, plants and forests, although the impacts of vegetation depend also on the availability of water and nutrients. For warming of more than a few degrees, the effects are expected to become increasingly negative, especially for vegetation near the warm end of its suitable range.

3 **Water Resources.** In a warming climate, extreme events like floods and droughts are likely to become more frequent. More frequent floods and droughts will affect water quality and availability. For example, increases in drought in some areas may increase the frequency of water shortages and lead to more restrictions on water usage. An overall increase in precipitation may increase water availability in some regions, but also create greater flood potential.

4 **Coasts.** If you live along the coast, your home may be impacted by sea level rise and an increase in storm intensity. Rising seas may contribute to enhanced coastal erosion, coastal flooding, loss of coastal wetlands, and increased risk of property loss from storm surges.

(continued)

Fifth division, and
as with the others,
something that
affects everyone.

Sixth division:
wildlife also are
affected.

5   **Energy.** Warmer temperatures may result in higher energy bills for air conditioning in summer, and lower bills for heating in winter. Energy usage is also connected to water needs. Energy is needed for irrigation, which will most likely increase due to climate change. Also, energy is generated by hydropower in some regions, which will also be impacted by changing precipitation patterns.

6   **Wildlife.** Warmer temperatures and precipitation changes will likely affect the habitats and migratory patterns of many types of wildlife. The range and distribution of many species will change, and some species that cannot move or adapt may face extinction.

Questions for Discussion and Writing

1. The EPA selected specific ways that climate change might affect readers. Can you think of any other ways in which climate change might affect the world?
2. Do you agree with this analysis? Why or why not?
3. What was the most interesting or surprising piece of information in this analysis?
4. Does this analysis make you want to learn more about climate change? Why or why not?

Everyday Writing Activity: A Brief Analysis

You just read a piece analyzing climate change and its effects. There are many other things that can be similarly analyzed, and one of them is the qualities of someone you know. In your journal, answer these questions. Consider a person who has inspired you and helped make you who you are today.

- What qualities might you list about that person, if you were to analyze him/her? (You are using the rhetorical strategy of division to list his/her various qualities.)
- If you were to classify those qualities, how would you explain how they functioned together to affect who you are, today?

Your instructor may want you to share your responses with the rest of the class.

WRITING ASSIGNMENTS

Your instructor will ask you to complete one of the following analysis assignments. Be sure to use the rhetorical strategies of *division* and *classification* to write your analysis.

Writing Assignment One: Analyze Local Opportunities to Volunteer

For this assignment, write a paper that analyzes opportunities for volunteer work in your college and community. Start by listing all the opportunities available to residents of your town, *dividing* them into the kinds of work volunteers are asked to perform. You might end up with a list including jobs such as

- Picking up used furniture.
- Delivering supplies.
- Clerking at a Goodwill store.
- Repairing broken items that had been donated.
- Cleaning.
- Sorting donated food.
- Making sandwiches at a local soup kitchen.
- Fundraising.
- Doing administrative or office tasks.

Once you have a list, you can then *classify* the tasks in various ways: perhaps by the kind of work (driving, delivery, office work), or the time commitment (hours per week), or the type of organization (cultural, social services), and so on. Choose a classification scheme that is meaningful to you.

Writing Assignment Two: Analyze the Requirements of Your College Major

For this assignment, consider your own college plans: what subject do you plan to major in? Analyze that major: how do the parts of it (the college courses you will take) work together to provide the end result (a college degree that will help you get a job doing what you want to do)?

For instance, perhaps you hope to become a paramedic, which requires an Associate of Science (AS) degree. Before you commit to this, it would be valuable to analyze the various courses the degree asks you to take (as well as any potential elective classes and internships), so you can understand how everything "fits together," how the coursework you will do in those classes works together to get you to the degree you want. To do so, you would use *division* to examine all of the classes you need to take and any other requirements, and then you would *classify* them and explain how they function to create the degree program you need.

In this example, the AS degree requires 60 hours of coursework, so you could break up or *divide* that work by listing the courses. Then, you would *classify* those courses into groups; you might end up with something like this (based on Glendale Community College in Arizona):

Group 1: Foundation Courses

Applied Practical Skills
Advanced Concepts
Cardiology
Vehicular Extrication
Trauma Patient Management
Field Internship
Pharmacology
Hazardous Materials
Anatomy and Physiology

Group 2: Level 1 Paramedic Courses

Paramedic 1
Didactic 1

Group 3: Level 2 Paramedic Courses

Paramedic 2
Didactic 2
ACLS
PEPP
Individualized Plan

Group 4: Clinical / Vehicular Practice

Clinical / Vehicular
Individualized Plan
National Registry Prep

Classifying the courses into groups helps you see how they work together, as well as what courses need to be taken first, and so on.

Writing Assignment Three: Analyze Local Attractions

In your writing class, you are asked to analyze local attractions that might appeal to tourists—a visitor's guide, so to speak.

You would first list all the events and attractions that might interest tourists, and then divide them into component parts. (A lake, for example, might offer boating, fishing, picnic locations, and hiking trails. A local museum might have various exhibits, some of which might interest adults and others that might interest children.) Then you would classify each attraction, perhaps by kind of attraction—outdoors/indoors—or attractions for adults/children, or by cost, or by general location.

Optional Multi-Modal Assignment: E-mail

Assume you are given writing assignment three, which asks that you analyze local attractions that might interest tourists. If you were to construct an e-mail message that summarized your analysis, what would you include in the e-mail? What would you leave out? Would you attach or include illustrations?

Critical Thinking Activity: Questions to Ask before You Start

Spend some time now considering the assignment and planning your analysis so your task will be easier. In your journal, answer these questions:

1. Your purpose in writing is to analyze something (volunteer opportunities, your college major, or local tourist attractions). What aspects of your subject work together to make it function? How might these parts be arranged, or classified, into groups?
2. How you would describe the audience for your analysis?
3. When someone tells you about something they have analyzed, what kinds of details and examples and visual aids are the most useful to you, to understand what they mean? How might answering this question help you as you write your own paper?
4. Consider what research you might conduct to help you explain the various aspects of your subject and how they are related to one another. Who could you talk with? What kinds of observations can you make? Are there books or articles that could provide you with information for your analysis?

LO3

Use invention
and discovery
strategies to
come up with
ideas and
details

Invention and Discovery Activities

A good way to get started on any writing assignment is to use **invention/ discovery activities**—brief pieces of writing that get some of your ideas onto paper. There are a number of ways you can help yourself (and your paper) by getting started with invention activities. **Listing** is a particularly useful technique for analysis. (For more details on invention activities, see pages 80–88).

Student Writing: Rebecca Tremble's Listing

In her marketing class, student Rebecca Tremble was assigned a semester-long project, in which she had to examine a small business and the various aspects of running that business. Put another way, she was asked to do a detailed analysis of all parts of running a small business.

As one aspect of that assignment, Rebecca decided to analyze how advertising methods in her local community might work together to help the business grow. Note that Rebecca is not evaluating the ways to advertise (then she would try to determine which ways would be better than others), but rather she wants to use them all, collectively, for the business's advertising.

Rebecca decided to start with a simple list of all of the possible ways to advertise:

1. Local daily newspaper ad
2. Local radio station ad
3. Local mailing service, for direct mail to potential customers
4. Local marketing agency, specializing in e-mail to potential customers
5. Local college newspaper ad
6. Facebook ad

Everyday Writing Activity: Listing

In your journal, create a list to get started on your own analysis. For example, if you were writing for assignment two, you might go through your college catalog and make a simple list of the classes you need to take (and the possible electives) for your college major.

Now, take the list you just made, and classify those courses by the focus of the class (as near as you can tell by its title and the brief catalog description). Your instructor may ask you to share your list and classification with the rest of the class.

Remember that the idea behind any invention/discovery activity is to help you get started with your writing. Using a number of invention activities—listing, freewriting, brainstorming, clustering—will help you get some ideas onto paper and develop a preliminary **thesis statement** for your analysis.

LO4
Write a thesis statement that states the point of your essay

Writing a Thesis Statement for Your Analysis

You may not know the point of your analysis (your thesis) until you get some drafting and revision done. For student writer Rebecca Tremble, until she conducts research and gets some of what she learns onto paper, she will not know what her final thesis or point is. At this stage, Rebecca might start with a tentative thesis for her analysis that says:

> There are many ways to advertise to our local community, and they all have to work together to create an effective advertising campaign.

We suggest that you delay writing your final thesis statement until you have conducted research and written a draft. Start with a tentative thesis statement—that will help you get going—but understand that you may change your point of view as you write and revise.

Sometimes, students think their topic is the same as their thesis statement, but they really are different. Your topic is the subject you are focusing on (in student writer Rebecca Tremble's case, it is how various ways of local advertising can work or function together to end up as an effective marketing strategy). Your thesis statement is the point you want to make about this topic. For example, student writer Tremble's analysis might determine that all of the business's advertising should have a common theme to work together effectively. If so, her thesis statement might read:

> For the company's advertising to be most effective, all aspects must share a common theme.

LO5
Organize and write your first draft

Organizing and Writing Your First Draft

Now you have some ideas on paper in the form of listing, or perhaps you constructed a cluster diagram showing how your ideas relate to one another, or perhaps you have a few pages listing the various general classifications of your topic. How can you take what you have so far and organize it into an effective analysis?

Most often in an analysis, you will define the subject of your analysis, show how it is divided into parts or pieces, and then explain how all of those pieces work together to create the subject itself. Of course, you can reverse this approach and explain how the various parts work together, then explain each division or part of your subject.

Which organization is better? Only you, the writer, can decide that, and one way to do so is to try one and then the other, as writing a page or two will give you some sense of which might be best for the particular subject you are analyzing, your audience, and so on.

Here is an example of the first approach:

An Organizational Plan for an Analysis Essay: From the Whole to Its Parts

Introduction: Define and describe your subject.

In Rebecca's case, she would need to define what makes an effective advertising campaign—it could be as simple as saying that more potential customers can be reached using various media.

First way to advertise: the local newspaper

Second way to advertise: local radio station

Can this method relate to and support newspaper advertising? *Hint:* Can the company run ads that say, "Watch for our discount coupon in the local paper"?

Third way to advertise: direct mail

Can this method relate to and support newspaper and/or radio advertising? *Hint:* Can the business run ads that say, "Watch for our discount coupon in the mail"? Or ads that say, "Combine the mail coupon with the newspaper coupon and save more"?

After showing the different parts of her subject, Rebecca can then explain how each piece of the subject works together to create the whole. This would mean emphasizing that all aspects of the campaign repeat the same message and reinforce one another.

Another organizational approach is to begin with the various aspects of your subject and then explain how each contributes to the whole subject as well as how they might relate to one another:

An Organizational Plan for an Analysis Essay: From the Parts to a Whole

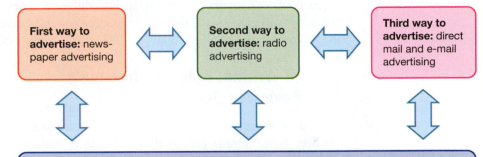

First way to advertise: newspaper advertising

Second way to advertise: radio advertising

Third way to advertise: direct mail and e-mail advertising

Overall goal: to get the message to as many potential customers as possible
Thesis: All advertising must work together

Student Writing: Rebecca Tremble's Introduction

Here is the introduction to student writer Rebecca Tremble's first draft of her analysis paper for her marketing class:

> In our community, there are many ways a business can advertise, including hard-copy (newspaper), electronic (radio, e-mail, Web site). The small business, *Too Cool Clothing!*, which caters to female college students, decided to use every method possible to reach potential customers.
>
> As we read in our marketing textbook, advertising is more effective if (1) it is consistent, and (2) all parts of an advertising campaign work together. This analysis will examine the various types of advertising available to *Too Cool Clothing!*, categorize them, and show how they all would work together to help *Too Cool Clothing!* increase sales.

Note that Rebecca immediately lets her readers know that her main rhetorical strategies will be *division* (all the kinds of advertising) and *classification* (how they group together) to increase sales for the small business, *Too Cool Clothing!*

LO6
Revise your essay, and prepare a final draft

Revising: The Key to Effective Papers

As you learned in Chapter 8, once you have a first draft of a paper, you need to revise it, because it is impossible to say exactly what you want to in any first draft. If possible, set your draft aside for a day or longer, and then reread it.

Your instructor may provide feedback on your work and will most likely ask you and your classmates to help each other, by providing suggestions on each other's papers. There are several different ways to do this (your instructor will guide you), and there are some general questions he/she may ask you to respond to as you read your classmate's papers (see page 114).

Student Writing: Rebecca Tremble's Peer-Reviewed Draft

Several of student writer Tremble's classmates read and responded to her first draft. Here is part of that draft along with their comments and suggestions. What suggestions would you have made on this part of Rebecca's introduction?

This wording seems confusing to me. Maybe bullet points? They make it easier to show a list. Interesting plan; I can see where you're heading with this.	In our community, there are many ways a business can advertise, including hard-copy (newspaper), electronic (radio, e-mail, Web site). The small business *Too Cool Clothing!*, which caters to female college students, decided to use every method possible to reach potential customers. As we read in our marketing textbook, advertising is more effective if (1) it is consistent, and (2) if all parts of an advertising campaign work together. This analysis will examine the various types of advertising available to *Too Cool Clothing!*, categorize them, and show how they all would work together to help *Too Cool Clothing!* increase sales.

The important thing about getting feedback and comments on your analysis is that those comments represent *real readers* responding to your ideas. Take their suggestions and comments seriously.

Here is how student writer Tremble responded to readers' suggestions. One reader suggested that if Rebecca was going to list types of advertising, bullet points might make them easier to read. For her first paragraph, another reader wrote that he thought some of her wording was "confusing." It is hard to know what such a comment means (certainly Rebecca did not intend to write a "confusing" sentence), but after rereading her work, Rebecca changed both her first and second sentences:

A classmate thought the wording was confusing, so Rebecca revised it.

Rebecca used bullet points to make the items easier to read.

In our community, there are many ways a business can advertise. The small business *Too Cool Clothing!* decided to use hard-copy advertising, such as

- Newspaper
- Direct mail
- Posters and signs

It also used electronic ways to advertse, including

- Radio
- E-mail
- Web site
- Text-messaging

 ## Writing Style Tip: Using Bullet Points

Student writer Tremble got a comment from a classmate that said that he was confused and suggested using bullet points for listing parts of the analysis. In any analysis, you are dividing up your subject into its component parts, and then putting those parts into general categories (classifying them) to help show how all the parts work together. Often, if you put all those parts into a paragraph structure, it is difficult for readers to see and to understand what you mean.

For example, if you wanted to analyze a professional sports team, think of how a reader might respond to this paragraph:

An analysis of the New York Giants football team will focus on the elements that make up that team, including players, coaches, the weekly game plan, supporting staff on the field and in the office …

It probably is easier for readers to see these various aspects if you use bullets:

An analysis of the New York Giants football team will focus on the elements that make up that team, including

- Players
- Coaches
- The weekly game plan
- Supporting staff on the field
- Supporting staff in the office

(continued)

Such an approach also lets you classify general categories and then add more specific details:

- Offensive players
  - Quarterbacks
  - Running backs
  - Receivers
  - Tackles
  - Guards
- Defensive players
  - Linebackers
  - Defensive ends
  - Cornerbacks

Another way to list items is to use numbers and letters rather than bullets:

1. Offensive players
   a. Quarterbacks
   b. Running backs
   c. Receivers
   d. Tackles
   e. Guards
2. Defensive players
   a. Linebackers
   b. Defensive ends
   c. Cornerbacks

When you use numbers, you create kind of a "most important" (1) to least important (2, 3, etc.) design. There is nothing wrong with putting the aspects of your analysis into an order, especially if you will show how the players are the most important, the coaching is next important, and so on.

 ## Critical Thinking Activity: Questions to Ask before You Revise

Now you have a first draft of your analysis, and have reread it several times, and most likely, you also have received comments and suggestions from your classmates (and perhaps from your instructor, family members, or friends). You will recall from Chapter 8 that *revision* means to reconsider and to reenvision your text—not just to fix surface errors. So consider:

1. Did any of the suggestions I received say anything about me not achieving my *purpose?* Did I perhaps misunderstand or misrepresent the information and details my *audience* needed to understand my analysis?
2. Did any of the suggestions I received indicate that I might want to reorganize my paper? If so, what *organizational approach* might be more effective? (For more on organizational approaches, see pages 186–187).
3. Did anyone tell me that they did not understand or seem to have misunderstood the *thesis statement* of my analysis? How can I clarify it?
4. Did any of those suggestions ask for more *examples and details* to help readers see how all the parts of my subject functioned together? Are there places in the paper where I can show what I mean, rather than just tell about it?

Student writer Rebecca Tremble used the following checklist to "check off" what she had done and also to make some notes to herself on what she wanted to add or change, for her final draft.

Revision Checklist for Your Analysis	
As you think about writing the final draft of your paper, consider the parts of it that you want to make sure to include:	
Part of Your Paper	**Check √**
Title for your paper that gets your readers' attention	
Introduction with a clear thesis statement	
Supporting paragraphs, each with a topic sentence, evidence or examples, and a transition to the next paragraph (all information must relate to your analysis showing how all parts of your subject work together)	
Visual aids if they will help the readers understand your analysis	
Conclusion that summarizes your main points and restates your thesis about your analysis	

Student Writing: Rebecca Tremble's Final Draft

Here is student writer Rebecca Tremble's final draft of her analysis. As you see, she has added two visual aids. Do both illustrations help Rebecca's paper? Why or why not? Can you suggest more effective illustrations?

Tremble 1

Rebecca Tremble

Professor Carol Hammond

Marketing 114

15 Mar. 2011

Advertising Analysis: Working Together

There are many aspects to a successful business, and the goal for any business is to increase sales and therefore to increase profits. Even a brief business analysis demonstrates that all businesses want to provide exciting new products, that advertising and marketing are a critical part of increasing sales, that the business needs to plan and then put its plan into effect—all leading to success. This analysis centers on the small business *Too Cool Clothing!* and how all aspects of its advertising might work together to help increase sales. It seems clear that any effective advertising campaign must include all kinds of advertising methods (newspaper, radio, etc.) and they all must work together to create that effective campaign.

In any community, there are many ways for a business to advertise. The business *Too Cool Clothing!* decided to use hard-copy advertising, such as

- Newspaper
- Direct mail
- Posters and signs
- Door flyers

Tremble 2

It also decided to use electronic ways to advertise, including

- Radio
- E-mail
- Web site
- Text-messaging
- Blogging/Tweeting/Facebook

The key is to understand how all these various aspects or parts of an advertising plan can work together, collectively, to help *Too Cool Clothing!* increase sales (and thus profits).

Newspaper advertising is the most traditional kind of advertising. *Too Cool Clothing!* has two local venues: the community paper, *The Star-Citizen*, and the community college paper, the *Collegian*. Both venues need to work together, so advertisements run in one newspaper should also appear in the other.

Other print media (door flyers, mailers) also need to mirror the newspaper advertisements, and one way all print ads can "work together" is to use a common picture and theme (the same model making a "shh" gesture) on every advertisement it buys:

(continued)

Tremble 3

This photograph must appear in each print advertisement (and on the Web, too), so that when readers see it, they will associate it with the business, instantly.

In addition, the various kinds of print advertising connect to the advertising plan by referring to other print advertisements. For example, any discount coupon *Too Cool Clothing!* has printed in one of the papers, or mailed out or put on a door flyer, should say it can be *combined* with one other coupon, for an even larger discount. Radio advertisements also should refer to coupon combining.

Of course, *Too Cool Clothing!* cannot show its photo on the radio, but it can use the "Shh!" sound in its commercials. In addition, the company can use the photo on its Web page, and attach it to every e-mail advertisement *Too Cool Clothing!* sends out. The company also should use the same font, where possible, in e-mail and blog entries. The photograph should be on the business's Facebook page, of course.

Put another way, when the owners of *Too Cool Clothing!* analyze the company's advertising, they want to make sure that there is one thing that "connects" all of it together, so every advertisement functions as part of the company's complete strategy. Even with electronic advertisements, such as its radio spots, the "Shh!" part of *Too Cool Clothing!*'s marketing has to come through, as that is another way to connect all of its ads. In the end, all of the various kinds and types of advertising (newspaper, mailers, electronic) function together to create an overall effective advertising campaign.

Critical Thinking Activity: Questions to Ask as You Reflect on Your Writing

It is always a good idea to reflect on your writing, if only to think about what worked effectively and what you might improve and change the next time you face a similar writing situation. Your instructor may ask you to answer some or all of these questions in your journal:

1. How did you decide what topic to focus on?
2. How did you go about *dividing* and *classifying* the parts of your subject?
3. What kinds of invention/discovery activities did you do? What was the most helpful for your analysis? The least helpful? Why?
4. Did you try out different ways to organize your analysis?
5. What could your classmates do next time to make their comments and suggestions more useful to you?
6. What did you learn about your own writing process through the process of writing this analysis?
7. Did you use visual aids? If so, what did you learn about using them that will help you in future assignments? If you did not use visual aids, do you think if you had, they may have improved your analysis?
8. Did you procrastinate at starting your paper? What might you do differently next time?
9. What did you learn from writing this paper that will help you as you write other papers, especially analysis texts, in the future?

Readings That Analyze

The following readings are all analyses and will give you a sense of what an effective analysis essay looks like and how it functions.

Note: words highlighted **in blue** are terms used in the "Improve Your Vocabulary" activities that follow each reading.

Women Less Likely Than Men to Fake Soccer Injuries, Study Finds

Thomas H. Maugh II

Thomas H. Maugh II has been a science and medical writer for the Los Angeles Times *for over twenty years. In this article, he reports on a study of fake soccer (or football, as it is known in most of the world) injuries.*

time-honored: traditional; customary

albeit: even if; even though

disrupt: confuse; throw into disorder

denouncing: publicly declare something to be bad or wrong

simulation: pretending

eradicate: eliminate

scourge: widespread disease or affliction

writhing: squirming; wriggling

anguished: agonizing

apparent: seemingly obvious; easy to see

1   Faking injuries is a **time-honored**—**albeit** widely frowned-upon—way to slow down an athletic event, catch a breather or **disrupt** an opponent's rhythm. A new study issued Thursday hints that the practice may be somewhat testosterone-driven. Women soccer players, the study finds, are significantly less likely than men to fake an injury on the field, researchers from the Wake Forest University School of Medicine in Winston-Salem, N.C., reported.

2   "Injuries are common in women's soccer and seem to be on the rise at the international level," said Dr. Daryl A. Rosenbaum, an assistant professor of family and community medicine at Wake Forest. Faked injuries also seem to be on the rise, to the point that the International Federation of Assn. Football (FIFA), soccer's governing body, issued a directive calling for "the football family to unite in **denouncing** injury **simulation** and working to **eradicate** this **scourge** from the game." FIFA's concern may be justified, he said.

3   In 2010, Rosenbaum and his colleagues studied videotapes of international men's soccer matches and concluded that there were an average of 11.26 apparent injuries per match, in which players were **writhing** or rolling on the ground, grabbing a body part, yelling, having an **anguished** facial expression or hiding their face. They concluded that only 7.2% of the apparent injuries were "definite" injuries — that is, the player withdrew from the contest within five minutes or blood was apparent.

4   Now Rosenbaum's team has performed the same analysis for women's soccer. The researchers analyzed 47 televised games from two international women's tournaments. They reported in the journal Research in Sports Medicine that they observed only half as many **apparent** injuries as they previously saw in men's games, an average of 5.74 per game. And they concluded that 13.7% of those apparent injuries were definite injuries, twice the proportion

corroboration: to confirm something

as in men's soccer. As **corroboration** of their findings, they noted that they observed an average of six apparent injuries per match in the 2007 Women's World Cup, but that team physicians reported only 2.3 injuries per match.

5 The researchers speculated about possible causes for the higher apparent injury rate in the men's game. "Perhaps the higher visibility or financial stakes of the men's game creates greater incentives for **gamesmanship**," they wrote. "Another theory could be that the men's game may have greater frequency and force of physical contact as it involves larger, faster players.

gamesmanship: gaining improper advantage

contusions: bruises

6 Collisions could lead to initially painful injuries like **contusions** that do not require a player to withdraw, or more frequent contact situations could mean that there are more opportunities to try and influence the referee through simulation."

7 One piece of good news, they concluded: There was no evidence that injuries, either faked or real, affected the outcome of the games.

Questions for Discussion and Writing

1. If you play sports, have you ever faked an injury? Why?
2. What part of Maugh's analysis surprised you? Why?
3. Do you agree with the conclusion that females fake sports injuries less often than males?
4. How to you relate Maugh's note that "the men's game may have greater frequency and force of physical contact as it involves larger, faster players" (paragraph 5) to the data he provides on fake injuries by male players?

Improve Your Vocabulary

In your journal, use the highlighted and defined words from "Women Less Likely Than Men to Fake Soccer Injuries, Study Finds" in a sentence or in a paragraph.

Language Change
National Science Foundation

The National Science Foundation produces reports, including this excerpt from their special report on Language and Linguistics. Researchers who study linguistics focus on many things, including how humans learn language, and they also consider language variation and change. The National Science Foundation notes that

> *Language is common to all humans; we seem to be "hard-wired" for it. Many social scientists and philosophers say it's this ability to use language symbolically that makes us "human."*
>
> *This special report touches on nearly all of these areas by answering questions such as: How does language develop and change? Can the language apparatus be "seen" in the brain? Does it matter if a language disappears? What exactly is a dialect? How can sign language help us to understand languages in general?*

This section of the report focuses on language change. As you read this excerpt, think about your own language use and how it changes over time.

albeit: although

evolved: changed over time

1   In some ways, it is surprising that languages change. After all, they are passed down through the generations reliably enough for parents and children to communicate with each other. Yet linguists find that all languages change over time—**albeit** at different rates. For example, while Japanese has changed relatively little over 1,000 years, English **evolved** rapidly in just a few centuries. Many present-day speakers find Shakespeare's sixteenth century texts difficult and Chaucer's fourteenth century Canterbury Tales nearly impossible to read.

Why They Change

2   Languages change for a variety of reasons. Large-scale shifts often occur in response to social, economic and political pressures. History records many examples of language change fueled by invasions, colonization and migration. Even without these kinds of influences, a language can change dramatically if enough users alter the way they speak it.

drive: move

3   Frequently, the needs of speakers drive language change. New technologies, industries, products and experiences simply require new words. Plastic, cell phones and the Internet didn't exist in Shakespeare's time, for example. By using new and emerging terms, we all **drive** language change. But the unique way that individuals speak also fuels language change. That's because no two individuals use a language in exactly the same way. The vocabulary and phrases people use depend on where they live, their age, education level, social status and other factors. Through our interactions, we pick up new words and

integrate: become part of

sayings and **integrate** them into our speech. Teens and young adults for example, often use different words and phrases from their parents. Some of them spread through the population and slowly change the language.

No two individuals use a language in exactly the same way. The vocabulary and phrases people use are linked to where they live, their age, education level, social status and sometimes to their membership in a particular group or community.

Types of Change

aspects: parts of

4   Three main **aspects** of language change over time: vocabulary, sentence structure and pronunciations. Vocabulary can change quickly as new words are borrowed from other languages, or as words get combined or shortened. Some words are even created by mistake. As noted in the Linguistic Society of America's publication *Is English Changing?,* pea is one such example. Up until about 400 years ago, pease referred to either a single pea or many peas. At some point, people mistakenly assumed that the word pease was the plural form of pea, and a new word was born. While vocabulary can change quickly, sentence structure—the order of words in a sentence—changes more slowly. Yet it's clear that today's English speakers construct sentences very differently from Chaucer and Shakespeare's contemporaries. Changes in sound are somewhat harder to document, but at least as interesting. For example, during the so-called "Great Vowel Shift" 500 years ago, English speakers **modified** their vowel pronunciation dramatically. This shift represents the biggest difference between the pronunciations of so called Middle and Modern English.

modified: change

Agents of Change

internalize: make part of one's self

propagate: distribute

5   Before a language can change, speakers must adopt new words, sentence structures and sounds, spread them through the community and transmit them to the next generation. According to many linguists—including David Lightfoot, NSF assistant director for social, behavioral and economic sciences—children serve as agents for language change when, in the process of learning the language of previous generations, they **internalize** it differently and **propagate** a different variation of that language.

Questions for Discussion and Writing

1. What new or interesting information did you learn from this analysis?
2. What rhetorical strategies can you point to that are used in this analysis?
3. Paragraph 3 notes that "Plastic, cell phones and the Internet didn't exist in Shakespeare's time, for example." Can you think of words you now use that "didn't exist" when you were young?
4. In paragraph 3, this analysis claims, "By using new and emerging terms, we all drive language change." Do you agree? Can you provide examples of how your own language has changed over time?
5. Do you agree that there are three major categories of change (why, types, agents of change) as covered in this analysis?

Improve Your Vocabulary

Use the highlighted and defined words from "Language Change" in a sentence or in a paragraph.

The Truth About Lying

Judith Viorst

Judith Viorst has published fiction and nonfiction, both for adults and children. She is well known for her children's book about the death of a pet, The Tenth Good Thing About Barney. Do you see yourself or anyone you know in any of the situations she describes?

intrigues: interest in

intolerant: unaccepting

ultimate: final

1   I've been wanting to write on a subject that **intrigues** and challenges me: the subject of lying. I've found it very difficult to do. Everyone I've talked to has a quite intense and personal but often rather **intolerant** point of view about what we can—and can never—tell lies about. I've finally reached the conclusion that I can't present any **ultimate** conclusions, for too many people would promptly disagree. Instead, I'd like to present a series of moral puzzles, all concerned with lying. I'll tell you what I think about them. Do you agree?

Social Lies

brutish: animal-like; thug

incorruptible: perfect

2   Most of the people I've talked with say that they find social lying acceptable and necessary. They think it's the civilized way for folks to behave. Without these little white lies, they say, our relationships would be short and **brutish** and nasty. It's arrogant, they say, to insist on being so **incorruptible**

and so brave that you cause other people unnecessary embarrassment or pain by compulsively **assailing** them with your honesty. I basically agree. What about you?

assailing: forcing something on someone

3 Will you say to people, when it simply isn't true, "I like your new hairdo," "You're looking much better," "It's so nice to see you," "I had a wonderful time"?

4 Will you praise hideous presents and homely kids?

5 Will you decline invitations with "We're busy that night—so sorry we can't come," when the truth is you'd rather stay home than dine with the So-and-sos?

evasion: hiding

6 And even though, as I do, you may prefer the polite **evasion** of "You really cooked up a storm" instead of "The soup"—which tastes like warmed-over coffee—"is wonderful," will you, if you must, proclaim it wonderful?

7 There's one man I know who absolutely refuses to tell social lies. "I can't play that game," he says; "I'm simply not made that way." And his answer to the argument that saying nice things to someone doesn't cost anything is, "Yes, it does—it destroys your **credibility**." Now, he won't, **unsolicited**, offer his views on the painting you just bought, but you don't ask his frank opinion unless you want *frank*, and his silence at those moments when the rest of us liars are muttering, "Isn't it lovely?" is, for the most part, eloquent enough. My friend does not **indulge** in what he calls "flattery, false praise and **mellifluous** comments." When others tell fibs he will not go along. He says that social lying is lying, that little white lies are still lies. And he feels that telling lies is morally wrong. What about you?

credibility: believability

unsolicited: unasked for

indulge: give in to desire

mellifluous: sweet

Peace-Keeping Lies

8 Many people tell peace-keeping lies; lies designed to avoid irritation or argument; lies designed to shelter the liar from possible blame or pain; lies (or so it is rationalized) designed to keep trouble at bay without hurting anyone.

9 I tell these lies at times, and yet I always feel they're wrong. I understand why we tell them, but still they feel wrong. And whenever I lie so that someone won't disapprove of me or think less of me or holler at me, I feel I'm a bit of a coward, I feel I'm dodging responsibility, I feel … guilty. What about you?

10 Do you, when you're late for a date because you overslept, say that you're late because you got caught in a traffic jam?

11 Do you, when you forget to call a friend, say that you called several times but the line was busy?

12 Do you, when you didn't remember that it was your father's birthday, say that his present must be delayed in the mail?

13 And when you're planning a weekend in New York City and you're not in the mood to visit your mother, who lives there, do you conceal—with a lie, if you must—the fact that you'll be in New York? Or do you have the courage—or is it the cruelty?—to say, "I'll be in New York, but sorry—I don't plan on seeing you"?

(continued)

14 (Dave and his wife Elaine have two quite different points of view on this very subject. He calls her a coward. She says she's being wise. He says she must assert her right to visit New York sometimes and not see her mother. To which she always patiently replies: "Why should we have useless fights? My mother's too old to change. We get along much better when I lie to her.")

15 Finally, do you keep the peace by telling your husband lies on the subject of money? Do you reduce what you really paid for your shoes? And in general do you find yourself ready, willing and able to lie to him when you make absurd mistakes or lose or break things?

16 "I used to have a romantic idea that part of intimacy was confessing every dumb thing that you did to your husband. But after a couple of years of that," says Laura, "have I changed my mind!"

17 And having changed her mind, she finds herself telling peace-keeping lies. And yes, I tell them too. What about you?

Protective Lies

18 Protective lies are lies folks tell—often quite serious lies—because they're convinced that the truth would be too damaging. They lie because they feel there are certain human values that supersede the wrong of having lied. They lie, not for personal gain, but because they believe it's for the good of the person they're lying to. They lie to those they love, to those who trust them most of all, on the grounds that breaking this trust is justified.

19 They may lie to their children on money or marital matters.

20 They may lie to the dying about the state of their health.

21 They may lie about adultery, and not—or so they insist—to save their own hide, but to save the heart and the pride of the men they are married to.

22 They may lie to their closest friend because the truth about her talents or son or **psyche** would be—or so they insist—utterly devastating.

23 I sometimes tell such lies, but I'm aware that it's quite **presumptuous** to claim I know what's best for others to know. That's called playing God. That's called manipulation and control. And we never can be sure, once we start to juggle lies, just where they'll land, exactly where they'll roll.

24 And furthermore, we may find ourselves lying in order to back up the lies that are backing up the lie we initially told.

25 And furthermore—let's be honest—if conditions were reversed, we certainly wouldn't want anyone lying to us.

26 Yet, having said all that, I still believe that there are times when protective lies must nonetheless be told. What about you?

27 If your Dad had a very bad heart and you had to tell him some bad family news, which would you choose: to tell him the truth or lie?

28 If your former husband failed to send his monthly child-support check and in other ways behaved like a total rat, would you allow your children—who believed he was simply wonderful—to continue to believe that he was wonderful?

psyche: mental health

presumptuous: assumes something without being asked to do so

29 If your dearly beloved brother selected a wife whom you deeply disliked, would you reveal your feelings or would you fake it?

30 And if you were asked, after making love, "And how was that for you?" would you reply, if it wasn't too good, "Not too good"?

31 Now, some would call a sex lie unimportant, little more than social lying, a simple act of courtesy that makes all human intercourse run smoothly. And some would say all sex lies are bad news and unacceptably protective. Because, says Ruth, "a man with an ego that fragile doesn't need your lies—he needs a psychiatrist." Still others feel that sex lies are indeed protective lies, more serious than simple social lying, and yet at times they tell them on the grounds that when it comes to matters sexual, everybody's ego is somewhat fragile.

dissemble: not telling the whole truth

32 "If most of the time things go well in sex," says Sue, "I think you're allowed to **dissemble** when they don't. I can't believe it's good to say, 'Last night was four stars, darling, but tonight's performance rates only a half.'"

33 I'm inclined to agree with Sue. What about you?

Trust-Keeping Lies

34 Another group of lies are trust-keeping lies, lies that involve triangulation, with *A* (that's you) telling lies to *B* on behalf of *C* (whose trust you'd promised to keep). Most people concede that once you've agreed not to betray a friend's confidence, you can't betray it, even if you must lie. But I've talked with people who don't want you telling them anything that they might be called on to lie about.

35 "I don't tell lies for myself," says Fran, "and I don't want to have to tell them for other people." Which means, she agrees, that if her best friend is having an affair, she absolutely doesn't want to know about it.

36 "Are you saying," her best friend asks, "that if I went off with a lover and I asked you to tell my husband I'd been with you, that you wouldn't lie for me, that you'd betray me?"

37 Fran is very pained but very adamant. "I wouldn't want to betray you, so … don't ask me."

38 Fran's best friend is shocked. What about you?

39 Do you believe you can have close friends if you're not prepared to receive their deepest secrets?

40 Do you believe you must always lie for your friends?

41 Do you believe, if your friend tells a secret that turns out to be quite immoral or illegal, that once you've promised to keep it, you must keep it?

Watergate: apartment in Washington, D. C. where a burglary took place during the Nixon presidency; that crime helped lead to President Nixon's resignation

42 And what if your friend were your boss—if you were perhaps one of the President's men—would you betray or lie for him over, say, Watergate?

43 As you can see, these issues get terribly sticky.

44 It's my belief that once we've promised to keep a trust, we must tell lies to keep it. I also believe that we can't tell **Watergate** lies. And if these two statements

(continued)

strike you as quite contradictory, you're right—they're quite contradictory. But for now they're the best I can do. What about you?

45   Some say that truth will come out and thus you might as well tell the truth. Some say you can't regain the trust that lies lose. Some say that even though the truth may never be revealed, our lies **pervert** and damage our relationships. Some say … well, here's what some of them have to say.

pervert: modify in a negative manner

46   "I'm a coward," says Grace, "about telling close people important, difficult truths. I find that I'm unable to carry it off. And so if something is bothering me, it keeps building up inside till I end up just not seeing them any more."

47   "I lie to my husband on sexual things, but I'm furious," says Joyce, "that he's too insensitive to know I'm lying."

48   "I suffer most from the misconception that children can't take the truth," says Emily. "But I'm starting to see that what's harder and more damaging for them is being told lies, is *not* being told the truth."

49   "I'm afraid," says Joan, "that we often wind up feeling a bit of contempt for the people we lie to."

50   And then there are those who have no talent for lying.

51   "Over the years, I tried to lie," a friend of mine explained, "but I always got found out and I always got punished. I guess I gave myself away because I feel guilty about any kind of lying. It looks as if I'm stuck with telling the truth."

52   For those of us, however, who are good at telling lies, for those of us who lie and don't get caught, the question of whether or not to lie can be a hard and serious moral problem. I liked the remark of a friend of mine who said, "I'm willing to lie. But just as a last resort—the truth's always better."

53   "Because," he explained, "though others may completely accept the lie I'm telling, I don't."

54   I tend to feel that way too.

55   What about you?

Questions for Discussion and Writing

1. Did Viorst's title get your attention? Why?
2. Do any of Viorst's situations seem true and accurate to you? Which ones?
3. At the end of her first paragraph, Viorst asks, "Do you agree?" with her conclusions. Do you?
4. What did you learn from Viorst's essay that was new or surprising?
5. How effective is Viorst's division and classification of the kinds of lies (social, peace-keeping, etc.)? Can you think of others that could be added?

Improve Your Vocabulary

Use the highlighted and defined words from "The Truth About Lying" in a sentence or in a paragraph.

MyWritingLab™ For support in meeting this chapter's objectives, log in to www.mywritinglab.com and select **Essay Development—Division/ Classification.**

Chapter 12

Writing to Explain Why
Using Cause and Effect

Learning Objectives

In this chapter, you will learn to:

LO1 Consider the writer's situation, and determine your purpose and audience

LO2 Use the rhetorical strategy of *cause* and *effect* to explain something

LO3 Use invention and discovery strategies to come up with ideas and details

LO4 Write a thesis statement that states the point of your essay

LO5 Organize and write your first draft

LO6 Revise your essay, and prepare a final draft

206

What happens at a state college or university when state funding for education decreases? Most likely tuition goes up. Put another way, at least one *cause* of tuition increases is a drop in state support for education.

One useful way to think of **cause** and **effect** relationships is to remember the "cause" in the word "because." That explains why something happened:

- Because state aid to education dropped, tuition increased.
- Because Harry missed his last shot, we lost the basketball game.
- Because I studied hard last weekend, I did well on the test.
- Because I worked yesterday, I don't have to work this Saturday.

Another way to think of cause and effect is that when something happens *(effect)*, there are reasons that it happened: those reasons are the *causes* of that *effect*.

Consider this: Do you agree with all of the preceding statements? You probably thought, yes, you do agree with them, but there is a problem: it is not easy to prove *cause and effect*, and any one *effect* often has many *causes*, many reasons why. We usually think of cause and effect sequentially: and it is pretty simple and obvious to say that when state funding for education decreased, that caused tuition to increase. But, consider:

- **One effect might have multiple causes.** Tuition can increase for many reasons, not just because state funding dropped (inflation, high enrollment means the college needs more teachers, utility costs, and so on). Or, consider the earlier example of Harry: is Harry the only reason the team lost the game? Probably not—there can be any number of reasons, including that many other players probably missed shots, too.
- **One cause might have multiple effects.** Think about the third example: you studied hard so you did well on a test. Good for you! But another effect might be that now, you will study hard for *every* test, right? Another effect of that hard studying might be that your GPA will improve, and you will be awarded a scholarship next semester.

Our point is, of course, that cause and effect is rarely as simple as one thing that causes one effect: more often than not, there are multiple causes that cause multiple effects.

The ability to write an effective cause and effect essay will be important to you not only in this class, but in your other classes and once you have graduated from college. Most often, you will use cause and effect to *explain* something. In a history or political science class, for example, you may write about the causes of a military conflict. As a parent, you may write about the causes of problems in your child's school or about the effects of increased class size. As an employee, you may write a memo about the effects of changing a procedure. *Cause and effect* is a common rhetorical strategy.

Everyday Writing Activity: Analyzing Cause and Effect Statements

With a classmate, consider each of the statements on page 207. Could there be more than one cause for each of the effect(s)? In your journal, list the possibilities you think of. We have done the second one for you as an example:

- Be<u>cause</u> Harry missed his last shot, we lost the basketball game.
  - But there are other possible reasons your team lost the game: It could also be be<u>cause</u>
    - Everyone else missed shots.
    - The other team outplayed us.
    - The other team was just better than we were.
    - Joe got hurt in the first quarter and didn't play after that.
    - Our coach made some bad decisions.
    - The referees didn't call enough fouls on the other team.
- Be<u>cause</u> I studied hard last weekend, I did well on the test.
  - Other reasons might include: _____
- Be<u>cause</u> I worked yesterday, I don't have to work this Saturday.
  - Other reasons might include: _____

Your instructor may ask you to share your responses with the rest of the class.

LO1 Consider the writer's situation, and determine your purpose and audience	# The Writer's Situation

Was that difficult, trying to explain why something happened? Did you come up with some reasons you did not think of to start with?

Any time you try to explain why something happened (what causes an effect), the first step is to consider your **purpose:** to explain why one or more things or events cause some effect or several effects. Anything that does not relate to this purpose does not belong in your paper. Therefore, defining and describing the effect is critical: unless readers understand the effect (or multiple effects) none of the causes or reasons you suggest will make any sense (for more on the rhetorical strategies of *definition* and *description*, see Chapter 5).

As you consider what your purpose is, you also need to think about your **audience:** what do they already know about the cause(s) and effect(s) you are focusing on? How much detail or other information would help them understand those causes and effects?

LO2

Use the rhetorical strategy of *cause* and *effect* to explain something

Explaining Why Using Cause and Effect

This activity does what we teachers often like to do: "complicate the situation." To help you think about cause and effect relationships, consider whether one thing really does in fact cause another (and maybe even yet other effects), and whether there can be many causes to create one effect. We usually think of cause and effect as one event causing another, which causes another, and so on in a causal chain:

Causal Chain

| Mario found a $20 bill. | → | Mario spent it on candy. | → | Mario ate all the candy. | → | Mario got really sick. |

Cause and effect is rarely this simple, of course. Consider any event, for example: how many causes might there be? For example, a large tsunami caused many people to perish. The tsunami seems to be the clear *cause* for the *effect* (the loss of life), but might there be other causes?

One Effect, Many Causes

Cause: An earthquake caused the tsunami; that was the real cause of the large loss of life.

Cause: Poor planning by the government delayed rescue efforts and contributed to the loss of life.

Effect: Many people lost their lives.

Cause: Many countries promised aid but did not deliver. This is at least partly responsible for the loss of life.

Cause: Government and private rescue agencies didn't collaborate, which contributed to the loss of life.

Cause: Medical facilities were destroyed by the tsunami, so that is another reason for the loss of life.

While an earthquake might have been the main culprit, there are other possible, additional reasons why people might lose their lives following a tsunami.

Likewise, one *cause* may have multiple *effects*:

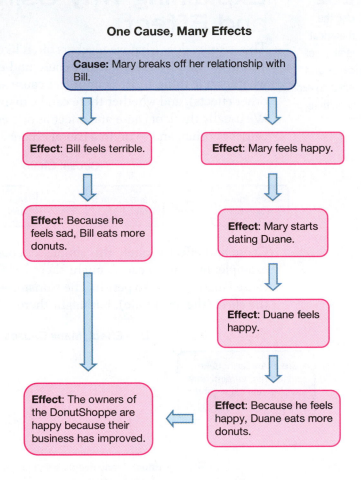

One Cause, Many Effects

Cause: Mary breaks off her relationship with Bill.

Effect: Bill feels terrible.

Effect: Mary feels happy.

Effect: Because he feels sad, Bill eats more donuts.

Effect: Mary starts dating Duane.

Effect: Duane feels happy.

Effect: The owners of the DonutShoppe are happy because their business has improved.

Effect: Because he feels happy, Duane eats more donuts.

Because showing cause and effect can be complex, the first rule of thinking about any cause and effect connection is to really examine what the *effect* is: how would you define or describe or show it? (Remember that *definition* and *description* are rhetorical strategies—see Chapter 5.)

When you have determined the effect you want to focus on, and then have determined some of the possible causes of that effect, your next step is to consider how you might demonstrate that those causes really do in fact cause the effect you are writing about.

Five Surprising Reasons You're Gaining Weight

Kathleen Zelman, MPH, RD, LD

Read the following excerpt from WebMD, a health Web site, on how people might gain weight even though they exercise. Kathleen Zelman is the director of nutrition for WebMD, where she oversees diet, nutrition, and food information. Think about whether the causes listed and explained here really cause the effect of gaining weight. Do you agree with all of Zelman's reasons for weight gain?

Does the title of this article make you want to read it? Why?

A list of all of the "usual suspects" that explain why we gain weight. Do you agree with this statement?

For you as a reader, would it have helped if writer Zelman did explain what she meant by "weight gain"? Or could Zelman assume that her readers will more or less know what the term means? Good question!

Note there are several *causes* suggested for the one *effect* of gaining weight.

Have you heard of this reason? Do you agree that this is a possibility?

Do you eat more when you're tired? Do you sleep this much? Have you heard of this reason for gaining weight?

Extra calories may not be the only cause of weight gain

1   It's no mystery that a diet full of fried foods, giant portions, decadent desserts, alcohol, and sugary soft drinks will lead to weight gain. And there's little question why the pounds pile up when you take in more calories than you burn in physical activity. But how do you explain weight gain when your lifestyle includes regular exercise and a healthy diet that is controlled in calories? Gaining weight is absolutely maddening, especially when you really don't understand why the needle on the scale keeps going up.

2   Several things should be considered if you are gaining weight while watching calories and being physically active. More than likely, it's a variety of things working together that have resulted in the weight gain.

3   "Weight gain is so complicated; there are so many factors that can impact your weight. It is more likely a combination of things more than just one factor," explains Michelle May, MD, author of *Am I Hungry? What to Do When Diets Don't Work.*

4   Here are five factors that can cause the scale to creep up when you least expect it.

1. You Might Be Gaining Weight Because of Lack of Sleep

5   The body functions best when well rested. "When you don't get enough sleep, your body experiences physiological stress and, biochemically, you store fat more efficiently," says May.

6   When you're tired, you also don't handle stress as well, so you may reach for food as a coping mechanism. Further, you may be taking in extra calories from late-night snacking. Some people think eating might help them get back to sleep, but all it really does is add more calories to their daily total.

7   Symptoms that you may not be getting enough rest include fatigue, low energy levels, nodding off easily, and feeling irritable.

8   Strive to get eight hours of sleep each night.

9   "Add about 15 minutes to your bedtime and see how you feel," suggests May. "Continue to experiment with additional 15-minute increments until you find the … amount of sleep that is right for you."

(continued)

Do you eat more when you're stressed?

If her title had been "Five Surprising Reasons You're Gaining a LOT of Weight," what else might she have included in this paper?

10   When you develop good sleeping rituals and get regular exercise, you sleep better, she adds.

2. You May Be Gaining Weight Because of Stress

11   We live in a society that demands we do more, be more, and achieve more. Stress moves us forward and helps cope with life's demands, but it also affects our mood and emotions.

12   "Stress response, whether it is 'fight-or-flight,' juggling too many responsibilities, or coping with financial pressures, triggers a biochemical process where our bodies go into survival mode," explains May. "Our bodies store fuel, slow down metabolism, and dump out chemicals [cortisol, leptin, and other hormones] which are more likely to cause … obesity in the abdominal region."

13   Many people reach for food to help ease the stress. But, of course, this doesn't work in the long run.

14   "Food is a temporary fix because it does not deal with the real stressors that must be addressed in order to reduce the trigger for eating and fix the problem," says May.

15   Susan Bowerman, MS, RD, assistant director of the UCLA Center for Human Nutrition, says stress eaters tend to prefer high-carbohydrate foods because these foods trigger an increase in the brain chemical serotonin, which has a calming effect. "It is almost like self-medicating," she says. "Many people binge on starchy foods to make themselves feel better."

16   Both May and Bowerman recommend relaxation techniques as well as exercise, which also burns calories and provides other health benefits.…

Questions for Discussion and Writing

1. Did Zelman make an effective cause and effect connection? Point out her most effective example.
2. Do you agree with Zelman's reasons for why people gain weight? Why?
3. What was the most surprising or interesting piece of information in this essay?
4. The writer does not define "weight gain" in any detail. Does that hurt the effectiveness of the essay?
5. Several times in the essay, you read about advice for not gaining weight. Do you think that such causes (like getting more sleep) will really have the desired effect (not gaining weight)?

Everyday Writing Activity: Adding Your Own Reasons

This WebMD essay outlines five reasons for weight gain—we've shown only the first two. What other causes might there be? In your journal, describe at least three other possible causes, as if you were continuing the essay:

1. You may be gaining weight because _____

2. You may be gaining weight because _____

3. You may be gaining weight because _____

Your instructor may ask you to share your responses with the rest of the class.

WRITING ASSIGNMENTS

All of the following writing assignment options ask you to write about a cause and effect relationship: why and how one or more things cause something to happen.

Writing Assignment One: Explaining Why a Relationship "Works"

For this assignment, assume that in your psychology class you are assigned to write a paper explaining why a relationship "works." You can focus on

- **General relationships:** why does a particular friendship work? This could be a friendship you are involved with, or one you have observed.
- **Parental relationships:** why does your parent's (or someone else's) marriage work?
- **Business relationships:** why does a particular salesperson/customer relationship work?

Stay away from writing about intimate relationships, as they are too private.

In any of these assignments, of course, you will have to define what you mean by "work" as you explain how a relationship functions.

Writing Assignment Two: Explaining What Makes a Good Employee

For this assignment, write an essay explaining what makes a good employee. Think about people you know: what makes them good employees for the company they work for? Especially consider your own immediate relatives: if your mom or dad or brother or sister or cousin has a job, what makes them good employees? What characteristics would you choose to focus on? How would you define those characteristics and qualities? What examples would you provide to show what you mean?

As you think about the qualities of a good employee, also be sure to explain *why* those qualities are important to a business. For example, you may write that a good employee is one who is

- **Punctual.** What does that mean, and why is being punctual important to a business?

- **Courteous.** What does that term mean, and why is being courteous a valuable quality for an employee?
- **Able to work well with others.** How would you define this quality, and why is it important to any business?
- **Honest.** How might you define this term, and why is it important for a business to have honest employees?

Writing Assignment Three: Explaining Good School Performance

In your Academic Success class, you are asked to construct a paper that explains the cause and effect relationship between study habits and classroom success: the reasons some students succeed and others do not.

To write this paper effectively, you will have to describe what "study habits" are as well as to define what "classroom success" means. You might look at study habits in a general way, considering

- Planning when to study (and where, and what, and with whom).
- How students study (do they read and watch TV, text someone at the same time, do they interact with the text etc.? (See Chapter 2 for more information on actively reading a text.)
- Whether students study differently for different subjects.
- Whether or not students participate in study groups.
- Time of day or night.
- Background noise; food; whether roommates are around; and so on.

Is "classroom success" just getting a good grade, or does it mean something else? Could it also mean that the student really knows the material (and how could you determine this)? Being actively involved in classroom discussions? Being able to explain concepts to another student?

Optional Multi-Modal Assignment: Blogging

Assume you are given writing assignment three, which asks that you define/describe a successful college student, and then explain the reasons behind that success.

Construct a blog on which your classmates can share their "how to succeed in college" advice, and also respond to the suggestions and ideas that others post there.

Critical Thinking: Questions to Ask before You Start

If you spend some time now considering the assignment you have been asked to construct, and to do some planning about how you will work at that assignment, your overall task will be easier. So answer these questions in your journal:

1. Your *purpose* in writing is to explain the cause(s) of some effect(s): why one thing causes another. What information will you need to supply about the (a) effect or effects or (b) cause or causes to really show your readers that one or more causes do in fact cause the effect or effects?
2. How would you describe the *audience* for this paper?
3. When someone tells you about a cause and effect situation, what kinds of *details and examples* and *visual aids* are the most useful to you, to understand what they mean? How might answering that question help you as you write your own paper?
4. Consider what *research* you might conduct to help you explain the cause and effect relationship you will write about. Who might you talk with? What kinds of observations can you make, personally? Are there books or articles that could help provide you with evidence for your cause and effect assertions?

LO3

Use invention and discovery strategies to come up with ideas and details

Invention and Discovery Activities

A good way to get started on any writing assignment is to use **invention/discovery activities**—small pieces of writing that get some of your ideas onto paper. Here are a number of ways you can help yourself (and your paper) by getting started with discovery activities, including brainstorming, freewriting, listing, clustering, and others. (For more details on invention/discovery activities, see pages 80–88.)

Student Writing: Shannon Owens's Cluster Diagram

Shannon Owens was assigned a cause and effect paper for her Communication class that asked her to examine the causes behind this statement:

> Academically, female college students are better than male college students.

Shannon decided to sketch a small diagram that might illustrate some of what she saw as the causes behind the effect.

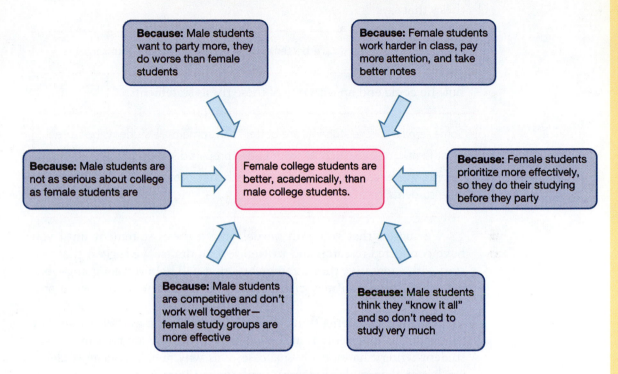

Everyday Writing Activity: Clustering

In your journal, create a cluster diagram to show how one event might cause another. Consider "sports teams":

Our [team] will win more games this year because_____ .

Or consider something more personal:

I will do better in school this year because_____ .

Your instructor may want you to share your cluster diagram with the class.

LO4

Write a thesis statement that states the point of your essay

Writing a Thesis for Your Cause and Effect Paper

In much of your writing, you really will not know how you will end up until you get some drafting and revision done. For student writer Shannon Owens, until she conducts research and gets some of what she learns as well as her own ideas onto paper, she will not know what her final thesis or point is. At this stage, Shannon could easily end up with a thesis that says

> Female college students are better students than their male counterparts.

But she could end up with one of these thesis statements:

> Some female college students are better than some male students because …
>
> Most female college students seem better prepared in class because …
>
> Overall, my female classmates are always better prepared for class than the male students, because …

We suggest that you plan on delaying a thesis statement until you have conducted research and written several drafts. We suggest that you start with a tentative thesis statement—that will help you get going—but understand that you may change your point of view as you write and revise.

Sometimes, students think their **topic** is the same as their thesis, but they really are different. Your **topic** is the subject you are focusing on (in student writer Shannon Owens' case, it is why female college students are better than male students), while your **thesis** is what you want to focus on, about that topic (based on what she learns from her research, Shannon may want to suggest that "most of my female classmates are better students than my male classmates, for several reasons").

LO5
Organize and write your first draft

Organizing and Writing Your First Draft

Now you have some ideas on paper in the form of brainstorming or freewriting, or perhaps you constructed a cluster diagram showing how your ideas relate to one another, or perhaps you have a few pages listing definitions of your topic. So, where do you go from here? How can you take what you have so far and start to organize it into an effective cause and effect paper?

Most often in a cause and effect paper, you will want to describe the effect first. That way, readers can better understand how the reasons (causes) you provide for the effect do in fact cause it. Of course, you can reverse this approach and list one reason, then another, then another, and so on, leading up to the effect. But this organizational approach assumes that readers can follow along with you and remember all the causes. So, for most cause and effect papers, you will use a linear organizational approach, where you define and explain the effect first, followed by explanations of how each cause contributes to that effect.

Here is an example of this approach, which essentially is a "here is the effect" and then "here is one cause" and then "here is another cause" and then "here is another cause" organization:

Organizational Plan for a Cause and Effect Essay

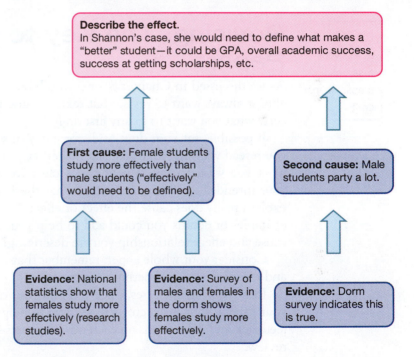

Describe the effect.
In Shannon's case, she would need to define what makes a "better" student—it could be GPA, overall academic success, success at getting scholarships, etc.

First cause: Female students study more effectively than male students ("effectively" would need to be defined).

Second cause: Male students party a lot.

Evidence: National statistics show that females study more effectively (research studies).

Evidence: Survey of males and females in the dorm shows females study more effectively.

Evidence: Dorm survey indicates this is true.

Student Example: Shannon's Introduction

Here is the introduction to student writer Shannon Owens' first draft of her paper that outlines some of her ideas about why female students are better than their male counterparts:

Just in looking around in my college classes, it becomes obvious that female students always seem to be better prepared and ready for class. They have done the reading. They have written the papers. They have

(continued)

done the homework assignments. And in asking them about their college work, they seem to get really good grades, perhaps better grades than my male classmates. I wonder why this is? So first, I will define what I think makes a "better student" and then will explain the reasons why female students, generally, are better students than the male students are.

Note that Owens immediately lets her readers know that her main rhetorical strategies will be *definition* followed by *cause and effect*.

<table>
<tr><td>

LO6

Revise your essay, and prepare a final draft

</td><td>

Revising: The Key to Effective Papers

As we discussed in Chapter 8, once you have a first draft of a paper, you almost always want to revise that text, because it is impossible to say exactly what you want to in any first draft.

</td></tr>
</table>

If possible, set your draft aside for a day or so, and then reread it. As you reread your first draft, consider whether you really say, in your thesis, what you want to say. Is your thesis clear to any and all readers? Will your intended audience understand that thesis and how each cause you explain really does cause the effect or effects? Can you think of any more examples or details you could add to help your audience understand the cause and effect relationship you are describing?

Consider your whole paper: remember that revising means rethinking and reconsidering and perhaps reorganizing.

In most writing classes, once you and your classmates have a draft of your papers, your instructor will ask you to help each other by providing feedback and suggestions on each other's papers—this is often called peer review.

There are several different approaches to do this; your instructor will guide you. (For more on effective responding, see Chapter 8. For more on what *to do* with the comments and suggestions that you receive, see the following sections.)

Student Writing: Peer-Reviewed Draft

Several of student writer Owens' classmates read and responded to her first draft. Here is part of her draft along with their comments and suggestions. What suggestions would you have made on her work?

I don't like the "looking around" here—awkward.

"In asking" seems awkward.

I'd put your "plan" differently—some teachers don't like students to say I'll do this, then I'll do that ... Also, do you want to use "I"?

I like this list—it's helpful.

Is a good student smarter than a bad student?

Just in looking around in my college classes, female students always seem to be better prepared and ready for class. They have done the reading. They have written the papers. They have done the homework assignments. And in asking them about their college work, they seem to get really good grades, perhaps better grades than my male classmates. I wonder why this is? So first, I will define what I think makes a "better student" and then will explain the reasons why female students, generally, are better students than the male students are.

What makes for a good student? I think there are several important parts. Good students

1. Attend class
2. Do their homework
3. Are prepared for class
4. Aren't afraid to ask questions when they have some
5. Get their work done on time
6. Follow directions for assignments
7. Do their work before they party

The important thing about getting feedback and comments on your cause and effect paper is those comments represent *real readers* responding to your ideas. Take their suggestions and comments seriously.

Here is how student writer Owens responded to a reader's suggestions: for her first paragraph, a reader wrote that he or she didn't like the "looking around" first line. Here is Shannon's revised section:

Shannon deleted "looking around."

She replaced the awkward "in asking."

Shannon changed the wording of her plan but kept "I" and "we" since her instructor didn't mind personal pronouns.

When I consider the students in my college classes, female students always seem to be better prepared and ready for class. They have done the reading. They have written the papers. They have done the homework assignments. When I ask my female classmates about their college work, they tell me that they get really good grades, perhaps better grades than my male classmates. I wonder why this is? There are many qualities that make for a "better student" and once we have a solid definition, we can consider why female students are—overall—better than male students.

 ## Writing Style Tip: Awkward Sentence Construction

Student writer Owens got a comment from a classmate that said that he or she didn't "like" the way she started: Shannon's first draft said "Just in looking around in my college classes."

Shannon reread that section of her work and saw that it *did* sound awkward—but what does that mean? "Awkward" is one of those comments that writers sometimes get without any explanation. We think that "awkward" means that there is something odd or out of place for the readers, even if they do not tell the writer exactly what it means or how to fix it.

One way to work at changing your sentences when a peer reviewer or teacher notes that it is awkward is to try out different ways to say the same thing. Shannon might write that

> When I listened to my classmates, it was clear that female students had better answers than the male students …
>
> When I read their papers, it was obvious that papers from female students were better …

As she wrote what she wanted to say in these other ways, Shannon realized that "looking around" just did not say what she wanted to say, and she finally decided to write,

> When I consider the students in my college classes …

Note how "consider" describes things more effectively, because now Shannon can "consider" who seems prepared, who asks questions, who has answers, and so on—all the aspects she might consider as to what makes a better student.

Critical Thinking Questions to Ask before You Revise

Now you have a first draft of your cause and effect paper and have reread it several times, and most likely, you also have received suggestions from your classmates (and perhaps from your instructor, family members, or friends). You will recall from Chapter 8 that *revision* means to reconsider and to reenvision your text—not to just fix surface errors. So consider:

1. Did anyone indicate that they did not understand the *effect* I was defining and/or describing?

2. Did any of the suggestions I received say anything about me not achieving my *purpose?* Did I perhaps misunderstand what information and details my *audience* needed to show these causes really cause the effect?
3. Did anyone tell me that they did not understand or seem to have misunderstood my *thesis statement?* How can I clarify it?
4. Did any of those suggestions ask for more *examples and details* to help readers see the cause and effect relationship? Are there places in the paper where I can "show" what I mean, rather than just "tell" about it?

Use this checklist to see whether your revised paper is finally done or whether you need to make further changes before printing a final draft.

Revision Checklist for Your Cause and Effect Paper	
Part of Your Paper	**Check √**
Title for your paper that gets your readers' attention	
Introduction with a clear thesis statement	
Supporting paragraphs, each with a topic sentence, supporting evidence or examples, and a transition to the next paragraph (all information must relate to showing how the causes you discuss really do cause the effect(s) you are focusing on)	
Visual aids if they will help the purpose of your cause and effect paper	
Conclusion that summarizes your main points and restates your thesis about the cause and effect relationship	

Student Writing: Shannon Owens' Final Draft

Here is student writer Shannon Owens' final draft of her cause/effect paper. As you see, she has added what she learned from a survey she conducted. (For more on surveys, see Chapter 15) Does that information help Shannon's paper? Why or why not?

Shannon Owens

Dr. Michael Vincent

ENG 090

15 Mar. 2011

Female Students Are Better than Male Students: Why?

When I consider my college classmates, female students always seem to be better prepared and ready for class. They have done the reading. They have written the papers. They have done the homework assignments. When I ask my female classmates about their college work, they tell me that they get really good grades, perhaps better grades than my male classmates. I wonder if this is true and if it is, why? There are many qualities that make for a "better student" and once we have a solid definition, we can consider why female students are—overall—better than male students.

What makes for a good student? I think there are several important parts. Good students

1. Attend class
2. Do their homework
3. Are prepared for class
4. Aren't afraid to ask questions when they have some
5. Get their work done on time
6. Follow directions for assignments
7. Do their work before they party

Of course, none of those reasons mean that females are better than male students, because *all students* can do all of those things. But why are female students more successful in college? There seem to be two main reasons: good grades and graduation rates, and hard work. This essay discusses these reasons.

For college students, success has a pretty basic definition: students need to pass their classes with good grades and then graduate. In a survey in my WRT 101 class, I asked everyone what their GPA is and learned that female students had, on average, higher GPAs than the male students in that class did.

Owens 2

One reason for this seems to be that women pay more attention in class and take better notes. One female student who I surveyed said that she listens carefully to what the teacher says and takes a lot of notes for future use, while a male student reported that he doesn't "really pay attention" in any of his classes. Nor does he take many notes, he admitted. The female student's current GPA is 3.4, while the male's GPA is 2.72.

Of course, my survey was small (22 students) but that information was validated by data from the U.S. Department of Education, showing "that men, whatever their race or socioeconomic group, are less likely than women to get bachelor's degrees—and among those who do, fewer complete their degrees in four or five years. Men also get worse grades than women" (Lewin). Both of those things are factors in a student's success, so both indicate that women are better students than men because of grades and their graduation rates.

In the survey I also asked some of my classmates, both male and female, how much they studied: how hard did they work at their classes? A female student reported that she averages about three hours every day, reading and studying, and if she has an upcoming test or a paper to write, she skips weekend parties thrown by her friends. Another female student says she studies about two hours every day and more on the weekends and admits she does not socialize much.

By contrast, a male student says he only studies "maybe" one hour per day, and his roommate claims he "never or hardly ever reads the book." Both male students also said they would rather hang out with their friends than study. Tamara Lewin confirmed this, noting that in national studies, "college men reported that they studied less and socialized more than their female classmates." Both of these reasons—studying more and partying less—are reasons for students to be successful, and men clearly are less successful as college students than female students are.

(continued)

Owens 3

Both my own research and Lewin's research, therefore, come to the same conclusion: as students, men are less successful than women because of lower grades and longer graduation times, as well as because they study less and party more. I feel male students should make better use of the opportunities that education brings, so that this gender gap can be narrowed.

Owens 4

Works Cited

Lewin, Tamara. "At Colleges, Women Are Leaving Men in the Dust." *New York Times*. 9 July 2006. Web. 1 Mar. 2011.

Owens, Shannon. "Study Habits." Survey. 6 Mar. 2011.

 # Critical Thinking Activity: Questions to Ask as You Reflect on Your Writing

Please respond to the following questions in your journal. Your instructor may want you to share your responses with the rest of the class:

1. How did you decide what topic to focus on?
2. How did you go about *defining* the *effect* you centered on?
3. What kinds of research did you conduct to determine all cause and effect connections? What would you do differently next time?
4. What kinds of invention/discovery activities did you do? What was the most helpful for your cause and effect paper? The least? Why?
5. What could your classmates do next time to make their comments and suggestions more useful to you?
6. What editing problems did you have with this paper? What did you do to solve them?
7. What did you learn from writing this paper that will help you as you write other papers, especially papers that explain why something happened, in the future?

Readings That Explain Why

These texts will help you get some sense of how other writers explain why a cause or multiple causes do in fact cause some effect.

Note: Words highlighted **in blue** are terms used in the "Improve Your Vocabulary" activity after each reading.

The Surprising Causes of Those College Tuition Hikes

Kim Clark

Journalist Kim Clark focuses on economic issues, especially on student financial aid. She not only contributes her expertise to US News & World Report, but also has appeared on television discussing financial aid issues. Her article describes some of the causes for rising tuition costs—and some of the reasons she argues for might surprise you.

1   Why has college tuition been rising so high and fast? Will college costs ever drop back to more affordable levels?

2   Those questions have been frustrating parents and students for years. A new report provides some surprising answers that will, unfortunately, probably only frustrate and anger them even more. At public colleges, tuition has generally been driven up by rising spending on administrators, student support services, and the need to make up for reductions in government subsidies, according to a report issued by the Delta Cost Project, a nonprofit based in Washington, D.C.

3   In some cases, such as at community colleges (which educate about half of the nation's college students), tuition has risen while spending on classroom instruction has actually fallen. At public colleges especially, the current economic troubles will likely only **accelerate** the trend of rising prices and classroom cutbacks, says Jane Wellman, the author of the report. After analyzing income and spending statistics that nearly 2,000 colleges reported to the federal government, Wellman concludes: "Students are paying more and, arguably, getting less in the classroom."

accelerate: moving faster

4   Among the more surprising findings:

- The main reason tuition has been rising faster than college costs is that colleges had to make up for reductions in the per-student subsidy state taxpayers sent colleges. In 2006, the last year for which Wellman had data, state taxpayers sent $7,078 per student to the big public research universities. That's $1,270 less (after accounting for inflation) than they sent in 2002.

reining in: holding back

flagship: main state university

- Public universities have been **reining in** overall spending per student in recent years. **Flagship** public universities' spending per student has

(continued)

risen from about $12,400 in 1995 to $13,800 in 2006 after accounting for inflation. But since 2002, spending at public colleges has generally not exceeded inflation.

- Increases in spending were driven mostly by higher administration, maintenance, and student services costs. Public universities spent almost $4,000 per student per year on administration, support, and maintenance in 2006, up more than 13 percent, in real terms over 1995. And they spent another $1,200 a year on services such as counseling, which was up 23 percent. Meanwhile, they spent about $8,700 a year on classroom instruction for each student, up about 9 percent.

- Big private universities, powered by tuition and endowment increases, have increased spending dramatically while public schools have **languished**. Total educational spending per student at private research universities has jumped by almost 10 percent since 2002 to more than $33,000. During that same period, public university total spending was comparatively flat and totaled less than $14,000 a year.

languished: slowed-down

5 That growing gap between rich schools and poor schools worries observers like Wellman. The cost of attending a public university, even after subtracting out aid and inflation, rose more than 15 percent in the last five years, according to the College Board. But almost all of the recent price increases at public universities are "**backfilling** for cuts in state funds," Wellman says.

backfilling: making up for

6 Some college presidents say the report shows they haven't been raising prices irresponsibly.

7 "Virginia Tech" explained David Hodge, president of Miami University of Ohio. "Everybody expects us to do a lot more security. Students are coming with more physical disabilities and emotional needs. There are greater expectations for career services," he says. And that kind of administrative and support spending "is a really good investment. It helps the students."

8 In addition, public schools tend to serve many low-income students and minority students who need more remedial classes and extra counseling services than better-prepared students who attend elite private universities, says F. King Alexander, president of California State University—Long Beach.

9 One of the reasons that Duke University costs about $51,000 a year is that the elite schools are in a bidding war for top faculty and better services for students, says college spokesman Michael Schoenfeld. In addition, competition for the best students forces schools to offer bigger and bigger scholarships, which means few students actually pay the full sticker price, he notes. Duke's record-breaking flood of applications for the next academic year shows there's still plenty of demand for what private universities offer, he says.

10 But as more and more states facing budget crises consider further subsidy cuts and tuition hikes for public schools, parents and students are increasingly objecting to price increases for any reason. "Enough is enough," says James Boyle, president of the College Parents of America. A tsunami of applications

at lower cost schools such as the California State University campuses shows that students and parents are voting with their feet. "The changing market for higher ed will cause colleges to hold down their expenses and state legislators to increase their subsidies," Boyle predicts.

Questions for Discussion and Writing

1. What is your initial reaction to this essay? Do you agree with Clark's conclusions?
2. What rhetorical strategies can you point to in Clark's essay?
3. In paragraph 2, Clark writes, "At public colleges, tuition has generally been driven up by rising spending on administrators, student support services, and the need to make up for reductions in government subsidies." Were you surprised at any of those reasons? Why?
4. How are you paying for your college tuition costs? How about other college costs, such as books or transportation?
5. How much consideration did you give to tuition costs, before you selected your own college or university?
6. What other causes can you think of (athletics, health/workout centers, etc.) that might impact tuition costs?

Improve Your Vocabulary

Use the highlighted and defined words from "The Surprising Causes of Those College Tuition Hikes" in a sentence or in a paragraph.

What Is Keeping Italian Men at Home?

Claudio Lavanga

Claudio Lavanga is a news editor and reporter. He has reported for Al Jazeera International and has been a producer for DateLine NBC for NBC News. This piece was prepared for NBC News.

1   ROME—For most Italian single men, inviting a girlfriend home is a dangerous affair: If the visit is not planned carefully, they run the big risk of bumping into the other woman in their lives—their mother.

(continued)

umbilical cord: the cord that connects a baby to its mother

Oedipal complex: psychological theory that a child wishes to possess its parent of the opposite sex

chronic: constant; continual

wedlock: being married

dolce vita: the good or sweet life

2   Italian men, in fact, still find it too difficult to cleanly sever the **umbilical cord**, and end up staying at home with their parents well into their 30s.

3   Now experts believe that the nationwide **Oedipal complex** might cause more serious damage than the endless complaints of aspiring wives: men's **chronic** refusal to move on might be responsible for the drastic decline of Italy's birth rate.

Drop in Italian birth rate

4   At least this is the conclusion of the experts at the Population Reference Bureau, a non-profit association that studies population trends.

5   The annual study recently released by the private organization found that despite the fact that the world's population will increase approximately 50 percent by mid-century, Italy is projected to actually lose 10 percent of its population by 2050.

6   "Many young men live at home with parents until their late 20s because it is less acceptable to live with someone and raise a family out of **wedlock**," said Carl Haub, author of the report. "As a result, many young Italians either don't get married or leave the country entirely."

7   So where does the stereotype of the Italian *mamma's boy* end, and reality begin? The answer lies in the many recent surveys that all come to the same conclusion: more than half of Italian men between the age of 25 and 35 still live with their mother. But why?

Why move out of a luxury hotel?

8   "I just don't see the point of leaving my parents' home," said Luca Orsenigo, a 30 year-old software analyst from Milan. Despite the fact that his income is higher than average, he is not ready to give up his **dolce vita** yet.

9   "Right now I am single, so why would I give up traveling, my bike, the car, the clothes to waste money on rent? I would only start making such sacrifices when I find the right woman," Orsenigo said.

10   His mother doesn't seem to share his view.

11   "I keep telling him that it is time to find his own place," Enrica Turconi said. "He's become a burden, and he behaves like a guest in a hotel: I wash and iron, cut the grass and paint the walls, no wonder he doesn't want to leave."

Italian ladies have had it

12   Luca's behavior is so widespread that many Italian women aren't waiting any longer. Cristina Guidi, a 30-year-old flight coordinator, has just bought a one-bedroom apartment for herself.

13   "Relationships are not what they used to be. Both men and women have become unreliable, so it's not unusual for girls to decide to buy their own place," Guidi said.

14   On one issue, she agreed with Luca. "Still, I had to wait until I could afford to buy my own place, as I didn't want to throw away money on rent," she said.

initiative: a project; usually a project designed to change or improve something

15   If Italy is not used to single men living alone, a female "going solo" might prove too much to bear.

16   "Every time I have to deal with bricklayers, estate agents or carpet layers, I get asked the same thing: 'Where is your husband?' Nobody seems to believe that I can take care of myself," Guidi said.

17   Is money, rather than cultural tradition, the real hurdle keeping Italians from independence and making babies?

18   Not according to an **initiative** by a small village in the southern province of Salerno, where local authorities promised to give parents $12,000 for every newborn. Despite the offer, so far only one child has been born.

19   Another sign that no check is big enough to entice Italian men away from their nests.

Questions for Discussion and Writing

1. What is the most interesting thing you learned from Lavanga's text?
2. Did Lavanga provide enough *causes* to explain the end result, the *effect*?
3. Where in the text did Lavanga use the rhetorical strategies of *compare* and *contrast*?
4. What do you think about living at home when you are, say, 30 years old?

Improve Your Vocabulary

Use the highlighted and defined words from "What Is Keeping Italian Men at Home?" in a sentence or in a paragraph.

Illegal Immigration to the United States

Udall Center for Studies in Public Policy

The Udall Center for Studies in Public Policy was established in 1987, and sponsors policy-relevant, interdisciplinary research and forums that link scholarship and education with decision making.

The Udall Center specializes in issues that focus on: (1) environmental policy, primarily in the Southwest and U.S.-Mexico border region (2) immigration policy of the United States (3) Indigenous nations policy. (From http://udallcenter.arizona.edu/more.php.)

Q&A: What are the main causes of illegal immigration to the United States?

1   The number of illegal, or unauthorized, immigrants entering the United States is estimated to have increased over the past several decades,

(continued)

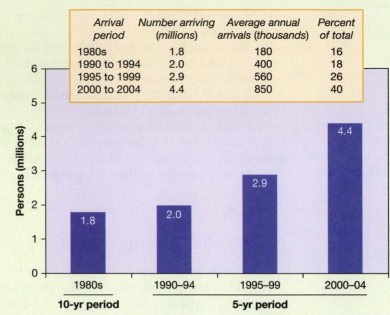

Arrival period	Number arriving (millions)	Average annual arrivals (thousands)	Percent of total
1980s	1.8	180	16
1990 to 1994	2.0	400	18
1995 to 1999	2.9	560	26
2000 to 2004	4.4	850	40

Arrivals of unauthorized immigrants by time period, 1980–2004.
Source: Passel, Jeffrey S.1

substantially: for the most part; significant

fundamental: essential to; basic

migrate: move from one place to another

channels: avenues; pathways

global economic integration: companies involved with and selling around the world

liberalized: made easier

NAFTA: North American Free Trade Agreement

from approximately 180,000 per year in the 1980s to as many as 850,000 per year since 2000.[1]

2   The reasons for this are both simple and complex. Simply stated, most immigrants who come to the United States illegally—especially those from less-developed nations—do so because U.S. employers hire them at wages **substantially** higher than they could earn in their native countries. This much is clear. But, on a more **fundamental** level, illegal immigration is a symptom of the fact that the U.S. immigration system is seriously out of step with global political and economic realities that drive people to **migrate** and pushed U.S. employers to hire these migrants. The three main drivers of this process are:

> 1) global economic change, 2) the inadequacy of **channels** for legal economic migration, and 3) ineffective employer sanctions.

Global Economic Change

3   The current wave of **global economic integration**—or "globalization"—is one cause of illegal immigration. But globalization involves more than **liberalized** trade (such as through treaties like **NAFTA** and World Trade Organization conventions). Additional changes in today's global economy include information and

[1]Passel, Jeffrey, 2006. "The Size and Characteristics of the Unauthorized Migrant Population in the U.S.: Estimates Based on the March 2005 Current Population Survey," March 7, 2006. Washington, DC: Pew Hispanic Center. p. 2.

foster: encourage

transportation technologies that **foster** internationalized production, distribution and consumption, and labor. India, China, and the former Soviet republics have opened their economies to outside investment, thereby greatly increasing the number of low-skilled workers participating in global labor markets and making low-skilled labor markets all the more competitive. Further, developed countries are shifting away from manufacturing-based to knowledge-based economies.

realigning: changing the direction of; adjusting to match something more precisely

4   All of these factors have significantly shifted global competitive advantage, **realigning** economic activity around the world. This, in turn, has resulted in increased labor mobility. Labor has become more international as individuals have migrated seeking work, in spite of attempts by government to control this migration.

Inadequate Channels for Legal Economic Migration

incentives: rewards for doing something

trumped: to beat someone; to win

embedded: inside of; part of

5   A second cause of illegal immigration derives from the fact that the U.S. immigration system, whose structure was created in 1965, provides only limited channels for legal permanent economic migration, especially of low-skilled workers. And due to this shortage of legal channels, economic **incentives** have **trumped** legal structures, creating a large pool of low- skilled immigrants in the country illegally and **embedded** in the U.S. economy. Reflecting the political and economic realities of 40 years ago, the U.S. immigration system rests on just three pillars:

> 1) family reunification, 2) provision for scarce labor such as agricultural and specific high-skilled workers, and 3) protecting American workers from competition with foreign workers.

compensate: pay for

6   The U.S. education system creates relatively few people who either lack a high-school diploma (low-skilled workers) or who hold Ph.D.s (especially in math and science). The U.S. immigration system attempts to **compensate** for shortages in these areas by providing for temporary immigration by farm workers and seasonal low-skilled workers and for permanent immigration of high-skilled workers, such as bioscience researchers and computer programmers (Pillar 2). The system otherwise strictly limits permanent legal immigration by other categories of workers (Pillar 3). These existing legal channels have not been adequate to fill specific gaps in both the size and the composition of the U.S. labor force that result from recent trends.

7   The claim that immigrants are doing jobs American workers won't do has significant truth to it. Industries such as construction, meat-packing, and service industries need large numbers of non-seasonal, low-skilled workers. But it is also the case that immigrants are doing jobs that American workers aren't available to do. The native-born population is growing slowly and is aging. Since 1990, over half of the growth in the U.S. labor force occurred through immigration and 1 of 8 U.S. workers today is an immigrant, up from 1 in 16 in 1970.[2]

[2]Mosisa, Abraham T., 2002. "Foreign-Born Workers in the U.S. Economy," Monthly Labor Review. Vol. 125, no. 5.

(continued)

mechanism: a way to do something

8   Because the current system makes it nearly impossible for low-skilled workers to legally and permanently enter the country to work, illegal entry is the **mechanism** whereby migrants respond to the lure of jobs in the United States that pay much more than could be earned at home.

Ineffective Employer Sanctions

sanctions: penalty

9   A third cause of illegal immigration is the ineffectiveness of employer **sanctions** for illegal hiring. This assures that immigrants who are in the country illegally can readily find employment.

10   There are at least three reasons why employer sanctions are ineffective:

1) absence of reliable mechanisms for verifying employment eligibility, 2) inadequate funding of interior immigration enforcement, and 3) absence of political will due to labor needs of the U.S. economy.

Verification

11   It has been unlawful since 1986 to knowingly hire an immigrant in the country illegally, but the law simply requires that employers determine whether documents presented as proof of eligibility to work appear authentic. There are no reliable mechanisms or legal requirements for employers to verify whether they actually are authentic.

fraudulent: fake; not real

12   Consequently, widespread use of unverifiable, **fraudulent** documents has made it easy for employers to comply with little more than the paper-work provisions of the law[3] and immigrants in the country illegally have become embedded in the economy. Because little is spent by the United States on worksite enforcement, even those flagrantly violating the law have little to fear.

Interior Enforcement and Political Will

apace: to continue as before

sovereignty: supreme power

13   Public concern over illegal immigration has meant that the budget for patrolling the border skyrocketed from $700 million in 1985 to $2.84 billion by 2002,[4] although illegal immigration has continued **apace**. Why? Competing political pressures are at work. Legitimate public concern about **sovereignty** and violations of U.S. law compels attempts to stop illegal border crossing. At the same time, legitimate public desire for strong economic performance works against disrupting the economic activity that workers in the country illegally make possible. The result of these competing political pressures has been that enforcement has overwhelmingly focused on the U.S.-Mexico border while the budget for interior enforcement is tiny compared to the U.S. economy.

[3]Bach, Robert L. and Howard Brill, 1991. Impact of IRCA on the U.S. Labor Market and Economy: Final Report to the U.S. Department of Labor. Institute for Research on Multiculturalism and International Labor, State University of New York at Binghamton. pp. 124-128.
[4]Meyers, Deborah Waller, 2005. "U.S. Border Enforcement: From Horseback to High-Tech," Migration Policy Institute Insight: Independent Task Force on Immigration and America's Future, No. 7. Washington, DC: Migration Policy Institute. p. 21.

disrupt: impede; stop from functioning

14   The budget for interior enforcement increased between 1987 and 2002, from $109 to $458 million – still a small portion of the overall enforcement budget. In comparison, the worksite enforcement portion of the budget has been miniscule. As of 2002, fewer than 200 agents nationwide and less than three percent of the budget for patrolling the border were used for worksite enforcement.[5] In fact, worksite enforcement has decreased between 1992 and 2002: employer investigations were nine percent of the interior enforcement budget in FY1991 and only two percent in FY2003. While interior enforcement has increased recently and there have been a few highly-publicized raids at specific worksites around the country, spending on interior enforcement remains a small fraction of spending at the border.

15   In other words, there has been little consistent political will to **disrupt** the economic activity fueled by immigrants in the country illegally. Focusing enforcement at the border rather than at the worksite responds to two conflicting political pressures: to do something about illegal immigration, but to avoid disrupting economic activity.

[5]Jacoby, Tamar, 2005. "An Idea Whose Time Has Finely Come? The Case for Employment Verification," Migration Policy Institute Policy Brief: Independent Task Force on Immigration and America's Future, No. 9. Washington, DC: Migration Policy Institute.

Questions for Discussion and Writing

1. What is your initial reaction to this essay? Do you agree with the causes provided for illegal immigration?
2. What rhetorical strategies can you point to in this essay?
3. How effective is this essay as a cause and effect essay?
4. How does the chart help readers understand the information it illustrates?
5. What did you find surprising in this essay?

Improve Your Vocabulary

Use the highlighted and defined words from "Illegal Immigration to the United States" in a sentence or in a paragraph.

MyWritingLab™ For support in meeting this chapter's objectives, log in to **www.mywritinglab.com** and select **Essay Development—Cause and Effect.**

Chapter 13

Writing to Evaluate
Using Comparison and Contrast

Learning **O**bjectives

In this chapter, you will learn to:

LO1 Consider the writer's situation, and determine your purpose and audience

LO2 Use the rhetorical strategies of *comparing* and *contrasting* to evaluate something

LO3 Use invention and discovery strategies to come up with ideas and details

LO4 Write a thesis statement that states the point of your essay

LO5 Organize and write your first draft

LO6 Revise your essay, and prepare a final draft

U.S.News WORLD REPORT

usnews.com   Sunday, September 05, 2010

Home | Politics & Policy | Health | Money | Education | Science | Travel

Best Colleges 2011

Home > Education > Best Colleges

 BEST COLLEGES 2011   **Find the Best College for You**

Get exclusive rankings of 1,400 schools. Use our tools to search for your perfect fit. And find details on scholarships, loans, and grants. » See ranking category definitions

National University Rankings

1 Harvard University
Cambridge, MA
2 Princeton University
Princeton, NJ
3 Yale University
New Haven, CT
› Full ranking

National Liberal Arts College Rankings

1 Williams College
Williamstown, MA
2 Amherst College
Amherst, MA
3 Swarthmore College
Swarthmore, PA
› Full ranking

Regional Rankings

. Regional Universities
. Regional Colleges

Other Rankings and Lists

. Business Programs
. Engineering Programs
. Great schools at great prices
. A+ schools for B students
. Up-and-coming colleges
. Academic programs to look for
. Historically black colleges and universities
. Best undergrad teaching
. Unranked specialty s

College Rankings by High School Counselors

. National Universities
. National Liberal Arts

When we think of **evaluating** something, we often think of choosing a product or a service: a flat-screen television, a car, a hair stylist, or a movie. But evaluation is something we do all the time, not just when we purchase something. We **evaluate**, or judge, our friends and our neighborhood, our community and our schools, even political issues and elected officials.

All evaluations have one thing in common: they have **criteria**, or characteristics, on which they are based. For example, *price* is a easy criterion to use when deciding where to purchase something: if you find an item at store A and it costs less than the same item at store B, your evaluation is complete—store A is better for making that purchase. *Color* is another easy criterion: if you want a blouse to go with your favorite red skirt, you will evaluate blouses and choose a color that matches the skirt. Any evaluation, then, begins with a determination of the criteria on which that evaluation will be based. Of course, we do not always base our evaluations on the best criteria. For example, we may eat that banana-marshmallow-chocolate sundae because we know it will taste good (a criterion), but perhaps we should not eat it based on the number of calories it contains (another criterion).

As shown on the image at the start of this chapter, one thing that many students evaluate is the college they attend. How and why did you decide to enroll at *your* college?

Everyday Writing Activity: Why Are You Here?

Briefly outline why you decided to attend this college. On what did you base your decision?

Did you consider how close or far the college was to where you lived? Cost? The financial aid you received? Friends who attend the same school? The college's reputation? A specific program you wanted to enroll in? Did you make a list of plusses and minuses of various colleges, to help you decide where to attend?

In your journal, list the criteria on which you made the decision to come to school here. Your instructor may want you to share your responses with the rest of the class.

It is often useful to look back at a decision you made and think about *why* you decided one way rather than another: that can help with future decisions.

Here is an example: assume that you just saw the latest *Star Trek* film and really liked it. Why? If we asked you to explain, you might tell us that your criteria for judging an action film (like *Star Trek*) include:

1. The film must be *exciting*.
2. The *villains* should be *interesting*.

3. The *actors* must do a *terrific job*.
4. The *storyline* must keep the viewer's *interest*.

Now if we asked you to give us some examples from *Star Trek* to show what you mean for each of these criteria, you could do so. For instance, for the first criterion, you might say that the film was exciting *because*

a. The opening showed the *Enterprise* in a battle with two enemy ships; the *Enterprise* was disabled and was sliding off into a black hole . . .
b. Inside on the deck, the Captain was injured; the whole room was filled with smoke and fire and the computers were clicking off . . .
c. The *Enterprise* sounded the "abandon ship" message . . .
d. And that was all in the opening two minutes of the film!

If we asked you for another reason that Star Trek was a good action movie, you might tell us that the villains were interesting. You could provide examples and details and scenes to support your judgment that the villains in *Star Trek* fit this criterion.

You just constructed a brief but helpful film evaluation, by first explaining the criteria on which you based your evaluation, and then explaining how well the film matched up to that criteria.

You probably constructed your evaluation at least partly by using the rhetorical strategies of *description:* what the characters looked like, how they acted, and so on, along with *narration:* what happened in the story.

But the most useful strategy, and the one used most often in evaluations, is to *compare and contrast:* in this example, how *Star Trek* is similar to or different than other movies. You almost always will **compare** and **contrast** whenever you evaluate anything (this item is bigger than that item; this costs less than that; this idea is better than that idea; an so on). (For more on rhetorical strategies, see Chapter 5.)

Finally, when you use criteria to evaluate something, some of them are more important than others. For example, you might give the criterion "film must be exciting" the greatest weight when evaluating an action movie. The quality of the acting, our third criterion, might be far less important to you.

LO1

Consider the writer's situation, and determine your purpose and audience

The Writer's Situation

As you were thinking of the criteria you might use for a film evaluation, did you consider your **purpose**: to provide an evaluation (a judgment about the subject of your evaluation) based on the criteria and to show how well (or poorly) the film matches-up with that criteria? Did you think about who might be the **audience** for your evaluation, and what they might need to know, from your text, to agree with your evaluation?

Did you consider what rhetorical strategies (like *comparing and contrasting*) might most effectively show the match between your criteria and the subject of your evaluation?

Evaluating Using Comparing and Contrasting

Writing an evaluation begins with useful criteria on which you will base your judgments. Then, through the process of *comparing* and *contrasting* the various aspects of your subject, you construct an evaluation. When you compare and contrast, you are in essence matching up the properties of the thing you are evaluating with your criteria.

Comparing and contrasting is, of course, only one rhetorical strategy to use to write an evaluation—but it is the most common. You can also use:

- *Description*. You need to describe the subject of your evaluation. Note how Roger Ebert *describes* some of the parts of *Shutter Island* in the following reading.
- *Argumentation*. If you want to make a point, perhaps your evaluation will show that one program of study will help you more in your planned career than another.
- *Examples*. Specific examples and details will illustrate how the subject of your evaluation "matches up" to your criteria. For instance, if one of the criteria for evaluating a college class is a professor's past student evaluations, then you would want to provide examples of those evaluations in your own text.

Notice how film critic Roger Ebert effectively uses several rhetorical strategies in his review, but especially relies on *comparing* and *contrasting*.

Shutter Island
Roger Ebert

Ebert provides the main cast of characters (if you recognize some of the names, that alone may encourage you to see the film).

cast & credits

Teddy Daniels: **Leonardo DiCaprio**
Chuck Aule: **Mark Ruffalo**
Dr. Cawley: **Ben Kingsley**
Dr. Naehring: **Max von Sydow**
Dolores: **Michelle Williams**

(*continued*)

Rachel 1: **Emily Mortimer**
Rachel 2: **Patricia Clarkson**
George: **Jackie Earle Haley**
Warden: **Ted Levine**

Paramount Pictures presents a film directed by Martin Scorsese. Written by Laeta Kalogridis, based on the novel by Dennis Lehane. Running time: 138 minutes. Rated R (for disturbing violent content, language and some nudity).

Ebert sets the stage, noting the setting is "ominous and doomy" (is doomy a word?). Note how Ebert *compares Shutter Island* to how other horror films function

1   "Shutter Island" starts working on us with the first musical notes under the Paramount logo's mountain, even before the film starts. They're ominous and doomy. So is the film. This is Martin Scorsese's evocation of the delicious shuddering fear we feel when horror movies are about something and don't release all the tension with action scenes.

Ebert tells us what kind of a film this is and compares it to *King Kong*.

If you've seen *King Kong*, you can relate to Ebert's comment.

2   In its own way it's a haunted house movie, or make that a haunted castle or fortress. Shutter Island, we're told, is a remote and craggy island off Boston, where a Civil War-era fort has been adapted as a prison for the criminally insane. We approach it by boat through lowering skies, and the feeling is something like the approach to King Kong's island: Looming in gloom from the sea, it fills the visitor with dread. To this island travel U.S. marshal Teddy Daniels (Leonardo DiCaprio) and his partner Chuck Aule (Mark Ruffalo).

A bit about the plot and one of the actors, Sir Ben Kingsley.

3   It's 1954, and they are assigned to investigate the disappearance of a child murderer (Emily Mortimer). There seems to be no way to leave the island alive. The disappearance of one prisoner might not require the presence of two marshals unfamiliar with the situation, but we never ask that question. Not after the ominous walls of the prison arise. Not after the visitors are shown into the office of the prison medical director, Dr. Cawley, played by Ben Kingsley with that forbidding charm he has mastered.

A little about the basic plot, comparing it to Poe's gothic stories. If you have read any of Poe's work, you will relate to this comment.

4   It's clear that Teddy has no idea what he's getting himself into. Teddy—such an innocuous name in such a gothic setting. Scorsese, working from a novel by Dennis Lehane, seems to be telling a simple enough story here; the woman is missing, and Teddy and Chuck will look for her. But the cold, gray walls clamp in on them, and the offices of Cawley and his colleagues, furnished for the Civil War commanding officers, seem borrowed from a tale by Edgar Allan Poe.

Instructive comments about the director's work; note that Ebert refers to him as a "craftsman."

5   Scorsese the craftsman chips away at reality piece by piece. Flashbacks suggest Teddy's traumas in the decade since World War II. That war, its prologue and aftermath, supplied the dark undercurrent of classic film noir. The term "post-traumatic shock syndrome" was not then in use, but its symptoms could be seen in men attempting to look confident in their facades of unstyled

suits, subdued ties, heavy smoking and fedoras pulled low against the rain. DiCaprio and Ruffalo both affect this look, but DiCaprio makes it seem more like a hopeful disguise.

More comparisons to what horror films include.

6   The film's primary effect is on the senses. Everything is brought together into a disturbing foreshadow of dreadful secrets. How did this woman escape from a locked cell in a locked ward in the old fort, its walls thick enough to withstand cannon fire? Why do Cawley and his sinister colleague Dr. Naehring (Max von Sydow, ready to play chess with Death) seem to be concealing something? Why is even such a pleasant person as the deputy warden not quite convincingly friendly? (He's played by John Carroll Lynch, Marge's husband in "Fargo," so you can sense how nice he *should* be.) Why do the methods in the prison trigger flashbacks to Teddy's memories of helping to liberate a Nazi death camp?

Evaluative comments about characters in horror films.

Comparison about visuals.

7   These kinds of questions are at the heart of film noir. The hero is always flawed. Scorsese showed his actors the great 1947 noir "Out of the Past," whose very title is a noir theme: Characters never arrive at a story without baggage. They have unsettled issues, buried traumas. So, yes, perhaps Teddy isn't simply a clean-cut G-man. But why are the others so strange? Kingsley in particular exudes menace every time he smiles.

8   There are thrilling visuals in "Shutter Island." Another film Scorsese showed his cast was Hitchcock's "Vertigo," and we sense echoes of its hero's fear of heights. There's the possibility that the escaped woman might be lurking in a cave on a cliff, or hiding in a lighthouse. Both involve hazardous terrain to negotiate, above vertiginous falls to waves pounding on the rocks below. A possible hurricane is approaching. Light leaks out of the sky. The wind sounds mournful. It is, as they say, a dark and stormy night. And that's what the movie is about: atmosphere, ominous portents, the erosion of Teddy's confidence and even his identity. It's all done with flawless directorial command. Scorsese has fear to evoke, and he does it with many notes.

Ebert critiques the ending.

9   You may read reviews of "Shutter Island" complaining that the ending blindsides you. The uncertainty it causes prevents the film from feeling perfect on first viewing. I have a feeling it might improve on second. Some may believe it doesn't make sense. Or that, if it does, then the movie leading up to it doesn't. I asked myself: OK, then, how *should* it end? What would be more satisfactory? Why can't I be one of those critics who informs the director what he should have done instead?

10   Oh, I've had moments like that. Every moviegoer does. But not with "Shutter Island." This movie is all of a piece, even the parts that don't appear to fit. There is a human tendency to note carefully what goes before, and draw logical conclusions. But—what if you can't nail down exactly what went before? What if there were things about Cawley and his peculiar staff that were hidden? What if the movie lacks a reliable narrator? What if its point of view isn't omniscient but fragmented? Where can it all lead? What does it mean? We ask, and Teddy asks, too.

Questions for Discussion and Writing

1. What did you learn from Ebert's review?
2. Did his review make you want to see the film? Why or why not?
3. Go back through Ebert's review and list all of the criteria he used for his film evaluation. Do you agree with all of them?
4. We indicated some places where Roger Ebert used *comparison* and *contrast* in his review. Can you find other times where he used *comparison* and *contrast* to explain his review of *Shutter Island*?
5. Can you find places where Roger Ebert used *description* or *narration* to explain his review of *Shutter Island?*
6. If you saw this film, do you agree with Ebert's review? Why?

While we have used a film review as an example of an evaluation (as film reviews are something most people are familiar with), the concept of making an effective evaluation will be important to you not only in this class, but in your other classes and in your professional life. Now, of course, you will participate in end-of-semester evaluations of your college classes and teachers. Those evaluations may have implications for which teachers get rehired, or possibly, which receive raises. Likewise, your work is evaluated by your professors (you call them *grades* and essentially, they are evaluations). In your work you are and will continue to be evaluated; you also will evaluate others, who you may supervise. So while we have focused on a film evaluation, because that is interesting and fun, other evaluations you will be involved with can carry real and serious consequences.

Everyday Writing Activity: What Might You Evaluate?

Think about the last few days and what you might have evaluated during that time. A restaurant? A college course? A trip? A film? A novel? A short story? An art exhibit? A song? A music video?

Select something you evaluated, even informally, within the last few days. In your journal, jot down your answers to these questions:

1. What criteria did you use to make your decision?
2. How did you "weight" each criteria—how did you decide what was most important, next in importance, etc.?
3. Would you change any of those criteria now, after the fact? Why?

Your instructor may want you to share your responses with the rest of your class.

WRITING ASSIGNMENTS

The writing assignments that follow all ask you to write to evaluate: to describe to your readers the criteria on which you will base your evaluation, to explain those criteria in detail, to explain how the criteria "match up" to the subject of your evaluation, and to outline the conclusion and judgment you came to.

You also need to consider what rhetorical strategies might be the most effective for your evaluation. In Roger Ebert's review of *Shutter Island*, he often uses the rhetorical strategy of *compare* and *contrast* to relate the film to other movies, or to horror films in general. (For more on rhetorical strategies, see Chapter 5.)

Writing Assignment One: Evaluating a Web Site

For this assignment, assume that in your Transition to College class you have been asked to evaluate the Web site of a campus club or organization. Part of the reason for the assignment, your instructor explains, is to give you the chance to explore what groups are available on campus, groups you might yourself be interested in joining. The writing part of the assignment asks you to consider how effective those groups' Web sites are in terms of giving you the information a potential member might need and want. One way to consider such information is to ask, after reading what this group or that organization has on its Web site, do I want to join the group? What questions do I still have about them?

Those large questions might give you a sense of what smaller questions to ask (which in effect become the criteria on which you will base your evaluation). For example, think about what you would like to know about a campus group or organization. You might consider if the Web site

- Explains the purpose for the group and, if they have a "mission statement," whether that statement is clear and understandable.
- Outlines what the group does—activities and events.
- Explains the benefits and costs of being in the group.
- Details whether or not the group is connected to a national organization and if there are benefits to such a connection.
- Explains if there are costs (membership dues) involved.

In other words, on what criteria would you evaluate such a Web site? For this assignment, determine and explain the criteria you think should be used, and then evaluate the Web site of a campus group at your own college or university.

Writing Assignment Two: Evaluating a Local Art Exhibit or Live Performance

For this assignment, assume that you have been asked to go to several local art exhibits, select one you like, and evaluate that exhibit. Or, that you have been asked to evaluate a live performance (a play, concert, etc.).

Then, consider the following: What makes a good art exhibit or live performance? Is it just the art or the placement and how paintings (as an example) are hung and displayed, or how a performance is staged? What role does lighting play in either the exhibit or performance? The seating? What criteria would be important to evaluate an art exhibit or live performance?

For this assignment, construct and explain criteria, and evaluate a local art exhibit or live performance.

Writing Assignment Three: Evaluating a Friend's Work Ability in a Reference Letter

A good friend told you that he was applying for a job and asked if he could list you as a reference. Of course, you agreed. Now you have received a request for a letter of recommendation. Start by determining the criteria on which you will base your letter of recommendation: what qualities should a good employee have? Should an employee

- Be trustworthy?
- Be a hard worker?
- Be honest?
- Be able to work well with others?
- Have past work experience?
- Be able to solve problems?

What can you say about your friend (and you must be honest) that will help *show* a potential employer how good of any employee he is likely to be? Remember that as with any evaluation, your friend might be excellent in several criteria areas, but not as wonderful in others.

Optional Multi-Modal Assignment: Tweeting

Assume you were asked to complete writing assignment two, which asks you to evaluate a local art exhibit or live performance. As an optional assignment, tweet as you experience the art exhibit or performance that you decide to evaluate. Focus on explaining how you determined your evaluation criteria and your initial reactions to how well (or not well) the art exhibit or performance matches up with your criteria.

 ## Critical Thinking Activity: Questions to Ask before You Start

If you spend some time considering your evaluation before you start writing, your end result will be more effective. In your journal, answer these questions:

1. Your *purpose* in writing is to evaluate an organization's Web site, an art exhibit, or your friend's qualities as an employee, but before you can do so, you need to determine, define and describe specific *criteria* on which to base your evaluation. Your criteria will, naturally, vary widely by what you are evaluating (you would not evaluate a college major, for example, using the same criteria that you would use to evaluate a television set). What are the criteria you will use?
2. How would you describe the audience for your evaluation?
3. What *rhetorical strategies* (like *compare* and *contrast*) might be most effective for your evaluation?
4. When someone tries to explain how their own evaluation of something is correct, what kinds of *details and examples* and *visual aids* are the most useful to you, to understand what they mean (and perhaps to then agree with their evaluation)? How might answering that question help you as you write your own evaluation?

LO3
Use invention and discovery strategies to come up with ideas and details

Invention and Discovery Activities

Remember that the purpose of any **invention/discovery activity** is to help you get started with your writing. For most of us, it is really hard just to sit down and write, so using several invention activities will help get some of your ideas onto paper.

Once you have some ideas on paper, they should help you determine the criteria on which you will base your evaluation. They also will help you decide what criteria are more important—how much importance you will give to your various criteria.

After you have some sense of the criteria you will use for your evaluation, more invention work (e.g., clustering) will help you see how your subject matches up with the criteria you set (for more on clustering, see pages 84–85). That can help you decide on your preliminary thesis statement.

Student Writing: Ken Bishop's Freewriting

In his LifePlan class, which is designed to help students consider what career paths might be best for them, student writer Ken Bishop decided to evaluate sports photography as a career. Is working as a sports photographer a good career choice? Ken wanted to know. Ken decided to freewrite to get some of his thoughts and questions down on paper:

> I love photography, but I wonder if anyone can make a career out of being a sports photographer. Is there any money in it? Wouldn't it be neat if someone actually bought some of my pictures or if they were published in the local paper or a magazine? Wow!
>
> I know there are different types of photographers (fashion photographer, journalist photographer, movie photographer, etc.), but I'm most interested in sports photography: taking photos at football and basketball and soccer games.
>
> What do they pay for that kind of work? Are there a lot of opportunities? Is the work steady? How much technical knowledge do you need? Are there classes to take that might help? Do you need to learn Photoshop or some way to manipulate pictures? How do people who <u>are</u> sports photographers like their job?

Note that Ken is already starting to develop some *criteria* on which he will base his evaluation.

Everyday Writing Activity: Freewriting

In your journal, freewrite for 10 minutes about the subject of your evaluation, without stopping or re-reading what you have written. If you cannot think of anything to write about your topic, write "I can't think of anything to write about." (For more on freewriting, see pages 83–84.) Your instructor may ask you to share your freewriting with the rest of the class.

LO4

Write a thesis statement that states the point of your essay

Writing a Thesis for Your Evaluation

One of the things to remember when you evaluate something is that you may need to start *without* knowing how you will end up. You will need to determine the criteria you will use for your evaluation, be able to explain them, and then see how the subject of your evaluation matches up (compares to) with your criteria.

If you have one simple criterion such as cost, then it is pretty easy to evaluate something: this chocolate bar is cheaper than that chocolate bar, so that makes it easy to decide which to buy. But if you are evaluating something on a more complex basis, then it is not as simple. *Cost* can certainly be one criterion when you evaluate which chocolate bar to buy, but *calories* might be another, *taste* may also be important (and harder to define), and so on. So, plan on delaying a thesis statement until you have developed good criteria, can explain them, and have tested the subject of your evaluation against your criteria. Then, you can construct a good thesis statement.

Students sometimes think their **topic** is the same as their thesis, but they really are different. Your topic is the subject you are focusing on (in student writer Ken Bishop's case, it is sports photography as a career), while your **thesis** is what you want to focus on, about that topic. Based on his criteria for a good career, Ken might end up determining that sports photography is interesting, but not a career at which he can make a living. His thesis, then, might be something like:

> An evaluation of sports photography shows that it is not the career for me.

LO5

Organize and write your first draft

Organizing and Writing Your First Draft

Now you have some ideas on paper. So, where do you go from here? How can you take what you have so far and start to organize it into an effective evaluation?

In your evaluation, you generally can select from two **organizational approaches**. The first asks that you outline your subject, explain each criterion, explain how your subject matches up to each criterion, and then give your conclusion (evaluation) about the subject. Visually, this approach looks like this (note that we list only three criteria; your evaluation may have many criteria):

An Organizational Plan for an Evaluation Essay: Evaluation Comes Last

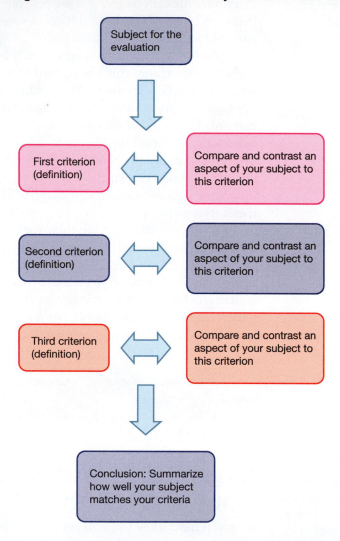

The second organizational approach essentially reverses the preceding process, so you start with your conclusion and then define your criteria and explain how each part of your subject matches up to it (note that we list only three criteria; your evaluation may have many criteria):

An Organizational Plan for an Evaluation Essay: Evaluation Comes First

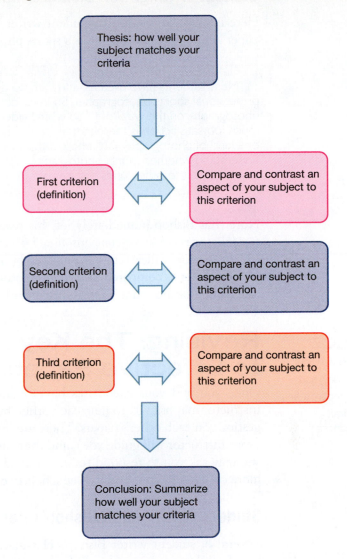

One secret of writing an effective evaluation is to try out each of these ways of organizing your work and see how they work for you, which seems to be the stronger, and what visual aids might help show what you mean.

Student Writing: Ken Bishop's Introduction

Here is the introduction to student writer Ken Bishop's first draft of his paper about a possible career as a sports photographer:

> Most students have dreams, and I am no different: I dream of being a professional sports photographer. So I wonder: can that be a career? Is still photography on the way "out," so would video make more sense? How much job satisfaction is there in that career? Is it harder to get started at one kind of photography (still photos) than another (video, Web)? To really understand whether sports photography might make a good career, I need to compare it to other kinds of careers in terms of several criteria.

Note that Bishop immediately lets his readers know that his main rhetorical strategy will be *comparison and contrast*, by asking questions that his evaluation will attempt to answer by matching up one thing (still photographer as compared to a video photographer as compared to someone who publishes on a Web site, etc.) with others.

LO6

Revise your essay, and prepare a final draft

Revising: The Key to Effective Papers

Once you and your classmates have a draft of your evaluations, your instructor may ask you to help each other, by providing feedback and suggestions on each other's papers. There are several different ways to do this (your instructor will guide you), and there are some general questions he/she may ask you to respond to, as you read your classmate's papers. (For more on effective responding, see Chapter 8.)

Student Writing: Ken Bishop's Peer-Reviewed Draft

Several of student writer Bishop's classmates read and responded to his first draft. Here is part of his draft along with their comments and suggestions. What suggestions would you have made? What rhetorical strategies can you see at work in his paper?

I like your questions as they make me want answers. More?

> Most students have dreams, and I am no different: I dream of being a professional sports photographer. So I wonder: can that be a career? Is still photography on the way "out," so would video make more sense? How much job satisfaction is there in that career? Is it harder to get started at one kind of photography (still photos) than another (video, Web)? To really

Good background.
I wonder if including some of your own pictures would be interesting and show what you mean?

Combine these sentences?

Now you're starting to develop criteria—that's good. More explanation?

understand whether sports photography might make a good career, I need to compare it to other kinds of careers in terms of several criteria.

I have been taking pictures now for about five years, and some are pretty good. I have tried a number of different types, including children's birthday parties and downtown on the plaza, where all sorts of people hang out, play chess, read, and so on. I've never been asked to photograph a wedding, though. Maybe I'm too young. And I am pretty good at what is called "nature" photography: flowers and birds and such.

I think a lot about the kind of work I would like to do after I graduate from college. I always come back to sports photography—basketball and soccer and football and tennis. That is what I enjoy the most, and what I seem to do the best.

The one main criterion for any kind of career has to include how much someone would earn doing that career. For a sports photographer, there are those with a job (like for a newspaper or magazine—imagine working for *Sports Illustrated*!)—or freelancers. The job would bring a steady income, but the freelance approach lets you take pictures of what you want to take pictures of. You wouldn't be assigned to take pictures of certain things, some of which you may not like.

Here is how student writer Bishop responded to a reader's suggestions. In his second paragraph, a reader wrote that he wondered if an example would help show what Bishop meant, so he added one of his photographs. Here is his revised section:

Student writer Bishop, responding to his classmate's comments, added a photograph.

I have been taking pictures now for about five years, and some are pretty good. I have tried a number of different types, including children's birthday parties and downtown on the plaza, where all sorts of people hang out, play chess, read, and so on. I've never been asked to photograph a wedding, though. Maybe I'm too young. And I am pretty good at what is called "sports" photography. Here is a photo I took of my friend Duane.

✓ Writing Style Tip: Sentence Combining

Student writer Bishop got a comment from a classmate that said, "Combine these sentences?" Ken thought about what his classmate suggested and so changed his text for his final draft by combining the first two sentences and deleting the names of the sports:

> I think a lot about the kind of work I would like to do after I graduate from college, and I always come back to sports photography. That is what I enjoy the most and what I seem to do the best.

It often is a good idea to combine your sentences, in order to increase the kinds and lengths of sentences in your evaluation. Any text filled with similar sentences quickly gets boring to readers (imagine reading a text where each sentence was five or six words long!).

For more on sentence variety, see simple, compound, and complex sentences in the Handbook, pages 427–428.

Critical Thinking Activity: Questions to Ask before You Revise

Now you have a first draft of your evaluation, have reread it several times, and most likely you also have received comments and suggestions from your classmates (and perhaps from your instructor, family members, or friends). You will recall from Chapter 8 that *revision* means to rethink and to reenvision your text—not to just fix surface errors. So consider:

1. Did any of the suggestions I received say anything about me not achieving my *purpose*? Did I perhaps misunderstand or misrepresent the information and details my *audience* needed to understand my evaluation?

2. Were readers convinced that my evaluation was correct? That is not my major goal, but it will help me understand what other evidence I might supply, to be more convincing.

3. Did any of the comments I received indicate that I might want to reorganize my evaluation? If so, what *organizational approach* might be more effective? (For more on organizational approaches, see pages 247–249.)

4. Did anyone tell me that they did not understand or seem to have misunderstood the *thesis statement* for my evaluation? How can I clarify it?
5. Did anyone suggest a *visual* (chart, graph, table, photograph, etc.) that might help improve my evaluation?

As you think about revising your paper, consider each part of it and decide whether revisions are needed before your final draft.

Revision Checklist for Your Evaluation	
Part of Your Paper	**Check √**
Title for your paper that gets your readers' attention	
Introduction with a clear thesis statement	
Criteria for your evaluation that are defined/ described, so readers know and understand on what you are basing your evaluation	
Supporting paragraphs, each with a topic sentence, supporting evidence or examples, and a transition to the next paragraph (all information must relate to your evaluation, your point)	
Visual aids if they will help the purpose of your evaluation (charts, graphs, tables, etc.)	
Conclusion that summarizes your main points and restates the thesis of your evaluation	

Student Writing: Ken Bishop's Final Draft

Here is student writer Ken Bishop's final draft of his evaluation of a career in sports photography. Note that he added more visual aids and explained his criteria in detail.

Bishop 1

Ken Bishop

Dr. Camille Newton

ENG 090

3 Mar. 2011

(continued)

Bishop 2

A Career Taking Pictures?

Most students have dreams, and I am no different: I dream of being a professional sports photographer. So I wonder: can that be a career? Is still photography on the way "out," so would video make more sense? How much job satisfaction is there in that career? Is it harder to get started at one kind of photography (still photos) than another (video, Web)? How would I evaluate sports photography as a possible career?

I have been taking pictures now for about five years, and some are pretty good. I have tried a number of different types, including children's birthday parties and downtown on the plaza, where all sorts of people hang out, play chess, read, and so on. I've never been asked to photograph a wedding, though. Maybe I'm too young. And I am pretty good at sports photography. Here is a photo I took of my friend Duane.

I think a lot about the kind of work I would like to do after I graduate from college, and I always come back to sports photography. That is what I enjoy the most, and what I seem to do the best.

One main criterion for any kind of career has to include how much someone would earn doing that career. For a sports photographer, there are those with a job (like for a newspaper or magazine—imagine working for *Sports Illustrated*!)—or freelancers. The job would bring a steady income, but the freelance approach lets you take pictures of what you want to take

Bishop 3

pictures of. You wouldn't be assigned to take pictures of certain things, some of which you may not like.

The hard part is figuring out how to make any money with photography, but that is my main criterion: can I make a living selling photographs? I could not find a lot of specific information on what sports photographers earn, but in terms of what they can "bill" a customer, I found out that hourly billing rates were pretty good.

A Web site, *HotGigs,* collects billing rates from lots of sports photographers. A billing rate of $55 per hour equals a total of $2,200 per week, if I could work as a photographer all week long. Even if I could only work half-time, the business would provide a pretty good income. In an interview by Alex McRae, Ross Kinnaird, a sports photographer who works for the Getty Agency (a worldwide photographic agency), reports that "A photographer at Getty might start out on £20,000 a year" (about $30,000). That would be a good starting point for me, and working in Europe would be wonderful.

In addition to income, another thing that is important is how well sports photographers like their jobs, the work they do. Ross Kinnaird notes that "I still get a huge buzz from seeing my pictures published. There's nothing better than taking a picture one day, and seeing it in the newspapers the next" (McRae). But Kinnaird also notes that there is a downside to his career, as a professional sports photographer is away from home a lot, and "You see a lot of hotel rooms and airports, but not much of the cities you're going to, so the travelling can get monotonous" (McRae). On the other hand, I interviewed Joseph Williams, the sports photographer for our local newspaper *(The Clarion)* and he does not travel much, so he did not voice the same complaint that Kinnaird did.

(continued)

Bishop 4

Based on these two essential things—income and job satisfaction—I think a sports photography career might be perfect for me.

Bishop 5

Works Cited

McRae, Alex. "I Want Your Job: Sports Photographer." *The Independent*. 3 Aug. 2006. Web. 27 Feb. 2011.

"Sports Photographer Hourly Bill Rates." *HotGigs.com*. 2010. Web. 22 Feb. 2011.

Williams, Joseph. Personal interview. 22 Feb. 2011.

 ## Critical Thinking Activity: Questions to Ask as You Reflect on Your Writing

In your journal, answer these questions about the writing assignment you just completed. Thinking and writing about your work on a writing assignment will make your next writing task easier, as you will learn from this one.

1. How did you decide what to evaluate?
2. How did you decide what criteria to use for your evaluation?
3. How did you think about what your audience needs to understand about those criteria? How did you *describe* or *define* your criteria?
4. What kinds of invention/discovery activities did you do? What was the most helpful for your evaluation? The least? Why?
5. Did you try out different ways to organize your paper? How did you decide how to organize the first draft of your evaluation?

6. What could your classmates do next time to make their comments and suggestions more useful?
7. Did you use visual aids in your evaluation? If so, what did you learn about using them that will help you in future assignments? If you did not use visual aids, do you think if you had, they may have improved your paper?
8. Did you procrastinate at starting your paper? What might you do differently next time?
9. What did you learn from writing this paper that will help you as you write other papers, especially evaluations, in the future?

Readings That Evaluate

These texts will help you get some sense of what effective evaluative writing looks like and how it functions.

Note: Words highlighted **in blue** are terms used in the "Improve Your Vocabulary" activity following each reading.

Best Places to Work 2010

Christina Breda Antoniades

Christina Breda Antoniades is a freelance journalist who writes frequently about children and families. Her work has appeared in the Washington Post, Parenting, *and* AAA World *magazine. This excerpt appeared in* Baltimore Magazine, *and it focuses on the top places to work in that area. As you read through this section of the essay, consider: do you agree with the criteria for what makes a "great place" to work? If you could design the perfect place for you to work, what would that place look like? Where would it be? What would you do and what would your coworkers do?*

hunkered-down: waiting

pink slips: piece of paper given to someone who is fired from a job

foosball: game

retain: keep

rounded up: collected

digs: slang for buildings

patootie: rear-end

stellar: outstanding

sought: wanted; searched for

parental leave: time off from work when a child is born

1   If you spent 2009 **hunkered down** in your cubicle, hoping to avoid the HR manager's **pink slips**, you weren't alone. Forget the **foosball** table, the sweet view, and the free cola, it was a year to be thankful just to have the pleasure of pulling in a paycheck.

2   Fortunately, even in the worst of times, the smartest employers recognize that to attract and **retain** the very best, they've got to pony up for more than just the basics. And the good news is that, after a rocky year or two, many of those companies now seem positioned to grow, which means more opportunity for you, those ambitious employees-to-be they so covet.

3   As part of our regular efforts to bring you the skinny on who's best, we **rounded up** 20 first-rate employers. They offer great benefits, competitive pay, family-friendly policies, a commitment to professional development, inspiring leadership, great **digs**, or all of the above. And, you guessed it, they're all hiring. So, whether you're just curious or actively seeking a new place to park your **patootie** from 9 to 5, read on to learn what these **stellar** employers have to offer.

How We Found Them

4   We started our process with a round of calls to the professionals who deal with employers firsthand: recruiters, business development leaders, community leaders, and, of course, employees. To be considered, employers then filled out our detailed questionnaire, which **sought** information on 401(k) programs, health benefits, diversity initiatives, career development offerings, maternity and **parental leave**, and much more. In considering companies, we worked to end up with a mix of large and small companies from a variety of industries. As always, companies had to be financially healthy and hiring in the coming year. Our list is not ranked; the employers are listed in random order.

Ascend One

Employees: 735 total; 455 in Maryland.

privately held: owned by a family or small group of people

Who they are: A *privately held* family of businesses—including CareOne Services, Amerix and 3CI—that help consumers get out of debt and manage their finances.

What we love: A virtual work option that lets employees work from anywhere.

Best benefits: Formal mentoring, tuition assistance of up to $5,000 per year, adoption assistance, up to four weeks' vacation in the first year of employment.

5   Getting from her Baltimore County home to Ascend One's Columbia offices used to be a one-hour haul for Raenice Bains, a quality specialist who has been with Ascend One for seven years. Evenings were worse. The commute to her Coppin State college classes often meant crawling bumper to bumper for more than an hour and a half.

6   "It was awful," says Bains, 33. "Stressful mornings, stressful evenings, no time to study."

7   But these days, it takes her about 30 seconds to get to work: That's because Bains is part of Ascend One's vast virtual workforce, and her commute takes her no farther than the second floor, to a home office that once was a den. There she logs on to the company's network and monitors the calls of Ascend One's customer service representatives, 80 percent of whom also work from home.

intranet: computer network restricted to employees of a business

8   To stay in touch with workmates, she uses the company's newly updated **intranet,** The Vibe, and only occasionally visits the office.

9   "It's been a great experience," says Bains, who has been working from home for about two years. "It helps me to be more involved in my school work and gives me time to study."

commute: trip to your work

10   And while the super-short **commute** may be the biggest bonus, Bains also credits telecommuting with allowing her to pitch in more for her parents, with whom she shares a home, especially her father. "My father's been sick, so working from home has helped me to help him," she says.

11   And Ascend One's tuition reimbursement program has been icing on the cake for Bains: It's paying for part of her schooling and gives her one more reason to love her job. "I wouldn't trade it for the world," she says.

CareFirst BlueCross BlueShield

Location: Canton, Owings Mills, and other locations regionally.

Employees: 5,250 total; 2,891 in the Baltimore area.

Who they are: A not-for-profit health insurer.

What we love: Solid benefits, family-friendly policies.

Best benefits: Six weeks paid maternity leave, on-site fitness center, tuition assistance up to $4,000, flexible work arrangements, on-site dining, bank, and dry cleaners.

(continued)

12   If you're looking for an example of how CareFirst helps its employees move up the ladder, you need look no farther than Julie Fisher, who started working for the organization nearly 25 years ago as a claims examiner.

13   "I was actually collecting unemployment and had just gotten out of the army," says Fisher, who today is senior director of service and operations technical support. "It's such a big company with so much opportunity." It helped, too, that Fisher's immediate bosses focused heavily on development and often acted as mentors, both formally and informally.

14   In fact, their mere presence was inspirational. "I would see different women here in the company being very successful and progressing and being valued," says Fisher. "There are a number of females in significant roles here and they are very **accessible**."

accessible: easy to get to

15   In fact, 62 percent of CareFirst's management team is female. And the organization has long had family-friendly policies in place—like flexible scheduling. "I've always had management that was very flexible," says Fisher, who had four children while working at CareFirst and at times had to take advantage of that flexibility. "In turn, I've made it a practice to ensure that that flexibility was there as well" for other employees.

16   And now that her children are in college, Fisher is equally grateful for the company's benefits, including its retirement and savings plans. "Their benefits overall here are very, very rich," she says.

10 Fun Places to Work

Orioles: Solid benefits and a culture of promoting from within, not to mention the ballpark views and free O's games.

The National Aquarium: The Aquarium has positions that range from "visitors' services" jobs to marine mammal trainers, and boasts an upbeat, **explorative** culture.

explorative: looking for new ideas

Maryland Institute College of Art: MICA has tuition reimbursement, a hearty 403(b) match, and you're surrounded by creativity.

Millennial Media: This Canton-based mobile advertising network offers up the fun, fast-paced culture you'd expect from a **startup,** plus ample benefits.

startup: new business

Blue Sky Factory: This little Federal Hill tech company offers up solid benefits, bonuses, and a super-casual dress code.

Planit: The fast-paced advertising and marketing agency has a fun and funky workspace with fabulous harbor views, plus a beer-stocked bar.

Trader Joe's: This specialty grocer has a casual, energetic environment, plus a promote-from-within culture.

Baseball Factory: This Columbia-based organization trains players of all ages and advises high school baseball players on the recruiting process.

Ravens: The organization offers game tickets, use of the team's training facilities, and on-site meals served during the season.

The Baltimore Museum of Art: The BMA has impressive benefits, a collaborative culture, and it's one of the few cultural organizations that avoided layoffs last year.

...

Questions for Discussion and Writing

1. What is your initial reaction to this evaluation?
2. How do the personal examples help show what the writer is saying about these companies? Are the personal examples effective? Why?
3. What might be your most important criterion for a good place to work? Why?
4. How would you answer this question, from the *Book of Questions*: If all jobs paid the same, what would you do?
5. The author has a section titled "10 Fun Places to Work." What do you think of the criteria she uses for this section of her evaluation?
6. If you had to choose between a fun place to work and a drudge job that paid better, which would you select? Why?
7. Make a list of the criteria that writer Antoniades uses in her "10 Fun Places to Work" section. Which of these is the most important to you? Why?

Improve Your Vocabulary Activity

Use the highlighted and defined words from "Best Places to Work 2010" in a sentence or in a paragraph.

Travel for Distinction: UGA Study Abroad Offers Many Options

Eva Vasquez

This reading appeared in the University of Georgia's student newspaper, where writer Eva Vasquez evaluates the school's study abroad program and also compares its exchange program. Have you ever wanted to study abroad for a semester or year? Where would you like to do so? What would you study?

daydreaming: having a fantasy dream when awake

fulfilling: completing

time-consuming: taking a lot of time

1 For students who spend class **daydreaming** of far off destinations, studying abroad may be the perfect way to get an education while **fulfilling** dreams of exotic travel.

2 Finding the right fit can be a **time-consuming** process, but the benefits of a successful study abroad experience can be worth the time and effort. About 25 percent of University students decide to study abroad, said Kasee Laster, director of study abroad.

3 "The first advantage is that we believe it can help you be a better citizen for your country and the world," Laster said. "It increases your flexibility and adaptability, and it is a great way to learn a language."

(*continued*)

UGA: University of Georgia at Athens, GA

entail: include; require

immersion: fully a part of

Three Avenues

4   The team of study abroad advisors in the Office of International Education can help students take advantage of the many types of programs offered. There are three main avenues of doing so: **UGA** study abroad programs, UGA exchange programs and external programs.

5   "UGA has 100 faculty-led study abroad options—we have programs in about 50 or 60 countries a year," Laster said. "On top of that, we have 50 exchange partners around the world, where we trade students."

6   Exchange programs are typically longer than a study abroad program, lasting a semester or a year, and usually **entail** greater **immersion** into the country.

7   Students can also take part in programs from any other University System of Georgia School, and the University is now a member of the South Eastern Conference Academic Consortium, which allows students to engage in programs from other SEC members and pay in-state tuition.

8   Study abroad advisors such as Julie Escobedo and Colleen Larson help students make the right decision based on their individual needs.

9   "Usually students come in with an idea of either a location, or they have some academic requirements they want to fill and are looking for a program that specializes in that," Escobedo said.

10   Though academic requirements are a good starting point, students should not feel restricted by major requirements.

11   "There are creative ways to look at your degree—you can do your electives or core credits," Larson said.

University students take a study break at Oxford University. UGA at Oxford is one of a wealth of opportunities for students studying abroad.
Source: robjudgesstudying/Alamy

Specific Programs

12   One of the tried and true programs is UGA at Oxford.

13   "It has a lot to do with the variety of classes that they offer, as well as the structure and the academic system," Escobedo said.

14   Kalpen Trivedi, director of UGA at Oxford study abroad programs, takes great pride in the nearly 20-year-old program.

15   "The vast majority of our courses are taught by faculty at the University of Oxford, which allows us to draw on a large pool of faculty expertise and offer a significantly greater variety of courses than is usually the case with study abroad," Trivedi said. "The other thing to note is that we offer a **comprehensive** residential experience, and our students are completely **integrated** into college life in Oxford, which makes for a very good balance of challenging academics and varied social activity."

16   To build international bridges, UGA at Oxford has joined forces with the University's Washington semester program to offer a joint study abroad. Students will spend the month of June in Washington, D.C., and the month of July in Oxford, earning six semester hours of credit. Applications are now being accepted for summer 2010.

17   Another program that is growing in popularity is the study abroad in the South Pacific and Caribbean.

18   "They have **Maymesters** that go to Australia and New Zealand – they travel around a lot, and students get upper division, kind of elective credit," Escobedo said.

19   But those are only two out of a **plethora** of options.

20   "We offer afternoon information sessions three times a week that are designed to **acquaint** you with the options and then help you narrow it down with a small group of advisors," Laster said.

The Funding

21   Another critical aspect to consider is money.

22   Traditional study abroad programs are handled with **OASIS** like any other class, so the HOPE scholarship and academic credits are automatic. HOPE can still be used with exchange and external programs, but students must fill out a credit approval form, which allows students to receive credits during study abroad and ensures maintained status as a University student and financial aid eligibility.

23   Students should also look critically at program prices and understand that the listed price of each program does not cover the same expenses.

24   The same concept applies when students compare the costs of a study abroad program versus an exchange program.

25   "Do not discount a semester program," Larson said. An exchange program for a semester might have a bigger price tag than a shorter summer study abroad program, but students should take into account the per day cost and the amount of credits you are earning.

(continued)

comprehensive: complete

integrated: part of

Maymesters: brief study-abroad courses; usually only a few weeks long

plethora: lots of; too many of something

acquaint: to know

OASIS: student information and registration system at UGA

excursions: trip

26   "So a semester exchange program may be $5,000 more than a semester at UGA, but you might pay that much for a program fee," Larson said.

27   Exchange programs do not have the big package pricetag for extras—weekend **excursions**, sightseeing, food allowances—like a study abroad program may, so students can pick individual travel arrangements. However, the package of activities might be appealing to those who prefer more structure.

28   Many factors must be taken into consideration when studying abroad, but with the appropriate use of planning and resources, it can be an opportunity for any student willing to put forth the effort.

Questions for Discussion and Writing

1. Does this essay make you more or less interested in studying abroad? Why?
2. Were you surprised to read, in the second paragraph, that "About 25 percent of University students decide to study abroad"? What percentage of your own classmates do you think may want to study abroad?
3. Vasquez lists three main criteria for her evaluation: types of programs, specific programs, and funding. Which do you feel is the most important? Why?
4. Do you know anyone who has studied abroad? If so, how would you describe his/her experiences?
5. How effective is this text, as an evaluation? Why?

Improve Your Vocabulary Activity

Use the highlighted and defined words from "Travel for Distinction: UGA Study Abroad Offers Many Options" in a sentence or in a paragraph.

Community College vs. University

Jeren W. Canning

Jeren W. Canning is the former Editor-in-Chief of The Globe Newspaper *in Salt Lake City. Canning graduated from Salt Lake Community College with an Associate's Degree in Communication and the University of Utah with a Bachelor's Degree in Mass Communication. As you read his essay weighing two higher education options, think about why you selected the college or university you attended, and if you used any of the same criteria that Canning outlines below.*

SLCC: Salt Lake Community College

U: abbreviation for University of Utah

1   Three years ago, two friends graduated from high school. The first, Jason Lee, was accepted at the University of Utah. The second, J.D. Hooton, was also accepted, but opted to attend **SLCC** before transferring to the **U**.

2   Since his entrance at the U., Lee has spent much of his money being what he calls "just a number to the large university." He reduced his class load due to low finances and is currently considered a sopho-more, when he should now be considered a senior. After two years of struggling with the university he decided enough is enough and stopped taking classes.

in over my head: overwhelmed by something

3   "I figured I would be ahead of the game because I was accepted to the U., but I was **in over my head**," Lee said. "I simply wasn't ready for a University. I was only 17 and didn't know what I was getting myself into."

4   Hooton on the other hand has taken the easier, but just as academic route. He is currently finishing up his associate's degree at SLCC and will transfer to the University of Utah in January, where he will complete his bachelor's degree.

5   "My friends gave me a hard time for choosing SLCC over the U.," Hooton said. "At least I have a little money in my pocket after tuition, and now I feel I'm ready to take the next step."

synonymous: the same as

prestige: distinction; reputation

6   These stories are **synonymous** with many of the students across the state. When offered the chance to attend either a University or a Community College, it is a very difficult decision. A university has the **prestige**, but a community college has many advantages also.

7   Money is always a problem for college students. No matter which way you look at it, students will end up spending thousands of dollars each year for tuition. One positive is that SLCC is on the lighter side of the tuition scale. A full-time student at SLCC can expect to spend approximately $2,300 a year, where the **tab** at the University of Utah can tip the scale at about $5,000. More than double the cost, and for students on a budget $2,700 goes a very long way.

tab: cost of something; the bill

8   To get a quality education the size of classes can play a major role. A general education class at SLCC may consist of about 20 students, maybe as

(continued)

entrepreneur:
someone who starts a
business

high as 50 depending on the size of classroom. But no matter the size, the instructor of a class of only 20 students will have much more time to devote to each student. At the University of Utah, the size of a general education class could number in the hundreds, which truly makes students feel like "just a number."

9   As any business **entrepreneur** would say, "location, location, location." SLCC has a total of 13 different campuses all across the Salt Lake Valley, from Downtown Salt Lake to Draper. Everyone in the valley is within 15 minutes from a SLCC campus. Students of the U. are at least a 30 minute drive or public transit ride to the campus. Also take into account that the U has only one true campus.

10   As much as SLCC students complain about parking at each of the campuses, it is a lot easier than parking at the U. A full year parking pass to the U can cost as much as $120, depending on proximity to the buildings, and they are restricted to only a few lots across the campus. In contrast, a full year pass at SLCC is only $20, and is good for every parking lot at every campus.

clout: power

11   On the prestige front, of course the University of Utah holds more **clout** than SLCC, but there is something to be said for a person who spreads their education out over two or more institutions. SLCC, although, has grown in **notoriety** as of late, due to the school's more hands-on educational experience. As it is now, many graduates of SLCC choose to transfer to the U. to complete their educational experience. When they leave SLCC the students are many times half way to their Bachelor's degree, already having many of their general education requirements behind them.

notoriety: reputation;
sometimes a negative
reputation

12   "The junior college system is an excellent way for students to get started in the world of higher education," Jodee Taylor said. "Many students just aren't ready for the four-year university set-up, but by the end of their two-year degree they are definitely ready to go to the next level."

Questions for Discussion and Writing

1. What is your initial reaction to this evaluation?
2. Did you use any of the same criteria that Canning listed to decide where you would attend college?
3. Of the criteria listed, which is the most important? Why?
4. What rhetorical strategies (such as *compare and contrast*) can you point to in Cannning's evaluation?
5. What did you learn from this evaluation that was new?
6. How would you improve this evaluation? Would data or charts or graphs help you understand it better?

Improve Your Vocabulary Activity

Use the highlighted and defined words from "Community College vs. University" in a sentence or in a paragraph.

MyWritingLab™ For support in meeting this chapter's objectives, log in to www.mywritinglab.com and select **Essay Development—Comparison and Contrast**.

Chapter **14**

Writing to Persuade
Using Multiple Strategies

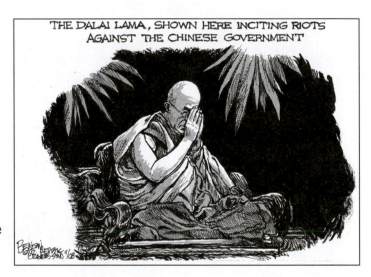

THE DALAI LAMA, SHOWN HERE INCITING RIOTS AGAINST THE CHINESE GOVERNMENT

Learning **O**bjectives

In this chapter, you will learn to:

LO1 Consider the writer's situation, and determine your purpose and audience

LO2 Use appropriate rhetorical strategies to *persuade* your audience

LO3 Use invention and discovery strategies to come up with ideas and details

LO4 Write a thesis statement that states your claim, or point of view

LO5 Organize and write your first draft

LO6 Revise your essay, and prepare a final draft

The Dalai Lama, as you probably know, is the spiritual leader of the people of Tibet. China considers Tibet to be a part of China and the Dalai Lama now lives in exile, in India. More than once, the Chinese government has accused the Dalai Lama of encouraging Tibetans to riot, and Steve Benson's cartoon focuses on that accusation. Could his praying actually cause a riot? Is this cartoon persuasive in some way? How?

To **persuade** someone, you hope that person will accept what you are saying: that they are convinced by your argument. Argument in college writing does not mean there is a winner and a loser (as there usually is in, say, a court trial). Rather an **argument** is an organized text that makes a **claim** (thesis statement) and provides **evidence** (data, quotations, statistics, etc.) to support that claim.

Often, you will try to persuade someone to act, and if they do what you suggest, they clearly have been persuaded. For example, if your best friend suggested that a particular film was one that you should see, and if you were persuaded by that person, then you would *believe* it was a good film and perhaps even go and see the film.

Everyday Writing Activity: Can a Cartoon Be Persuasive?

In your journal, briefly answer these questions about the Dalai Lama cartoon. Your instructor may want you to share your responses with the rest of the class.

1. Is cartoonist Steve Benson being serious or funny? What can you point to in the cartoon to support your answer?
2. What point is the cartoonist trying to make?
3. Do you think the cartoon is persuasive?
4. Do you like this cartoon? Why or why not?
5. Can a cartoon make an argument? Why?
6. Is a cartoon an effective way to make an argument? Why?

LO1

Consider the writer's situation, and determine your purpose and audience

The Writer's Situation

In this chapter, our focus is on helping you learn to use several rhetorical strategies to construct an effective argument. That way you will have more than one approach to use, depending on your audience, what points you are trying to make, and so on.

Consider for a moment that you may be asked to solve a problem by persuading readers that your solution to that problem is better than others, as the writing assignments in this chapter ask you to do. You might construct your argument by using the rhetorical strategies of

- *Description.* Before readers will accept your solution to solve a problem, they first have to understand and believe that there is a problem. So, first you would describe the problem, and the solution, in enough detail so readers can understand them.
- *Definition.* You would define any terms readers might not already know.
- *Exemplification.* You might provide examples to help readers see what you mean.
- *Comparison and contrast.* You might compare the problem to other problems. Or, you may explain how the solution you suggest compares and/or contrasts with other possible solutions.
- *Cause and effect.* How does the problem affect your school or community? How will implementing your proposed solution affect it?

If your instructor asks you to do the following Everyday Writing Activity, in which you contact your uncle to convince him to loan you some money, how might you *describe* your situation and why you need a loan? How might you *define* the terms of the loan? What *examples* would you provide to help convince your uncle to loan you the money you need?

The key to deciding which rhetorical strategy or strategies might be best for your argumentative paper is to "try some out"—try writing to describe your topic in detail, and you will see how that specific strategy is useful (or not) to making an effective argument.

Remember, too, that effective writing draws on the **rhetorical appeals**:

- *Ethos:* the credibility of the writer. In the following example, why should your uncle believe that you need the money and will repay him?
- *Logos:* logical reasons for your argument.
- *Pathos:* emotional arguments. Should you, in the following writing activity, try to make your uncle feel sorry for you so he will lend you money? Will such a strategy be effective, do you think?

For more on effectively using the rhetorical appeals, see Chapter 5.

Everyday Writing Activity: Borrowing Some Cash

Assume that you need some money and decide to try to borrow it from your Uncle Gordon. He has lent you money in the past, and in fact you still owe your uncle $200 from the last loan he gave you. But now you need some additional money for next semester's college costs. For this brief note, you get to decide how much money you need.

In effect, you are trying to persuade Uncle Gordon to loan you more money. Consider what rhetorical strategies (like *description* or *narration*) will help you convince your Uncle Gordon to give you the loan.

In your journal, write a brief note to your uncle asking for another loan. Some of the things you might want to include in your note may be:

- How much money you need, and exactly why. How much detail will Uncle Gordon need for him to decide to give you the cash? Can you say that you need $350, or will he need a detailed breakdown ($100 for books, $50 for a bus pass, etc.)?
- When you can pay back the loan and what the terms might be. Do you want to offer to pay interest? If so, how much? Would that make the whole loan idea too impersonal or would it make it more business-like?
- Do you want to explain why you have not yet repaid the previous loan? Would this be a place to use an emotional appeal?

Your instructor may want you to share your note with the rest of the class.

LO2

Use appropriate rhetorical strategies to *persuade* your audience

Persuading through Multiple Strategies

This essay was originally published in *Newsweek*, and writer Mary Sherry immediately gets readers' attention with her title—which actually refers to something other than what readers might expect. Do you agree with what Sherry has to say about failing high school students who do not perform satisfactorily? Why? As you read Sherry's essay, consider how she uses several rhetorical strategies to make her argument.

In Praise of the F Word

Mary Sherry

Sherry's thesis: Lots of students graduate without mastering high school subjects. This is the problem she wants to solve.

1 Tens of thousands of 18-year-olds will graduate this year and be handed meaningless diplomas. These diplomas won't look any different from those awarded their luckier classmates. Their validity will be questioned only when their employers discover that these graduates are semiliterate.

2 Eventually a fortunate few will find their way into educational-repair shops—adult-literacy programs, such as the one where I teach basic grammar and writing. There, high-school graduates and high-school dropouts pursuing

(continued)

Sherry argues that students have been cheated by the educational system: she is *describing* the problem.

Sherry provides *examples*—quotations from students—to show readers what she means.

Sherry uses *narration* to tell her own story and how it relates to her argument.

Sherry argues that one way to solve this problem is to threaten failure.

Sherry provides a personal example.

Sherry uses *exemplification* as well as *narration* in her argument.

Sherry argues that students must understand the stakes: if they believe they might fail and be held back, they will work harder. Is this an effective argument?

graduate-equivalency certificates will learn the skills they should have learned in school. They will also discover they have been cheated by our educational system.

3   As I teach, I learn a lot about our schools. Early in each session I ask my students to write about an unpleasant experience they had in school. No writers' block here! "I wish someone would have had made me stop doing drugs and made me study." "I liked to party and no one seemed to care." "I was a good kid and didn't cause any trouble, so they just passed me along even though I didn't read well and couldn't write." And so on.

4   I am your basic do-gooder, and prior to teaching this class I blamed the poor academic skills our kids have today on drugs, divorce and other impediments to concentration necessary for doing well in school. But, as I rediscover each time I walk into the classroom, before a teacher can expect students to concentrate, he has to get their attention, no matter what distractions may be at hand. There are many ways to do this, and they have much to do with teaching style. However, if style alone won't do it, there is another way to show who holds the winning hand in the classroom. That is to reveal the trump card of failure.

5   I will never forget a teacher who played that card to get the attention of one of my children. Our youngest, a world-class charmer, did little to develop his intellectual talents but always got by. Until Mrs. Stifter.

6   Our son was a high-school senior when he had her for English. "He sits in the back of the room talking to his friends," she told me. "Why don't you move him to the front row?" I urged, believing the embarrassment would get him to settle down. Mrs. Stifter looked at me steely-eyed over her glasses. "I don't move seniors," she said. "I flunk them." I was flustered. Our son's academic life flashed before my eyes. No teacher had ever threatened him with that before. I regained my composure and managed to say that I thought she was right.

7   By the time I got home I was feeling pretty good about this. It was a radical approach for these times, but, well, why not? "She's going to flunk you," I told my son. I did not discuss it any further. Suddenly English became a priority in his life. He finished out the semester with an A.

8   I know one example doesn't make a case, but at night I see a parade of students who are angry and resentful for having been passed along until they could no longer even pretend to keep up. Of average intelligence or better, they eventually quit school, concluding they were too dumb to finish. "I should have been held back," is a comment I hear frequently. Even sadder are those students who are high-school graduates who say to me after a few weeks of class, "I don't know how I ever got a high-school diploma."

9   Passing students who have not mastered the work cheats them and the employers who expect graduates to have basic skills. We excuse this dishonest behavior by saying kids can't learn if they come from terrible environments. No one seems to stop to think that—no matter what environments they come from—most kids don't put school first on their list unless they perceive something is at stake. They'd rather be sailing.

This part of Sherry's argument compares high school to adult students.

10   Many students I see at night could give expert testimony on unemployment, chemical dependency, abusive relationships. In spite of these difficulties, they have decided to make education a priority. They are motivated by the desire for a better job or the need to hang on to the one they've got. They have a healthy fear of failure.

11   People of all ages can rise above their problems, but they need to have a reason to do so. Young people generally don't have the maturity to value education in the same way my adult students value it. But fear of failure, whether economic or academic, can motivate both.

12   Flunking as a regular policy has just as much merit today as it did two generations ago. We must review the threat of flunking and see it as it really is—a positive teaching tool. It is an expression of confidence by both teachers and parents that the students have the ability to learn the material presented to them. However, making it work again would take a dedicated, caring conspiracy between teachers and parents. It would mean facing the tough reality that passing kids who haven't learned the material—while it might save them grief for the short term—dooms them to long-term illiteracy. It would mean that teachers would have to follow through on their threats, and parents would have to stand behind them, knowing their children's best interests are indeed at stake. This means no more doing Scott's assignments for him because he might fail. No more passing Jodi because she's such a nice kid.

Sherry restates her thesis and summarizes her argument.

13   This is a policy that worked in the past and can work today. A wise teacher, with the support of his parents, gave our son the opportunity to succeed—or fail. It's time we return this choice to all students.

Questions for Discussion and Writing

1. Did Sherry's title get your attention and make you want to read her essay?
2. What did you learn about writing an effective persuasive essay from this essay?
3. Do you agree with Sherry's claim about "meaningless" diplomas (paragraph 1)? Why?
4. Do you think of students in this way—that they are cheated by America's educational system (paragraph 4)?
5. Do you know anyone who has been *passed along* when he/she should have failed a class? Has that ever happened to you?
6. How effective is Sherry's use of the various rhetorical strategies in her argument?
7. Do you think it is better to pass a student who deserves to fail, rather than to fail and hold back that student? Why?

WRITING ASSIGNMENTS

We give you several options for a persuasive writing assignment in this section; all of them ask you to write about a problem and a possible solution. We think that **problem-solving** is a useful focus for a persuasive writing assignment, for several reasons:

- Solving a problem gives you a real situation to work with: here is the problem to solve (your purpose for writing), here is the audience you are writing for, here are some possible formats to use, and so on.
- Various kinds of problems ask you to employ **rhetorical strategies** in different ways; you will need to determine which strategies might help you persuade a specific audience.
- Finally, solving a problem lends itself to persuasive writing: you get to argue about what a problem consists of, why people should be concerned about it, and why your solution for solving it is better than other possible solutions.

We have tried to create situations that you might have been in or that you might find yourself involved with one day. These give you the chance to simulate possible problems and arguments about those situations, perhaps before you actually find yourself involved in one.

Writing Assignment One: Solving a Problem at Your School

For this assignment, assume that your writing instructor has asked you to consider a current problem on your campus and to write a persuasive paper that suggests how the problem might be solved. Possible problems you might consider include

- Parking issues.
- Dining options (food options; cost; availability).
- General cost issues (tuition; fees; books).
- Litter; graffiti; broken sidewalks; poor outdoor lighting in walkways; inadequate number of emergency call-boxes.
- Class availability (if you cannot take the required classes when you need to, how can you graduate?).

For this assignment, describe the problem in sufficient detail so your readers can understand it, explain your solution, and persuade your readers that yours is the best solution to the problem.

Writing Assignment Two: Solving a Consumer Problem

For this assignment, assume that you recently made a major purchase and now want to return the product for a refund. You know that businesses (naturally) do not want to refund the cost of a product, as that means cash out of their pocket—so they most likely will want to fix or replace your product. You, though, do not want a replacement or repair, but rather, a full refund. Write a letter to a fictitious company about your purchase, asking for a full refund. What rhetorical strategies (*definition*, *description*, etc.) will be the most effective to use? What rhetorical appeals (*ethos/your credibility*, *logos/ logical appeal*, *pathos/emotional appeal*) will help you get the refund you want?

Writing Assignment Three: Solving a Community Problem

For this assignment, assume that in your communication class you have been asked to construct an opinion essay for your local newspaper about a community problem and a solution to that problem. You want to persuade readers that the problem is important so they should be concerned about it and that your proposed solution will solve the problem.

Note: Opinion essays are slightly different than letters to the editor of a newspaper, because opinion essay are a bit longer and give you more time to develop your argument.

Optional Multi-Modal Assignment: E-mail

Assume you are given writing assignment three to describe/define a community problem and propose a solution to that problem. In an e-mail, describe/ define the problem and your proposed solution. Remember that e-mails are generally brief and to-the-point kinds of communication.

 **Critical Thinking Activity: Questions to Ask before You Start**

Spend some time now considering the persuasive assignment you have been asked to construct, and do some planning so your overall task will

(continued)

be easier. Consider how you might answer these questions, and answer them in your journal:

1. Your *purpose* in writing is to persuade readers about something (how to solve a school problem, a community problem, etc.). What evidence might help make your text persuasive for your audience?

2. How would you describe the *audience* for your persuasive text? What *rhetorical strategies* (*description, definition, narration,* etc.) might be most useful for your text?

3. When someone tries to convince you about something, what kinds of *details and examples* and *visual aids* are the most useful to help you understand what they mean (and perhaps be persuaded by their arguments)? How might answering that question help you as you write your own persuasive text?

4. Consider what research you might conduct to provide *evidence* for your persuasive text. Who could you talk with? What kinds of *research* might be useful?

LO3

Use invention and discovery strategies to come up with ideas and details

Invention and Discovery Activities

Remember that the idea with any kind of invention/discovery activity is to help you get started with your writing. Often, it is really hard to just sit down and write, so using several invention activities will help get some of your ideas onto paper.

Once you have done some invention work, once you have some ideas on paper, you should have some sense of what you would like to argue: your preliminary **thesis statement** for your persuasive paper. We use the word "preliminary" at this point because once you start writing, your argument might change; as you conduct more research, you may want to modify your thesis. So for now, consider that you need something to start with—your preliminary thesis statement—and understand that you might want to modify it as you draft and revise your paper.

Everyday Writing Activity: Brainstorming

In your journal, brainstorm about how you define or describe your topic: if you had to describe it to a friend, what would you say? What terms would you use? For example, if you were working on assignment three, how would you define and describe the community problem you want to focus on? (For more on brainstorming, see page 80.) Your instructor may want you to share your brainstorming with the rest of the class.

Student Writing: Marcie Willen's Brainstorming

Student writer Marcie Willen was assigned a persuasive paper for her writing class, but the instructor left the subject matter pretty open: "Write about a local or campus problem that interests you," the assignment said, "and explain the reasons that cause the problem, and suggest what you think is the best solution."

Many students have difficulty with such open assignments, and Marcie was no exception. She told her best friend that she "didn't have a clue" what to write about—and Marcie's friend suggested that Marcie brainstorm some possible problems. Here is part of her writing:

> How about a local problem, as that would be easy to focus on as compared some big issue. I wonder about
> - Why local residents are homeless.
> - Why is there always a traffic jam on Milton Road?
> - Why does tuition keep going up for us students?
> - What is that tuition spent on, anyway?
> - We used to have, I think, a fee for child care on campus. Why did that go away?
> - Do we even need child care on campus? Do we have a lot of working parents who would use it?
>
> Now that I'm writing about it, I wonder about campus child care. I don't have any children but if I did, it sure would be nice to bring them to campus while I was in class… but who would pay for that? And maybe we don't even need it here… I wonder if we have a lot of working parents who are students?

Note that Marcie is working her way through some ideas—brainstorming about them—and now has come to a problem and a question: Does her college need to provide childcare and if so, why? That gives Marcie a starting point for her paper.

LO4

Write a thesis statement that states your claim, or point of view

Writing a Thesis Statement for Your Persuasive Text

Once you have some ideas on paper, you probably will come to some conclusion about the point you want to make—your **thesis statement**. Sometimes students think their topic is the same as their thesis, but they really are different. Your **topic** is the subject you are focusing on (in student writer Willen's case, a child care facility on campus), while your **thesis** is what you want to argue for, about that topic (Marcie could argue "we need to have affordable childcare for our students who are parents"). Your thesis or point is just that: your main argument, distilled into one or two sentences.

Everyday Writing Activity: Thesis Statement

This activity is designed to help you figure out and get onto paper at least a little of what you think and believe about a topic you are considering— a possible thesis statement. This activity also asks you to start considering where you might learn more about your problem and to determine potential solutions.

One way to help you determine your own thesis is to complete these items in your journal:

I really believe that _____ is a serious problem for our college or community. If I had to describe or define the problem right now, I'd say _____.

I might learn more about this problem if I _____.
Now complete this statement:

If I had to argue about a possible solution to the problem, some solutions might be _____, _____, and _____.

I might learn more about potential solutions if I _____.

Thesis statements that indicate the problem and a possible solution might be worded this way: _____

Your instructor may want you to share your notes with the rest of the class.

As we noted earlier, at this point in the writing process, your thesis statement should not be set in stone. It is a good starting point for your first draft, but assume it might change as you learn more and as you construct your argument paper, through the writing itself.

For student writer Marcie Willen, until she conducts research and gets some of what she learns and her own ideas onto paper, she will not know what her final thesis or point is. At this stage, Marcie could easily end up with a thesis that says

> There are many reasons our campus needs to provide child care for students who have children and work, and here is how we could do so...

But—depending on what she learns through her research—Marcie also could end up with one of these thesis statements:

> Our campus needs and should subsidize child care for its working students, because...
>
> We need to provide child care for students who have children, and our Nursing Program students would benefit and learn from it because...

We suggest that you plan on delaying your final thesis statement until you have conducted research and written several drafts. Start with a tentative thesis statement—that will help you get going—but understand that you may change your point of view as you write and revise.

LO5
Organize and write your first draft

Organizing and Writing Your First Draft

Now you have some ideas on paper in the form of a list, or a cluster diagram showing how your ideas relate to one another, or a few pages of freewriting. You also have an initial idea for your thesis statement—the point you think you want to argue for. And, you have spent some time writing to try out several rhetorical strategies. So, where do you go from here? How can you take what you have so far and organize it into an effective argument?

One way to organize an argument, usually referred to as the "classical scheme," was first outlined by the Greek philosopher Aristotle about 2,500 years ago (Aristotle is the same person who described the rhetorical appeals discussed on pages 72–76). Aristotle listened to public speeches and determined how the best ones were organized. His organizational advice also works for a written argument.

In Aristotle's classical scheme of organization, you start with an introduction, so your readers will know what you are focusing on. Here is where your *main claim* or thesis statement goes—you want your readers, right off the bat, to understand your point. From a reader's viewpoint, they now have a road map to follow: they know what your main point is, and so now they will look for reasoning and evidence that supports that point. From your perspective as a writer, this helps you connect each idea that follows back to your main point—and if you cannot make that connection, then that idea does not belong in this paper, right?

The next section is usually the longest, because this is where you provide supporting reasons and evidence for those assertions—where, in other words, you make your argument and try to convince your readers that you have good ideas. The third section is where you list any objections to your claim, and refute those objections. Finally, you restate your claim in your conclusion.

Assume that you are writing a persuasive paper about the parking issues on your college campus. You might use the organizational plan shown on the next page. Note, though, that we have only shown three reasons why parking is a problem. If you were to write a paper about the parking problem on your campus, you may have several more reasons. Also, for this illustration we show only two pieces of evidence for each reason for the parking problem. You would want more evidence, because more evidence will help convince your readers.

The classical organizational approach looks like this.

Organizational Chart for a Persuasive Essay

Main claim or thesis: Parking on campus is a major problem.

First reason
There are 6800 students with 3100 cars and 2000 parking spaces.

Second reason
Both the campus and nearby neighborhoods are congested.

Third reason
No one gets tickets, so everyone parks wherever they want.

Supporting evidence
1. During popular class times, we have too many cars looking for too few spaces.

2. During rush hour, it's even worse.

Supporting evidence
1. There are only three ways to get off campus

2. The intersections inside the campus also are congested

Supporting evidence
1. Friends never get tickets, no matter where they park

2. The police department doesn't have the manpower to enforce parking rules.

Solutions
1. Add a new parking garage

2. Widen the intersections both on campus and leaving campus

3. Add a patrol officer to the campus police to ticket illegal parkers

The other side: Objections to your solutions
1. We cannot afford a new parking garage

2. We cannot afford to widen the intersections

3. We cannot afford to hire another person for the campus police

Refuting the objections to your solutions
1. A parking garage would pay for itself (cite data to show this)

2. The city will pay for changing the intersections

3. The tickets the new patrol officer would hand out will pay his or her salary

Conclusion
Our campus has a parking problem and these three actions will solve it.

Of course, there are other ways you might organize your persuasive text, but the classical approach is the most common—and very effective in most cases.

Student Writing: Marcie Willen's Introduction

Here is the introduction to student writer Marcie Willen's first draft of her paper that outlines some of her ideas about child care on her campus:

> At least three of my classmates are single parents, or parents who work, and it is difficult for them to attend college because of child care issues. Child care not only is expensive, it requires dropping-off and picking-up, often not at convenient times. Convenient for taking classes, that is. So they maybe take one or two classes a semester, hoping to get through. It seems to me that if our college had child care for its parent-students, it would be a good thing and more people could stay in school. I will start by defining what I mean by "child care." Then I will describe some of the people involved in this problem.

Note that Willen immediately lets her readers know that two of rhetorical strategies she will use include *definition* and *description*.

LO6
Revise your essay, and prepare a final draft

Revising: The Key to Effective Papers

Once you and your classmates have a draft of your persuasive papers, your instructor may provide feedback on your work or he/she may ask your class to help each other by providing feedback and suggestions on each other's papers. There are several different ways to do this (your instructor will guide you), and there are some general questions on page 114 that he/she may ask you to respond to as you read your classmate's papers.

Student Writing: Marcie Willen's Peer-Reviewed Draft

Several of student writer Willen's classmates read and responded to her first draft. Here is part of her draft along with their comments and suggestions. What suggestions would you have made on her work? Can you point out the rhetorical strategies she used in her paper?

I like your opening sentence; is there a title for your paper?

At least three of my classmates are single parents, or parents who work, and it is difficult for them to attend college because of child care issues. Child care not only is expensive, it requires dropping-off and

Confusing sentence— sounds like this interferes with the children's class.

picking-up, often not at convenient times. Convenient for taking classes, that is. So they maybe take one or two classes a semester, hoping to get through. It seems to me that if our college had child care for its parent-students, it would be a good thing and more people could stay in school. Without such a center, our students have to take their children to a facility and drop them off, perhaps at a time that interferes with their classes.

The important reason to get feedback and comments on your argument paper is those comments represent *real readers* responding to your ideas. Take their suggestions and comments seriously.

Here is how student writer Willen responded to a reader's suggestions: for her first paragraph, a reader wrote that one sentence seemed "confusing," because the reader did not understand the text. Here is Marcie's revised section:

A classmate was confused about dropping off and picking up children. Willen rewrote the sentence to clarify.

At least three of my classmates are single parents, or parents who work, and it is difficult for them to attend college because of child care issues. Child care not only is expensive, it requires dropping-off and picking-up, often not at convenient times. Convenient for taking classes, that is. So they maybe take one or two classes a semester, hoping to get through. It seems to me that if our college had child care for its parent-students, it would be a good thing and more people could stay in school. ~~Without such a center, our students have to take their children to a facility and drop them off, perhaps at a time that interferes with their classes.~~ This is really true in terms of picking children up from child care. What do parents do when the child care business closes before the parents' college classes end?

Writing Style Tip: Making Sure Pronouns Have a Clear Reference

Student writer Willen got a comment from a classmate that said "Confusing sentence—sounds like this interferes with the children's class" (have you ever received such a comment?). She reread that section of her work and saw that it *did* sound like she was writing about the children when she wrote

Without such a center, our students have to take their children to a facility and drop them off, perhaps at a time that interferes with their classes.

Who does "their" in "their classes" refer to? Because "children" is the noun closest to this phrase, it makes the sentence sound like the dropping off process refers to classes the children take, right? This is called an unclear pronoun reference because the pronoun "their" could refer to "children" or "our students."

Marcie really means it to refer to the students' classes. Here is Marcie's revision. Note how this change clarifies the original sentence.

> This is really true in terms of picking children up from child care. What do parents do when the child care business closes before the parents' college classes end?

For more on pronouns, see the Handbook pages 397–401.

 ## Critical Thinking Activity: Questions to Ask before You Revise

Now you have a first draft of your persuasive text, have reread it several times, and most likely you also have received comments and suggestions from your classmates (and perhaps from your instructor family members, or friends). You will recall from Chapter 8 that *revision* means to rethink and to reenvision your text—not to just fix surface errors. So consider:

1. Did any of the suggestions I received say anything about me not achieving my *purpose?* That I perhaps had misunderstood or misrepresented the information and details my *audience* needed to understand my argument?
2. Were readers convinced by my argument?
3. Did anyone tell me that they did not understand, or did anyone seem to have misunderstood, the *thesis statement* of my argument? How can I clarify it?
4. Did anyone suggest a *visual* (chart, graph, table, photograph, etc.) that might help improve my argument?

Use the following checklist to see whether your revised paper is finally done, or whether you need to make further changes before printing a final draft.

Revision Checklist for Your Persuasive Paper	
As you think about revising your paper, consider the parts of it that you want to make sure to include:	
Part of Your Paper	**Check √**
Title for your paper that gets your readers' attention	
Introduction with a clear thesis statement	

Part of Your Paper	Check √
Supporting paragraphs, each with a topic sentence, supporting evidence or examples, and a transition to the next paragraph (all information must relate to your argument, your point)	
Visual aids if they will help the purpose of your argument (charts, graphs, tables, etc.)	
Conclusion that summarizes your main points and restates your thesis	

Student Writing: Marcie Willen's Final Draft

Here is student writer Marcie Willen's final draft of her persuasive paper. Note also that Marcie has added a visual aid. Does the photograph help Marcie's paper? Why or why not? Can you suggest a more effective photograph?

Willen 1

Marcie Willen
Dr. Michael Vincent
ENG 099
15 Mar. 2011

Child Care for Our Student-Parents

At least three of my class-mates are single parents, or parents who work, and it is difficult for them to attend college because of child care issues. Child care not only is expensive, but parents have to get their children to the child care location. If we had child care on campus, it  would be open whenever we had classes meeting. But now, with transportation issues alone, there are some students who simply

(continued)

cannot attend school. Or, it will take them forever to finish, because of child care issues.

The term "child care" means providing a place and staff to take care of a student's child. The place should be on campus, so it's convenient for students to drop off and pick up their children. It should also be open when classes are meeting, and have trained staff members to take care of the children. Finally, the child care center should be cheap for student-parents.

There are several reasons why our college needs to provide this service for its students. First, a child care center will help students who have children to take classes. Without such a center, our students have to take their children to an off-campus facility. And often, the child care company has business hours different than when our classes are in session. This is really true in terms of picking children up from child care. What does a parent do when the child care business closes before the parent's college class ends? Maria, a classmate in my Anthropology class, ran into this problem last semester: her last class ended at 5:40, but the child care for her daughter ended at 5:00. Maria ended up dropping the Anthro class.

Maria also told me how expensive the child care was. For Maria's four-year-old daughter, child care was $35 a day. That may not seem like much, but Maria's classes were all M-W-F, so it added up to over $100 per week. If we had child care at our college, it should cost less. One reason why is because some of our students who wanted to be elementary teachers could staff it.

Such staffing would be inexpensive and give those future teachers some wonderful experience with working with children. Maybe some of our nursing students could help out with health issues. Both of those ideas would make our child care cost less. I interviewed Dr. Jensen, who is the head of our Education Program, and she thought such an idea—using her students to help staff the center—might "be doable," as she put it. "I really like the hands-on experience it would give our students," she told me.

Willen 3

Our college needs child care to help our working parent-students. One reason we need it is so that students could attend class and not have to worry about when they dropped off or picked up their child. Another would be that it costs less if our college provides it. Finally, our own students could get "real world" working experience in the child care center.

Willen 4

Works Cited

Jenson, Martha. Personal interview. 2 Feb. 2011.

Jones, Maria. Personal interview. 3 Feb. 2011.

 ## Critical Thinking Activity: Questions to Ask as You Reflect on Your Writing

In your journal, answer the questions your instructor assigns about the writing project you just completed. Thinking and writing about your work on a writing assignment will make your next writing task easier, as you will learn from this one.

1. How did you decide what topic to focus on?
2. How did you go about writing your initial thesis statement? Did that original thesis change by the time you constructed your final draft?
3. What kinds of invention/discovery activities did you do? What was the most helpful for your argument? The least? Why?
4. Did you use visual aids? If so, what did you learn about using them that will help you in future assignments? If you did not use visual aids, do you think if you had, they may have improved your paper?
5. Did you procrastinate at starting your paper? What might you do differently next time?
6. What did you learn from writing this paper that will help you as you write other papers, especially persuasive papers, in the future?

Readings That Persuade

Your instructor may ask you to read and perhaps discuss and write about one or more of these persuasive readings. We selected these texts to help you get some sense of what effective writing of this kind looks like and to help you understand how it works.

Note: Words highlighted **in blue** are terms used in the "Improve Your Vocabulary" activities that follow each reading.

Early Education Pays Off: High-quality Programs Are Good for Kids, for Society and for Business

James Fish

James Fish is vice president for Pennsylvania and West Virginia of Waste Management Inc. This opinion piece was published by the Pittsburgh Post-Gazette.

Pennsylvania Pre-K: pre-kindergarten program in Pennsylvania

Keystone STARS: Pennnsylvania program that promotes an early learning environment and positive child outcomes; stands for

- Standards
- Training/ Professional Development
- Assistance
- Resources and
- Support

indicator: points toward something

mitigated: fixed; made less severe

1   There are amazing returns on investment when we provide quality early education to our young children. In a time when all budgets are tight, investing in early education programs such as **Pennsylvania Pre-K** Counts, **Keystone STARS,** Child Care Works, Early Intervention, Head Start and Nurse-Family Partnership will help save money while preparing our children for a competitive workforce.

2   When kids start behind in school, they often stay behind. Research shows that third-grade performance is an **indicator** of whether a child will graduate or drop out of high school. A child's early learning experiences can affect whether they go on to get good grades, a good education and a good job–or instead get poor grades, drop out of school, get involved in crime or possibly end up on welfare, in jail or worse.

3   When our children fail, it hurts our communities. When they succeed, we all benefit. Many risk factors can contribute to a child having trouble in school. Some of them, such as living in a low-income family or having a mother with less than a high school education, can be **mitigated** through quality early education. Allegheny County children overall are considered at moderate to high risk of school failure because of these factors, with 36 percent living in low-income families.

4   We need a system that makes it possible for all children to succeed.

5   Research shows that brain development is most intense in the first five years. When we invest in early education, we promote healthy brains that can support the skills needed by adults, such as literacy, math and social awareness. After age six, development slows; it's harder to build the proper nerve

remediation: correction of a deficiency

connections. So we can invest now in quality early education or pay more later for special education and **remediation**–with worse results.

6   The benefits of early education are long-term. One highly regarded study followed at-risk children who received quality early education until they turned 40 and found that they were more likely to have graduated from high school, attended college and earned high incomes than individuals who did not have quality early education.

7   Pennsylvania is seeing improvements in early education programs that are very promising for our children's futures.

8   A 2006 study showed that Keystone STARS had reversed a negative trend of declining quality in child-care programs. In the first two years of Pennsylvania Pre-K Counts, nearly every child (94 percent to 99 percent) showed age-appropriate or emerging age-appropriate skills after participating in the program. And since 2003, classroom quality scores have continued to rise in STARS, Pre-K Counts and Head Start classrooms. We are seeing the results of public investment in quality early education in Pittsburgh, but it is only a start. For example, of the 308 preschoolers who received early-intervention services at 4 years old in 2008-2009, only 34 percent required special-education services when they entered kindergarten this past fall. At the end of last school year, 3.2 percent of Pittsburgh Public Schools kindergarten children were **retained**, but only 1 percent of those children who attended the district's early-childhood program were retained. This trend was consistent with the previous two years.

retained: kept (as in kept in school)

9   These positive results for children represent cost savings to our citizens and the potential of higher academic and career achievement as these children progress through school.

10   Pennsylvania's investment in early-education programs is working, but more resources are needed.

11   Only 40 percent of young children in Allegheny County have access to publicly funded high-quality early education. Less than 2 percent of young children are enrolled in Pennsylvania Pre-K Counts programs, approximately 6 percent in Head Start and less than 4 percent in STAR 3 and 4 programs.

12   Early education may not be a magic pill, but it can lay the foundation for future prosperity for generations. When these children reach adulthood they are more likely to succeed and, as a result, their children are at less risk to fail in school, too.

13   In the United States, we treasure education. With education and social skills supported in early childhood, a person can break the cycle of poverty and provide a brighter future for their children and grandchildren.

14   As a business leader, having more children grow up to earn college degrees and hold good jobs means more qualified candidates for employment and more potential customers. Strong communities are good for business. I encourage our policy makers to make quality early education a priority for Pennsylvania.

Questions for Discussion and Writing

1. Are you convinced by Fish's argument that early childhood programs make for better students and citizens later in life?
2. What is the most convincing part of Fish's essay? Why?
3. What did you learn from this essay?
4. What rhetorical strategies (*definition*, *description*, etc.) can you point to in Fish's essay?
5. Did you or someone you know benefit from an early-childhood program and if so, what were the benefits?
6. Would you pay more in taxes to support the kinds of programs that Fish argues for?
7. In the last paragraph, Fish writes

> As a business leader, having more children grow up to earn college degrees and hold good jobs means more qualified candidates for employment and more potential customers.

Would this sentence have been easier to understand if he had added "I think that" to it, (as shown in red) and if so, why?

> As a business leader, I think that having more children grow up to earn college degrees and hold good jobs means more qualified candidates for employment and more potential customers.

Improve Your Vocabulary Activity

In your journal, use the highlighted and defined words from Fish's essay in a sentence or in a paragraph.

Your Brain on Languages

Chris Livaccari

Chris Livaccari is the Associate Director, Chinese Language Initiatives, for the Asia Society. Before joining the Asia Society in 2009, he taught Chinese and Japanese in New York public schools. Livaccari's language classes have been featured on ABC News, NBC's Today Show, *and PBS. He is the co-author of the* Chinese for Tomorrow *textbook series, has studied Chinese and Japanese literature at Columbia University, and holds advanced degrees from the University of Chicago and New York University.*

integral: essential to something

competence: ability to do something well

facility: ability; skillfulness

cognitive: mental

potent: strong

fluency: skill in using language

divergent: not similar

1   Young Americans growing up and seeking their place in this global society need knowledge and skills that are significantly different from those of previous generations. An **integral** part of global **competence** is **facility** in world languages and cultures.

2   Beyond the clear economic and professional advantages of achieving facility in a language other than English, language learning also has clear **cognitive** benefits for students of all ages. There are many examples of people who start learning a language late in life who successfully achieve high levels of linguistic proficiency, but studies clearly show that there is a significant advantage for those who have the opportunity to start early. The human brain is more open to linguistic development in the years before adolescence, so children who learn a language during elementary school are more likely to achieve native-like pronunciation. In fact, there is good evidence to suggest that young children who are exposed to a richer variety of sounds at an early age are more likely to develop an ear for new languages in general as they get older.

3   Having more time in which to learn a new language is an obvious yet **potent** argument for early instruction. When students get an early start to a long sequence of language instruction, they can more easily achieve high levels of **fluency** than those who start learning a foreign language in high school. This extended sequences approach is especially important for the increasingly significant yet less commonly taught languages such as Chinese and Arabic, which take longer for students to master than European languages. According to the U.S. Department of State, it takes three or four times as many hours of study for an English speaker to reach an equivalent level of proficiency in Chinese, Japanese, Korean, or Arabic compared to languages like Spanish, French, or German.

4   Research also shows that learning another language early has other cognitive and academic benefits. Increased mental flexibility, the ability to shift easily between different symbol systems, improved **divergent** thinking, and, sometimes, higher scores on measures of verbal ability all correlate with early language learning. On standardized achievement tests, young language learners often outperform their peers who are not studying a foreign language. As anyone who has learned another language knows, it also enhances a student's

(continued)

understanding of the structure and patterns of English. Perhaps more importantly, the set of linguistic and communicative skills that students develop through learning one foreign language can be applied to the learning of other languages. Even if the languages in question are very different, such as Spanish and Chinese, an early education in one language will make it easier for students to learn another later in life. So, ultimately, the study of language generally is as, if not more important than achieving linguistic proficiency in one particular language.

No Child Left Behind: U. S. law that put an emphasis on standardized testing

urban: city; densely populated area

5   However, world language courses are dwindling in American schools. Only 25 percent of elementary schools in the United States offered any world languages in 2008, down from 31 percent in 1997, due to the increased focus on accountability in reading and math alone as a result of **No Child Left Behind**. American secondary schools offer more opportunities yet involvement is still low; currently, only half of all American high school students take even one year of a world language. Like many other academic advantages, language-learning opportunities are less available in **urban** schools than in suburban or private schools. For the past fifty years, school language choices have remained for the most part the same commonly taught European languages. The American language-education offerings contrast markedly with those of other countries where learning a second language is a higher priority. Twenty out of twenty-five industrialized countries start teaching world languages in grades K-5 and twenty-one of the thirty-one countries in the European Union require nine years of language study.

articulated: connected; coordinated

6   The "Excellence and Innovation in Language Learning Act" (HR 6036), new federal legislation introduced in July 2010, would dramatically expand teaching and learning of world languages and international education, allowing every young American to become proficient in a second language—in addition to English—within a generation. The goal of the bill is to provide every student access to quality world language instruction as part of **articulated** K-12 language sequences with the goal of graduating high school students with an advanced level of proficiency and to create a coordinated national and state role for foreign language instruction.

Questions for Discussion and Writing

1. What is your initial reaction to Livaccari's persuasive essay?
2. What was new and surprising to you in this essay?
3. Are you persuaded that American students need more foreign language instruction? Why?
4. Do you agree with Livaccari's claim that "language learning also has clear cognitive benefits for students of all ages" (paragraph 2)? Can you point to anything in your own experience to demonstrate this?

5. Author Livacarri writes that "Only 25 percent of elementary schools in the United States offered any world languages in 2008, down from 31 percent in 1997" and that "American secondary schools offer more opportunities yet involvement is still low; currently, only half of all American high school students take even one year of a world language" (paragraph 5). Were you surprised to read that information? Why?

Improve Your Vocabulary Activity

In your journal, use the highlighted and defined words from "Your Brain on Languages" in a sentence or in a paragraph.

Parent's Guide to Childhood Immunization
Centers for Disease Control

The Centers for Disease Control and Prevention (CDC) is a U.S. government agency dedicated to public health and the control and prevention of disease. The CDC provides health and safety information to a wide range of audiences, including parents. The following excerpt from one of the CDC's brochures focuses on the benefits of childhood immunization.

vaccination: taking a vaccine to prevent getting a disease

1   The most obvious benefit of **vaccination** is, of course, protection from disease. But there is more to it than that. There are really three types of benefit to vaccination—personal benefits, community benefits, and future benefits. It is worth looking at each of these separately.

a) Personal benefits

2   Vaccinating your child will protect him from a dozen or so potentially serious diseases.

3   But how likely is it that your child will actually get one of these diseases? Remember that vaccine-preventable diseases have been **declining** (thanks to vaccines), and that many of them are now at all-time lows. If the risk of disease is very low, isn't the benefit of vaccination also very low?

declining: going down

4   Good question. Statistically, the chance of your child getting a vaccine-preventable disease may be relatively low. You are making a wager.

5   If you choose vaccination you are betting that your child could be exposed to disease, so you accept the tiny risk of a serious vaccine **reaction** to protect him if that happens.

reaction: a response; in this context, something that happens because someone got vaccinated

(continued)

6   If you choose not to vaccinate, you are betting that your child probably won't be exposed to disease, or if he is, his illness won't be serious, and you are willing to accept the small risk of serious illness to avoid the small possibility of a vaccine reaction.

7   In our opinion, vaccinating is by far the safer bet. Even though diseases have declined, they haven't disappeared. A recent study showed that children who had not gotten **DTaP** vaccine were 23 times more likely to get whooping cough than children who had. Thirty-one children died from whooping cough in 2005. That might not be many, but the number wouldn't matter if your child were one of them.

DTaP: vaccine to protect against diphtheria, tetanus, and pertussis diseases

b) Community benefits

8   [Earlier] we said that a small percentage of children fail to develop immunity from vaccines. There are also children who cannot get certain vaccines for medical or other reasons, and those who are too young to be vaccinated. These children have no protection if they are exposed to someone who is infected with a **communicable** disease.

communicable: transferrable from one person to another

9   When most children in a community are immune, even if one child gets sick, the disease will probably not spread. That's because it will have nowhere to go—if the sick child comes in contact only with children who are immune, the disease will die out. This is called herd immunity.

10   But when fewer children in a community are immune, it is easier for a disease to spread from person to person and cause an outbreak.

11   As this booklet was being written, Wales was experiencing a "massive" measles outbreak because of parents' failure to vaccinate their children. And outbreaks of measles, mumps, and whooping cough are occurring around the United States—often among groups of children whose parents have refused to get them vaccinated. Recently in California, a boy who contracted measles during a European vacation came back and infected 11 of his unvaccinated classmates.

10   In other words, you are not just protecting your own child by getting her vaccinated, you are protecting other children—adults, too.

c) Future benefits

11   Rates of vaccine-preventable diseases are very low in the United States. So the risk of an individual child getting, say, a case of measles is very low, too. What would happen, then, if we all just stopped vaccinating? We know what would happen because we have seen it in other countries. Diseases that have been declining for years would come back.

Example: In the mid-1970s, most Japanese children (about 80%) got **pertussis** vaccine. In 1974 there were only 393 cases of whooping cough in the entire country, and no one died from it.

pertussis: whooping cough

But then, because of a scare about the vaccine's safety, the immunization rate dropped to only about 10% over the next few years. By 1979 the country was in the grip of a whooping cough epidemic that infected more than 13,000 people and left 41 dead that year. When routine vaccination was resumed, the disease numbers dropped again.

12   The point is, we can't stop vaccinating, because even though disease rates are low, they are not zero. Even a few cases in a vulnerable population could touch off a major outbreak. This is why we still vaccinate against polio, even though we haven't seen it in this country for more than 10 years. One infected traveler from a country where polio hasn't been eliminated could set us back 50 years if our own population wasn't protected.

To summarize: When you vaccinate your child, you are not just protecting her. You are also protecting her friends and schoolmates and their families; and you are also protecting her children, her grandchildren, and all future generations.

Meet Riley

In most ways Riley is a typical eight-year old girl. She takes piano and gymnastics lessons, plays soccer, likes to swim, and gets into fights with her brothers.

But Riley has something most eight-year olds don't—another child's heart. She was born with a serious heart defect and had to get a transplant within days of her birth.

To Riley's immune system, her new heart doesn't belong, because it is "non-self," like a disease germ.

Her immune system would reject it if she didn't take special drugs. These drugs suppress her immune system, and because of this she can't get live-virus vaccines like measles, mumps, rubella, or chickenpox.

Consequently, Riley is not immune to these diseases.

She has to depend on the immunity of people around her for protection. If one of her schoolmates or playmates were to come down with a case of measles or chickenpox, Riley could easily catch it from them. And because her immune system can't fight off the infection, it could become very serious if not treated promptly.

Riley enjoys a normal life today, partly thanks to her friends who are protecting her from infections by getting all their shots.

Questions for Discussion and Writing

1. What is your initial reaction to this argument?
2. Are you convinced that vaccinating children is a good thing?
3. The CDC lists three areas of benefits (personal benefits, community benefits, and future benefits) that come from childhood vaccinations. Which of these did you find the most convincing? Why?

4. Did the "Meet Riley" part of the brochure help the CDC's argument to be more effective? Why?
5. In paragraph 4, the CDC writes that

> Statistically, the chance of your child getting a vaccine-preventable disease may be relatively low. You are making a wager.

Do you agree that parents are "gambling" with their children's health when it comes to deciding whether or not to vaccinate them? Why?

Improve Your Vocabulary

Use the highlighted and defined words from "Parent's Guide to Childhood Immunization" in a sentence or in a paragraph.

MyWritingLab™ For support in meeting this chapter's objectives, log in to www.mywritinglab.com and select **Essay Development—Argument**.

PART 3

Special Writing Situations

Chapter 15 Conducting Effective Research

Chapter 16 Documenting Your Sources

Chapter 17 Writing Timed Essay Examinations and Making Oral Presentations

Chapter 18 Writing E-mail, Job Application Letters, and Résumés

Chapter 15

Conducting Effective Research

Learning Objectives

In this chapter, you will learn to:

LO1 Choose and focus a research topic

LO2 Find and evaluate sources

LO3 Take notes from sources

LO4 Incorporate sources in your writing

College assignments often involve writing research papers that require you to visit your campus library. They will, in all likelihood, also require you to conduct research on the Internet.

What does conducting research mean? Broadly speaking, conducting research means that after you have a topic to write about, you locate outside sources for more information on the topic, read those sources to gather information, and then incorporate those sources in your writing, giving them proper credit.

LO1

Choose and focus a research topic

Developing a Research Topic

The first stage in writing a research paper, then, is to *have something to write about*, that is, a **topic**. Your topic may be assigned to you by the instructor; sometimes the class may be given a few topics from which students need to choose one. At other times, your instructor may give your class an option to write on any topic of the students' choice.

Choosing Your Own Topic

If you are free to choose your own topic, you need to find a topic that interests you, a topic on which you are willing to conduct research and then write. You may want to ask yourself the following questions as you decide on a topic:

- What kinds of topics interest me?
- Should I write about a topic of general interest?
- Should I write about a specialized topic?
- Should I write about a topic about which people are likely to want to know more?
- Should my topic reflect current social, political, economic, environmental, or global issues?

Some possible topics for a research paper may include the following:

The importance of a college education	The value of a liberal arts education
The role of sports in building a healthy mind	Women in science and engineering
The value of travel	Outsourcing jobs
The dangers of deforestation	Global warming
Obesity in America	The value of social networking
The dangers of fast food	Social stereotypes
Small families versus large families	The advantages and disadvantages of the internet
Government-subsidized health care	Environmental pollution

This list is not comprehensive, by any means; it is meant to give you ideas for possible topic choices if you are free to write on a topic of your choice.

Narrowing Your Research Topic

Once you have a topic, and if your professor has not specified what exactly about the topic you need to write about, you need to determine what aspect of the topic you are going to focus on. In other words, you must **narrow** or **focus** your topic to something manageable, so you can write about it in a few pages. If your topic is too broad or too general, it will lack focus and may become too vague to keep readers' attention. For instance, if your topic is the Internet, you should ask yourself what exactly about the Internet you are going to write about. You cannot write everything about the Internet, so you have to focus on something specific. Narrowing your topic will give it a particular focus that readers can follow. It will also make your own writing task much easier. If you are writing a research paper, it will make your task of researching much easier, because you will know what exactly you need to research.

If you are not sure how to narrow your topic, we recommend the following steps:

- Write down what you already know about the topic. From the material generated, try to decide what about the topic you would like to focus on specifically.
- Gather information about your topic. You can do this by:
  - Reading about it in books, encyclopedias, and the like.
  - Reading about it in newspapers and magazines.
  - Reading about it on the Internet.
  - Discussing the topic with your teachers, family members, and/or friends.
- Think about the thesis statement you would like to have for your essay and your topic, and let that thesis statement guide you toward narrowing your focus (for more on thesis statements, see pages 95–98). For example, if your topic is "college courses" and your thesis statement is, "All college students should be required to complete a foreign language course," you know right away that your topic needs to be narrowed down to "required foreign language courses in college." Once you have that decided, you can decide what to write about the narrowed-down topic, depending on the kind of essay you are writing, your thesis, and your purpose and audience for writing that essay.

- Make sure the topic isn't too narrow to write about. If it is, you will not have much to write about, and you will have to choose a different focus for your topic.

The following table provides some examples of broad and narrowed-down topics:

Broad Topic	Narrowed-down Topics
The Internet	Reasons for the increasing popularity of the Internet from 1990 to the present
	The value of the Internet in conducting research
	The dangers of the Internet for young children
Education	The cost of higher education in America
	The importance of getting a college education
	Successful teaching strategies at the elementary level
Music	The popularity of jazz
	The benefits of music therapy
	Comparing and contrasting the work of two famous musicians
Wildlife	Wildlife conservation methods
	The history and mission of the World Wildlife Federation
	Protecting the wildlife in the Arctic
Sports	The value of playing sports
	The popularity of baseball in America
	The sport of boxing

Everyday Writing Activity: Narrowing Your Topic

Assume you have three broad topic choices in mind:

- Social networking.
- Reading.
- Television.

In your journal, narrow down these topics to two aspects of each topic, something that can be researched and written about in a few pages. Your instructor may want you to share your responses with the rest of the class.

Finding and Evaluating Sources

Once you have decided on a topic for your research paper, you need to identify sources you can use in your paper. Because we live in the information age, finding sources is not a problem; both the library and the Internet contain a vast body of information. Unfortunately, along with all the good information, there is some information that may not always be wholly reliable. The challenge, then, is to locate the information that is reliable and that can safely be included in your paper.

Library Research

Your campus library most likely offers study space, computer workstations, and printers. You probably use the library quite often to study for exams, read course materials kept on electronic reserve, access your online courses, or even to do some quiet reading. While these services are all important for students, it is also important to realize that the library is *a vast storehouse of research*. Much of the information you would need to write a research paper on a topic of your choice is likely available at your library. However, you need to be able to locate that information. Follow these steps to be able to use your library's resources effectively:

- Speak to your librarian and ask him/her for help.
- Visit your library's Web site.
- Learn how to use your library's online database for books and articles effectively.

Consult Your Librarian. Your reference librarians are there to help you; feel free to speak to them when you need help. Some questions you may consider asking the librarians could include the following:

- Can you please show me how to use the library's database?
- Where is the best place to look for sources for my topic within the database?
- Once I have identified a source, how can I find it?
- If I want a printed copy of my source, how can I get it?
- How much does it cost to print copies of my sources at the library?
- I already have some sources, but I need some more. Where else should I look?
- How can I access the library's Web site from off-campus?
- Can I access the Internet for my research from the library?
- What should I do if I need sources not available at this library?

Visit Your Library's Web Site. Because college classes frequently require you to write research papers, it is a wise move on your part to make yourself familiar with your library's Web site, or its home page. While each library's home page is different, there are some common features, including valuable information such as:

- Library hours.
- Phone numbers of the Reference desk and Circulation desk (among others).
- Online tutorials on how to access books, articles, newspapers, etc.
- A search page with a search box where you can search for sources by keyword, title of source, or author name.
- Links to databases in various subjects such as Astronomy, Botany, Business, Geology, and Music.
- Links to different documentation styles (for a discussion on documentation, see Chapter 16).
- Interlibrary loan information, which allows you to "borrow" books from other libraries.
- Information about your account, such as how many books you have checked out, when they are due back at the library, if there is a recall on any one of them, and so forth.

Familiarize Yourself with the Library Database. It is vital for you to familiarize yourself with your library's database. This database lists everything held by the library. Most library databases are computerized, so they can be accessed from anywhere with an Internet connection. The database includes information such as book/journal title, author name(s), publication information (place of publication, publisher, date of publication, etc.), call number and physical location.

Once in the library database, you can search by author and/or title if known, or search by subject or keyword. For instance, if you are looking for sources on Chinese astronomy but do not know of any specific authors or titles on the topic, you can simply type "Chinese astronomy" in the search box. This will provide you with a list of all the sources on the topic that the library has. If you are looking for the book *American Cinema/American Culture*, and you know that the author is John Belton, you can search by the title of the book or by the author's name. If you have trouble finding your way around the database system, ask your reference librarian for help.

Locate a Book. A search on the topic of "International Students in America" brought up the following information on a book from one school's online library catalog:

Library Database Record for a Book

The international student's guide to going to college in America: how to choose colleges and universities in the United States, how to apply, how to fit in	
Personal Author:	Dalby, Sidonia	Author's name
Title:	The international student's guide to going to college in America: how to choose colleges and universities in the United States, how to apply, how to fit in / Sidonia M. Dalby, Sally Rubenstone, Emily Harrison Weir.	Title of book
Publication info:	New York: Macmillan USA, c1996.	Place of publication, publisher, and date
Physical descrip:	v, 170 p. : ill. ; 24 cm.	
General note:	"An Arco book" --T.p. verso.	
General note:	Includes index.	
Held by:	OREM	
Subject term:	Universities and colleges—United States—Admission—Handbooks, manuals, etc.	
Subject term:	Students, Foreign—United States—Handbooks, manuals, etc.	
Added author:	Rubenstone, Sally	
Added author:	Weir, Emily Harrison	
Holdings	Change Display	

Orem Campus	Copies	Material	Location	
LB2351.2 .D25 1996 120182	1	Book	Regular Collection, 4th Floor	Call number Location in the library's stacks

Usually, books are organized by subject, so once you use the call number to find the book on the shelves, there will be other books on the same topic nearby. It is always useful to spend some time looking at the nearby books—those books will be on the same topic, so they might provide useful research information for you.

If, after accessing the library's database, you find that the book you need is checked out, you may request it, which means the current borrower of the book will have to return it within a specified time so you can have it. It may also mean that the current borrower will not be able to renew the book because you have requested it.

If you find that a source you need is not available at your college library, ask the reference librarian if you can get it through an interlibrary loan (this means that your school can borrow it for you from another library).

Everyday Library Activity: Locating a Book

Visit your school library's Web site, and engage in the following activities. Please record your responses in your journal. Then, write a paragraph on how easy or difficult it was for you to locate the books.

1. Locate any book written by Maya Angelou. Note title of book, all publication information, and whether it is available in your campus library; if it is available, note the call number and its physical location.
2. Locate the book *The Positronic Man* by Isaac Asimov. Note all publication information and whether it is available in your campus library; if it is available, note the call number and its physical location.
3. Do a search for two books on the topic "The History of Mathematics." Note author names, all publication information, and whether they are available in your campus library; if they are available, note the call numbers and physical location.

Your instructor may want you to share your journal entries and/or your paragraph with the rest of the class.

Locate Periodicals and Specialized Indexes. The term **periodical** refers to magazines, journals and newspapers, because they come out *periodically*, that is, on a regular basis (every week, month, etc.). A magazine usually refers to popular periodicals like *Newsweek* or *Sports Illustrated*, while a journal is a more scholarly periodical, generally written by scholars and often based on research. In the library, periodicals can usually be found in online periodical databases that often include the full text of articles.

Some common periodical databases include:

- EBSCO Host's Academic Search Complete (general periodicals and scholarly journals).
- JStor (Journal Storage; contains back issues of academic journals).
- LexisNexis Academic (for news, business, and legal publications).

- EBSCO Host's ERIC (Educational Resource Information Center; for topics dealing with education).
- BioMedCentral (for scientific articles in medical research and biology).
- CQ Researcher (Congressional Quarterly Researcher; examines controversial topics and topics of current concern).
- MERB (Music Education Resource Base; for resources in music and music education).
- PsycINFO (for articles on psychology and related fields such as psychiatry, medicine, nursing, etc.).
- ScienceDirect (for articles in the scientific, medical, and technical fields).

So, if you decided to access Academic Search Complete to write a paper on "college education," and you did not have any specific focus yet or any author(s) or article titles in mind, you would type in the words "college education" in the Search box, and the first page would bring up several sources, as seen here. Each source will include author name(s), name of article, publication information such as year of publication, volume number and issue number of journal where the article was published, page numbers, and accession number.

Search Results from a Periodicals Database

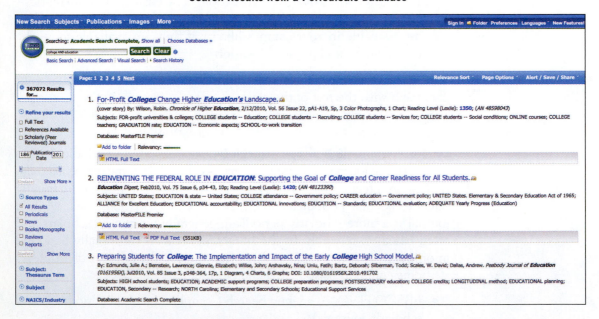

If you then decided to access entry 2, you would click on it for additional information. This is what would be pulled up:

Periodicals Database Record for an Article

REINVENTING THE FEDERAL ROLE IN *EDUCATION*: Supporting the Goal of *College* and Career Readiness for All Students.

Source:	Education Digest; Feb2010, Vol. 75 Issue 6, p34-43, 10p
Document Type:	Article
Subject Terms:	EDUCATION & state -- United States
	COLLEGE attendance -- Government policy
	CAREER education -- Government policy
	UNITED States. Elementary & Secondary Education Act of 1965
	ALLIANCE for Excellent Education
	EDUCATIONAL accountability
	EDUCATIONAL innovations
	EDUCATION -- Standards
	EDUCATIONAL evaluation
	ADEQUATE Yearly Progress (Education)
Geographic Terms:	UNITED States
Abstract:	The article presents a policy brief issued by the educational organization Alliance for Excellent *Education* which focuses on U.S. government policies to promote *college* and career preparation in students. The brief suggests that a reauthorization of the U.S. Elementary and Secondary *Education* Act (ESEA) should include provisions that would shift educational accountability to focus on career and *college* readiness, support improvement of high school *education* and encourage educational innovation through additional funding. The need for common educational standards and assessments, public statements by states reporting academic performance and progress monitoring through changes to adequate yearly progress (AYP) measurements is discussed.
Lexile:	1420
Full Text Word Count:	3567
ISSN:	0013127X
Accession Number:	48123390
Database:	MasterFILE Premier

As you can see, this gives you the abstract, or summary, of the article, so you can see what it focuses on. Because the full text is available, you can simply click on the title, and the article will open on your computer.

Everyday Library Activity: Searching for Journal, Magazine, and/or Newspaper Articles

Visit your school library's Web site, and engage in the following activities. Please record your responses in your journal. Then, write a paragraph on how easy or difficult it was for you to locate the articles. Your instructor may want you to share your journal entries and/or your paragraph with the rest of the class.

Assume that your instructor has asked you to write a research paper on the topic of "genetically modified foods." Also assume that he/she has asked you to locate one journal article, one magazine article, and one newspaper article on the topic. Do an online database search for each of these different kinds of sources, and write down your findings for each source. Make sure to include all relevant information, such as article name, author name, journal/magazine/newspaper name, volume number, issue number, page number, year of publication, and, in the case of the newspaper source, the date of publication.

Locate Encyclopedias and Dictionaries. Encyclopedias and dictionaries are often good places to start the research process because they help define a topic and/or provide a good overview of your research topic. While some of them are almost certainly available in hard copy in the Reference section of your library, they are also probably available in your library in electronic format. There might be a separate link on your library's home page that will take you to the list of references available electronically, or the references may be included as links in a list of the library's research

Home Page of Online Encyclopedia

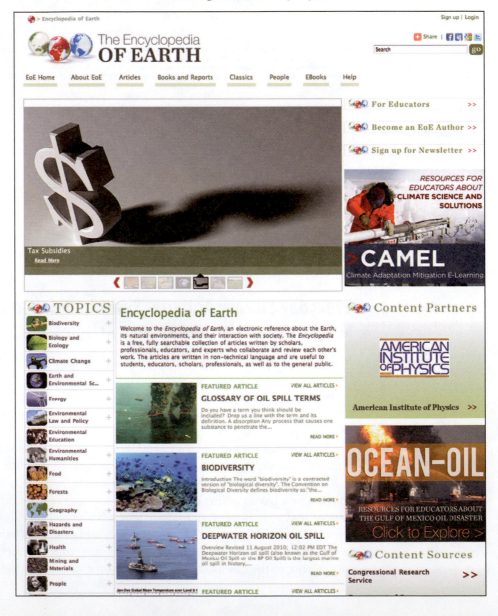

databases. Once you click on the link of your choice, you will be taken directly to the home page of your chosen reference source. For instance, if you click on the link to the *Encyclopedia of Earth*, you will be taken directly to its home page, where there will be a search box.

In that search box, you can type in keywords related to your topic. If you type in "Climate Change," for instance, you will see all the articles related to climate change the encyclopedia includes. From there, you select the article (s) of your choice:

Search Results for an Online Encyclopedia

Among encyclopedias and dictionaries, *Encyclopedia Britannica*, Funk and Wagnall's *New World Encyclopedia* and *Oxford English Dictionary* are well known, but there are also some specialized encyclopedias and dictionaries focused on a particular topic in a particular discipline, such as the *Encyclopedia of Earth* just mentioned. Some other examples of specialized encyclopedias and dictionaries include:

- *Oxford Dictionary of Art.*
- *Dictionary of Modern and Contemporary Art.*
- *Dictionary of Biology.*
- *Encyclopedia of the Middle Ages.*
- *Oxford Dictionary of Law.*
- *International Encyclopedia of Dance.*
- *Dictionary of Earth Sciences.*
- *Statistical Abstract of the United States.*

If you were writing a research paper related to the topic of art, you could begin by consulting the *Oxford Dictionary of Art* or the *Dictionary of Modern and Contemporary Art*, or both. After that, you would locate other sources such as books, journal articles, newspaper articles, and so on.

Everyday Library Activity: Searching for Encyclopedias and Dictionaries

Visit your college library's Web site, and engage in the following activity. Please record your responses in your journal. Then, write a paragraph on how easy or difficult it was for you to locate the sources. Your instructor may want you to share your journal entries and/or your paragraph with the rest of the class.

Locate at least two reference sources (encyclopedia and/or dictionary) on each of the following topics:

1. Folklore and mythology.
2. Music.
3. Religion.
4. Technology.

Internet Research

The Internet contains a vast body of knowledge on almost any topic and, therefore, can be very useful during the research process. Many of you probably already know how to use the Internet, but if you are new to using the Internet, here is some background for you:

- The Internet is a huge network that connects millions of computers around the world and is open to everyone who wishes to use it.
- The World Wide Web is located within the Internet; individual Web sites contain links to other sites, creating a kind of Web, hence the name *World Wide Web*.
- Each Web site has an address beginning with www. This address is known as the URL, or Uniform Resource Locator. For instance, the URL of the Library of Congress is www.loc.gov; the URL of the British Broadcasting Corporation is www.bbc.co.uk.
- To access the Internet from outside campus, you need a computer and a modem, which allows information to be transmitted electronically over a phone or a cable line. If you are accessing the Internet from campus, your school will likely have computer centers for students. Your library will probably also have computer stations at which you can work and from which you can access the Internet and/or your library's database of books, journals, magazines, newspapers, and so on.
- These days, wireless Internet access is available at many public places, including cafés, retail stores, airports, and the like.
- The Internet is generally accessed using Web browsers such as Internet Explorer, Google Chrome, or Mozilla Firefox. These browsers are software programs that allow your computer to retrieve and read the Web page(s) you are trying to access.
- If you are not sure how to access the Internet, ask your reference librarian to help you.

Use Web Search Engines. If you do not know the URL of pages related to your research topic, you can use Internet search engines to help you. Some of the commonest search engines include:

- Google (www.google.com).
- Yahoo (www.yahoo.com).
- Alta Vista (www.altavista.com).
- MSN (www.msn.com).

- Bing (www.bing.com).
- DogPile (www.dogpile.com).

To use any of these search engines, you need to type in a keyword or phrase in the search box that is provided within each search engine.

Everyday Internet Activity: Searching for URLs

Get on the Internet, select a search engine, and find the URLs of the following entities. Please record your findings in your journal. Your instructor may want you to share your findings with the rest of the class:

1. National Aeronautics and Space Administration.
2. National Geographic.
3. Association of African Universities.
4. Organization of Petroleum Exporting Countries.
5. Intel.

Use Keyword Searches. Most likely, your research will require you to search for more general topics, which will mean a **keyword search.** The search results are usually presented as a list and are called "hits." Because a keyword search can potentially pull up many thousands of hits, it is best if your keywords or phrases are narrowed down to be specific. If you are doing research on the topic of online education, you have probably already narrowed down your topic (see earlier discussion on pages 300–301 on narrowing a topic before writing). When you use a search engine to find sources related to your topic, simply typing in "online education" will bring up 393,000,000 hits, an unmanageable number. However, if you type in "online education advantages," the number is reduced to 24,100,000; it is still a big number, but more narrowed down, and the first few hits are probably most directly relevant to your research. The information pulled up through such searches may include books, Web pages, journal articles, newspaper articles, images, or other kinds of files.

A search of "texting and driving dangers" using Google brought up the following hits on the first page:

Google Search Results

As you can see, Google found more than 8 million "hits," and the top hits include news reports from the news channel, CBS, an article from the Web site caranddriver.com, and a government report from the FCC (Federal Communications Commission), among others. With a variety of sources available to you, can now pick and choose the sources that you think will be the most helpful to you as you write your research paper. You can save the addresses of these Web sites in your browser: in Explorer, click on the Favorites button in the upper left-hand corner; in

Firefox, click on the Bookmark button on the top of your screen. When you need to return to these Web sites again, you can simply select them from the saved list, instead of having to search for these sites again.

Everyday Internet Activity: Using Web Search Engines

Using any search engine, do a keyword search of the following topics. Note the first five "hits" for each topic. Record your responses in your journal. Your instructor may want you to share your responses with the rest of the class.

1. Online shopping.
2. The dangers of technology.
3. Electric cars.

Evaluate Web Sites. While the Internet is a wonderful resource for information, it is important to remember that its open nature can affect the quality and reliability of the available information. Anyone with a little bit of computer knowledge can create a Web site and post information that has not been verified for accuracy. This is very unlike books, articles in scholarly journals, newspapers, and the like, which have gone through a rigorous research and/or peer review process. It is, therefore, important to evaluate Web sites carefully before using them. Ask yourself the following questions while evaluating a Web site:

- Is the information reliable? How can I know?
- Is the information up-to-date? How can I know?

In both cases, the answer is that you need to look where the material was published (an online scholarly journal, a respected newspaper, etc.), the date it was published or last updated (if available), and who the author is. Is the author an expert on the subject, or is the author someone who is posting personal material or opinions? For instance, an article on reducing obesity levels in America, written by a professor of nutrition, is much more reliable than a personal account posted on a Web site by someone who has lost weight. It is also important to check the article for bias. Does it present only one point of view, or are all perspectives included? A reliable article is one that is objective, presents all sides of the issue, and uses evidence to support all claims.

A common way of evaluating Internet sources is to look at the Internet address. The URL extensions (the three letters after the dot) are known as the **Internet domain.** The most common domains are .com, .gov, .org, .edu, and .net. While a Web site's reliability cannot be exclusively determined by the domain, it can often act as a guide to the reliability of the source. The following chart can act as a guide to help you determine the validity of certain Web sites:

Guide to Evaluating Web Sites by Domain

URL Extension	Reliability	Example
.com This is a commercial or a personal site.	If the business is well known, it can be considered reliable although it will have a pro-business point of view; if not, the information provided on the home page of the business should be double-checked. Personal Web pages should also be checked for reliability.	Microsoft, www.microsoft.com Procter & Gamble, www.pg.com
.gov This indicates it is the Web site of a government agency.	Usually very reliable, because the information there is usually well researched and up-to-date.	Social Security Administration, www.ssa.gov U.S. Census, www.census.gov
.org This indicates it is the Web site of a nonprofit organization.	Usually reliable, though depends on the organization. The Web site will promote its viewpoints and interests.	Independence Hall Association in Philadelphia, www.ushistory.org
.edu This is the Web site of an educational institution.	Usually reliable; institutions generally provide accurate information about their school for parents and current and prospective students. Instructors also post course materials on the Web site, which may vary in quality.	University of Texas at Austin, www.utexas.edu
.net Like .com, this is usually a commercial site.	Reliability can vary based on how valid the source is. The source's home page should be checked out to establish validity.	www.fashion.net

Note that in mid-2011, news reports indicated that the Internet Corporation for Assigned Names and Numbers, or Icann, the nonprofit Internet coordinating body, announced that within about 18 months, anyone could apply for almost any kind of domain name, if they were willing to pay $185,000 and complete a several-hundred page application. Icann is making this change because the world is running out of Internet "addresses."

This change will make it more difficult for you as a student to evaluate Web sites, but if you follow the rules outlined in this chapter, you will be able to tell which sites are legitimate and have accurate information, and which do not.

Everyday Internet Activity: Looking at Web Sites

Spend some time investigating the following Web sites to determine their validity and reliability. What strikes you as interesting? Record your responses in your journal. Your instructor may want you to share your responses with the rest of the class.

1. www.foodnetwork.com
2. www.science.gov
3. www.alexanderpalace.org
4. www.nus.edu
5. www.teachers.net

Conducting Field Research

While the library and the Internet are the most common places to find materials to write a research paper, valuable information can also be gathered by conducting **field research,** that is, research that gathers material directly through observation, interviewing, and surveys, rather than relying on published material.

Observation. First-hand **observations,** where you watch and take notes yourself, are often important in writing a research paper; they can provide you with useful material for your writing. For instance, if your research topic is "daycare centers," you could make arrangements with a local daycare center (perhaps your campus daycare center, if there is one) to go and spend one hour on a specified day to observe the activities there. Such observation will require some preparation on your part: first, you will need to call/e-mail the daycare center to set up an appointment. Once there, you should be prepared to take notes on what you see. You may also want to take your camera or video camera to help document your observations. Additionally, such observation may require you to get permission from authorities at your school and the authorities at the daycare center, because human subjects are involved.

Interviewing. Interviewing experts on your research topic is an excellent way to gather material for your paper, because you are getting information directly from the primary source. The **interview** process includes the following: get in touch with the interviewee, explain your purpose in interviewing, and set up a mutually convenient time for the interview. Then, make a list of questions that you will ask during the interview. The questions must be carefully thought-out: they must be relevant to the topic, they must be designed so as to extract the maximum information from the person being interviewed, yet they must be flexible enough for the interviewee to feel comfortable answering them.

For instance, if you are researching the topic of whether daycare is beneficial for children or not, you could set up an interview with the director of the daycare center you are observing, and ask the following questions:

- What are the top three reasons you feel daycare is beneficial?
- Have you asked parents of children at your daycare whether they feel daycare is beneficial or not?
- If you were asked to name three reasons daycare is not beneficial, what would they be?
- Do you think we should expand the size of the campus daycare/open more daycares in our city?

You can record the interview responses by taking notes, or, with the permission of the person interviewed, you can record the answers on a recorder, or you may even videotape the whole process if the person being interviewed is willing to be filmed. If you wish to quote the person in your paper, confirm with him/her what exactly he/she said (see pages 321–322 on using quotations in a research paper).

If you wish to conduct a telephone interview instead of a face-to-face one, inform the interviewee that his/her comments are being recorded (and request his or her permission), and then follow the same procedure outlined above: have a list of questions prepared before the interview, take notes, and verify comments for possible use as quotations.

Conducting Surveys. Surveys, often in the form of a **questionnaire,** can be very useful in gathering material for your research paper. A successful survey is based around a central purpose. You must ask yourself what exactly is the information you want the survey to reveal. If you want to research students' study habits, then the survey questions must be focused around this topic, and not ask any unrelated questions. They must also be clearly stated, and unbiased, and it is a good idea to mention how much time it will take to complete the questionnaire so that the respondents feel prepared. You will probably want to ask questions like the following:

- How many hours every day do you study?
- Do you study on weekends?
- Do you like to study quietly, or do you study while listening to music, watching TV, or engaging in some other activity?
- Do you like to study by yourself or in a peer group?

The way survey questions are formulated is important; if they are too complicated, you may not get back too many responses. It is also preferable that the answers are elicited in the form of inserting check marks in boxes or yes/no questions. Questions that require lengthy answers are usually not suitable, because few people may be willing to take the time to write lengthy responses. Even so, usually the response rate of questionnaires is only at around 25 to 30 percent, so don't be disappointed if you don't get a high response rate. You can report results statistically, or come to logical conclusions about the survey results.

The following is part of a questionnaire administered by the Stanford University School of Medicine to patients suffering from chronic diseases:

1. Ethnic origin (check **only one**):
   - ❏ White not Hispanic
   - ❏ Black not Hispanic
   - ❏ Hispanic
   - ❏ Asian or Pacific Islander
   - ❏ Filipino
   - ❏ American Indian/Alaskan Native
   - ❏ Other: _____
2. Please circle the **highest** year of school completed:
   1 2 3 4 5 6 7 8 9 10 11 12 13 14 15 16 17 18 19 20 21 22 23+
   (primary) (high school) (college/university) (graduate school)
3. Are you currently (check **only one**):
   - ❏ Married
   - ❏ Single
   - ❏ Separated
   - ❏ Divorced
   - ❏ Widowed
4. Please indicate below which chronic condition(s) you have:
   - ❏ Diabetes ❏ Asthma ❏ Emphysema or COPD
   - ❏ Other lung disease *Type of lung disease:* _____
   - ❏ Heart disease *Type of heart disease:* _____
   - ❏ Arthritis or other rheumatic disease *Specify type:* _____
   - ❏ Cancer *Type of cancer:* _____
   - ❏ Other chronic condition *Specify:* _____

Planning Your Research

Once you have your topic defined in your mind, and you have familiarized yourself with your library's database and how to access materials in your library, as well as how to conduct Internet research, the next step is to collect your research materials. Will you need to do field research? How about library and Internet research? How many sources do you need? What kind of sources do you need? Your instructor may have specific instructions for you about these matters; check your assignment sheet. You need to follow the instructions given very carefully. If the instructions are to consult two books and an article from a magazine, as well as one Internet source, that is exactly what you should do.

If there are no specific instructions given by your instructor regarding the research materials to be consulted and included in your paper, you are free to choose your own materials. In this case, a good rule of thumb is to vary your source materials. For instance, if you wish to consult five different sources, you may want to look at a book, an article from a journal, an article from a magazine, an article from a newspaper, and an article from the Internet. Additionally, depending on your research topic, you may want to do some field research. Also depending on your topic, you may have to consult more books or more scholarly journals than other sources. This means that you need to be flexible during the research process.

Taking Notes

LO3
Take notes from sources

Doing research can be overwhelming. After you have located all your sources, and read through them, you might start to feel a little overwhelmed by all the information you have collected. You probably will not need to use all the information you have gathered in your paper, so you must identify the information you think you are likely to use. The best way to keep things organized is by **taking notes** on what you are reading, especially if it is information you may include in your paper.

You may take notes on regular index cards, either four-by-six-inch cards or five-by-eight-inch cards. You may also take notes in a journal or on loose sheets of paper. If you prefer taking notes on your personal laptop or desktop, that will work, too. Remember to save the notes as a file on your computer.

What kinds of notes should you take? If the article has one main point, and several subpoints, you will want to make a note of those. Of course, you can't write down everything, so you will have to condense, or **summarize,** the points that you would want to include later in your article (for more information on summarizing, see Chapter 3. If there are any **quotations** you want to include in your paper, you need to include those, word for word, in your notes. Remember, quotations duplicate the exact words of the author, so be careful to write them down in your notes exactly the way they are. You may also want to **paraphrase**—that is, put in your own words—the ideas in your sources while taking notes.

Whatever kind of notes you take, remember to keep them organized so they are easily accessible to you when you are actually writing your paper:

- If you are using index cards, use separate cards for each piece of information.
- Write a heading on each note card about what kind of information is included in the card. For instance, if your card includes a quotation by John Smith on the topic of international adoptions, write "Quotation from John Smith on international adoptions" on the top of the card. That way, you will be able to locate the quotation easily when you need to incorporate it in your paper, and you will not have to go through each card.
- Remember to take down bibliographic information about the source; you will need it during the documentation process, and recording it now will save you from having to look it up again (for a discussion of documentation, see Chapter 16). If you are taking notes in a journal or on loose sheets of paper, use a separate sheet for each piece of information, and use headings and documentation information, as mentioned earlier.
- If you are taking notes on your computer, you may want to create separate files based on the kind of notes you are taking. Most researchers organize their notes by topic or by source. For instance, if you are researching the topic of deep sea fishing, and you choose to write about the best places in the world for deep sea fishing, and the fishing gear needed, you could have two separate files within a folder, each file including the research for each of your subtopics. If you wish to organize by source, and the sources you consult during the research process include Mary Smith, William Henry, and Akiko Suzuki, you can have separate files for each source within a single folder. The entire folder can be titled "Research Sources."

Here is an example of one student's notes on a source she found using a Google search on "texting and driving dangers" from CBS News (see page 313):

Student's Notes on a Source

Note the image captures the title, author, and date posted—all this information will be needed for the citation.

> **Home** › **Blogs** › **Couric & Co.**
>
> **COURIC & CO.**
>
> September 29, 2009 4:18 PM
>
> ## Texting and Driving Dangers
>
> Posted by **Daniel Sieberg** 💬 **6 comments**
>
> http://www.cbsnews.com/8301-500803_162-5351287-500803.html
>
> Summary: We are all tempted to text when we drive (author included). Author did a story on bad accidents and some were caused by texting. So CBS News followed 40 students as they drove on a controlled course, and texted. The students could then understand the dangers of texting and driving.
>
> Full report was shown in CBS Evening News.

The student writer copied and pasted in the URL.

The student writer summarized the source.

LO4
Incorporate sources in your writing

Incorporating Sources in Your Writing

Now that you have gathered all the sources necessary for your research paper, and have read through them and taken notes on them, it is time to actually incorporate those sources in your writing. There are three major ways to integrate sources in a research paper:

- Quotation.
- Summary.
- Paraphrase.

Quotation

To *quote* is to use the exact words of your source in your writing, without making any changes at all. The quoted material is always enclosed within double quotation marks ("abc"), and the source's name is indicated either somewhere in the sentence, or within parentheses after the quotation (for more on in-text citations, see Chapter 16).

Usually, material is quoted under the following circumstances:

- The quotation belongs to an expert in the field, or a well-known person, and you want to highlight him/her as an authority on the subject. For instance, in a research paper on U.S. President Abraham Lincoln you should quote, rather than put in your own words, exactly what Lincoln said, because he is a respected personality: "Leave nothing for tomorrow which can be done today" (Lincoln).

- The quote is so appropriately worded that any attempt to put it in your own words will destroy the impact of those words. The words of the Lebanese-American poet Kahlil Gibran, "The veil that clouds your eyes shall be lifted by the hands that wove it" are very difficult to express in any other way; the beauty of the words and the impact the original words cannot, in all likelihood, be maintained. Thus, it is better to quote him in your paper.

Summary

Sometimes your source will contain a lot of information, and it will prove to be difficult for you to include all that information in your paper. In this case, you need to *summarize* the main ideas of the source (see Chapter 3 on writing a summary) and incorporate the condensed information in your paper. For instance, if you used the February 11, 2010, editorial "Global Warming Snow Job" from *The Washington Times* newspaper, you could summarize the entire article in the following way:

> The editorial argues that claims of global warming by the UN are misleading and not backed up by science; not enough academic studies have been cited to prove the theory of global warming. ("Global")

Paraphrase

To *paraphrase* is to restate somebody else's ideas in your own words. Unlike a summary, a paraphrase is usually around the same length as the original. Usually, you would paraphrase when you want to keep the original meaning of the writer, but when the writer's language can be easily restated in your own words. In the following two passages, the first passage is the original passage (part of the article "Inside the Knock-off-Tennis Shoe Factory" from *The New York Times Magazine*), and the second passage is the paraphrased one:

Original passage

In the last fiscal year, U.S. Customs and Border Protection seized more than $260 million worth of counterfeit goods. The goods included counterfeit Snuggies, DVDs, brake pads, computer parts and baby formula. But for four years, counterfeit footwear has topped the seizure list of the customs service; in the last fiscal year it accounted for nearly 40 percent of total seizures. (Electronics made up the second-largest share in that year, with about 12 percent of the total.) The customs service doesn't break down seizures by brand, but demand for the fake reflects demand for the real, and Nike is widely considered to be the most counterfeited brand. One Nike employee estimated that there was one fake Nike item for every two authentic ones. But Peter Koehler, Nike's global counsel for brand and litigation, told me that "counting the number of counterfeits is frankly impossible."

Paraphrase

The New York Times Magazine article, "Inside the Knockoff-Tennis-Shoe Factory," makes the point that while counterfeit goods such as Snuggies, DVDs, computer parts, and baby food are included in the almost $260 million worth of goods that was seized last year by U.S. Customs and Border Protection, almost 40 percent of the seizures in the last year have been counterfeit footwear, especially those of the Nike brand. According to Nike authorities, while it is impossible to know how many counterfeits are in circulation, it is estimated that the ratio of originals to counterfeits is two to one, indicating the popularity of the brand.

Everyday Writing Activity: Paraphrase Exercise

Write a paraphrase of the following paragraphs in your journal. Your instructor may want you to share your paraphrase with the rest of the class.

Hula dancing is the traditional art of movement, smooth bodily gestures, and vocals. You may notice that Hula dancing seems to have an incredibly smooth "flow" and the movements are extremely fluid. These movements are said to actually tell a story or represent movements of nature such as trees blowing in the wind or fish swimming smoothly in the ocean.

Traditionally, you will find both men and women wearing knee-level skirts made of palm leaves as well as flower leis around their arms, lower legs, and heads. However, prior to 1820, women wore skirts that were much shorter and men simply wore loin clothes. It was in 1820 that missionaries made them wear a less revealing wardrobe during their performances.

Integrating Sources in Your Research Paper: Strategies at a Glance	
Strategy	**When to Use It**
Quotation	• When you are quoting an expert, an authority figure or a well-known personality. • When the words of the quotation are so appropriate that they are difficult to express in any other way.
Summary	• When the passage is too long and you can easily present its main ideas in a condensed form.
Paraphrase	• When you want to keep the writer's idea(s), but want to restate them in your own words.

Everyday Writing Activity: Chapter Reflection

In your journal, please respond to the following prompts:

- List the five most important things you learned from this chapter.
- Write two paragraphs describing the process of conducting research to a friend who has never done so.

Your instructor may want you to share your responses with the rest of the class.

MyWritingLab™ For support in meeting this chapter's objectives, log in to **www.mywritinglab.com** and select **Research Process**.

Chapter 16

Documenting Your Sources

Learning Objectives

In this chapter, you will learn to:

LO1 Avoid plagiarizing when you write papers

LO2 Document sources and format a paper according to MLA style

LO3 Document sources and format a paper according to APA style

R esearch, as you learned in the previous chapter, is an important part of college writing. You will have to write research papers in many of your college courses, and to write these papers, you will consult many different sources such as books, journal articles, newspapers, magazines, government documents, and, of course, sources from the Internet. While it is easy to access such sources either by visiting the library or through the Internet, using sources properly in your own writing is a large part of your task as a college writer. In order to avoid charges of plagiarism, it is important to use your sources by correctly quoting, paraphrasing, and summarizing them (see Chapter 3 for summary, and Chapter 15 for using sources in your own writing) and by documenting those sources properly in your paper, as explained in this chapter.

<table>
<tr><td>

LO1

Avoid plagiarizing when you write papers
</td><td>

Avoiding Plagiarism

Plagiarism occurs when a writer uses words or ideas that are someone else's, not the writer's own, and does not credit the source. The term *plagiarism* comes from the Latin word "plagiurus," which means "manstealer." Thus, literally it means stealing or kidnapping someone else's work and presenting it as your own. It is considered a form of academic dishonesty, and it is a serious offense. Your college/university probably has its own plagiarism policy, and your professor and your institution will certainly penalize you in some way for plagiarism. You wouldn't like someone stealing your words or ideas, we are sure, so you have to be careful not to appropriate another writer's words or thoughts, intentionally or unintentionally.
</td></tr>
</table>

Examples of Plagiarism:

> **Original source:** "Education is the most powerful weapon which you can use to change the world."—Nelson Mandela

> **Plagiarism:** Education is a powerful weapon that one can use to change the world.

Note that though you may have changed a couple of words in the original sentence, using "a" instead of "the," "one" instead of "you," and "that" instead of "which," the bulk of the sentence is still Dr. Mandela's words and ideas. Additionally, Dr. Mandela's name is not cited.

> **Source used properly:** From time to time, several prominent personalities have commented on the importance of education. One well-known South African calls on his countrymen to make the world a better place through education: "Education is the most powerful weapon you can use to change the world" (Mandela).

Here is another example:

Original source: "The energy of the mind is the essence of life."—Aristotle

Plagiarism: In any discussion of evolution, consciousness, and life, it is said that the mind's energy is the most important thing in life.

Note that though you have changed the form and/or the order of the words of the original sentence, the idea is still the same, and no credit has been given to Aristotle.

Source used properly: In any discussion of evolution, consciousness, and life, we are reminded of the following famous words: "The energy of the mind is the essence of life" (Aristotle).

Tips for Using Sources Properly

1. Give credit when using someone else's words or ideas or even graphs, charts, drawings, and the like. This is true whether you are quoting, summarizing, or paraphrasing the original source.
2. Take careful notes (in a journal, on note cards or on the computer) while conducting research so that you are aware of what exactly the author is saying and can clearly distinguish between your ideas and those of the author's.
3. Carefully note all bibliographic information that you will need for your in-text citations and your Works Cited/References page. (For more on these, see pages 328–337 and 346–351.)
4. Know the conventions for citing sources. This chapter will help you with citing sources according to MLA and APA style.
5. When in doubt, provide a citation for your source.

What Is Documentation?

Documentation means to refer, in the appropriate places, to the sources used in your writing. This tells readers that you borrowed the material and where you borrowed it from. It will also help protect you from charges of plagiarism.

There are several different ways to document sources. Different academic disciplines often require students to use different documentation formats. Some of the most common documentation styles are:

- MLA (Modern Language Association), used in English and the humanities.
- APA (American Psychological Association), used in the social sciences.

- *The Chicago Manual of Style*, used in the humanities..
- AAA Style Guide (American Anthropological Association), used in anthropology.
- LSA Style Sheet (Linguistic Society of America), used in linguistics.
- CSE (Council of Science Editors), used in science and related subjects.

While these documentation styles can be considerably different from one another, all of them emphasize two things:

- *In-text citations*, that is, sources cited within the body of the writing, so readers know what material is borrowed and from whom.
- A *list of more detailed source information* at the end of the writing, which gives readers all the necessary publication information, such as place of publication, publisher, date, and so forth.

The following chart illustrates, in MLA format, what an in-text citation looks like and what a Works Cited entry looks like. More detailed information on MLA documentation is provided later.

In-text citation (in the body of a paper)	Corresponding Works Cited entry (at the end of the paper)
Mike Rose reminds teachers that "We are in the middle of an extraordinary social experiment: the attempt to provide education for all members of a vast pluralistic democracy" (238).	Rose, Mike. *Lives on the Boundary: A Moving Account of the Struggles and Achievements of America's Educationally Underprepared.* New York: Penguin, 1989. Print.

We will focus on the MLA and APA documentation formats in this chapter, because these are the ones you will be most likely to use in college papers.

<table>
<tr><td>

LO2

Document sources and format a paper according to MLA style

</td><td>

MLA Documentation Format

This section will first discuss using the **Modern Language Association (MLA) format** for **in-text citations.** After that, we will show you how to format the complete citation information for each source at the end of the paper (the **Works Cited** page). The following key shows

</td></tr>
</table>

the colors used to highlight different elements of the citations in this chapter:

Author

Article title

Periodical, Book, Movie, Web Site, or *Online Database Title*

Publication information: publisher, place of publication, edition, page numbers

Medium of publication (print, Web, DVD, CD, etc.) and access date for Web sources

MLA In-Text Citation Examples

In-text citations indicate that something has been taken from a source and inserted into the body of your writing. Direct quotations, summaries, and paraphrases (see pages 321–324 for a discussion of quotations, summaries, and paraphrases) are cited, while common knowledge (e.g., the earth orbits around the sun) is not. In-text citations are typically very brief because full details are available in the Works Cited list. Also, you want your readers to focus on your writing and not be distracted by long references within the writing to the sources used.

In MLA style, in-text citations usually consist of the writer's last name and the page number(s) where the material that has been used appears. If there is no author or no page number(s), then only the title of the work is used in the citation. The citation is placed as close to the borrowed material as possible. This means it can be placed anywhere in the sentence, including at the end. Each in-text citation refers to a complete entry in the Works Cited page.

The next sections show examples of in-text citations of sources according to MLA format. To see how in-text citations actually look in an essay, refer to the MLA format student paper on pages 338–344.

1. **Author name not mentioned in your writing.**

   When the author's name is not mentioned in your sentence, be sure to include the author's last name and the relevant page number(s), without any punctuation between them, in parentheses, and as close to the borrowed material as possible.

   It has been said that "traditionally ESL teachers have emphasized the need for ESL writers to think and write as completely as possible in English" (Friedlander 109).

Note that the ending quotation marks (" ") come at the end of the actual quotation, before the parentheses, and *not* at the end of your sentence. Those ending quotation marks are followed by the citation, in parentheses, and then the period ends your sentence.

2. Author name mentioned in the writing.

When the author's name is mentioned in your sentence, it is unnecessary to repeat it in the parenthetical citation. In this case, just use the page number(s).

> Friedlander has said that "traditionally ESL teachers have emphasized the need for ESL writers to think and write as completely as possible in English" (109).

3. A work with two or three authors.

When a source has two or three authors, the last names of all the authors should be included in your text or in the parenthetical citation. If there are two authors, the word *and* is used between the two names (and as discussed earlier, note that the ending quotation marks follow the actual quotation).

> Cohen and Cavalcanti remind us that student learners "may make changes according to what they think the teacher's values are, out of a belief that the teacher knows best" (155).

> Education researchers remind us that student learners "may make changes according to what they think the teacher's values are, out of a belief that the teacher knows best" (Cohen and Cavalcanti 155).

If there are three authors, remember to add commas and also *and* before the final name.

> Fitzgerald, Kingsley, and Kusko write about the "processes, devices, and systems associated with electro-mechanical energy conversion" (xiii).

> What is emphasized are the "processes, devices, and systems associated with electro-mechanical energy conversion" (Fitzgerald, Kingsley, and Kusko xiii).

4. A work with four or more authors.

When your source has four or more authors, you may list the last names of all the authors, or you may only use the last name of the first author followed by the phrase *et al.* (*et al.* is a Latin term meaning "and others").

More and more dissertations are being devoted to second-language writing (Matsuda, Cox, Jordan, and Ortmeier-Hooper 23-24).

More and more dissertations are being devoted to second-language writing (Matsuda et al. 23-24).

5. Two or more works by the same author.

If you use two different sources by the same author, then you must make clear which source you are referring to. The title of the work can be referred to either in the text or in the parenthetical citation. If the title is too long, and you are writing it in the parenthetical citation, include only the first one or two main words, excluding *A, An,* or *The,* which are not considered major words.

"Globalization, I want to suggest, must always begin at home" (Bhabha, *Location,* xv).

The *Location of Culture* is a book title; hence it is italicized.

There is an interdependence between the colonizer and the colonized (Bhabha, "Cultural," 6).

"Cultural Diversity and Cultural Differences" is an article title; hence quotation marks are used around the title.

6. Authors with the same last name.

When two or more of your source authors have the same last name, use the first initials of both authors in your in-text citations as a way to distinguish between them:

While the focus is on East Africa and the gathering war clouds (W. Smith), it is pitted against the claim that Botswana is one of the finest and most peaceful countries in the world (A. Smith).

There are no page numbers included because this is an online article that does not have any page numbers.

7. An anonymous work.

If one of your sources is an unsigned one, use the book or article title, either full or shortened, depending on whether you are citing it in parentheses or in-text:

The writer notes that difficulties in catching trout probably result from "not using the right fishing lure or bait" ("Fishing").

"Fishing: Trout Fishing with the Best Fishing Lures" tells readers having trouble catching trout that they are probably not using the right fishing lure or bait.

Note: As in the preceding example, there are no page numbers included because this online article does not have page numbers. If page numbers were available, they would have been included.

8. A work by entities such as a government department, an association, a committee, or the like.

If any of these groups is the author of your source, the source is cited using the entity's name:

> According to the World Health Organization, globally there are more than 1 billion overweight adults, at least 300 million of them obese (1).

> Globally there are more than 1 billion overweight adults, at least 300 million of them obese (World Health Organization 1).

9. An entire work

When you refer to an entire work, you do not need to refer to any page number(s) in the text; simply refer to the author's name, either in the text or in a parenthetical citation:

> Friedman focuses on globalization and the forces behind the process.

> One thesis is that individual countries must sacrifice some degree of economic sovereignty to global institutions (Friedman).

10. A source using two or more sentences and block quotations.

When your reference to a source is longer than a sentence, the author's name is usually used in the first sentence, and the parenthetical citation is placed at the end of the last sentence. This helps clarify boundaries for the reader:

> Brokaw writes that by 1944, twelve million Americans were in uniform. He adds that war production represented 44 percent of the Gross National Product, and that 35 percent of the workers were women (11).

For quotations of more than four lines, place the quoted text in a free-standing block of text and omit quotation marks. Start the quotation on a new line, with the entire quote indented one inch from the left margin, and maintain double spacing. Your parenthetical citation should come after the closing punctuation mark and an additional space after the punctuation:

> Foster and Gibbons make the following point:
> > The University of Rochester's River Campus Libraries are known as innovative and forward-thinking, especially in the areas of reference outreach, online catalogs, institutional repositories, and Web-based

> services. Still, the library staff wanted to do more to reach students and their instructors in support of the university's educational mission. But to do more, we realized we needed to know more about today's undergraduate students—their habits, the academic work they are required to do, and their library-related needs. In particular, we were interested in how students write their research papers and what services, resources, and facilities would be most useful to them. As Katie Clark, director of the Carlson Science and Engineering Library, remarked early in this project, "Papers happen," but we did not know how they happen. (6)

Note that you do not need quotation marks for a block quotation; when readers see it set off in a "block," they understand that it is a quotation.

11. Source with no page numbers

For sources with no page numbers (many of these will be online sources), use the last name of author in the parenthetical citation. If there is no author, use the first major word (as mentioned earlier, *a, an, the* are not considered major words) of the article title as the citation:

> Treadmill weight loss is one of the most successful methods of losing weight (Gresham).

> Rain develops when growing cloud droplets become too heavy to remain in the cloud and as a result, fall toward the surface as rain ("Rain").

Note: Parenthetical citations are usually placed before a punctuation mark:

> "A house divided against itself cannot stand" (Lincoln).

If the quotation ends in a question mark or an exclamation point, then the punctuation is used inside the closing quotation marks, followed by the parenthetical citation and the period:

> "Why does the universe go to all the bother of existing?" wonders physicist Stephen Hawking (192).

> "I write music with an exclamation point!" wrote German composer Richard Wagner (*Brainyquote.com*).

MLA Works Cited Examples

After you have finished writing your paper, you need to make a list that includes *all* the sources used as in-text citations. This list is known as the Works Cited page and is written on a separate page at the end of your paper. While the in-text citations are brief, the Works Cited entries contain the complete information about each source—that information lets your readers find and then read the article or book, if they want to. There are some rules to remember when you draft the Works Cited page:

- The sources should be arranged alphabetically, by the last name of the author(s). If there is no author, the source is alphabetized by the first main word of the title.
- If there is more than one author of a work, list the first author by last name, first name, and subsequent authors by first name, last name. Use commas to separate their names, with an "and" before the last name:

> Castellucci, Marion, Debbie Meyer, and Samantha Neary. *How to Write a Thriller*. New York: Pearson, 2012. Print.

- The entire list should be double-spaced, within the entries as well as between the entries.
- The second and subsequent lines of each entry are indented one half inch from the left margin. That makes it easier for readers to skim down the list, as they search for a particular author's last name.
- The publication medium for each source—such as print, Web, DVD—should be indicated, usually as the last item in the citation.

The following examples show how to list different kinds of sources in the Works Cited page. For a student's Works Cited page, see page 345:

1. **Book (print).**

> Goshgarian, Gary. *What Matters in America: Reading and Writing About Contemporary Culture*. 2nd ed. New York: Pearson, 2010. Print.

Name of author with last name first; title of the book in italics; book edition (if any); place of publication; publisher; year of publication; publication medium—in this case, Print.

2. **Dictionary entry (print).**

> "Compact." *Random House Webster's Collegiate Dictionary*. 1991. Print.

Entry name, placed within quotation marks; name of the dictionary in italics; the year of publication of the dictionary; publication medium.

3. **Newspaper article (print).**

> "Double-digit Inflation Spreads to Non-food Items." *India West* 18 June 2010: A35. Print.

Name of article, placed within quotation marks (because there is no author); name of newspaper, italicized; date of publication (in day month year sequence); page number; publication medium.

4. Journal article (print).

Rintakoski, K., J. Kaprio, and H. Murtoma. "Genetic and Environmental Factors in Oral Health Among Twins." *Journal of Dental Research* 89.2 (2010): 700-704. Print.

Names of authors, alphabetized by the last name of the first author; article title within quotation marks; name of journal in italics; volume number and issue number of journal; year of publication; relevant page numbers; publication medium.

5. Magazine article (print).

Hirsh, Michael. "Mortgages and Madness." *Newsweek* 2 June 2008: 38-40. Print.

Name of author; name of article within quotation marks; italicized name of magazine in which article is published; date of publication of the magazine; relevant page numbers; publication medium.

6. An entire Web site.

National Science Foundation: Where Discoveries Begin. National Science Foundation, June 2010. Web. 20 Sept. 2010.

Title of the Web site in italics; name of organization whose Web site it is; the latest date of update (if any); publication medium; date of access.

7. Journal article (Web).

Schneider, Julie, et al. "Hearing Loss Impacts on the Use of Community and Informal Supports." *Age and Ageing* 39.4 (2010). Web. 5 July 2010.

Name of the first author; name of article, placed within quotation marks; name of journal in italics; volume number and issue number of journal; year of publication; publication medium; date of access.

8. Journal article (online database).

Frakes, Dan. "Installing Snow Leopard: What You Need to Know." *MacWorld* 26.1 (2009): 48-53. *EBSCOHost.* Web. 20 June 2010.

Name of author; title of article within quotation marks; name of journal in italics; volume number and issue number of journal; year of publication of journal; relevant page numbers; name of online database in italics; publication medium; date of access.

9. Newspaper article (Web).

Yang, Jia Lynn. "Companies Are Hoarding Cash, Not Creating Jobs." *Washington Post.* Washington Post, 16 July 2010. Web. 16 July 2010.

Name of author; article name within quotation marks; name of newspaper in italics; name of publisher; date of publication; publication medium; date of access.

10. Magazine article (Web).

Gregory, Sean. "Athletic Edge: Does Practice Really Make Perfect?" *Time*. Time, 16 July 2010. Web. 16 July 2010.

Name of author; name of article within quotation marks; name of magazine in italics; name of publisher; date of publication; publication medium; date of access.

11. Government document (Web).

United Nations. "The Universal Declaration of Human Rights." *UN.org*. United Nations, n.d. Web. 10 Mar. 2010.

Name of government agency; name of document within quotation marks; name of Web site in italics; name of sponsor; no publication date indicated by n.d.; publication medium; date of access.

12. Encyclopedia article (Web).

"French Revolution." *Encyclopaedia Britannica Online*. Encyclopaedia Britannica, 2010. Web. 16 July 2010.

Name of encyclopedia entry within quotation marks; name of encyclopedia in italics; publisher; date of publication; publication medium; date of access.

13. An article in a wiki (Web).

"Traditional Pop Music." *Wikipedia*. Wikimedia, 26 Sept. 2010. Web. 3 Oct. 2010.

Entry title; wiki name; sponsor; publication date; publication medium (Web); date of access.

14. A blog entry (Web).

Oord, Thomas Jay. "Comparing Bible and Qur'an." *For the Love of Wisdom and the Wisdom of Love*. N.p., 20 May 2010. Web. 28 May 2010.

Name of author; title of entry within quotation marks; title of blog or site in italics; no sponsor (indicated by N.p.); publication date; publication medium; date of access.

15. A video (Web).

Utah Valley University, prod. *UVU: Wolverine Achievement Awards 2010*. *YouTube*. YouTube, 31 May 2010. Web. 1 June 2010.

Name of organization that produced the video; title of video in italics; title of site in italics; name of sponsor; date of production; publication medium; date of access.

16. An e-mail message.

Robertson, Jason. "Next Weekend." Message to the author. 10 Sept. 2011. E-mail.

Name of author; e-mail's subject heading within quotation marks; name of the recipient; date of message; publication medium. There is no need to include date of access.

17. A television program.

The Price Is Right. CBS. KPHO, Phoenix, 16 July 2010. Television.

Name of program, italicized; name of network; the call letters and city of the local station; program date; medium. If there were an episode title, it would be in quotation marks.

18. A radio program.

"The Incredible Shrinking Proton." Dir. Ira Flatow. *Science Friday.* NPR. 16 July 2010. Radio.

Episode title, placed within quotation marks; name of the episode's director; program title in italics; name of network; date of broadcast; medium.

19. A personal interview.

Chavez, Ernesto. Personal interview. 1 Feb. 2009.

Name of person interviewed; indicate that you conducted the interview; date of interview.

20. An advertisement (print).

Liberty Mutual. Advertisement. *Newsweek* 9 June 2008: 57. Print.

Name of the company or product advertised; the description *Advertisement*; publication source in italics; date of publication and page of publication; publication medium.

21. A film.

Roman Holiday. Dir. William Wyler. Paramount, 1953. Film.

Name of film, in italics; name of director; name of distributor; year, medium.

22. A DVD.

This Is Macbeth. Dir. Greg Watkins. 2008. DVD.

Title of DVD in italics; name of director; release date; medium.

Research Paper Formatted in MLA Style

Following is a sample paper written by a student for her college composition course. It is formatted in MLA style.

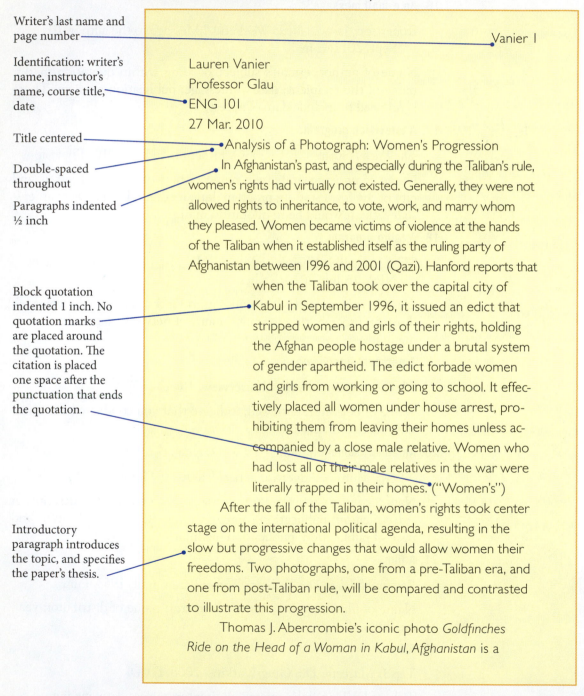

Writer's last name and page number

Identification: writer's name, instructor's name, course title, date

Title centered

Double-spaced throughout

Paragraphs indented ½ inch

Block quotation indented 1 inch. No quotation marks are placed around the quotation. The citation is placed one space after the punctuation that ends the quotation.

Introductory paragraph introduces the topic, and specifies the paper's thesis.

Vanier 1

Lauren Vanier
Professor Glau
ENG 101
27 Mar. 2010

Analysis of a Photograph: Women's Progression

In Afghanistan's past, and especially during the Taliban's rule, women's rights had virtually not existed. Generally, they were not allowed rights to inheritance, to vote, work, and marry whom they pleased. Women became victims of violence at the hands of the Taliban when it established itself as the ruling party of Afghanistan between 1996 and 2001 (Qazi). Hanford reports that

> when the Taliban took over the capital city of Kabul in September 1996, it issued an edict that stripped women and girls of their rights, holding the Afghan people hostage under a brutal system of gender apartheid. The edict forbade women and girls from working or going to school. It effectively placed all women under house arrest, prohibiting them from leaving their homes unless accompanied by a close male relative. Women who had lost all of their male relatives in the war were literally trapped in their homes. ("Women's")

After the fall of the Taliban, women's rights took center stage on the international political agenda, resulting in the slow but progressive changes that would allow women their freedoms. Two photographs, one from a pre-Taliban era, and one from post-Taliban rule, will be compared and contrasted to illustrate this progression.

Thomas J. Abercrombie's iconic photo *Goldfinches Ride on the Head of a Woman in Kabul, Afghanistan* is a

Vanier 2

First visual

strikingly detailed color photograph. It conveys a concise message about the subject, especially when one considers the social and political setting in which it was captured.

The Middle East in 1968 had, the previous year, experienced the infamous Six Day War that involved the entire region. What our current generation knows as a conflict ridden area has been called a "direct consequence" of this Six Day War. Although there were few civilian casualties, the resulting turmoil had been added to an already oppressive society. Women of the Middle East were (and still are, although not to the same extent) subject to segregation, denial of education and work, forced marriages, and female genital mutilation, among other dehumanizing gender barriers. In 1996, rights denial worsened with the rise of the Taliban, who made women objects of their violence. During this period, sexual assaults and abductions of women occurred on a large scale. They were forced to wear restrictive head to toe burqas, and were virtually banned from public life, as they were not allowed out unless they were supervised by a close male relative (Afary 109).

The focal point of the photograph is clearly the woman in the red burqa with the birdcage balanced on her head. She and the birds are the only presence in the photo. Detail is almost completely absent in the white background, although there is a horizontal line, which breaks the monotony of the backdrop. The tonality of her attire is in bright contrast to the white behind her. It is both colorful and intricate, being an electric red, with both contour and pleated lines in diagonals, verticals, and horizontals. The multidirectional lines are reflected in the bars of the birdcage. There is a shallow depth of field that results in the rich surface texture of the subject's dress, and also creates another dimension of how outstandingly singular the focal point is. The birds in the cage are also in sharp focus, as they are an essential part of the subject.

As the audience combines the contextual and compositional elements of the photograph, the message becomes undeniable. The birds in the cage are the most important factor in the interpretation of the photograph, and make it almost purely subjective. Without them, the photo would hardly be more than just a pretty display of Middle Eastern wear. Birds in a cage have been firmly rooted in many cultures as a metaphor for entrapment, of an inability to escape. The same idea is reflected literally and symbolically in the woman's burqa. She is literally veiled without even her eyes visible, and seems encased by her clothing. The wall behind her also adds another element of enclosure. The situation presented by her environment provides the symbolic aspect. Although Middle Eastern women today have an option as to whether they want to remain traditional in their dress, in recent history wearing such outfits was law, enforced by religious police. She did not have the option of expression, caged by her government and religious practices that made the law. This photograph is evidence of a "big-picture" idea. She is not the only one suffering from such oppression. Although the Six Day War left the area somewhat dismembered, it would be nothing compared to the savagery that the Taliban would later afflict upon women in Afghanistan. As far as a person coming from a free nation is concerned, living amidst such violence would be an incredibly hard "cage" to escape from.

Farzana Wahidy's *A Woman in a White Burqa Feeds a Pigeon after Paying Respect to Imam Ali at His Resting Place in Mazar-e Sharif*, 2008 (see next page) is an uplifting photograph which is a visual supplement when defining contemporary women's rights in Afghanistan. In addition to the iconic and symbolic image represented in the photograph, one must consider that the photographer is an Afghani woman who lived under the Taliban regime, forced to wear the burqa and unable to attend school like the rest. After the fall of the Taliban, she was offered a scholarship at a photojournalism college, and now has internationally recognized work on Afghan women's stories, which she hopes will further the cause for women's freedoms (Wahidy).

The focal point of the photograph is the woman in the burqa, and the pigeons eating from her hand. She is the only human presence in the photograph, so, again, there is an element of singularity, which helps to focus the audience's attention on her. The background is broken up by many white birds, and helps to create movement in the picture. The photograph contains a small palette of colors, but still creates a high range

Vanier 5

Second visual

of value, which reflect upon each other in different elements of the picture. White is the prominent color, as the subject is in a white head to toe burqa. The birds that constitute a generous portion of the background are of the same color. There are contrasting dark components, such as the subject's arm and the architecture in the background that allow the subject to further stand out. The blue sky brightens the picture, and is a crisp background that defines the detail in the woman's attire. The texture of the woman's burqa, along with the texture that the birds give the background, enrich this photograph with superb detail. This detail allows for engaging visual stimulation, and begs to be closely examined.

Vanier 6

As one considers the progression women in Afghanistan have made towards obtaining women's rights, the photograph grows into a statement of optimism for this oppressed minority group. We must first note that as the Taliban regime ceased to rule, wearing a burqa like the one in the photo became optional for Afghani women (Qazi). As this is a post-Taliban photograph, it is determined that the subject is choosing to don this attire. The subject is surrounded by white, which is typically interpreted as a peaceful color. Birds are everywhere, mulling about undisturbed. These two elements, when combined, give the viewer a sense of tranquility, something that would not be present in an oppressive, even violent, atmosphere. She is facing the sun, so that it appears as if the woman in the burqa is looking into a brighter future. One of the most important elements of the photo is the woman's exposed arm. Seven years before this photograph was taken, women could be severely beaten for something as little as an exposed bare wrist or ankle (Afary 112). Now, this woman is allowing someone to capture such a display in a picture, which is a radical change from the fear of being seen and beaten for this "offense." The somewhat dramatic flying birds and her upturned hand appear to be celebratory of a dawning era of freedom. Overall, the photograph becomes a composition that communicates a sense of rejoice and peace for the subject.

Thomas J. Abercrombie's 1968 photograph and Farzana Wahidy's 2008 portrait could be looked at as points on a timeline, each depicting Afghani women of their era. The woman in the red embraces herself, staying as small and confined as possible, while the woman in white reaches her arm outside of her burqa to interact with the environment around her. The juxtaposition of the birds in each photograph also appeal symbolically to the interpretation of both meanings. The birds in the 1968 photograph were caged, a symbol of entrapment, while the birds in the 2008 photograph contrast the others by flying, interpreted as freedom. The pre-Taliban woman is against a wall, and has an inability to escape from the even more oppressive and dismal future she faces under the Taliban. The contemporary picture is taken in an open area, which is another element that communicates her autonomy. Upon analyzing these two photographs we see that each perfectly illustrate and further define the state of women's rights in the time period in which each were captured. During the 40 years between the photographs, women's rights in Afghanistan first became more oppressed as the Taliban regime took control, and then, with the fall of the Taliban in 2001, began to progress to allow women many of the freedoms they were previously denied. As the promotion of Middle Eastern women's rights continue to gain momentum and hold an international spotlight, the women of this region have only a brighter future to look forward to. And as they look to expanded horizons, the rest of the world waits for the next defining photograph of the Middle East's slowly but surely evolving culture.

Vanier 8

New page for Works
Cited. Title Works
Cited centered.
Double-spaced
throughout. Sources
alphabetized by
authors' last names.

Photograph in an
illustrated book

Scholarly journal

A Web site

A Web site

An online photograph

Works Cited

Abercrombie, Thomas J. *Goldfinches Ride on the Head of a*
Veiled Woman in Kabul, Afghanistan. 1968. Photograph.
In Focus: National Geographic Greatest Portraits.
National Geographic, 2004. 297. Print.

Afary, Janet. "The Human Rights of Middle Eastern and
Muslim Women: A Project for the 21st Century."
Human Rights Quarterly 26.1 (2004): 106-125. Print.

Hanford, Cindy. "Women's Lives Under the Taliban."
National Organization for Women, 2001. Web. 20 July
2010.

Qazi, Abdullah. "The Plight of the Afghan Woman."
Afghanistan Online, June 2010. Web. 14 July 2010.

Wahidy, Farzana. *A Woman in a White Burqa Feeds a Pigeon*
after Paying Respect to Imam Ali at His Resting Place in
Mazar-e Sharif. 2008. Photograph. 22 July 2010.

LO3
Document sources and format a paper according to APA style

APA Documentation Format

Business, psychology, and some other social sciences use the **American Psychological Association (APA) format** to document sources in a research paper. As in the MLA style, sources in APA are cited in-text and on a separate page that provides complete bibliographic information of all the sources used. In APA, this page is known as the **References** page.

APA In-Text Citation Examples

Here are some examples of APA in-text documentation of sources:

1. Author not named in your text.

When the author is not named in the text, the author's last name, date of the source, and the page number (if available) are placed in parentheses, with each item being separated by a comma.

> "The readers likely to see your work—your **audience**—will often be specified or implied in a writing assignment" (Aaron, 2011, p. 7).

2. Author named in the text.

When the author's name is used in the text, the date is also placed in parentheses after the author's name, while the page number is placed after the borrowed material.

> Aaron (2011) reminds students that "The readers likely to see your work—your **audience**—will often be specified or implied in a writing assignment" (p. 7).

3. A work with two authors.

Within the text, both authors' names are used and are connected with the word *and*.

> Kotler and Andreasen (1987) apply the conceptual system of marketing to the marketing problems of nonprofit organizations.

4. In a parenthetical citation, the two authors' names are joined by an ampersand (&).

> One book (Kotler & Andreasen, 1987) applies the conceptual system of marketing to the marketing problems of nonprofit organizations.

5. A work with three to five authors.

Name all the authors in the first citation of a work with three to five authors. In second and subsequent references of the same work, give only the first author's last name, followed by *et al.*

Sullivan, Struve, and Mazzarella's (2007) *Elementary and Intermediate Algebra* is widely used in introductory mathematics courses.

Sullivan et al. (2007) emphasize training in mathematics in their book *Elementary and Intermediate Algebra*.

6. A work with six or more authors.

Even in the first citation of the work, use only the first author's name, followed by et al.

A very important study (Klein et al., 2010) focuses on the link between the measles-mumps-rubella-varicella vaccine and the risk of seizures.

7. An anonymous work, or a work without an author.

When a work has no named author, the first two or three words of the title are used. Use quotation marks around article titles, and capitalize the major words of the title.

The Australian shepherd is described as "animated, adaptable and agile" ("AKC Meet," 1993).

8. Two or more works by different authors.

When referring to two or more sources, list the sources in alphabetical order by the last name of the authors, with a semicolon between the sources.

Three important articles on Jewish rhetorical studies (Bernard-Donals, 2010; Handelman, 2010; Metzger & Katz, 2010) have recently been published.

9. An electronic source.

Electronic sources are often cited like print sources, with the author's last name and the year of publication.

It has been reported (Corbett Dooren, 2010) that Gilenia is an effective multiple sclerosis drug but that it has safety issues.

APA References Examples

As in MLA documentation style, in APA format there is a list of sources at the end of your paper (References) that provide full bibliographical information for each in-text citation. There are some rules to remember when you draft the References page:

- The sources should be arranged alphabetically, by the last name of the author(s). Use initials only instead of first and middle names. If there is no author, the source is alphabetized by the first main word of the article title. The entire list should be double-spaced, within the entries as well as between the entries.

- Each entry should begin at the left margin. The second and subsequent lines of each entry are indented one-half inch from the left margin.
- Each part of the reference (author, date, title, publication information) is separated with a period and one space.
- For works with up to seven authors, all authors are listed with last names first, with commas separating names and parts of names. Initials are used for first and any middle names and an ampersand (&) before the last author's name.
- The publication year is placed in parentheses after the author(s) name(s), followed by a period.
- Titles of books and journals are italicized. No quotation marks are used around the title of articles. Only the first word of book and article titles and subtitles and proper nouns are capitalized.
- If the journal article (or any other document) has a **Digital Object Identifier (DOI),** the DOI should be included instead of a URL or a database name. The DOI functions as an identifier of the source.

The following examples show how to list different kinds of sources in the References page.

1. A book (print).

Aaron, J. E. (2010). *The Little, Brown handbook.* Boston, MA: Longman.

Name of author; year of publication; title of book, italicized; city and state of publication; publisher.

2. A book with an editor (print).

Claiborne, C. (Ed.). (1961). *The New York Times cookbook.* New York, NY: Harper.

Name of editor, (Ed.) in parentheses, with periods inside the parentheses and outside it; year of publication; title of book, italicized; city and state of publication; publisher.

3. A later edition of a book (print).

Heward, W. L. (2008). *Exceptional children: An introduction to special education* (9th ed.). Upper Saddle River, NJ: Prentice-Hall.

Name of author; year of publication; title of book, italicized; edition number in parentheses, followed by a period; city and state of publication; publisher.

4. An article in a magazine (print).

Adler, J. (2008, June 9). The race for survival. *Newsweek*, 42-50.

Name of author; year and date of issue; name of article; magazine name, italicized; relevant page numbers.

5. An article in a newspaper (print).

Mundhra, S. (2010, June 18). On Father's Day: My father, the hero. *India West*, p. A10.

Name of author; year and date of publication; article name; newspaper name, italicized; page number preceded with *p.* or *pp.*

6. An article in a journal (print).

You, X. (2004). The choice made from no choice: English writing instruction in a Chinese university. *Journal of Second Language Writing, 13*(2), 97-110.

Name of author; year of publication; article name; journal name and volume number, italicized; issue number in parentheses; page numbers.

7. A government document (print).

U.S. Department of Labor. (2010). *State unemployment insurance benefits*. Washington, DC: Author.

Sponsoring agency as author—there is no individual author; year of publication; title of publication, italicized; place of publication; the word "author" (because the agency is both the author and the publisher).

8. An article in a journal with a DOI (Web).

Lewis, T. (2010). Branding, celebritization, and the lifestyle expert. *Cultural Studies 24*(4), 580-598. doi: 10.1080/09502386.2010.488406

Name of author, year of publication, name of article, name of journal and volume number italicized, issue number in parentheses, page numbers, digital object identifier (DOI). *Note:* No period is used after the DOI.

9. An article in a journal without a DOI (Web).

Rotimi, O. O. (2008). Knowledge and attitudes of students in a Caribbean medical school towards HIV/AIDS. *African Journal of Biomedical Research 11*(2). Retrieved from http://www.bioline.org.br/md

Name of author; year of publication; article name; name of journal and volume number italicized, issue number in parentheses; the URL of the journal's home page, beginning with the phrase *Retrieved from*.

10. An article in a newspaper (Web).

iPad overheats easily. (2010, July 28). *The Straits Times*. Retrieved from http://www.straitstimes.com/

Name of article (there is no author); year and date of publication; name of newspaper, italicized; the URL of the newspaper's home page, beginning with the phrase *Retrieved from*.

11. An article in a magazine (Web).

Almasi, M. A. (2010, July 27). The five best haircuts of all time. *Good Housekeeping*. Retrieved from http://www.goodhousekeeping.com/

Name of author; year and date of issue; name of article; name of magazine, italicized; the URL of the magazine's home page, beginning with the phrase *Retrieved from*.

12. A government document (Web).

United States. Department of Agriculture . (1998, December). *The USDA handbook on workplace violence prevention and response*. Retrieved from The US Department of Agriculture Web site: http://www.usda.gov

Name of organization; year and month of issue; title of document, italicized; the URL of the organization's home page, beginning with the phrase *Retrieved from*.

13. A report from the Web site of an organization.

Hansen, K. (2010, July). *Arctic voyage illuminating ocean optics*. Retrieved from the NASA Web site: http://www.nasa.gov/

Name of author; year and month of issue; title of document, italicized; the URL of the organization's home page, beginning with the phrase *Retrieved from*.

14. An article in a reference work (Web).

Magellanic cloud. (2010). In *Encyclopedia Britannica Online*. Retrieved from http://www.britannica.com/

Name of article (there is no author); year of publication; name of reference work, italicized; the URL of the reference work, beginning with the phrase *Retrieved from*.

15. An article in a wiki.

Superstition. (2010, July 25). Retrieved July 27, 2010, from
Wikipedia: http://www.wikipedia.org/

Name of article (there is no author); year, month and date of publication; retrieval date (because the source information is likely to change); the URL of the source

16. A film or video recording (Web).

National Taiwan University. (Producer). (2009).
National Taiwan University [Video file]. Retrieved from http://www.youtube.com/watch?v=XydRpAtmpU0

Name of film/video producer, the title *Producer* in parentheses; year of production; name of video file italicized; the URL, beginning with the phrase *Retrieved from.*

17. A motion picture.

Murphy, R. (Director). (2010). *Eat, pray, love* [Motion picture].
United States: Columbia.

Name of movie director, the title *Director* in parentheses; year of release in parentheses; name of movie, in italics; the medium (motion picture) in parentheses; place of release; name of company that released the movie.

Research Paper Formatted in APA Style

Following is a sample paper written by a student for her college composition course. It is formatted in APA style.

Shortened running header in capital letters on all pages

Running head: DRUG USE ON COLLEGE CAMPUSES 1

Prevalence of Drug Use on College Campuses

Lauren Vanier

ENG 101

Professor Glau

May 15, 2010

Shortened running head in capital letters on all pages

Double spaced throughout

Topic of paper introduced

Thesis statement

APA style in-text citation used throughout

DRUG USE ON COLLEGE CAMPUSES   2

Prevalence of Drug Use on College Campuses

It is said that college is a time of experimentation. What is it that we are supposed to experiment with? Many try different fields of study; others participate in various school organizations, such as intramurals. Whatever the case, a generous portion of these students experiment with other, more illicit activities. Drugs have become a prominent aspect of college life; according to the Almanac of Policy Issues, almost half of America's college student population uses drugs or binges on alcohol at least once a month (2002). Since it concerns a large body of people in the United States, the effects of such use is vital to understanding the health of those college students who may be our siblings or peers.

The Almanac of Policy Issues reports that the rate of current illicit drug use among full time college students is 20.6%, compared to 10.7% among 12 to 17 year olds, and 4.2% in people ages 26 and older (2002). As of 2005, the three most popular drugs among college students were marijuana, cocaine, and hallucinogens. Recently, prescription drugs have exploded among the college population, the most popular being analeptics, or prescription amphetamines that are used to treat attention deficit hyperactivity disorder (Jacobs, 2005). Each comes with its own purpose, set of effects, and level of risk when using.

The most common illicit drug of choice is marijuana (*cannabis sativa*). In a study conducted over decades at one college, it was reported that in 2000, about 7% of students used it on a weekly basis (Pope, Ionescu-Pioggia, & Pope, 2005). In another statistic, 33.3% of college students had reported using marijuana at least once in 2005 (Leinwand, 2007). Short-term effects include loss of memory, a heightened appetite, and slower reaction time, none of which have any adverse effects on a user's health. Few studies have produced conclusive evidence on its long-term use, but possible effects, pointed out by the Alcohol and Drug Abuse (ADA) Web site, include loss of memory and cellular changes in the lungs called metaplasia, suspected to be pre-cancerous (1984). DrugWarFacts.org reports that in the United States, there are zero reported deaths in a year as a result of marijuana use, compared to the 435,000 tobacco related and 85,000 alcohol related deaths (2007). As no definite results have been produced regarding marijuana as a dangerous or high risk drug, one should consider whether America's higher educated are deserving of being thrown in jail for up to a year, and face being penalized another $2,000 for possessing a small amount (1 kg or less) of cannabis.

What is more concerning than the number of people trying marijuana each year is the fact that the second most frequented drug, cocaine, can be lethal. The Web site National Institute on Alcohol Abuse and Alcoholism reports that about 1% of the college student population reported being current cocaine users (2005), and 5.7% reported having tried it at least once in the year 2005 (Leinwand, 2007). The drug's short-term effects, according to the U.S. Drug Enforcement Administration, include a sense of euphoria and mental alertness, especially to the senses of sight, sound, and touch. It typically wears off within a few minutes. The short-term effects include constricted blood vessels, dilated pupils, and increased heart rate and blood pressure. Some users may experience tremors and paranoia, among other similar effects. Sudden death is possible, and is often the result of cardiac arrest or seizures, followed by respiratory arrest, which most commonly occurs among frequent users, although first time instances have been reported (2006). Because it is highly addictive, people may have trouble controlling their use, and could develop a tolerance. This means that it would take an increasingly greater amount for a frequent user to get high, putting him/her at a higher risk of overdose.

DRUG USE ON COLLEGE CAMPUSES   4

DrugRehabs.org estimates that about half of all drug related
emergency room visits are related to cocaine (2002). Although
cocaine can cause death and be harmful enough to make a person feel as if they need medical attention, there were hardly any
readily available death statistics as a result of its use.

Hallucinogens are the third most frequently used drug
by college students, as 5% of the college population had
tried them at least once in the year 2005 (Leinwand, 2007).
They are a group of drugs that cause an alteration in per-
ception, thought, or mood. This group includes, but is not
limited to, LSD, PCP, and Psilocybin mushrooms. Marijuana
is also classified as a hallucinogen, but is not included in
the statistics reported. Hallucinogens are used less habitu-
ally than marijuana or cocaine, as the high takes longer to
recede. Many college students use this drug to "expand
their minds," or go on a creative trip. They are considered
neuro-toxic (poisonous to nerve tissue), but the more immediate threats are impaired judgment, which can result in
accidents. Hallucinogen-related deaths are very rare, as a
person would have to ingest massive amounts in order for it
to become lethally toxic (Brenner & Dribbens, 2006). More
common are "bad trips," in which a person may experience
sensations that may induce panic and a feeling of loss of
control. These effects wear off with the drug. Some mental
changes can occur, such as impaired memory and attention
span, mental confusion, and difficulty with abstract thinking, observed in heavy LSD users. According to the ADA
Web site, it is not known whether or not these effects are
permanent (1984). As long as hallucinogens are used in a
responsible manner, there is no imminent danger to the user.

Prescription drugs have taken the spotlight on college
campuses nationwide. Most commonly used are "analeptics,
the class of prescription amphetamines that is used to treat

attention deficit hyperactivity disorder" (Jacobs, 2005). While the drugs previously discussed are used recreationally, analeptics such as Adderall and Ritalin are being taken as part of a recipe for academic success. These increase focus, and are used by students to write papers or study for exams, among other academic exercises. As many as 20% of college students have reported using either of these two drugs, rivaling the percent of students who have tried marijuana. They are cited as possibly being as commonplace as the stimulant energy drink, Red Bull (Jacobs, 2005). Although they carry side effects such as an increased heart rate or insomnia, they are safe drugs distributed by doctors to those who need them. The general standpoint of the student is that Adderall and Ritalin are ways to enhance academic performance, and the primary issue with it today is the illegality of taking prescription drugs, and the question of whether or not it gives students who use it an unfair advantage over those who do not use.

Despite the fact that a large portion of college students have used or currently use drugs, it may be just a phase, as a significant number stop after leaving college. The four most popular are marijuana, cocaine, hallucinogens, and prescription pills. As marijuana, hallucinogens, and analeptic pills pose very little threat to the student's life, authorities should focus on cocaine trafficking, which carries the risk of potentially life threatening side effects. To control the market would result in less of these drugs available to college students, which is more reasonable than focusing on finding the drugs within the college community. It seems that dealing with the source would be more efficient than jailing those who will progress to become some of the nation's next innovators and leaders.

DRUG USE ON COLLEGE CAMPUSES   6

References

New page for References. Title References centered. Double-spaced throughout. Sources alphabetized by authors' last names or first names of organizations.

ADA. *Fact sheet: Marijuana.* (1984). Retrieved from http://www.well.com/user/woa/fspot.htm

Almanac of Policy Issues. (2002, September 5). *Drug abuse in America: 2001.* Retrieved from http://www.policyalmanac.org/crime/archive/drug_abuse.shtml

Brenner, S., & Dribbens, B. (2006, August 17). *Toxicity, hallucinogens-LSD.* Retrieved from http://emedicine.medscape.com/

Article from a Web site (Web)

Article from the Web site of an organization (Web)

DrugRehabs.org. (2002). *Cocaine statistics.* Retrieved from http://www.drug-rehabs.org/drug-statistics.php

DrugWarFacts.org. (2007, March 15). *Annual causes of death in the United States.* Retrieved from http://drugwarfacts.org/cms/?q=node/30

Jacobs, A. (2005, July 31). The Adderall advantage. *New York Times.* Retrieved from http://www.nytimes.com/

Leinwand, D. (2007, March 15). College drug use, binge drinking rise. *USA Today.* Retrieved from http://www.usatoday.com/

Article from a journal (Web)

Pope, H. G, Ionescu-Pioggia, M., & Pope, K. W. (2001). Drug use and life style among college undergraduates: A 30-year longitudinal study. *Psychiatry Online.* Retrieved from http://ajp.psychiatryonline.org/

Article from the Web site of a government agency

U.S. Drug Enforcement Administration. (2006). *Cocaine.* Retrieved from http://www.usdoj.gov/dea/concern/cocaine.html

Everyday Documentation Activity: Citing Sources in MLA and APA Style

Using the following information, create a Works Cited page using MLA style documentation. Then, use the same information to create a References page using APA style documentation.

1. A book

   Author: Mary Stewart
   Title: Launching the Imagination: A Comprehensive Guide to Basic Design, 3rd edition
   Publisher: McGraw-Hill
   Year of publication: 2007
   Place of publication: New York, NY

2. A book

   Authors: Patricia A. Potter, Griffin Perry
   Title: Fundamentals of Nursing
   Publisher: Mosby
   Year of publication: 2008
   Place of publication: St. Louis, MO

3. A newspaper article on the Web

   Author: Hasan Mansoor
   Title: Malaria rising in Pakistan's provinces as new flood threatens
   Newspaper: The Sydney Morning Herald
   Date: August 31, 2010
   Date of access: August 31, 2010
   URL: http://www.smh.com.au/world/malaria-rising-in-pakistans-provinces-as-new-flood-threatens-20100830-147bt.html

4. Journal article

   Authors: Peter Adams, Sarah Gearhart, Robert Miller, Anne Roberts
   Title: The Accelerated Learning Program: Throwing Open the Gates

Journal: Journal of Basic Writing
Publication information: Volume 28, Number 2,
    Fall 2009
Pages: 50-69

5. Journal article from an online database

Author: Estelle R. Jorgensen
Title: School Music Education and Change
Journal: Music Educators Journal
Publication information: Volume 96, Issue 4, p. 21-27, June 2010
DOI: 10.1177/0027432110369779
Online database: Academic Search Premier
Date of Access: September 1, 2011

6. Encyclopedia article on the Web

Title: Stem Cell
Year: 2010
Source: Encyclopaedia Britannica
URL: www.britannica.com
Date of access: September 15, 2011

7. Magazine article

Authors: Mark Hosenball and Eve Conant
Title: A Secret Side to the Secret Service
Magazine: Newsweek
Publication information: June 2, 2008, Vol. 22, pp. 32-33

8. Video on the Web

Title: Big Cats
Producer: National Geographic
Date: June 7, 2007
URL: http://www.youtube.com/watch?v=BYm_Mn7Hxag

9. Government document on the Web

Author: U.S. Department of Health and Human Services
Title: HIV and AIDS: Medicines to Help You
Date of publication: 2008

(continued)

Date of access: June 30, 2009
URL: http://www.fda.gov/downloads/ForConsumers/ByAudience/
ForWomen/FreePublications/UCM132807.pdf

10. Movie

Title: The Blind Side
Director: John Lee Hancock
Year: 2009
Distributor: Warner Bros. Pictures

MyWritingLab™ For support in meeting this chapter's objectives, log in to www.mywritinglab.com and select **Research Process.**

Chapter 17

Writing Timed Essay Examinations and Making Oral Presentations

Learning Objectives

In this chapter you will learn to:

LO1 Write effective in-class or timed essay examinations

LO2 Create and make an effective oral presentation

In addition to writing essays for your college classes, there are many other assignments you will be asked to do, ranging from timed writing examinations to making oral reports or presentations. The purpose of this chapter is to help you learn the basic elements of these various kinds of tasks, and to help you succeed when you are asked to construct one.

LO1

Write effective in-class or timed essay examinations

Writing Timed or In-Class Essay Examinations

In some of your college classes, you will be asked to write essay examinations. These are fairly quick, in-class answers to specific questions, within a specific time limit. Most often, you will be allowed one class period of time to write the examination.

Most college classes are either 50 or 75 minutes long, neither of which gives you much time to write, much less go through the process you have learned in this text—invention and discovery activities, drafting, asking for feedback, revising, getting more feedback, revising, and finally editing and polishing your paper. There are some secrets, though, to writing effective essay examinations. One secret is to use the classical way to organize your paper (for more on the classical approach to organization, see pages 279–281).

The classical organizational approach includes four parts:

- **Introduction.** This is where you put your main answer to the examination question.
- **Main Body.** In the longest part of your essay answer, you explain in as much detail as possible what you pointed out in your introduction.
- **Refutation.** In this section, you list any objections to your own argument, or arguments for the other side, and try to refute those arguments. If you are not writing an argument, this section is not necessary.
- **Conclusion.** Here you restate your point and connect the parts of your argument.

Before you start to write, think about where in your text you will want to put aspects of your answer:

- What part(s) of your answer belong in your **introduction?**
- What part(s) of your answer belong in the **main body** of your text, where you explain your reasoning and any evidence that supports your answer?
- What part(s) of your answer belong in the "**refutation**" part of your text, where you explain (and refute) any objections to your claims?

Another secret is to use the writing processes you have learned in this textbook (figuring out what to write about, drafting, etc.) but to use them more quickly, often giving yourself a specific time limit.

There are two major steps you will want to take when you are assigned an in-class timed writing examination.

Step 1: Determine What the Examination Asks You to Do

In any writing assignment, as you know, the first thing you want to do is to determine your **purpose** for writing, and for an in-class or timed essay examination, that means to read and fully understand the question you are asked to write about. So start by reading the examination question(s) and determining what the timed examination asks you to *do*.

This **checklist** will help before you get started and as you answer the examination question(s):

Examination Planning Checklist		
The examination asks you to:	**Key things to consider before you get started and as you write your answer**	**Rhetorical strategies you can use**
Evaluate something.	Determine on what criteria you will base your evaluation. Then narrow down that list to the most important criteria.	*Define* your criteria, so readers clearly understand what you base your evaluation on. Then use *compare and contrast* to show how the subject of your evaluation matches up to your criteria
Explain why something happened.	Make a list of all causes of the event that you can think of. Then narrow down that list to the causes that seem most important.	Explaining *why* using *cause and effect* is the main strategy you will rely on. Also, *narration*—telling the story of the event—is often useful.
Analyze a subject.	Brainstorm all of the component parts of your subject, and how they work together.	*Division* is always a main strategy to use when you analyze, as you want to explain the various parts or components of your subject.

(continued)

The examination asks you to:	Key things to consider before you get started and as you write your answer	Rhetorical strategies you can use
Argue for or against something.	Brainstorm all of the evidence for all "sides" of the argument. Determine which side you want to argue. Decide which evidence is the most effective to make your case. Consider the other sides to the argument.	*Describing* the issue you are arguing about helps readers see and understand the subject. If you are arguing about a problem, *defining* the problem in detail is critical. What evidence and *examples* can you provide to support your argument?

Note that for most, if not all, timed writing assignments, there is no time allowed for you to conduct any research. You will have to rely on your memory or notes (if your teacher allows you to use notes).

Step 2: Plan Your Time

You know that you have a limited amount of time for the in-class exam, so once you understand what the examination asks you to do, consider how to best use your time. Be sure to allow some time to get ideas onto paper and also some time to go back and revise your work—and to do a quick final proofreading and editing.

As an example, you may decide to divide your time in this manner:

Time Planning Checklist		
For a 50-minute exam	**For a 75-minute exam**	**For a 120-minute exam**
10 minutes to brainstorm your ideas	**15 minutes** to brainstorm your ideas	**20 minutes** to brainstorm your ideas
30 minutes to write your examination answer	**45 minutes** to write your examination answer	**80 minutes** to write your examination answer
10 minutes to revise, edit, and proofread your examination	**15 minutes** to revise, edit, and proofread your examination	**20 minutes** to revise, edit, and proofread your examination

Student Writing: Debbie Larsen's Timed Writing Examination

Student writer Debbie Larsen was allowed a 50-minute class period to answer this examination question for her Transition to College class:

> Evaluate student dining options on campus. Be sure to explain your criteria. Your audience will be the marketing department for our college's Student Outreach Program—I will forward all of your comments to them, to give them feedback on what students think about their dining options.

Debbie immediately knows, when she reads these instructions, that she is writing an *evaluation*, and she also understands how important her *criteria* will be, because the professor specifically makes a note about this. Debbie also understands that she has a real audience for this writing assignment, someone who will read her (and her classmates') comments.

Brainstorming and Planning. Debbie considers her time and spends a few minutes brainstorming:

> I guess I should start by listing the places available to eat on campus. But they will have to be only the ones I'm familiar with, as there is no time to do research. The places I can think of include
>
> Campus Coffee Bean
> The Wild Guys Burgers and Fries
> Oscar's Pizza by the Ounce
> Salad Dayz
> Erica's Eats
>
> I know there are more but that might be enough. Now, what to evaluate them on? What possible criteria can I use? I guess
>
> - Cost or value
> - Quality (how to determine?)
> - Times they're open
> - Convenience (they're all close together, so this is not a good criteria)
> - Atmosphere (how to define?)
>
> I'll also use compare and contrast as a way to show how these places are different or the same, to help decide on my evaluation.

Writing a Draft. Student writer Larsen now has a starting point, and she spends about 30 minutes writing her first draft:

Any evaluation of restaurant options on campus necessarily starts with the criteria on which one might evaluate those options. There are a lot of possible ways to evaluate a restaurant. This evaluation will center on several of the most important ones.

The food in any restaurant is key to the success or failure of that business, so taste, quantity, and quality of menu items is critical. Taste, of course, is a personal opinion. However, if at least several customers say the same thing about taste, then their comments are probably accurate.

Quantity is something you could measure, but no one would bring a scale to a restaurant to weigh the food. Even a general idea of quantity, which one could determine by noting if most customers take food home after eating, would be useful. The quality of the food is another issue, too, and customers could determine that, at least to some extent, by finding out where the food was purchased.

A restaurant's general atmosphere is also important: is it noisy? Are the tables close together? How are customers treated when they walk in, and when they are served? Finally, cost is always a factor in any student's budget.

There are five restaurants on campus that give students a range of menu options:

Campus Coffee Bean
The Wild Guys Burgers and Fries
Oscar's Pizza by the Ounce
Salad Dayz
Erica's Eats

In terms of the taste of food, several of my dormmates have eaten at all five of these restaurants. They report that the Campus Coffee Bean has by far the best-tasting food for breakfast, lunch, and even for dinner. Mary even mentioned at one time that she would eat there even if she was not a student.

Also at the Campus Coffee Bean, there always is leftover food to take home. That was another thing everyone always mentions, that the amount of food you get is always more than you can eat. That is true even for the guys we eat with sometimes.

There is a sign at the Campus Coffee Bean, and also at Salad Dayz, that they buy local products at the Farmer's Market. That says that their quality should be excellent, as the Farmer's Market produce is always organic. Overall, the Campus Coffee Bean is best on taste and quantity of food. It and Salad Dayz both have the best quality food. They are not too noisy, either.

Cost is a hard factor to compare, but for a quarter-pound burger and fries, no one can beat The Wild Guys Burgers and Fries. That is what they do, after all, and when a business really has a tight focus, they often have the best price, too. Overall, though, my dormmates always seem to spend less at the Campus Coffee Bean, and several of them have even mentioned how whatever we all eat there, our meals seem to cost less at the "Bean."

In the end, overall, the Campus Coffee Bean seems to best place, at least based on two of the major criteria items focused on here: taste, quantity, and quality of food and cost.

Final Revising and Editing. Student writer Larsen now will spend her last 10 minutes going back over her paper, to proofread and to correct any spelling or other errors she spots. For example, when she read through her paper again, the word "dormmates" just did not seem quite right, so she changed it to "dorm mates." Debbie also understands that real revision (see Chapter 8) means "re-seeing" and "rethinking" her paper, and while she did not have time to do a lot of revision, she did revise her last two paragraphs, as shown in red:

Cost is a hard factor to compare, but for a quarter-pound burger and fries, no one can beat The Wild Guys Burgers and Fries. That is ~~what they do~~ the focus of their business, after all, and when a business really has a tight focus, they often have the best price, too. Overall, though, my dorm mates always seem to spend less at the Campus Coffee Bean, and several of them have even mentioned how ~~whatever~~ whenever we all eat there, our meals seem to cost less at ~~the~~ our favorite hangout, the "Bean."

In the end, overall, the Campus Coffee Bean seems to be the best place, at least based on ~~two~~ three of the major criteria items focused on here: taste, quantity, and quality of food ~~and cost~~.

Everyday Writing Activity: Your Own Restaurant Evaluation

If you were given the same timed writing assignment that student writer Debbie Larsen received, what criteria would you use to evaluate your own campus restaurants? In your journal, define at least three criteria in detail. Your instructor may want you to share your criteria with the rest of the class.

LO2

Create and make an effective oral presentation

Making an Effective Oral Presentation

In your college classes, and in your working world, you may be asked to construct and present various kinds of reports: laboratory or other scientific reports, business reports, and so on. And as you learned in Chapter 3, you sometimes will write a summary report. In high school, you may have summarized a book you read, for example, while in college, you may summarize some of your college reading assignments.

Because you are not likely to be asked to focus on business and lab reports in your college writing class, we are not going to examine them here. But one kind of report you may be asked to work with in your writing class is, of course, an oral presentation. Oral presentations are part of many college classes, and once you graduate, will likely continue to be a part of your career. While oral presentations do not have a specific format (like business or scientific reports do), there still are essential elements they include. To effectively make an oral presentation, you need to

- **Know what you are talking about.** Being prepared by really knowing your subject means that you are an authority on that topic. Listeners will want to hear what you have to say, so they can learn from you.
- **Organize your presentation.** Once again, the classical approach to organization (see pages 279–281) is often the best way to organize your material:
  - Here is the point and why it is important to you, my audience.
  - Here is my evidence that supports the point.
  - Here are some other thoughts that might disagree with my ideas, but mine are better because...
  - Therefore (summarize your conclusions).
- **Pay strict attention to the time you have.** Usually in a classroom setting, several students make their oral presentations, one after the other, during a class period. If yours runs too long, your classmates will not be able to present theirs. The same is true in the business world, where—as the saying goes—time is money. The way you can tell the length of your presentation is to practice it and to time yourself: make sure you can present your information in the time you are allowed.
- **Practice, practice, practice.** We cannot stress this enough: the more you practice your presentation, the better it will be. Entertainers have a rule about how they practice, too: real practice means a real run-through. Put another way, pretend you are actually making your

presentation in front of your audience. If you fumble part of it, do not start over, but rather continue through the whole presentation.

Perhaps a better word for practice is *rehearsal*. Were you ever part of a stage play or other performance? Then you know about how important it is to rehearse: to start from the beginning and run through the whole performance. If someone misses a line or goes to the wrong location on stage, the performance keeps going. The same is true when you rehearse your oral presentation: go through the whole thing just as if you were in front of an audience.

If you have a tape or digital or video recorder, **record** yourself and your presentation. Or get some friends to serve as an audience as you practice—and be sure to ask them for suggestions on how you can make your presentation more effective.

- **Visualize what you want to happen as you practice.** How do you expect your audience to react (laugh, nod, take notes)? Such positive visualization helps you make a good presentation.
- **If you use PowerPoint slides or other visual aids, learn how to correctly present the information.** Essentially, you want any visual aid (like a PP slide) to show only the highlights of your presentation. Then, you discuss that information in detail. You do *not* read the PP slide; there is nothing that can kill a presentation more quickly!
- **Be prepared for technology problems.** If you plan to use PowerPoint slides, be sure to bring your presentation in several electronic forms (a CD, a flash drive, etc.) because you never know what technology you might be faced with. If you bring overhead slides, also bring handouts you can point to, if the overhead projector does not work.
- **Pay attention to your audience.** Are they attentive, nodding at what you say, laughing when they are supposed to, etc.? Speak to the listener who is the furthest away from you—then you know you will be loud enough. Also, make eye contact with members of your audience. They will pay more attention if you look directly at them.
- **Save time for questions.** It often is useful to save a few minutes at the end of your presentation to give the audience the chance to ask questions.

Everyday Oral Presentation Activity: Your Own Restaurant Evaluation

Prepare a brief (three- to five-minute) oral presentation, evaluating one dining option on your campus. What would you say about that restaurant in such a brief time? Your teacher may ask you to make your brief presentation to a small group, or to the rest of the class.

Everyday Writing Activity: Writing to Reflect on This Chapter

In your journal, please respond to the following prompts. Your instructor may ask you to share your responses with the rest of the class.

- I learned that for in-class timed examinations I need to plan _____.

- I learned that a useful way to organize my essay exam is to use _____.

- I learned that a good way to organize my oral presentation is to use _____.

- I learned that some things to consider as I plan an oral presentation include _____.

MyWritingLab™ For support in meeting this chapter's objectives, log in to **www.mywritinglab.com** and select **Timed Writing and Essay Exams**.

Chapter 18

Writing E-mail, Job Application Letters, and Résumés

Learning Objectives

In this chapter, you will learn to

LO1 Write effective e-mail using the proper etiquette

LO2 Write an effective job application letter

LO3 Write an effective résumé

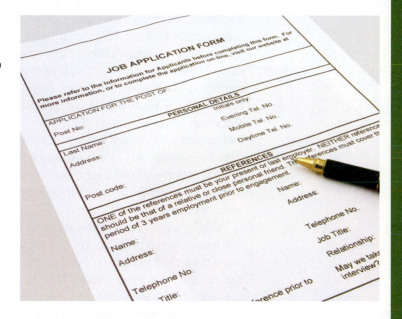

In addition to writing essays for your college classes, you will need to write other documents, ranging from e-mails to job application letters to résumés. The purpose of this chapter is to help you learn the basic elements of these workplace writing tasks.

Writing Effective E-mail

E-mail is often used by students to communicate with their instructors. It is also used in the workplace to communicate among employees, customers, and vendors.

E-mail Etiquette in College

One complaint that we writing teachers hear from our colleagues around campus is that many students do not use proper e-mail etiquette and do not understand the right way to construct an e-mail. Their most frequent comment is that students seem to consider that e-mail is informal and anonymous correspondence, and thus, students are not respectful in their e-mails. If students think of e-mail as kind of a note they write to someone, their tone becomes very informal and perhaps too familiar. Addressing a professor in an e-mail as "Hey, Dude," is too informal. Addressing a professor as "Hi, Mike," is also too familiar. So, unless your instructors specifically tell you to call them by their first names, always start an e-mail with "Dear Professor [Last Name]." Addressing an e-mail in that manner should set a formal tone for the rest of that e-mail. So, instead of writing "Whats due tomorrow?" a better way is to ask, "What assignment is due tomorrow?"

While e-mail may seem anonymous, it certainly is not—people can tell who it is from. So, never say something in an e-mail that you would not say to that person in person. Also, unless your e-mail is to a friend, emoticons (like smiley faces ☺) are not appropriate. Likewise, because it is easy to forward e-mail, never say something in an e-mail that you would not like forwarded to someone else. The rule is the same: never say anything in an e-mail that you do not want anyone else to read, or that you would not say to the person face-to-face.

E-mail in the Workplace

E-mail essentially has replaced what everyone used to write in the workplace: memos. A memo is a brief document that includes these elements:

- **Date.** The date the memo was sent.
- **To.** The person to whom the memo was addressed, including people who got copies.

- **From.** The writer of the memo.
- **Subject.** What the memo was about

All these elements are put at the beginning of the memo, which makes it easy to see the intended audience, author, etc. Now, of course, they are included in an e-mail heading.

Here is a typical e-mail. Note that it includes all of the elements of a memo's heading except the date and who it is from, which are automatically added by the e-mail program:

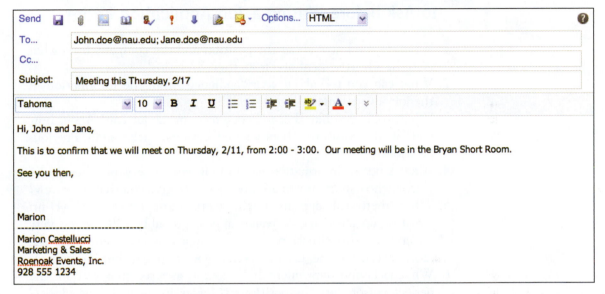

Note one other critical feature of a memo that has carried over to e-mail: both memos and e-mails are brief and to the point. The rule of thumb is that an e-mail should be no more than one "page" long—readers should be able to read the entire e-mail without scrolling down the computer screen. Now, clearly, such brevity is not always possible, but it should be something you strive for in your e-mails.

Finally, consider what rhetorical strategies might best help you get across to your reader (your audience) what you most need to accomplish (your purpose) for the e-mail: *description, narration, providing examples, comparing/contrasting,* and so forth.

LO2
Write an effective job application letter

Writing an Effective Job Application Letter

Sometime soon—probably sooner than you may think—you will graduate and want to find a job. That means you will need to write job application letters, which are often attached to e-mails or to electronic job applications). In an application letter, you are not asking for the job but rather to be *considered* for the position. Thus, your purpose is to land a job interview. You must demonstrate in the letter how your qualifications fit the job description outlined in the advertisement or online posting. If you are a good fit, then it is likely the company will want to interview you.

 ## Critical Thinking Activity: Questions to Ask before Writing a Job Application Letter

1. What do you know about the position and the company from what is in the advertisement and from their Web site?
2. What can you tell about your "audience" from the information in the job advertisement?
3. What would you like this audience to know about you? About how you "fit" the position? About your educational background? Previous positions?
4. What kinds of information would help convince your reader—the person who can grant you an interview—to give you that interview?
5. What rhetorical appeals might work most effectively? (Hint: Creating an *emotional* or *pathos* appeal probably will not be very effective in this situation. An *ethos* appeal may be effective: the more *credible* you are, the more likely you are to get that interview.)
6. What facts and data might help your reader see that you are the perfect person for this position? (Grades in your college classes? Particular classes you have taken that will help you do the job? Past work experience in similar positions?)
7. What rhetorical strategies might you use (*description, definition,* etc.) to help you get that interview?

Your job application letter needs to include this information:

1. **Why you are writing.** Indicate the position for which you are applying and how you learned of the organization or position.
2. **Basic information about your background and why you are a good match for the job.** Explain why you are interested in the position and how you fit the qualifications for the job, as outlined in the job advertisement. While you normally will also

send along your résumé, your letter is an opportunity to highlight elements in that résumé that show how you match what the employer is looking for.

If your work experience or educational background does not fit the job exactly, explain how you have done something similar. For example, if you are applying for a position teaching English 101—and you have not taught English 101—you might indicate that "while I have not taught English 101, I did teach English 100, a course very similar to your English 101 class." Or, if you are applying for an auto tech position at a Ford dealership and you never worked on the latest Ford models, you might say that "While I do not have experience with the latest Ford products, I have worked on and have a good deal of experience with Fords made before 2009."

Always focus on what you can bring *to* the business, how you can help them, not what *you* hope to gain. For example, instead of writing "I hope to work in agriculture, as that has been my lifelong dream," you are better served to write, "My college major in Agricultural/Environmental Science will be of benefit to your company, because…" Instead of writing, "I love working with children," it is better to say, "My three years of working at ChildLuv DayCare Center gave me useful experience that will help your company in the position of…" To put it bluntly, when someone at a firm reads a letter that focuses on the applicant's desires and needs ("I've always loved working on cars" or "I hope to earn a good income" or "I always wanted to live in Houston"), the response may be, "Who cares? What can you do for my business?"

3. **A request for an interview.** Ask for what you want the next step to be, which usually is a job interview. Indicate when you are available and if you are willing to travel to the company for that interview ("I will be in Houston on…"). Let the employer know that you are willing to provide other information ("I can send you reference letters" or "I can send you an example of…").

4. **Closing.** Be sure to thank your potential employer for considering your application. Then sign the letter *Sincerely*. Add your handwritten signature if the letter is a paper document. Be sure to put your name and contact information.

Always remember that the purpose of any job application letter is to show how your qualifications match up to the job requirements and, of course, to indicate how you are the *best* possible applicant.

Here is an example of a job advertisement from a fictional newspaper, the *Atlanta Herald*, followed by an example application letter:

Job Advertisement	Key Elements of the Advertisement
Administrative Assistant—Atlanta Office	Job title
Mid-sized contracting firm is seeking an Administrative Assistant.	Information about the company and position
Administrative Assistant candidate must have at least one year working in a construction office environment. Excellent communication skills are a must. Some accounting duties.	Required qualifications
Bachelor's degree preferred.	Desired qualifications
Salary up to $37,000--includes excellent benefits package.	Salary information
Please send your résumé (attention Randall Bucci) to PO Box 230, Atlanta GA 30305 for immediate consideration.	Process to use for your application

Here is an example of an effective job application letter.

1111 East Hope Street
Atlanta, GA 30301
June 15, 2012

Randall Bucci
PO Box 230
Atlanta, GA 30305

Dear Mr. Bucci:

I am applying for the position of administrative assistant, as recently advertised in the *Atlanta Herald.*

I have attached my résumé. As you will note, for the past two years I have been employed at Donner Road Construction, one of Atlanta's largest contracting companies, as an administrative assistant. My duties at Donner include a good deal of customer contact, both in person and over the telephone. I pride myself on my customer communication skills, which I continue to refine.

At Donner, part of my work also involves data entry and accounting using QuickBooks software. My AA degree is in accounting (Atlanta Central Community College), and I have 90 hours toward a bachelor's degree in computer science.

I am available for an interview at your convenience. Please email me at mary.redding@email.com or call me at 404-555-4579. I hope to hear from you soon.

Sincerely,

Mary Redding

Mary Redding

Everyday Writing Activity: Write a Job Application Letter

Find a job advertisement in your local or campus newspaper or online for which you are qualified. Write an application letter for that position. Your instructor may want you to share your letter with the rest of the class.

Writing an Effective Résumé

Do you have a résumé? If not, you should, because eventually you will need one and having one now, even while you are in college, gives you a place to list and track your experiences. There should be two versions of your résumé:

1. **A working résumé.** This is a list of any work experience, volunteering, course, project, or performance that you may eventually want to use to help you get a job. So, if you hope for a career in art, list every art class as well as every art exhibit your work appears in. If you plan to teach, list every class and any teaching or tutoring experience. Each time something new happens in your life that relates to possible future work opportunities, add it to your working résumé.
2. **An application résumé.** This is the résumé you will send to a potential employer. You will *select* specific information from your working résumé to include, put it in a readable format, and send it to the employer.

Using a Working Résumé

You will use your working résumé as the starting point for your application résumé. Here is what we mean: to get started with your working résumé, you want to list every relevant class you are taking in college. That gives you a complete record. But, of course, that list will eventually get really long (and will match your college transcript, which potential employers often request). After you graduate, you would not list every college class on your actual résumé, but instead would list your degree. But you may want to mention some of your classes in your letter, and list them on your résumé, if they fit a particular job you were applying for. For an EMT position, for instance, you may want to mention in your application résumé something like

Classes specializing in medical flight emergencies:

EMT 311: In-flight Care

EMT 312: In-flight Technologies

Creating a Résumé for a Job Application

There are any number of possible résumé formats, but all have the same rhetorical purpose: to highlight your achievements, especially as they relate to the job you are applying for. You usually will have several sections in your résumé: work objectives, education, work experience, skills, and so on. Most résumés list education and background in chronological order, with the most recent items on the top of each section. Some résumés highlight skills rather than show a chronological record.

What to Include. You always want to include these sections on your résumé:

- **Your contact information.** How people can reach you, including telephone numbers (home, work, cell), mailing address, e-mail address.
- **Educational background.** Begin with your most recent class (or degree). If you are just starting college, you can list key high school classes. List your college or university and when you graduated or expect to graduate. Be sure to note whenever you make the Dean's List or receive some other educational honor.
- **Work experience.** Again, begin with your most recent work experience. List the company you worked for, where it was located, the work you performed, and the dates you worked for them. If the work experience relates to the job you are applying for, be sure to include it.
- **References.** While you need not put your references on your résumé, you should be prepared with a list. References should be past employers or teachers (potential employers usually do not care that "a good friend" is a reference). Always be sure to ask someone if you can list them as a reference *before* putting his or her name on your list. Also, be sure to obtain the complete contact information for each reference. On your résumé, just say "References available on request."
- **Optional sections** can include your work objectives ("To make a difference in the lives of patients with major sports injuries"). Other possible sections might include a list of any particular skills you have ("Proficient with Microsoft Office for PCs and Macs"), as well as listing any special honors or awards ("National Honor Society").

That earlier "short of space" comment brings up a good point: how long should a résumé be? The rule of thumb has always been that a business résumé should be no longer than one page, but that is a hard rule to follow, and no one is sure where that rule really came from. The sense today is that résumé length can and will vary by the applicant's experience and the position applied for. A new college graduate will have a briefer résumé than someone who has an AA, a BA, and an MA and who has been working for several years. Our advice, then, is to list on your résumé what you need to have there to give you the best chance to get an interview. If you always think, "Will this piece of information help me get an interview?" before you list something on your résumé, you will be well served.

How to Format a Résumé. We also think that any résumé must be easy to read, which means you need to use type and white space attractively. If a résumé is difficult to read, it will not be read. So, for instance, which is easier for you to read?

Educational Experience	Educational Experience
1. Bachelor of Arts Degree, 2012. Northern Arizona University. Major: English. Minor: Spanish. 2. Associate of Science Degree, Mesa Community College, 2010. Emergency Medical Technician (EMT) II Degree. With Honors.	**Bachelor of Arts Degree,** 2012. Northern Arizona University. Major: English. Minor: Spanish. **Associate of Science Degree,** Mesa Community College, 2010. Emergency Medical Technician (EMT) II Degree. With Honors.

We are guessing that the section on the right is easier—why? Because the most important words—the names of the degrees—are much easier to see. They are not numbered, appear in bold type, and start at the left margin. Note also that the entry on the right allows a reader to skim down easily, spotting first the degrees (which, after all, are what applicants want readers to see). The entry on the left forces the reader to read through each complete entry before he/she gets to the next one.

Remember, too, that you want to foreground and highlight what is important to a potential employer. In the following two entries, what seems to be the most important information?

Educational Experience	**Educational Experience**
Bachelor of Arts Degree, 2012. Northern Arizona University. Major: English. Minor: Spanish.	**2012: Bachelor of Arts Degree,** Northern Arizona University. Major: English. Minor: Spanish.
Associates of Science Degree, Mesa Community College, 2010. Emergency Medical Technician (EMT) II Degree. With Honors.	**2010: Associates of Science Degree,** Mesa Community College. Emergency Medical Technician (EMT) II Degree. With Honors.

The entry on the left lists the degrees first; the one on the right lists the dates of those degrees first, thus highlighting the date rather than the degree. We think the degrees are more important than the date of those degrees, so they are the first item in each line.

A well-formatted résumé is shown on page 382.

Richard Collins
1411 East Farview Lane
Prescott, AZ 86301
Home: 928-555-5685
Cell: 928-555-1331
RCollins@Yahoo.com

CAREER OBJECTIVE

To make a difference in the lives of patients with major injuries, specifically as an Emergency Medical Technician

EDUCATION

Associate of Science Degree, Mesa Community College, 2010.

- **Emergency Medical Technician (EMT) II Degree**, with Honors and Full EMT certification.
- **Extra classes** taken for EMT 211 (medical transfer), EMT 215 (emergency issues), and EMT 231 (distance transfer issues).
- **Internship**, Mesa Community College (EMG 311 class). Worked nights and weekends with an EMT crew.

WORK EXPERIENCE

Baywood East Emergency Room. EMT, June 2010-present. In-training EMT; advanced to night EMT December 2010; advanced to weekend EMT April 2011.

Mesa County Hospital. In-service training, August 2008-May 2010.

Borders Books and Music. Part-time sales associate, June-August 2007.

HONORS AND AWARDS

Employee of the Month. Baywood East, March 2011.

Dean's List. Mesa Community College (each semester).

REFERENCES

Available on request.

Everyday Writing Activity: Write a One-Page Résumé

Write a one-page résumé for yourself. Be sure to include any educational background as well as work-related experience you have had. Your instructor may want you to share your résumé with the rest of the class.

Everyday Writing Activity: Reflecting on This Chapter

Please respond to the following questions in your journal. Your instructor may ask you to share your responses with the rest of the class.

- I know that e-mails to professors need to be more formal than those to my friends. That means _____.
- I want to make sure to include, in any job application letter: _____.
- My résumé needs to include _____ .
- If I was asked to write an application letter (earlier activity), I learned I should _____.
- If I was asked to write a résumé (earlier activity), I learned I should _____.

MyWritingLab™ For support in meeting this chapter's objectives, log in to **www.mywritinglab.com** and select **Standard and Non-Standard English.**

PART 4

Handbook of Grammar and Style

Chapter **19** Nouns

Chapter **20** Verbs

Chapter **21** Pronouns

Chapter **22** Adjectives, Adverbs, Prepositions, Conjunctions, and Interjections

Chapter **23** Articles

Chapter **24** Sentence Elements

Chapter **25** Types of Sentences

Chapter **26** Sentence Agreement

Chapter **27** Improving Your Sentences

Chapter **28** Periods, Question Marks, and Exclamation Points

Chapter **29** Commas

Chapter **30** Other Punctuation Marks

Chapter **31** Abbreviations and Numbers

Chapter **32** Spelling

Chapter **33** Word Choice

Chapter **34** English Idioms

verb
adverb
noun
pronoun
adjective
vowel
consonant

Part 4 focuses on some of the most common sentence-level errors made when writing. These errors can generally be divided into four groups: grammatical errors, punctuation errors, errors related to vocabulary, and mechanical errors, and these four categories will be the focus of this handbook. While the content of any writing is, of course, very important, presenting that content without sentence-level errors is also important. If your writing contains surface errors, it will certainly reflect negatively on your writing, and it may even prevent your message from being properly communicated to your readers. Your purpose for writing will, then, certainly suffer. Therefore, we recommend that you use this section of the book as a valuable resource that can guide you toward error-free papers, especially during the proofreading stage, as well as any time you are unsure about an issue related to grammar, or punctuation, or word choice or any other mechanical difficulty you may be having while writing.

Specifically, this handbook will help you to

- Clarify any sentence-level questions or doubts you may have.
- Get a lot of practice avoiding common sentence-level errors.
- Reduce, perhaps eliminate completely, any errors in your writing.
- Improve the quality of your communication with your readers.

Chapter 19

Nouns

Learning Objectives

In this chapter, you will learn to:

LO1 Identify and use proper nouns

LO2 Identify and use common nouns

LO3 Identify and use countable and uncountable nouns

Before we begin with nouns, it is important to remember that English grammar consists of eight parts of speech, and each word is a part of speech. The same word can also be a different part of speech depending on how it is used in a sentence.

The eight parts of speech are:

- Noun
- Verb
- Adjective
- Adverb
- Pronoun
- Preposition
- Conjunction
- Interjection

A **noun** is a word used to name a person, place, thing, or idea/emotion. The underlined words in the following examples are nouns:

- <u>Akiko</u> is studying at an American university. (a person)
- <u>Paris</u> is a city I would love to visit. (a place)
- A <u>car</u> is something many people like to have. (a thing)
- <u>Jealousy</u> is not good for human health. (an emotion)

There are two major kinds of nouns: proper nouns and common nouns.

Proper Nouns

Proper nouns are indicated with a capital letter because the noun represents the name of a specific person, place, a religion, a day of the week, the name of a school or a company or an organization, and so forth. The underlined words below are all proper nouns:

- <u>Jane</u> is on her way to school. (a person)
- <u>Cairo</u> is a very big city. (a place)
- One of the world's principal religions is <u>Buddhism</u>. (a religion)
- <u>Monday</u> is probably the least favorite day of the week for many people. (a day of the week)
- <u>Harvard University</u> is one of the best universities. (name of a school)
- <u>Microsoft Corporation</u> has its headquarters near Seattle. (name of a company)

Common Nouns

Common nouns refer to persons, places, things, ideas/emotions, conditions, and so on—in general—and are not capitalized unless they begin a sentence. The following underlined words are all common nouns:

- <u>Teachers</u> want their students to succeed. (persons)
- The <u>beach</u> is often a favorite vacation destination for many people. (a place)
- <u>Textbooks</u> can be expensive, but they are necessary. (things)
- <u>Kindness</u> should be practiced by all of us. (an emotion)
- <u>Countries</u> around the <u>world</u> (places) are working to eradicate <u>disease</u> and <u>poverty.</u> (conditions of human beings)

Everyday Grammar Activity: Nouns

In the following sentences, identify the nouns by underlining them, and then indicate whether they are proper nouns or common nouns. Write P for proper nouns and C for common nouns:

1. It was getting late, and the babysitter started feeling impatient.
2. Jack is doing his homework.
3. The crowd greeted the politician enthusiastically.
4. I would like to buy a Japanese car.
5. Watching television can take up a lot of time.

LO3
Identify and use countable and uncountable nouns

 ## Grammar Spotlight: Countable and Uncountable Nouns

Some nouns in English are **countable,** which means they can be counted, while others are **uncountable,** which means they cannot be counted. "Uncountable," then, means that whether you have one or several of the same thing, the word remains the same. In the following example, the noun "equipment" stays the same, no matter how many pieces of equipment the sentence refers to:

Those <u>students</u> should study hard. (countable noun)

Do not remove the <u>equipment</u>. (uncountable noun)

The following is a list of some uncountable nouns in English:

gas	furniture	water	noise	light
oxygen	luggage	soda	time	paper
carbon	music	coffee	wealth	laughter
love	bread	foreign	poverty	sadness
hate	milk	power	health	difficulty
anger	salt	information	money	ease
greed	sugar	evidence	darkness	comfort

Sometimes, the same noun can be both countable and uncountable.

Drinking <u>soda</u> is not good for health. (Here, *soda* is an uncountable noun.)

Will you please get me two <u>sodas</u>? (Here, *soda* is a countable noun.)

<u>Furniture</u> can be difficult to move. (Here, *furniture* is an uncountable noun.)

The handyman easily moved the two pieces of <u>furniture</u> to the next room. (Here, *furniture* is plural, even though it doesn't directly take the plural form—we cannot say *two furnitures.*)

Everyday Grammar Activity: Countable and Uncountable Nouns

In the following sentences, identify the nouns by underlining them, and then indicate whether they are countable nouns or uncountable nouns. Write C for countable nouns and U for uncountable nouns:

1. The workers worked hard all day.
2. Food is getting more and more expensive each day.
3. The current Student Council president is determined to work well.
4. Mrs. Martinez has been teaching for a long time.
5. Health is more important than wealth.

MyWritingLab™ For support in meeting this chapter's objectives, log in to www.mywritinglab.com and select **Nouns**.

Chapter 20

Verbs

Learning **O**bjectives

In this chapter, you will learn to:

LO1 Use different verb tenses

LO2 Use different verb forms

LO3 Use irregular verbs properly

LO4 Avoid split infinitives in your writing

A **verb** is often described as a "doing" word; verbs express the actions of a subject. The underlined words in the following examples are verbs:

- Melanie <u>rides</u> her bike to work every day. (The verb *rides* describes the action Melanie takes.)
- Mr. Cho <u>watches</u> a movie at least once a week. (The verb *watches* describes the actions of Mr. Cho.)
- On average, college students <u>commute</u> to campus at least three days a week. (The verb *commute* describes the actions of college students.)
- The weatherman <u>has predicted</u> rain for this weekend. (The verb *has predicted* describes the actions of the weatherman.)

LO1

Use different verb tenses

Verb Tenses

There are three basic verb tenses: past, present, and future.

The **past tense** expresses a situation that occurred in the past and that no longer exists. Past tense is often expressed with an *–ed*.

- Mitsuo <u>walked</u> the dog last night.

The **present tense** expresses an action that is ongoing, or a situation that presently exists, or something that is a widespread truth.

- The Turkish lira <u>is</u> the currency of Turkey.

The **future tense** expresses an action that will occur in the future. The future tense is often expressed using the words *will* and *shall*.

- The children <u>will start</u> school next week.

Everyday Grammar Activity: Verb Tenses

In the following sentences, provide the appropriate tense of the verb (verb in parentheses):

1. Asha (wait) all day for Danny to call.
2. Spring (be) here soon, and the flowers (be) bloom.
3. My grandfather (like) to garden in the spring and summer.
4. The police sirens (be) loud, indicating a chase is on.
5. Mrs. Smith (want) to visit her grandchildren in Cyprus last year.

LO2

Use different verb forms

Verb Forms

English verbs come in four main forms: simple, progressive, perfect, and perfect progressive.

The **simple form** of a verb expresses an action in the past, present or future.

- Rodger <u>ate</u> his meal in a hurry. (past)
- We <u>eat</u> breakfast at the same time every morning. (present)
- The Hardy family <u>will eat</u> dinner around 6 p.m. tonight. (future)

The **progressive form** of a verb describes an ongoing action in the past, present or in the future.

- John <u>was eating.</u> (past progressive)
- Rahul <u>is riding</u> his bike. (present progressive)
- Mohammed's cousin <u>will be visiting</u> him tomorrow. (future progressive)

The **perfect form** of a verb uses *had/has/have/will have had* to express an action that took place in the past or that is continuing in the present or that will take place in the future before another action.

- I <u>had eaten</u> by the time they arrived. (past perfect)
- Scientists <u>have planned</u> several more experiments in order to collect research data. (present perfect)
- I <u>will have eaten</u> my dinner by the time they arrive. (future perfect)

The **perfect progressive form** describes an ongoing action that occurred in the past, is continuing into the present, or will continue into the future. It uses *has/have been* and the verb (the verb form ending in *–ing*).

- Sandra <u>had been waiting</u> in the rain for 10 minutes before her friends arrived. (past perfect progressive)
- The athlete <u>has been considering</u> not participating in this year's Olympic games because of an injury. (present perfect progressive)
- By the time summer comes around, Derek <u>will have been learning</u> Italian for almost six months. (future perfect progressive)

The following table shows the different forms the verb *work* takes based on tense and form:

At a Glance: Verb Tenses and Verb Forms			
Verb: WORK	**Past**	**Present**	**Future**
Simple	worked	work	will work
Progressive	was/were working	am/are/is working	will be working
Perfect	had worked	have worked	will have worked
Perfect progressive	had been working	has been working	will have been working

Everyday Grammar Activity: Verb Forms

In the following sentences, provide the appropriate verb forms (verb in parentheses):

1. Both Marilee and Yoko (work) hard all morning.
2. Students (get) their diplomas at the ceremony next week.
3. It (be) two years next month since Sam moved to the Bahamas.
4. The bus driver (wait) at the railroad crossing for 10 minutes before the train finally passed.
5. The employee (prepare) the invoice as his boss instructed him to.

Grammar Spotlight: Irregular Verbs

Sometimes, verbs in English can be very irregular. A *regular verb* is formed by simply adding *–ed* to the verb to indicate the past tense.

> I wan<u>ted</u> to travel to Africa. (past tense)

However, not all verbs follow this pattern and thus become irregular verbs. For instance, the verb *eat* becomes *ate/has eaten* in the past tense.

> Henri <u>ate</u> some cereal for breakfast today. (not Henri *eated* some cereal for breakfast today)
>
> Henri <u>has eaten</u> cereal for breakfast today. (not Henri *has eated* some cereal for breakfast today)

The following is a list of some common irregular verbs in English, along with their past tense.

see	saw	put	put	bite	bit
write	wrote	know	knew	buy	bought
drink	drank	sleep	slept	run	ran
teach	taught	be	was	speak	spoke
sit	sat	drive	drove	fly	flew

Everyday Grammar Activity: Verb Tenses

Identify the verbs by underlining them, and then indicate the verb tense: past, present, or future. After you have done so, change the verb to a different tense, and rewrite the sentence. The first one is done for you.

1. My roommate Akbar <u>is speaking</u> to his family in Lebanon (present tense). My roommate Akbar <u>spoke</u> to his family in Lebanon yesterday (past tense).
2. Dr. Smith performed surgery on his neighbor's son last week.
3. Elias will meet with his counselor tomorrow morning.
4. Marta is working on her math homework.
5. Parents love their children unconditionally.

Everyday Grammar Activity: More Verb Forms

In the following sentences, identify the verbs by underlining them, and then indicate the verb form: simple, progressive, perfect, or perfect progressive.

1. Leon has been waiting at the airport for the last two hours in order to catch his next flight.
2. All faculty have finished their grading for this semester.
3. Aunt Shelley will be cooking Thanksgiving dinner this year.
4. Noor wants to go home to Morocco during Christmas vacation.
5. The police were waiting behind the building to catch the thieves.

LO4

Avoid split infinitives in your writing

Split Infinitives

An infinitive is a verb form that is usually preceded by the word *to:*

- to go
- to eat
- to sleep
- to write

When a word or a phrase comes between the infinitive marker "to" and the verb, it is considered a **split infinitive** because the verb is now separated from the infinitive marker.

- Roy decided <u>to</u> quickly <u>eat</u> his meal. (Incorrect; here, the adverb *quickly* comes between the infinitive form of the verb "to eat," and the verb, and, therefore, a split infinitive is created.)
- Roy decided <u>to eat</u> his meal quickly. (correct)
- The audience wanted <u>to</u> clearly <u>register</u> their disagreement with what the speaker was saying. (Incorrect; here, the adverb "clearly" comes between the infinitive form of the verb "to register," and, therefore, a split infinitive is created.)
- The audience wanted <u>to register</u> their clear disagreement with what the speaker was saying. (correct)

It is often considered poor grammar to split an infinitive because it is seen as a single unit.

Everyday Grammar Activity: Split Infinitives

Each of the following sentences contains a split infinitive. Write out the correct form of the sentence:

1. To forcefully argue to make a point is not a bad thing.
2. The couple decided to gracefully dance the night away.
3. In order to better organize my closet, I decided to throw away things I don't use much.
4. The gardener was always ready to lovingly nurture the plants in his garden.
5. Doctors and nurses are taught to sympathetically speak to their patients.
6. The electrician had to quickly repair the fault in the electrical circuit.
7. Older citizens at the retirement home are encouraged to slowly walk around the building for exercise.
8. The parents wanted their children to not go to the movies yesterday evening.
9. The artist started to very skillfully paint his portrait of Michelangelo.
10. To always be hungry could be a sign of a hidden disease.

MyWritingLab™ For support in meeting this chapter's objectives, log in to **www.mywritinglab.com** and select **Verbs, Tense, Subjects and Verbs,** and **Regular and Irregular Verbs**.

Chapter 21

Pronouns

Learning Objectives

In this chapter, you will learn to:

LO1 Use the major kinds of pronouns properly

LO2 Use subject and object pronouns and singular and plural pronouns properly

A **pronoun** is a word that replaces a noun or another pronoun. Pronouns are useful because they help to make sentences less repetitive. The underlined words in the following examples are pronouns:

- Marcelino gets good grades in college because <u>he</u> studies hard for all his classes. (*He* replaces the proper noun *Marcelino*.)
- Susan and Anita wish <u>their</u> roommate was less noisy. (*Their* replaces the proper nouns *Susan* and *Anita*.)
- The car could not be repaired because <u>it</u> was too badly damaged. (*It* replaces the common noun *car*.)
- Because Kenny and Roger were in financial trouble, their Aunt Gretchen loaned <u>them</u> some money. (*Them* replaces the proper nouns *Kenny* and *Roger*.)

Everyday Grammar Activity: Pronouns

Identify the pronouns in the following sentences by underlining them:

1. Ameena wondered whether she would make it to the meeting.
2. The babies at the daycare center seemed to not miss their parents.
3. The television set is old; I will recycle it and buy a new one instead.
4. The two friends were driving along the road when Jacques' car hit their car from behind.
5. At first, Julian did not know what to do with his lottery winnings.

LO1

Use the major kinds of pronouns properly

Types of Pronouns

There are seven major kinds of pronouns: personal pronouns, reflexive pronouns, demonstrative pronouns, interrogative pronouns, relative pronouns, possessive pronouns, and indefinite pronouns.

A **personal pronoun** refers to a specific person or thing. *I, me, you, he, him, she, her, it, we, us, they, them* are all personal pronouns.

- <u>We</u> were glad that the weather was forecasted to be good for the trip.
- Loretta will meet <u>me</u> in front of the library.

A **reflexive pronoun** refers to the subject of a sentence. *Myself, yourself, himself, herself, itself, ourselves, yourselves, themselves* are all reflexive pronouns.

- We are to blame for being robbed because we did not protect <u>ourselves</u> enough. (The pronoun *ourselves* refers back to the personal pronoun *we*.)
- Foreigners often find <u>themselves</u> struggling to understand the local language. (The pronoun *themselves* refers back to the uncountable noun *foreigners*.)

A **demonstrative pronoun** points to specific things. *This, that, these,* and *those* are demonstrative pronouns. *This* and *that* refer to singular nouns, while *these* and *those* refer to plural nouns.

- <u>This</u> is really interesting.
- I do want <u>those</u>.

An **interrogative pronoun** asks questions. *Who, whom, which, what,* and *whose* are interrogative pronouns.

- <u>Who</u> wants to take the train?
- <u>Whom</u> should we ask for directions?
- <u>Which</u> music album are you referring to?
- <u>What</u> did he do?
- <u>Whose</u> books are those?

A **relative pronoun** "relates" a subordinate clause (such a clause is not a sentence) to the rest of the sentence. *Who, whom, whose, that, which, whoever, whomever,* and *whichever* are relative pronouns.

- <u>Whoever</u> leaves the building last should make sure the front door is locked. (The relative pronoun *whoever* relates the unnamed subject to the rest of the sentence.)

- The book <u>that</u> I left on the desk is missing. (The relative pronoun *that* relates the subject, *book*, to the rest of the sentence.)
- The girl with <u>whom</u> I was speaking last night is planning to major in chemistry. (The relative pronoun *whom* relates the subject, *girl*, to the rest of the sentence.)
- Sam, <u>whose</u> uncle is a professor, is sitting in the front row. (The relative pronoun *whose* relates the subject, *Sam*, to the rest of the sentence.)

A **possessive pronoun** shows ownership. *Mine, yours, his, hers, its, ours, yours,* and *theirs* are possessive pronouns.

- Is this <u>yours</u> or <u>mine</u>?
- Our camp leader was sure the tents were not <u>ours</u>.
- That is <u>his</u> book, not <u>ours</u>.
- That car is <u>theirs</u>, not <u>ours</u>.

An **indefinite pronoun** refers to an identifiable but not specified person or thing. Some common indefinite pronouns are *each, everyone, some, somebody, someone, all, any, anyone, anybody, everyone, few, many, none,* and *several.*

- <u>Someone</u> brought in the lost dog to the pet shelter.
- As a teacher, I hope that <u>all</u> students will come to class.
- I noticed that <u>several</u> people were sitting down.
- <u>Anybody</u> can come to the community dance tonight; it is free.

At a Glance: Pronouns

Personal Pronouns	Reflexive Pronouns	Demonstrative Pronouns	Interrogative Pronouns	Relative Pronouns	Possessive Pronouns	Indefinite Pronouns
I, me, you, he, him, she, her, it, we, us, they, them	myself, yourself, himself, herself, itself, ourselves, yourselves, themselves	this, that, these, those	who, whom, which, what whose	who, whom, whose, that, which, whoever, whomever, whichever	mine, yours, his, hers, its, ours, yours, theirs	each, every-one, some, somebody, someone, all, any, anyone, anybody, everyone, few, many, none, several

Grammar Spotlight: Subject and Object Pronouns; Singular and Plural Pronouns

Remember to distinguish between subject pronouns and object pronouns; even though both are personal pronouns, they can be confusing.

A **subject pronoun** functions as the subject of a sentence. *I, you, he, she, it, we,* and *they* are subject pronouns.

> <u>We</u> will go on an African safari next year. (You cannot say *Us* will go on an African safari next year.)
>
> <u>She</u> should save some money out of every paycheck. (You cannot say *Her* should save money out of every paycheck.)

An **object pronoun** serves as the object of a verb. *Me, you, him, her, it, us, you,* and *them* are object pronouns.

> He asked <u>me</u> to help him. (You cannot say He asked *I* to help him.)
>
> I invited <u>him</u> to speak at the reception. (You cannot say I invited *he* to speak at the reception.)

The pronouns *which* and *that* refer to things, while *who* and *whom* refer to humans.

> That computer, <u>which</u> costs $1,000, is the one I like. (You cannot say That computer, *who* costs $1,000, is the one I like.)
>
> My friend Gary, <u>whom</u> you met last night, is moving to Germany. (You cannot say My friend Gary, *that* you met last night, is moving to Germany.)

Singular and plural pronouns can often be very different:

Singular	Plural	Singular	Plural
I	we	myself	ourselves
me	us	yourself	yourselves
my	our	himself/herself/itself	themselves
mine	ours	his/her/its	their
this	these	that	those

Everyday Grammar Activity: Pronouns

Identify the pronouns in each sentence by underlining them, and for each pronoun, indicate what kind of pronoun it is:

1. She wants to travel to Asia after graduation.
2. This book is not mine.
3. Have you seen them recently?
4. Jim and Bob spoke to her for a few minutes last night.
5. Everyone should take responsibility for what happened.
6. You can discuss the proposed changes with whomever you wish.
7. Which movie are you going to be watching this weekend?
8. Mrs. Jacobs wants that dress, not this one.
9. Commuters in New York City often find themselves in a traffic jam.
10. Several students commented on the teacher's classroom policies.

MyWritingLab™ For support in meeting this chapter's objectives, log in to www.mywritinglab.com and select **Pronouns, Pronoun–Antecedent Agreement, Pronoun Reference and Point of View,** and **Pronoun Case.**

Chapter 22

Adjectives, Adverbs, Prepositions, Conjunctions, and Interjections

LO1

Identify adjectives and use them properly

Adjectives

An **adjective** is a word that modifies—that is, provides additional details—about a noun or a pronoun in a sentence, usually through description. The adjective is often placed before the noun or the pronoun that is being modified. The underlined words in the following examples are adjectives:

- The <u>old</u> lady was trying unsuccessfully to cross the street. (The adjective *old* describes the lady by providing additional details about her.)
- The Incas were an <u>ancient</u> people belonging to South America. (The adjective *ancient* describes the Incas by providing additional details about them.)
- The <u>sub-tropical</u> Mediterranean climate is Europe's warmest climate. (The adjective *sub-tropical* describes and provides additional details about the Mediterranean climate.)

- Koalas are <u>slow-moving</u> animals. (The adjective *slow-moving* describes and provides additional details about the koalas.)

The following table provides a list of some common adjectives:

At a Glance: Adjectives		
Adjectives Describing Appearance	**Adjectives Describing Emotion**	**Adjectives Describing Condition**
attractive, beautiful, blonde, bright, dark-haired, fat, graceful, handsome, pretty, short, slim, tall, thin	annoyed, anxious, brave, confused, cowardly, cheerful, excited, fun-filled, happy, merry, morose, nervous, sad	dull, expensive, famous, foolish, helpful, important, inexpensive, infamous, middle-class, new, old, poor, proud, rich, shiny

Everyday Grammar Activity: Adjectives

In the following paragraph, identify the adjectives by underlining them. Then indicate which noun or pronoun is being modified.

The young boy, dressed in a blue T-shirt and corduroy jeans, noticed the little girl lying on the hardwood floor. He picked her up, smoothed her ruffled dress, and asked her name. She did not say anything, but her blue eyes seemed to smile at him. He saw that she had long hair and was wearing ballet shoes. He wondered where her parents were.

LO2

Identify adverbs and use them properly

Adverbs

An **adverb** usually describes when, where, why, and under what conditions things happen or how something happened. Adverbs modify verbs, adjectives, and other adverbs. The underlined words in the following examples are adverbs:

- Fatima speaks <u>softly</u>. (How does Fatima speak? This is an example of an adverb modifying a verb, *speaks*.)

- Fatima is wearing a <u>very</u> beautiful dress. (How beautiful is Fatima's dress? This is an example of an adverb modifying an adjective, *beautiful*).
- Fatima spoke <u>quite</u> clearly to the rest of the group. (How clearly did Fatima speak? This is an example of an adverb modifying another adverb, *clearly*).

Words ending in –*ly* are often, though not always, adverbs.

- They live in a <u>friendly</u> neighborhood. (*Friendly* is an adjective.)

The following table lists some common adverbs:

At a Glance: Adverbs			
Adverbs of Place (describe *where* something happens)	**Adverbs of Time (describe *when* something happens)**	**Adverbs of Purpose (describe *why* something happens)**	**Adverbs of Manner (describe *how* something happens)**
upstairs, downstairs, here, there, somewhere, anywhere, above below, beneath, inside, outside	yesterday, today, tomorrow, before, after, later, earlier, now, then, soon	because, since, so, so that	fast, quickly, slowly, loudly, quietly, easily, carefully, carelessly, lovingly, patiently, impatiently, warmly

Everyday Grammar Activity: Adverbs

Read the following paragraph. Then identify the adverbs by underlining them and for each adverb, indicate what kind of adverb it is.

John drove carefully on the rain-soaked streets to Mary's house. When he reached the front door, he knocked softly. Soon, Mary opened the door. John went inside, and both he and Mary walked downstairs to her basement. Mary showed John the two boxes of books she had stored there. He laughed loudly when he saw that she had kept even her favorite book of nursery rhymes. Because it was getting late, John took the boxes and left. Tomorrow, he would deliver them to the neighborhood children's library.

Prepositions

LO3

Identify prepositions and use them properly

A **preposition** is a linking word, linking nouns, pronouns, and phrases to other parts of a sentence. Prepositions usually indicate the time when something happened and the location where something happened. They also indicate action and movement. Words such as *on, at, over, under, for, before, behind, in front of, during, below, beside, for, from, by, within, without, since, to, through, throughout, until,* and *upon* are prepositions. The underlined words in the following examples are prepositions:

- Harry sat <u>beside</u> his friend Cervando in class. (preposition of location)
- The old lady slowly climbed <u>up</u> the hill. (preposition of action and movement)
- I was at the concert two hours <u>before</u> it actually started. (preposition of time)
- Scared by the sound of thunder, the cat hid <u>under</u> the bed. (preposition of location)

At a Glance: Prepositions		
Prepositions of Location	**Prepositions of Time**	**Prepositions of Action and Movement**
in, on, at, over, under, above, below, in front of, behind, beside, between, with, among, near	before, after, since, during, until, by, at, on	on, at, by, into, from, off, out of, onto, toward, up, down

Sometimes prepositions are used unnecessarily.

- The pen fell off ~~of~~ her desk. (Eliminate *of.*)
- Where is your house ~~at~~? (Eliminate *at.*)
- There was no light inside ~~of~~ the house. (Eliminate *of.*)
- Where are they going ~~to~~? (Eliminate *to.*)

Grammar Spotlight: One Preposition, Several Functions

Prepositions can be troublesome because the same preposition can have different functions:

At can indicate a specific time:

We will meet <u>at</u> 5 p.m. outside City Hall.

(continued)

At can indicate a specific place:

I live <u>at</u> 1234 Main Street, Best City, South Africa.

On can indicate days:

I will leave for Kenya <u>on</u> Friday.

On can indicate dates:

The family will meet <u>on</u> January 10, 2012.

On can indicate names of streets:

They live <u>on</u> Main Street.

In can be used for unspecified times:

The bus will leave <u>in</u> a few minutes.

In can be used for unspecified times during the month:

Jane has a music recital <u>in</u> February.

In can be used for unspecified times during the year:

We are planning a trip to Europe <u>in</u> 2013.

In can be used for names of cities:

My boss lives <u>in</u> Detroit.

In can be used for names of countries:

Julia's grandparents live <u>in</u> Scotland.

In can be used for names of continents:

There is a lot of snow <u>in</u> Antarctica.

Sometimes prepositions are not used:

We should go inside. (not We should go <u>to</u> inside)
The children are going upstairs. (not The children are going <u>to</u> upstairs)
Mrs. Yang is driving downtown. (not Mrs. Yang is driving <u>to</u> downtown)
I am going outside. (not I am going <u>to</u> outside)

Some idiomatic expressions use prepositions (see Chapter 34 for a discussion of idioms):

Agree <u>to</u> a proposal, <u>on</u> a price, <u>in</u> principle.
Argue <u>on</u> a matter.
A blessing <u>in</u> disguise.
A chip <u>on</u> your shoulder.
A drop <u>in</u> the bucket.
A piece <u>of</u> cake.
A slap <u>on</u> the wrist.
A taste <u>of</u> your own medicine.
An axe <u>to</u> grind.
The apple <u>of</u> my eye.

Everyday Grammar Activity: Prepositions

Identify the prepositions in each sentence by underlining them, and for each preposition, indicate what kind of preposition it is.

1. The thief hid behind the building so nobody could see him.
2. We arrived at the football stadium before they did.
3. The politician walked quickly toward the speaker's podium.
4. Brad dropped the ingredients into the pot and stirred them.
5. The captain held the team trophy in front of him.

(continued)

6. The already waterlogged streets turned into streams as more rain fell.

7. The audience talked during the entire performance.

8. Computers have become very popular since the 1990s.

9. Don't worry; you are among friends.

10. The children hoped they could play until the sun went down.

Conjunctions

LO4

Identify conjunctions and use them properly

A **conjunction** is a "joining" word, connecting different parts of a sentence. Thus, conjunctions are very important for sentence construction. There are three major kinds of conjunctions: coordinating conjunctions, subordinating conjunctions, and correlative conjunctions.

A **coordinating conjunction** joins two main parts of a sentence that are equally important. *And, but, for, so, or, yet,* and *nor* are coordinating conjunctions.

- Jae Song worked all morning <u>and</u> is feeling tired now.
- Charlie would like to cook dinner, <u>but</u> his roommate Jon wants to order pizza.
- It is after midnight, <u>yet</u> the party shows no signs of breaking up.

A **subordinating conjunction** connects a dependent clause (a phrase with a subject and verb but that is not a complete sentence) with an independent clause (a phrase that has a subject and verb and that can act as a complete sentence). Subordinating conjunctions are placed *before* the dependent clause. *As, although, because, if, since, than, that, though, till, until, while,* and *whether* are subordinating conjunctions.

- Rea is still awake, <u>although</u> it is late.
- They are planning a trip to Europe this summer <u>if</u> they have the money.
- The tired mother is getting some sleep <u>while</u> the babysitter takes care of the child.

A **correlative conjunction** combines with other words to join together similar parts of a sentence (phrase + phrase; clause + clause). *Whether/or, either/or, neither/nor, not only/but also, both/and,* and the like are correlative conjunctions.

- <u>Whether</u> Lee takes Algebra <u>or</u> Calculus next semester will depend on what his advisor thinks he should do.
- <u>Neither</u> Jeremy <u>nor</u> Michiko know how to drive a car with manual transmission.
- <u>Both</u> Sybil <u>and</u> Stefani are avid bird watchers.

At a Glance: Conjunctions		
Coordinating Conjunctions	**Subordinating Conjunctions**	**Correlative Conjunctions**
and, but, for, so, or, yet, nor	as, although, because, if, since, than, that, though, till, until, while, whether	whether/or, either/or, neither/nor, not only/but also, both/and

Everyday Grammar Activity: Conjunctions

Identify the conjunctions in each sentence by underlining them, and for each conjunction, indicate what kind of conjunction it is.

1. My uncle Nate is interested in buying either a Toyota or a Honda for his next vehicle.
2. It is not only expensive but also of poor quality.
3. The electricians will not rest until power has been restored in all areas.
4. Whether medical researchers should focus on finding a cure for cancer or for heart disease is often debated.
5. Haiti and the Dominican Republic are both Caribbean countries.
6. My neighbor lives very frugally, although he has inherited a lot of money.
7. Either Heather will go to the airport to pick up her mother or her sister Beth will.
8. Issa is feeling better, though he is still tired after the surgery.
9. Dee is a student of British literature, yet American literature is his favorite.
10. Neither the teacher nor the student thought the answer was correct.

LO5

Identify interjections and use them properly

Interjections

An **interjection** is a sudden, usually short, utterance that expresses some emotion. The emotion is often expressed through the use of an exclamation point. Words such as *Ah! Alas! Oh! Really! Wow! Aloha! Bravo! Gosh! Hello! Hurray! Indeed! Ouch! Whew! Lo and behold! Voila! Yay!* and the like are interjections. The underlined words in the following examples are interjections:

- <u>Hush</u>! You will wake the baby.
- <u>Phew</u>! For a moment, it looked like the car would not be able to stop.

- I woke up, and <u>lo and behold</u>! there was my lost wallet on the nightstand.
- <u>Indeed</u>! I had no idea.

Everyday Grammar Activity: Interjections

Identify the interjection in each sentence by underlining it.

1. See you soon. Bye!
2. Ahoy! Let's set sail.
3. Oops! It's almost midnight. We should be going now.
4. I will be in touch with you soon. Cheers!
5. Physics is not my strong subject. My word, am I finding my physics class difficult this semester!
6. Ooh! That is one scary movie.
7. We must head home now. So long!
8. Yippee! No school tomorrow because it's a holiday.
9. What! Do you really mean that?
10. That looks disgusting. Yuk!

MyWritingLab™ For support in meeting this chapter's objectives, log in to www.mywritinglab.com and select **Adjectives, Adverbs,** and **Prepositions**.

Chapter **23**

Articles

Learning Objectives

In this chapter, you will learn to:

LO1 Identify and use the definite article *(the)*

LO2 Identify and use indefinite articles *(a, an)*

Articles are words that modify nouns. English has two different kinds of articles:

- Definite article—the word *the*
- Indefinite articles—the words *a* and *an*

Definite Article

LO1
Identify and use the definite article *(the)*

The **definite article** indicates a specific noun. It can be used before both singular and plural nouns as long as the noun is specific.

- <u>The</u> dog sat on <u>the</u> mat. (Here, *the* refers to a specific dog and a specific mat, and both *dog* and *mat* are singular nouns.)
- <u>The</u> neighbors don't seem to be home right now. (*The* refers to specific neighbors, which is a plural noun.)

Indefinite Articles

LO2
Identify and use indefinite articles *(a, an)*

Indefinite articles indicate nouns that are nonspecific.

- <u>A</u> dog is <u>a</u> human's best friend. [Here, *a* indicates any dog and any human being in general, not a specific dog, or a specific human. (Both *dog* and *human* are nouns.)]
- It was <u>an</u> error in judgment. [Here, *an* is very nonspecific; it refers to errors in general. (*Error* is a noun.)]

A or *An?*

How do we know whether to use *a* or *an?* Here are the rules:

a. *A* is used in front of a singular noun beginning with a consonant.
- <u>a</u> student
- <u>a</u> teacher
- <u>a</u> meeting
- <u>a</u> house

b. *A* cannot be used in front of a plural noun. We cannot say, for example, *a* students or *a* teachers.

c. *An* is used in front of a singular noun beginning with a vowel.
- <u>an</u> animal
- <u>an</u> emergency
- <u>an</u> ice-cream cone
- <u>an</u> orange

d. Sometimes, but not always, in words where *h* is not pronounced, *an* is used.
- <u>an</u> honest man (However, we do not say He was *an* hungry man; instead we say He was *a* hungry man.)

e. If a noun beginning with a vowel is modified by an adjective, the sound of the adjective determines whether *a* or *an* should be used.
- <u>a</u> new automobile
- <u>a</u> loud argument
- <u>an</u> enlightening discussion

Grammar Spotlight: Using Articles Correctly

Article use can be troublesome, so here are a few pointers:

1. Using articles with countable and uncountable nouns:
   a. *The* can be used with both countable and uncountable nouns:

   > Ekaterina put on <u>the</u> skates. (skates: countable noun)
   >
   > The chef spilled <u>the</u> soup. (soup: uncountable noun)

   b. *A/an* can be used only with countable nouns:

   > The patient had <u>a</u> bowl of soup for dinner. (bowl: countable noun)
   >
   > Can you make me <u>an</u> omelet? (omelet: countable noun)

2. *A/an* are often used to introduce nouns for the first time, while *the* is used to refer to nouns that have already been introduced:

> Pavel rode <u>a</u> bike to school today. <u>The</u> bike belongs to his friend Ramsey.
>
> <u>A</u> library is necessary in every town, so the new mayor decided to set up <u>the</u> Pottstown library.

3. *The* is used when there is only one of that noun:

> <u>The</u> sun rises in <u>the</u> east and sets in <u>the</u> west.
>
> <u>The</u> Pope lives in Vatican City.
>
> She is <u>the</u> president's wife.

4. *A/An* can be used when there are many of the same noun:

> He is <u>a</u> student at St Michael's college.
>
> My aunt Esther is <u>an</u> insurance adjuster.

5. *The* is used before:
   a. Names of mountain ranges:

> <u>the</u> Himalayas
>
> the Alps
>
> the Pyrenees

   b. Names of rivers:

> <u>the</u> Potomac
>
> <u>the</u> Ganges
>
> <u>the</u> Volga

   c. Names of deserts:

> <u>the</u> Sahara
>
> <u>the</u> Kalahari
>
> <u>the</u> Gobi

(continued)

d.   Names of oceans and seas:

the Pacific Ocean
the Arabian Sea
the Mediterranean Sea

e.   Names of a specific geographic locality:

the Arctic
the Hawaiian islands
the Cayman islands

f.   Names of organizations/institutions:

the Organization of African Unity
the United Nations
the International Monetary Fund

6. *The* is not used before:

a.   Names of mountain peaks:

Mt. Kilimanjaro
Mt. Rainier
Mt. Everest

b.   Names of lakes:

Lake Tanganyika
Lake Winnipeg
Lake Erie

c.   Names of continents:

South America
Africa
Australia

d. Names of streets:

Michigan Avenue

Cypress Street

Southern Avenue

e. Names of cities:

Paris

Nairobi

Johannesburg

f. Names of most countries:

Guyana

Mauritania

Pakistan

Exceptions: the Philippines, *the* Netherlands, *the* United States, *the* Dominican Republic, *the* Cayman Islands, etc.

7. Sometimes articles are omitted in front of some nouns:

a. Before the names of some academic subjects:

English

mathematics

biology

b. Before the names of some sports:

hockey

tennis

baseball

c. Before the names of languages:

Farsi

Mandarin

German

(continued)

d. Before the names of nationalities:

> Swedish
>
> Chilean
>
> Algerian

Everyday Grammar Activity: Articles

Fill in the blanks with the appropriate articles. In some cases, you may not need to use articles:

1. _____ protesters marched into _____ Panama City and gathered in front of _____ Agriculture Ministry.

2. _____ Bengali is the mother tongue of most citizens of Bangladesh.

3. There was _____ loud argument in the next apartment, followed by _____ sound of a door closing, and I noticed _____ elderly woman leaving hurriedly.

4. Owning _____ house is nice, but it is also _____ lot of work, because _____ house has to be maintained properly.

5. _____ Russia is _____ largest country in the world by area. Moscow is _____ most important economic center, though it is not _____ capital of _____ country. _____ Russians are used to much cold and snow. _____ Russian is the major language of Russia.

6. Please pick up _____ bag of fruit for me from the store, along with _____ kind of wheat bread that I like.

7. _____ Nile is the longest river in Africa. Africa has two of _____ 10 longest rivers in the world, _____ Congo being _____ other one. _____ Amazon in _____ South America is _____ second longest river in the world.

8. _____ friend from elementary school is visiting this weekend. He lives in _____ California, near _____

San Diego. He said he does not yet have _____ car, but plans to get one next year. He would like to get _____ newest Toyota Prius model, but fears it might be too expensive.

9. _____ tennis is played between two players (singles) or between two sets of players (doubles). _____ US Open Tennis Championships is _____ tennis tournament that is widely followed. Other well-known tennis tournaments are _____ Wimbledon Championships, _____ French Open, and _____ Australian Open.

10. Mrs. X is _____ chief executive officer of Design Incorporated. It is a company that designs textiles for export to other countries. Sweden is _____ old customer of _____ company. Mrs. X is hoping to expand her business to _____ Canary Islands in _____ next six months and to _____ Mauritius next year.

MyWritingLab™ For support in meeting this chapter's objectives, log in to www.mywritinglab.com and select **Articles**.

Chapter **24**

Sentence Elements

Learning **O**bjectives

In this chapter, you will learn to:

LO1 Identify the parts that make up a sentence: subject and predicate

LO2 Identify direct and indirect objects

LO3 Identify and use dependent and independent clauses

LO4 Use active and passive voice properly

A sentence is a group of words arranged in particular way to make meaning for the reader.

- It is a hot day today.

If the words in this sentence are arranged differently, it may not make sense.

LO1

Identify the parts that make up a sentence: subject and predicate

Subjects and Predicates

A complete sentence consists of two main parts: a subject and a predicate.

The **subject** of a sentence is who or what the sentence is about. The subject can be easily be identified by first locating the verb and then asking the questions "who" or "what" about it. Often, but not always, the subject can be found at the beginning of the sentence.

The **predicate** of a sentence is the part of a sentence that says something about the subject. The predicate always includes the verb.

The firefighters *put out the flames very quickly.*

(Subject)   (Predicate)

The verb is *put out*. Asking the question "who put out?" identifies the subject of the sentence: <u>the firefighters</u>. The predicate *put out the flames very quickly* tells readers something about the subject (<u>the firefighters</u>).

 ## Grammar Spotlight: Identifying the Subject

Some sentences in English can be confusing because it can be hard to identify the subject.

> Do your homework.

This sentence really means "You do your homework." *You* is the subject of the sentence. However, *you* is not written out; it is understood.

> There were two students doing their homework.

Even though the sentence begins with there, the subject of the sentence really is *two students*. The verb is *were doing*. If we ask, "who were doing?", we get the correct subject of the sentence, *two students*.

Everyday Grammar Activity: Subject and Predicate

Identify the subject and predicate in the following sentences:

1. John used a ladder to climb up to the roof.
2. Three students and a teacher traveled to Brazil as part of a cultural exchange program.
3. There are many fans waiting in line to glimpse the movie star.
4. Abena is a West African name meaning "born on Tuesday."
5. Coffee is one of the most popular drinks worldwide.

LO2
Identify direct and indirect objects

Direct and Indirect Objects

Sentences frequently have an object. The **object** of a sentence is the person or thing affected by the action of the verb. There are two types of objects:

- Direct object
- Indirect object

Both direct and indirect objects are always either a noun or a pronoun.

The **direct object** is what is affected by the action of the verb. It is usually identified by asking *whom* or *what* after the verb.

- The construction workers built the <u>house</u>.

Here, *the house* is the direct object affected by the verb *built*. (What did the construction workers build?)

- Melinda wants to meet <u>Jim</u>.

Here, *Jim* is the direct object affected by the verb *wants*. (Whom does Melinda want to meet?)

The **indirect object** is the person or thing that receives the direct object. It is usually indicated by asking *to whom?*, *to what?*, *for whom?*, or *for what?* after the verb.

- The bank teller gave <u>Takahashi</u> the check.

Here, *Takahashi* is the indirect object because he receives the check, which is the direct object. (To whom did the bank teller give the check?)

- The grandparents saved their money for their <u>grandchildren</u>.

Here, *grandchildren* is the indirect object, because they receive money, which is the direct object. (For whom did the grandparents save their money?)

Everyday Grammar Activity: Object of a Sentence

In the following sentences, identify the object of each sentence and indicate whether it is a direct object (D) or an indirect object (I). Some sentences may have both a direct object and an indirect object.

1. The Red Cross distributed food and clothing to the flood victims.
2. The school principal distributed the prizes.
3. Doctors prescribe medications for their patients.
4. Jane bought a music album for her brother Anders.
5. Meteorologists study weather patterns.

Transitive and Intransitive Verbs

A verbs that has an object is known as a **transitive verb.**

- Denny bought some lunch meat.

Here *bought* is a transitive verb because it has a direct object (<u>lunch meat</u>).

An **intransitive verb** is one that is not followed by an object.

- They sang.

Here, the verb *sang* has no object. However, *sang* becomes a transitive verb in the following sentence because it has an object (*a Bob Dylan song*).

- They sang a Bob Dylan song.

Everyday Grammar Activity: Transitive and Intransitive Verbs

In each of the following sentences, underline the verbs and indicate whether they are transitive (T) or intransitive verbs (I):

1. The Colombian football team celebrated their victory.
2. We lost?
3. The villagers plant crops every season.
4. The Andes mountains are in South America.
5. He is sleeping.

Sentence Complements

Sentence complements are of two kinds:

- Subject complement
- Object complement

A **subject complement** provides more information about the subject.

- The train is traveling fast. (*Fast* is the subject complement; it tells us the manner in which the train is traveling.)
- Eleann works for IBM. (*For IBM* is the subject complement; it gives us more information about the subject, *Eleann*.)

An **object complement** provides more information about the object.

- The butcher carved the meat into two. (*Into two* is the object complement; it provides additional information about *meat*, the direct object.)
- Shelley painted her office blue. (*Blue* is the object complement; it provides information about Shelley's *office*, the direct object.)

Everyday Grammar Activity: Sentence Complement

In each of the following sentences, identify the sentence complements and indicate whether it is a subject complement (SC) or an object complement (OC).

1. The children threw the ball into the river.
2. The audience is waiting impatiently.
3. The teacher spoke clearly.
4. The mother dressed the little girl in pink.
5. The boy snapped the twig in half.

LO3

Identify and use dependent and independent clauses

Dependent and Independent Clauses

A clause is a group of words that contain a subject and a verb. Clauses are of two main kinds: dependent clause and independent clause.

A **dependent clause** is a group of words that has a subject and verb but that does not indicate a complete thought. This means that a dependent clause can never be a sentence.

- When they are ready to go out

The thought is incomplete, even though there is a subject, <u>they</u>, and a verb, *are ready*; we are not told what will happen when they are ready to go out.

An **independent clause** is a sentence that contains a subject and a verb and expresses a complete thought.

- When they are ready to go out, they will call for a cab.

The thought is complete, because we know what will happen when they are ready to go out (they will call for a cab).

Some words when added to the beginning of an independent clause, convert it to a dependent clause. These words are known as **dependent marker words.**

- <u>When</u> they are ready to go out

When is the dependent marker word here, turning the independent clause *They are ready to go out* into a dependent clause.

Dependent Marker Words
after, although, as, as if, as soon as, because, before, besides, but, even if, even though, if, in case, in case of, since, though, unless, until, when, which, while, whether

Independent marker words are used at the beginning of an independent clause and join together two independent clauses. Often a semicolon is needed before the independent marker word if it stands at the beginning of the second independent clause.

- Mr. Ortiz left work early to return home; <u>however</u>, he was caught in a traffic jam.

However is the independent marker word joining together the first independent clause (Mr. Ortiz left work early to return home) with the second independent clause (he was caught in a traffic jam). Because it stands at the beginning of the second independent clause, a semicolon is needed before it.

Note: Independent clauses can also be joined together with a coordinating conjunction, such as *and, but, for, or, nor, so* and *yet*, with a comma used before the coordinating conjunction.

- Mr. Ortiz left work early to return home, <u>but</u> he was caught in a traffic jam.

Everyday Grammar Activity: Dependent and Independent Clauses

Identify each of the following sentences as either a dependent clause (D) or an independent clause (I). Then take each sentence you have marked with a D, and convert it to an independent clause.

1. When you finish your homework, you can watch television.
2. Although they were hot and thirsty.
3. As if being late for the flight was not enough.
4. Jamal and Andrew were hot and thirsty, yet they were not ready to give up.
5. Whether it rains or not tomorrow.

Passive and Active Voice

Voice in grammar refers to the relationship between the action expressed by the verb and the subject and object of a sentence. Verbs have two voices: active and passive. Active voice is more commonly used than the passive voice.

A verb is said to be **active** when the subject of the sentence is the doer of the action.

- The nanny pushed the stroller. (*Nanny* is the subject of the sentence, and the doer of the verb *push*; the stroller is the receiver of the action.)

A verb is said to be **passive** when the subject is the receiver of the action (or is "passive"). It usually consists of a form of the verb *to be* and the past participle of another verb, and the word *by*, indicating who/what performed the action.

- The stroller was pushed by the nanny. [*The stroller* becomes the subject, while the action (*was pushed*) is performed by the nanny.]

Active Voice or Passive Voice?

How can you decide whether to use the active voice or the passive voice? Each has its own benefits, and your choice will depend on your writing situation and what you want to communicate to your reader. Following are some features of both voices, which will help you make a decision when you write.

Active Voice

1. More direct than the passive voice.
   - Maria made some spaghetti. (active voice)

     vs.

   - Spaghetti was made by Maria. (passive voice)
2. Less ambiguous because the subject is the doer of the action.
   - The bank teller (subject) deposited the check. (active voice)

     vs.

   - The check was deposited by the bank teller (passive voice)
3. Less wordy and easier to read than the passive.
   - Henry threw the trash in the dumpster. (active voice)

     vs.

   - The trash was thrown by Henry in the dumpster. (passive voice)

Passive Voice

1. When the person/thing receiving the action is more important than the doer of the action, the passive voice is used.
   - The family was informed of the disappearance of the little boy.
2. When the writer does not want to mention the person/thing performing the action or does not know the agent of the action, the passive voice is used.
   - Their house was broken into.
3. The passive voice is used when it is not necessary to mention the agent because the agent is already known.
   - The iPad was available for sale in stores in early 2010.

Changing from the Active Voice to the Passive Voice and Vice Versa

How can you change voice in a sentence?

1. Locate the verb of the sentence.
2. Locate the doer of the action.

Active to Passive

- Gita washed the car. (*Washed* is the verb, and *Gita* is the doer of the action.)

The passive form of the sentence is:

- The car was washed by Gita.

Passive to Active

- The song was sung beautifully by the church choir. (*Sung* is the verb, and *church choir* is the subject)

The active form of the sentence is:

- The church choir sang the song beautifully.

Everyday Grammar Activity: Active and Passive Voice

1. Identify each of the following sentences as either active or passive voice. Indicate sentences in the active voice with an A and sentences in the passive voice with a P.
   a. The French fries were eaten by Jadiel.

(continued)

b. Magda likes jewelry.

c. Ian delivered the pizza to the apartment.

d. The Olympic Games were watched by millions of television viewers around the world.

e. Professor Macias is grading homework and tests.

f. Mrs. Tomas was congratulated by her colleagues on her promotion.

g. Most children like ice cream and candy.

h. The mountaineers climbed Mt. McKinley in Alaska.

i. Winning the lottery would be nice.

j. The housekeeper prepared lunch.

2. Now take each of the sentences, and convert them to the other voice. Thus, you will convert sentences in the active voice to the passive voice and sentences in the passive voice to the active voice.

MyWritingLab™ For support in meeting this chapter's objectives, log in to **www.mywritinglab.com** and select **Fragments, Subjects and Verbs,** and **Consistent Verb Tense and Active Voice**.

Chapter 25

Types of Sentences

Learning Objectives

In this chapter, you will learn to:

LO1 Identify and use simple, compound, and complex sentences

LO2 Identify and use declarative, exclamatory, imperative, and interrogative sentences

Sentences can be distinguished from one another by their structure (simple, compound, or complex) and by the purposes they serve (to declare, to exclaim, to order, and to question).

LO1

Identify and use simple, compound, and complex sentences

Simple, Compound, and Complex Sentences

Sentences (by structure) can be divided into three major types, depending on the number and kind of clauses in the sentence:

- Simple sentence
- Compound sentence
- Complex sentence

A **simple sentence** is a sentence that has one independent clause.

- Dr. Matthews is a heart surgeon.
- The pizza looks delicious.

A **compound sentence** has two independent clauses. These clauses are joined by:

1. A coordinating conjunction
   - Dr. Matthews is a heart surgeon, <u>but</u> Dr Price is an oral surgeon.

2. An adverb such as *however, therefore*.
   - Dr. Matthews is a heart surgeon; <u>however</u>, Dr Price is an oral surgeon.
3. A semicolon. (See pages 458–459 for a discussion of semicolons.)
   - The pizza looks delicious<u>;</u> it has three of my favorite toppings.

A **complex sentence** consists of one independent clause to which is attached a dependent clause through the use of a subordinating conjunction or a relative pronoun.

- <u>Before</u> we could say "Smile," our pictures were taken. (dependent clause, independent clause; subordinating conjunction *before*)
- This is the cottage <u>that</u> was built in 1985. (dependent clause, independent clause; relative pronoun *that*)
- Dr Matthews is a surgeon <u>who</u> is very much liked by his patients. (independent clause, dependent clause; relative pronoun *who*)

Everyday Grammar Activity: Types of Sentences (by Structure)

Identify the kinds of sentences in the following, writing S for simple sentences, CO for compound sentences, and COM for complex sentences:

1. Jay does not feel well, but he is going to take the exam anyway.
2. Vanuatu is an island nation.
3. Marie prefers public transportation although her friend Jose prefers to drive.
4. Spring is around the corner.
5. There are leather seats in the car that Sonja bought last month.
6. Athletes work very hard; however, some people think they are paid too much money.
7. Ralph is the student whose name the teacher forgot.
8. Jared is the coworker who I try to avoid.
9. The Niger River is the main river in Western Africa; it is about 2,600 miles long.
10. Brown rice is healthier than white rice.

LO2

Identify and use declarative, exclamatory, imperative, and interrogative sentences

Declarative, Exclamatory, Imperative, and Interrogative Sentences

Sentences can be divided into four major types by their purpose:

- Declarative sentences
- Exclamatory sentences
- Imperative sentences
- Interrogative sentences

A **declarative sentence** is a sentence that declares something or makes a statement about something. It is factual in nature, and is the most common type of sentence structure in English.

- Tasmania is an Australian island and state.
- Madrid is the capital city of Spain.

An **exclamatory sentence** is a sentence that expresses feeling or emotion. It is usually accompanied by the exclamation point (!).

- How dare you!
- It is beautiful!

An **imperative sentence** is a sentence that expresses a command. It can seem that imperative sentences don't have a subject; however, the subject of imperative sentences is usually "you," because the command is usually given directly to the person being spoken to. In other words, the subject is "understood" in an imperative sentence, even though it may not be directly stated.

- Put on your coat. (You put on your coat.)
- Clean your room. (You clean your room.)

However, the speaker can also say:

- Alyssa, put on your coat.

In this sentence, Alyssa is the subject of the imperative sentence.

An **interrogative sentence** is a sentence that asks a question. It is always followed by the question mark sign (?).

- Is lunch ready?
- What is the climate of Armenia like?

Everyday Grammar Activity: Types of Sentences (by Purpose)

In each of the following sentences, identify the type of sentence it is. Write D for declarative sentence, E for exclamatory sentence, IM for imperative sentence, and INT for interrogative sentence.

1. Where is the country of Mali?
2. My advisor is helping me choose classes for next semester.
3. Not again!
4. Drive safely.
5. Venezuela is located on the northern coast of South America.
6. It's cold here!
7. What is your favorite sport?
8. Turn off the lights.
9. Islam is the major religion of Kazakhstan.
10. What a performance!

Everyday Grammar Activity: Purposes of Sentences

Write the following sentences:

1. Two declarative sentences.
2. Two exclamatory sentences.
3. Two imperative sentences.
4. Two interrogative sentences.

MyWritingLab™ For support in meeting this chapter's objectives, log in to **www.mywritinglab.com** and select **Sentence Structure** and **Sentence Patterns**.

Sentence Agreement

Learning Objectives

In this chapter, you will learn to:

LO1 Write sentences with proper subject–verb agreement

LO2 Write sentences with proper pronoun–antecedent agreement

Sentence agreement means that different parts of a sentence must be "in agreement" with one another or match one another. If the sentence parts don't match, the sentence will sound awkward and will be considered an error.

There are two main forms of sentence agreement:

- Subject–verb agreement
- Pronoun–antecedent agreement

LO1

Write sentences with proper subject–verb agreement

Subject–Verb Agreement

Subject–verb agreement means that the subject of a sentence must agree with its verb in number. Thus, a singular subject must take a singular verb, while a plural subject must take a plural verb. Here are some examples.

Singular Subject–Singular Verb

- <u>Mrs. Smith</u> *sings* in her church choir. (The third-person singular subject <u>Mrs. Smith</u> is in agreement with the third-person singular verb *sings*.)
- <u>He</u> *is* a good speaker. (The third-person singular subject <u>he</u> agrees with the third-person singular verb *is*.)

Plural Subject–Plural Verb

- <u>Persian carpets</u> *are* usually made of wool. (The third-person plural subject <u>Persian carpets</u> takes the third-person plural verb *are*.)
- <u>Dogs</u> *are* a man's best friend. (The third-person plural subject <u>dogs</u> takes the third-person plural verb *are*.)

A **subject–verb agreement** error occurs when the subject and the verb do not agree in number:

- <u>Mrs. Smith</u> *sing* in her church choir. (<u>Mrs. Smith</u> is a third-person singular subject, while *sing* is the third person plural form of the verb *to sing*.)
- <u>Dogs</u> *is* a man's best friend. (<u>Dogs</u> is a third-person plural subject, while *is* is the third-person singular form of the verb *to be*.)

Grammar Spotlight: Special Types of Subjects

Sometimes subject–verb agreement can be confusing for the following reasons:

1. A plural subject can sometimes function as a singular subject and so take a singular verb rather than a plural verb.

   <u>Peanut butter and jelly</u> *is* Wanda's favorite sandwich filling. (Here, <u>peanut butter and jelly</u> is a singular subject, not a plural one, and so takes the third-person singular verb *is*.)

2. Titles are always singular and so they always take the singular verb, even if they "look" plural.

   PCs for Dummies *is* a must-have book for anybody interested in learning how to use computers. (Even though the title refers to more than one PC and more than one "dummy," it is the title of one book, and so takes the third-person singular verb *is*.)

3. Singular subjects connected by *either/or*, *neither/nor*, and *not only/but also* take a singular verb because the connecting words indicate that only one subject of the two is being chosen.

   Either <u>Uncle Gustav</u> or <u>Aunt Birgitt</u> *is* going to represent the family at the funeral in Norway. (Here, only one person will represent the family—Uncle Gustav or Aunt Birgitt, and so the subject is singular; therefore, it takes the third-person singular verb *is*.)

4. If the subject is made up of two or more nouns or pronouns connected by *or, nor, not only,* and *but also,* then the verb agrees with the noun or pronoun closest to it.

> Neither Mrs. Kwan nor her <u>neighbors</u> *are* willing to pay more property taxes. (Here, <u>neighbors,</u> the closest noun, is a plural subject, so the sentence takes the third-person plural verb *are.*)

5. Words and/or phrases that come between a subject and a verb should be ignored; the subject and the verb should be in agreement.

> The best <u>book</u> out of all three categories *wins* the top prize. (Here, the singular subject <u>book</u> takes the third-person singular verb *wins.*)

Everyday Grammar Activity: Subject–Verb Agreement

In the following sentences, identify the correct verb by underlining it.

1. The people of Macau [is/are] mainly of Chinese origin.
2. The skiers, regardless of the weather, [is/are] determined to compete.
3. The garage [need/needs] cleaning.
4. *Pride and Prejudice* [is/are] a famous novel by Jane Austen.
5. Neither the store manager nor the cashier [know/knows] why the cash register will not open.
6. Either Paula or David [need/needs] to work the late night shift.
7. Fish and chips [is/are] a popular British food.
8. Neither my mother nor my aunts [is/are] going to Cynthia's potluck.
9. The children [is/are] playing outside.
10. A leopard [has/have] short legs, a long body, and a large skull.

LO2

Write sentences with proper pronoun–antecedent agreement

Pronoun–Antecedent Agreement

On page 397, we defined a **pronoun** as a word that takes the place of a noun. An **antecedent** is a word for which a pronoun stands (*ante* = before). The pronoun is known as the "referent" because it refers back to the antecedent. Just as when, in a sentence, a subject must agree with its verb in number, in the same way, a pronoun must agree with its antecedent in number. This is known as **pronoun–antecedent agreement.** The following sentence is an error because the pronoun and the antecedent do not agree in number:

- Grizzly <u>bears</u> live in North America, <u>its</u> historical home.

Bears is a plural antecedent, while *its* is a singular pronoun. Therefore, the sentence is incorrect. The correct form of the sentence is:

- Grizzly <u>bears</u> live in North America, <u>their</u> historical home.

Here are more examples of correct pronoun–antecedent agreement:

- The math <u>teacher</u> delivered <u>his</u> speech on the importance of learning math. (The pronoun *his* refers back to the *teacher*, which is the antecedent. Because *teacher* is singular, it uses the singular pronoun *his*.)
- The <u>visitors</u> left <u>their</u> passports at the information desk. (The pronoun *their* refers back to *visitors*, which is the antecedent. Because *visitors* is plural, it uses the plural pronoun *their*.)

 ## Grammar Spotlight: Pronoun Problems

Sometimes pronoun–antecedent agreement can be confusing, but follow these rules:

1. Words and/or phrases that come between a pronoun and the antecedent should be ignored; the pronoun and the antecedent should be in agreement.

> The <u>book</u> on economic reforms has been returned to <u>its</u> rightful owner. (Here, the singular antecedent *book* takes the singular pronoun referent *its*.)

2. Singular indefinite antecedents always take singular pronouns, while plural antecedents always take plural pronouns.

> Each <u>person</u> must take responsibility for <u>his</u> or <u>her</u> own actions. (Here, the singular antecedent *each* takes the singular pronoun referent *his* or *her*.)

> Both <u>students</u> have done <u>their</u> homework. (Here, the plural antecedent *both* takes the plural pronoun referent *their*.)

3. Uncountable antecedents are treated as singular and, therefore, use a singular pronoun referent.

Some of my happiness lost its edge when I found out I would have to leave tomorrow. (Here, *some of my happiness* is uncountable, so it is treated as a singular antecedent and takes the singular pronoun referent *its*.)

4. Countable antecedents are treated as plural and, therefore, use a plural referent pronoun.

Some of the books have lost their covers. (Here, *books* are countable, so they are treated as a plural antecedent and take the plural pronoun referent *their*.)

5. Compound subjects joined by *and* take a plural referent.

Wasim and Pedro are looking forward to their summer vacation. (Here, *Wasim and Pedro* are plural antecedents, so they take the plural pronoun referent *their*.)

6. When the antecedents are joined by *or/nor*, the antecedent closer to the pronoun determines the number of the pronoun referent.

Neither the child nor her parents had their coats. (Here, the plural antecedent *parents* determines that the plural pronoun referent *their* should be used.)

7. Some antecedents are singular or plural, depending on meaning:

The crowd made clear its views to the speaker. (Here, *crowd* functions as a singular antecedent, so it takes the singular pronoun referent *its*.)

Some members of the crowd made their views clear to the speaker. (Here, *members* is a plural antecedent, so it takes the plural pronoun referent *their*.)

8. Titles of books, names of countries, and organizations are singular antecedents and so take the singular pronoun referent.

The Adventures of Huckleberry Finn portrays its characters well. (Here, *The Adventures of Huckleberry Finn* is a singular antecedent, so it takes the singular pronoun referent *its*.)

(continued)

> The United Kingdom cherishes its important role within the European Union. (Here, *The United Kingdom* is a singular antecedent, so it takes the singular pronoun referent *its*.)
>
> The United Nations focuses its aims on promoting international peace and cooperation. (Here, *The United Nations* is a singular antecedent, so it takes the singular pronoun referent *its*.)

9. Some antecedents look plural but are singular in nature and so take the singular pronoun referent.

> The Olympic Games has lived up to its name. (Here, the *Olympic Games* is a singular antecedent, so it takes the singular pronoun referent *its*.)

10. *Every* or *many* require a singular referent.

> Every action has its own reaction. (Here, only one action is being referred to, so it uses the singular pronoun referent *its*.)

> Many a woman wishes she had a Gucci handbag. (Here, *many a* is a singular antecedent, so it uses the singular pronoun referent *she*.)

11. *A number of* is plural and so takes the plural referent.

> A number of students are registering for their classes today. (Here, the plural pronoun referent *their* is used.)

12. *The number of* is singular and so takes the singular referent.

> The number of students registering for classes today is at its peak. (Here, the singular pronoun referent *its* is used.)

Everyday Grammar Activity: Pronoun–Antecedent Agreement

In the following sentences, identify the correct pronoun to be used by underlining it:

1. Parents love [its/their] children.
2. The latest NHL (National Hockey League) news is available on [its/their] Web site.

3. The ASEAN (Association of Southeast Asian Nations) records [its/their] aims and purposes in the ASEAN Declaration.

4. Neither Jennifer nor Yu-Na had [her/their] homework done.

5. Some members of the community donated [its/their] money to set up a neighborhood patrol.

6. Each citizen must recycle [his or her/their] garbage in a responsible manner.

7. The scientists explained [its/their] research to the panel of experts at the meeting.

8. A number of homeless people have been sleeping in [his or her/their] cars lately.

9. Mrs. Javez and Mrs. Herrera have [her/their] eyes set on the same dress.

10. Their sadness is matched in [its/their] intensity by their enemies' happiness.

MyWritingLab™ For support in meeting this chapter's objectives, log in to **www.mywritinglab.com** and select **Subject–Verb Agreement, Pronoun–Antecedent Agreement, Pronoun Reference and Point of View,** and **Pronoun Case**.

Chapter 27

Improving Your Sentences

Learning Objectives

In this chapter, you will learn to:

LO1 Correct comma splice errors

LO2 Avoid run-on sentences

LO3 Avoid sentence fragments

LO4 Correct dangling modifiers

LO5 Avoid misplaced modifiers

LO6 Avoid double negatives

LO7 Use transitions correctly

Sentences can sometimes be troublesome because there are some common sentence errors that writers may make. Knowing about these errors will help you write more accurately, and, therefore, perform better in college.

There are seven major kinds of sentence errors:

- Comma splice errors
- Run-on sentences
- Sentence fragments
- Dangling modifiers
- Misplaced modifiers
- Double negatives
- Transition errors

LO1

Correct comma splice errors

Comma Splice

A **comma splice** error occurs when a comma is used between two independent clauses.

- <u>My friend Anastazja lives in Poland</u>, <u>I want to visit her there.</u>

       (independent clause)   (independent clause)

There are several ways to fix this problem:

1. The comma can be replaced by a period, thereby creating two independent clauses:
   - My friend Anastazja lives in Poland. I want to visit her there.
2. The comma can be replaced by a semicolon:
   - My friend Anastazja lives in Poland; I want to visit her there.
3. One clause can be made dependent by using a dependent marker word:
   - <u>Because</u> my friend Anastazja lives in Poland, I want to visit her there.
4. The comma can be replaced by a coordinating conjunction:
   - My friend Anastazja lives in Poland, <u>and</u> I want to visit her there.

Everyday Grammar Activity: Comma Splice Errors

Each of the following sentences contains a comma splice error. Correct the error in the sentences, and write out the correct form of the sentences.

1. Olive oil is a fruit oil obtained from the olive, it is most widely used in the Mediterranean region.
2. Sam and Alex have an exam tomorrow, they are studying.
3. Engineers apply science and math to solve technical problems, there are many branches of engineering.
4. I love eating stuffed mushrooms, I love to stuff them with cheese, sausage, crab meat, and more.
5. Afghanistan is a landlocked country, its people are known as Afghans.
6. Student loans pay for a college education, however they have to be paid back.
7. Traffic was backed up for miles on the highway, there was an accident involving two cars.
8. Clowns are an important part of a circus, they help to entertain spectators.
9. Hans' alarm clock is really loud, it never fails to wake him up.
10. Moose are large antlered animals, they can weigh between 800 and 1,000 pounds.

Run-on Sentence

A **run-on sentence,** also known as a **fused sentence,** happens when two independent clauses are not separated by any kind of punctuation.

- The native people of Australia are known as aborigines (independent clause) they make up about 2 percent of Australia's total population. (independent clause)

There are several ways to fix this problem:

1. By using a period to separate them into two independent clauses:
   - The native people of Australia are known as aborigines. They make up about 2 percent of Australia's total population.
2. By using a semicolon to separate them into two independent clauses:
   - The native people of Australia are known as aborigines; they make up about 2 percent of Australia's total population.
3. By adding a coordinating conjunction:
   - The native people of Australia are known as aborigines, and they make up about 2 percent of Australia's total population.
4. Depending on the sentence, a dependent marker word can also be used to separate a run-on sentence:
   - The entrée looks delicious; moreover, it is easy to prepare.

Everyday Grammar Activity: Run-on Sentences

Each of the following sentences contains a run-on error. Correct the error in the sentences, and write out the correct form of the sentences.

1. The Republic of Senegal is a country in Western Africa it has a population of approximately 14 million people.
2. The Grand Canyon is visited by nearly 5 million people each year the South Rim is the most visited part of this national park.
3. Construction of the Great Wall of China began in the 7th century B.C. it is more than 3,700 miles in length.
4. Mercedes-Benz is a German car it has a reputation of being a reliable and long-lasting car.
5. Tuyen is a Vietnamese name for a girl it means angel.
6. Paragliding is a flying sport it has become popular in many places.
7. Yoga requires no special equipment it has many health benefits.
8. Elementary education is the first stage of formal education it is often preceded by some form of preschool.

9. The real estate market outlook is bleak it may be years before the market picks up.
10. The 2010 football World Cup was held in South Africa the 2014 World Cup will be held in Brazil.

LO3

Avoid sentence fragments

Sentence Fragment

A **sentence fragment** is an incomplete sentence not expressing a complete thought.

- When Darren bought a new car.

There are two ways to fix this problem:

1. By combining it with other words to make a complete thought:
   - When Darren bought a new car, his friends came over to see it.
2. By removing the dependent marker *when*:
   - Darren bought a new car.

Everyday Grammar Activity: Sentence Fragments

Each of the following items is a sentence fragment. Correct the error in the sentences, and write out the correct form of the sentences.

1. The Palau islands, located in the western Pacific Ocean, 528 miles southeast of the Philippines.
2. The Republic of Panama, whose capital is Panama City.
3. One reason it is important to read.
4. Brussels and Antwerp two of Belgium's largest cities.
5. The fastest way to poach an egg.
6. The leaves on the trees.
7. Before the Wilson family went on vacation to the Caribbean.
8. Airline pilots.
9. Influences on Serbian food.
10. Going to Honduras.

LO4

Correct dangling modifiers

Dangling Modifier

A **modifier** is a word, phrase, or clause that describes, defines, and/or provides more details about something. Adjectives and adverbs are common modifiers.

When a word or phrase or clause modifies a word that is not part of a sentence, it is called a **dangling modifier** because the meaning of the sentence is left "dangling." In other words, the meaning is unclear because the modifier is not clearly linked to the word or phrase it modifies.

- After some practice, driving was learned (incorrect). (The subject of the action ("driving") is unclear in the participle ("after some practice"); therefore, the participle is said to be a dangling modifier.)
- After some practice, Francois learned to drive (correct). (The subject of the action ("Francois") is identified in the main clause; therefore, this sentence does not have a dangling modifier.)
- Having driven so much, tiredness was felt (incorrect). (The subject of the action ("having driven") is unclear in the participle "having driven"; therefore, the participle is said to be a dangling modifier.)
- Having driven so much, you felt tired (correct). (The subject of the action ("you") is identified in the main clause; therefore, this sentence does not have a dangling modifier.)

Revising Dangling Modifiers

There are several ways to fix this problem:

1. Name the subject in the main clause:
   - Having studied seriously, test preparation was complete. (incorrect)
   - Having studied seriously, Norma was completely prepared for the test. (correct)
   - Having put in so many hours at work, a long vacation was due. (incorrect)
   - Having put in so many hours at work, Mr. Ahmed was due for a long vacation. (correct)
2. Name the doer of the action in the phrase that dangles, thereby converting it to a complete introductory clause:
   - Without attending class, it was difficult to do well. (incorrect)
   - Because Salma did not attend class, it was difficult to do well. (correct)
   - Without paying the entrance fees, it was impossible to get into the museum. (incorrect)
   - Because the Johnson family did not pay the entrance fees, it was impossible for them to get into the museum. (correct)
3. Combine the dangling modifier and the main clause into one sentence:
   - To improve in math, tutoring sessions were attended. (incorrect)
   - Joey improved in math by attending tutoring sessions. (correct)
   - To learn driving, driving lessons were taken. (incorrect)
   - Mimi learned driving by taking driving lessons. (correct)

Everyday Grammar Activity: Dangling Modifiers

Each of the following sentences has a dangling modifier. Correct the errors in the sentences and write out the correct form of the sentences.

1. Sitting on the porch, the beautiful sunset was seen.
2. Dancing excellently, the audience was entertained.
3. Having given birth to triplets, Mr. Bishop felt anxious about his wife.
4. Deciding to go to college in a faraway city, my mother felt anxious.
5. Flashing lights, the criminal saw the police car approaching.
6. When an infant, my grandmother passed away.
7. Biking to school, the thunder and lightning scared Omar.
8. Hoping to travel abroad, excitement was felt.
9. On entering the room, the party was well under way.
10. At the age of nine, my father found work.

Misplaced Modifiers

Misplaced modifiers are a subtype of dangling modifiers; they are "misplaced," that is, they are not positioned correctly in a sentence. As a result, they do not modify the noun they are supposed to modify and can cause confusion in a sentence—and sometimes make the sentence sound irrational.

- Jasmine declared last week she traveled to France. (It is not clear whether Jasmine told everybody last week that she had traveled to France earlier or whether Jasmine traveled to France last week.)

- I read the book in my pajamas. (It almost sounds like the book is inside the pajamas!)

Revising Misplaced Modifiers

Misplaced modifiers are usually corrected by moving the modifier next to the word being modified:

- Last week, Jasmine declared that she had traveled to France.

or

- Jasmine declared that she had traveled to France last week.

- I read the book wearing my pajamas.

Everyday Grammar Activity: Misplaced Modifiers

Each of the following sentences has a misplaced modifier. Correct the errors in the sentences and write out the correct form of the sentences.

1. Mr. Ivanov said on Friday there would be a meeting.
2. The student turned in a paper to the teacher that was well-written.
3. The old lady put her clothes in the washing machine that she had worn.
4. We saw a statue at the museum made of wax.
5. The twins sat quietly at the back of the room wearing red dresses.
6. The guests entered the room carrying gifts quietly.
7. The store advertised a sale for shoppers with a discount of 20 percent.
8. The chef prepared a hot dish for the dinner guests of soup.
9. It would be nice to be able to afford those pearl ladies earrings.
10. They planned a tour of the Grand Canyon biking.

Double Negatives

LO6

Avoid double negatives

A **double negative** occurs when two negatives are used in the same sentence. It is a grammatically incorrect form, because one negative can express the idea just as well. The following words are considered negative words, and using them once in a sentence is adequate to convey negation:

At a Glance: Words Indicating Negation			
no	nobody	hardly	won't
not	nowhere	scarcely	wouldn't
none	nothing	barely	couldn't
no one	neither	don't	haven't

However, it is not uncommon to see sentences using double negatives.

- Paul is not going nowhere. (incorrect)
- Paul is not going anywhere. (correct)

- Even though they were poor, the men didn't want nothing. (incorrect)
- Even though they were poor, the men didn't want anything. (correct)

- There is barely nothing in the cupboard. (incorrect)
- There is barely anything in the cupboard. (correct)

Everyday Grammar Activity: Double Negatives

Each of the following sentences has a double negative. Correct the error in the sentences and write out the correct form of the sentences:

1. The cousins were not interested in seeing no movie.
2. I was so excited, I couldn't hardly wait.
3. Sammy didn't know no one in the room.
4. "I am not going to no bed so early," the teenager declared.
5. The boss scarcely couldn't hide his anger at his employees.
6. We haven't no bread for dinner.
7. Neither Lori nor Mikasa don't know the plans.
8. No one shouldn't plagiarize their papers in college.
9. No one should travel nowhere there is a security risk.
10. The students couldn't hardly believe their ears when the teacher told them that everybody in the class had got an A.

LO7

Use transitions correctly

Transitions

Transitions are words or phrases used in writing that help the writer move, or "transition," from one idea to another logically while maintaining the flow of the writing. They help keep the writing coherent, maintaining continuity for readers. Without them, your writing can become a series of disconnected sentences or paragraphs. You can view transitions as the "glue" that holds the writing together, or as a bridge between different ideas.

Transitions can be used to connect sentences, paragraphs and/or sections of the paper. They can be placed anywhere in the sentence they are appropriate.

Transitions between Sentences

- Dinner was ready, and the table was set. We wanted to wait until Larry and Chang arrived. (sentence without transition)

- Dinner was ready, and the table was set. <u>However,</u> we wanted to wait until Larry and Chang arrived. (sentence with transition word, *however*)

Transitions between Paragraphs

-     John and Rob had been friends for many years. They grew up in the same neighborhood, shared toys, books, bikes and school lunches. When one of them was sick, the other one was miserable.

When one of them had a stroke of luck, the other one was as happy as if he had had the same good fortune.

There was an underlying tension in this friendship. John was a talented violin player in school, while Rob could not really play any musical instrument. He envied John his talent, and in high school, went so far as to damage John's violin. (Here we have two disconnected paragraphs; there is no logical connection between the first paragraph and the second paragraph.)

- John and Rob had been friends for many years. They grew up in the same neighborhood, shared toys, books, bikes and school lunches. When one of them was sick, the other one was miserable. When one of them had a stroke of luck, the other one was as happy as if he had had the same good fortune.

  <u>At the same time,</u> there was an underlying tension in this friendship. John was a talented violin player in school, while Rob could not really play any musical instrument. He envied John his talent, and in high school, went so far as to damage John's violin. (Here we have the transitional phrase, *At the same time*, which creates a logical relationship between the first paragraph and the second paragraph.)

Transitional Expressions

There are several different transitional expressions you can use, depending on the kind of relationship (addition, compare and contrast, similarity, etc.) you want to indicate between sentences, paragraphs, or sections of your writing. You should become familiar with these expressions. The following list indicates some of the more common transitional expressions.

At a Glance: Transitions	
Relationship Expressed/Logical Connections	**Transitional Expressions**
Similarity	comparable to, similarly, in similar fashion, like, likewise, also, in the same way, in the same manner, so too
Difference	as opposed to, despite that, however, in contrast, on the contrary, on the other hand, in spite of, notwithstanding, nevertheless, though, otherwise, unlike

Relationship Expressed/Logical Connections	Transitional Expressions
Sequence/order	first, second, third, fourth, then, finally, lastly, next, generally…furthermore…finally
Time	after a while, at length, at last, as soon as, earlier, eventually, before, before long, currently, during, after, afterward, during, earlier, following, finally, later, lately, meanwhile, in the meantime, next, now, soon, thereafter, then, recently, simultaneously, subsequently, sometimes, first…second…third…
Emphasis	certainly, indeed, in fact, of course, surely, truly, undoubtedly, unquestionably, obviously, for this reason, to emphasize, in other words, with this in mind
Example	for example, for instance, to illustrate, namely, that is, to demonstrate
Cause/effect	because, for that reason, since, consequently, as a result, hence, thus, therefore, so
Additional support	in addition, additionally, also, further, furthermore, moreover, equally important, too, even more
Conclusion	finally, in brief, lastly, on the whole, therefore, to sum up, in summary, thus, therefore

Everyday Writing Activity: Transitions

Use the appropriate transition(s) in each of the following sentences in a manner that establishes a logical connection between the sentences:

1. They did not attend the meeting. They had not been told about it.
2. The chairperson made some lengthy comments at the annual general meeting of the corporation. He summed up the main points of his speech.
3. Hann-Jing is taking Physics 101, History 300, and English 1100 at the university. He is taking French 101 at the local community college.

(continued)

4. The microwave is a very useful kitchen appliance. It has certain limitations. You can't boil an egg in it.

5. John worked all day, went to his parents' house for dinner. He went home around midnight.

6. Shiraz is a very good student. There are few students who are as strong academically as he is.

7. Here is the plan for today. We will go for a stroll in the park. We will have lunch. We will do some shopping. We will go to my grandmother's house to see how she is doing.

8. It is snowing heavily, and there is dense fog. The airport did not shut down.

9. Elena loves to swim. Her friend Hyacinth likes to swim.

10. Elias and Sophie have applied for passports. They will leave for a trip to Australia.

MyWritingLab™ For support in meeting this chapter's objectives, log in to www.mywritinglab.com and select **Run-Ons, Fragments,** and **Misplaced or Dangling Modifiers**.

Chapter 28

Periods, Question Marks, and Exclamation Points

Learning Objectives

In this chapter, you will learn to:

LO1 Use periods correctly

LO2 Use question marks correctly

LO3 Use exclamation points correctly

Did you know that September 24 is National Punctuation Day? The day celebrates the importance of using proper punctuation.

Punctuation consists of marks that are part of writing conventions in English. They make writing more effective because they help to make communication clearer, and all good writers in English use them because they indicate specific things in a piece of writing. Punctuation rules guide our writing, just as the rules of the road guide our driving. They tell us when to stop, when to start, and when to pause, and they also help us provide additional information or express an emotion. In the next few pages, we will discuss some of the most common punctuation marks because they are the ones that you will use most often in your writing.

The most common punctuation marks used in writing are:

- Period
- Comma
- Semicolon
- Colon
- Question mark
- Apostrophe
- Dash and hyphen
- Exclamation point
- Quotation marks
- Parentheses
- Ellipses

In this chapter, we will focus on what is known as "end punctuation," that is, punctuation marks used to "end" a sentence, or bring it to a close: period, question mark, and exclamation point.

LO1

Use periods correctly

Period

A **period** is a mark that is used to punctuate a text. It is indicated by a single dot (.). It is the most common punctuation mark used to indicate the end of a sentence (and the end of a thought), though it can be used for other purposes, too. A sentence without a period is like a street without traffic lights; imagine the confusion there would be if readers did not know where the sentence boundaries were. When periods are not used, then we have run-on sentences (see page 440).

There are some common rules related to the use of the period that you should be familiar with:

1. The period is placed at the end of a declarative sentence:
   - All students should have registered for classes before the first day of school.
   - All drivers need to follow traffic rules.

2. The period is also often used at the end of imperative sentences:
   - Make sure that your homework is turned in on time.
   - Sweep away the dust.

3. Periods are placed after an abbreviated word:
   - All govt. officials need to be re-trained in paperwork handling procedures.
   - Jan. is the coldest month of the year.

4. Periods are used after initials:
   - My coworker's full name is Rose W. Clark. (Here, the first letter of the middle name, <u>W</u>, is initialized, and is followed by a period.)
   - H. L. Mencken was an American journalist and essayist. (The initials H and L are followed by periods.)

5. Periods are not used when a sentence concludes with an abbreviated word that ends in a period:
   - The whole family is moving from Nigeria to the U.S.A.. (incorrect)
   - The whole family is moving from Nigeria to the U.S.A. (correct)

6. Periods, rather than question marks, are used after indirect questions:
   - Grandpa asked Grandma if he should get anything from the grocery store.
   - Fran enquired after her friend Majid's health.
7. Periods are used after numbers, Roman numerals, or alphabets in a list or outline:

   1.
   2.
   3.

   or

   I.
   II.
   III.

   or

   a.
   b.
   c.

8. Periods are not used after individual letters in an acronym (an acronym is an abbreviation formed by using the first alphabet of each individual word):
   - E.S.L. (for *English as a Second Language*) (incorrect)
   - ESL (correct)

Everyday Punctuation Activity: Periods

In the following sentences, insert periods in the appropriate places.

1. Make sure to visit the Taj Mahal when you go to India
2. Jill's cousin Mary, who is an M D, is accepting new patients
3. Stefan dreams of working for NASA one day
4. The following students are absent from class today:
   a   Marta
   b   Akbar
5. President John F Kennedy was a well-known American president
6. The teacher asked if there was anything else she needed to explain
7. ACCT 110 is a required course for accountancy majors
8. The province on Canada's west coast is British Columbia, also known as B.C.
9. The show starts at 7 pm You can catch the later show at 9 pm
10. The music store is on University Ave

LO2

Use question
marks correctly

Question Mark

The **question mark**, indicated by the sign **?**, is commonly used to indicate that a question is being asked. The question mark sign comes directly after the question that is being asked. There are some common rules related to the use of the question mark that you should be familiar with:

1. The question mark is most commonly used at the end of an interrogative sentence:
   - What is the capital city of South Africa?
   - What is the currency of Kuwait?

2. Question marks are not used at the end of indirect questions:
   - The supervisor asked his employees if they wanted to work overtime the following week? (incorrect)
   - The supervisor asked his employees if they wanted to work overtime the following week. (correct)
   - The teacher asked the students what they thought about the previous day's homework reading? (incorrect)
   - The teacher asked the students what they thought about the previous day's homework reading. (correct)

3. Rhetorical questions (questions that are asked without an answer really being expected) end with a question mark:
   - Shakespeare was a great poet and playwright, wasn't he?
   - It is windy today, isn't it?

4. If a question includes a series of brief questions within itself, then question marks are used at the end of each of those brief questions:
   - Which sports does Leah play? Tennis? Basketball? Softball? All three?
   - When are you going on vacation? May? June? July?

5. When a tag question is used (a tag question turns a statement into a question), the question mark is placed after the tag question:
   - The price of new houses is expected to rise, isn't it?
   - You are expecting to leave tomorrow, aren't you?

6. A question mark can be used to turn a statement into a question without using a tag question:
   - Lucy didn't pass her Chemistry exam?
   - The movie theater ran out of tickets for the matinee?

7. When a question is inserted into a statement, a question mark is placed after the question:
   - The worried parent wondered, was her teenage son following all the traffic rules on his first night out alone with the car?
   - The truck driver asked himself, should he stop for the day or drive 25 more miles to the next big town?

8. If the question comes at the beginning of a sentence, the question mark directly follows the question:
   - Was her teenage son following all the traffic rules on his first night out alone with the car? the worried parent wondered.
   - Should he stop for the day or drive 25 more miles to the next big town? the truck driver wondered.

9. Question marks are used to indicate requests:
   - Would you please take some notes about this meeting?
   - Will you please drop Jude off at the gas station?

10. Question marks are sometimes included within parentheses to indicate uncertainty:
    - The Battle of Phyle took place in 404 B.C. (?).
    - Grandpa Morrison bought the farm in 1960 (?).

11. Usually, a question mark is enough to end the sentence; a period or any other kind of punctuation is not used after the question mark:
    - When is the book due at the library?. (incorrect)
    - When is the book due at the library? (correct)
    - Who is going to the violin performance?. (incorrect)
    - Who is going to the violin performance? (correct)

12. If the question ends with an abbreviation that ends with a period, a question mark is placed after the period:
    - Didn't the Greek philosopher Plato live in the fourth century B.C.?
    - Didn't Aristotle write *Poetics* in 335 B.C.?

13. If a question mark is part of a quoted text, then the question mark is placed within the quotation:
    - Once caught, the thief kept pleading with the policemen, "Please let me go, will you?"
    - The mother kept asking her son, "You drank the milk, didn't you?"

14. If a question mark is not part of the quoted text, but applies to the whole sentence, then the question mark is placed outside the quotation:
    - Didn't the thief keep pleading with the policemen, "Please let me go"?
    - Didn't the little boy keep saying, "I didn't do it"?

15. When a question is enclosed within a statement and the question is placed within parentheses, the question mark is placed within the parentheses if it is an independent clause:
    - Latisha is planning a trip to France and Germany this summer (isn't that going to be expensive, though?).
    - Jimmy and his friend Charlie should be back around midnight (isn't that late, though?).

16. When the text within the parentheses is not an independent clause, then the question mark is placed at the end of the sentence, and outside the closing parenthesis:
    - Is Latisha planning a trip to France and Germany this summer (despite it being so expensive)?
    - Aren't Jimmy and his friend Charlie going to be back around midnight (even though that's very late)?

Everyday Punctuation Activity: Question Marks

In the following sentences, insert question marks in the appropriate places.

1. You are leaving for Germany tomorrow, aren't you
2. The pharmacy will close early tomorrow night (isn't that going to inconvenience patients, though)
3. At what time is Renee's flight tomorrow
4. Will you please close the door on your way out
5. What is the price range of the furniture that is on sale $200–$400, $500–$700, $1,000 and above
6. "Will you have time to read my paper for some feedback" the student asked the teacher
7. Isn't Viktor's surgery supposed to start at 7 a.m.
8. The ice cream didn't melt, despite the heat
9. Isn't this beautiful weather
10. Is your mind set on going to college in Italy (even though it will be so far from home)

LO3

Use exclamation points correctly

Exclamation Point

An **exclamation point** (!) is a common punctuation mark. There are some rules related to the use of the exclamation point that you should be familiar with.

1. An exclamation point is usually used to express strong emotions like astonishment, joy, sorrow etc.:
   - Oh my goodness! Look at that!
   - So sorry!

2. An exclamation point can be used to issue commands:
   - Go now!
   - Wait!

3. An exclamation point can be inserted within parentheses to emphasize a certain word within a sentence:
   - There are some strange (!) noises coming from inside the deserted house.
   - That is really weird (!), don't you think?

4. If a sentence ends with an exclamation point, a period is not used to end the sentence; the exclamation point ends the sentence:
   - Polynesian dances are a pleasure to watch!. (incorrect)
   - Polynesian dances are a pleasure to watch! (correct)
   - What a bargain!. (incorrect)
   - What a bargain! (correct)

5. If the exclamation point is part of the title, italicize or underline it, depending on whether the title is underlined or italicized. If it is not part of the title, do not italicize or underline it:
   - *Oh, The Places You'll Go!* by Theodor Geisel is a children's book that adults can enjoy reading as well. (Here, the exclamation point is part of the title.)
   - You lost the book *College Algebra*! (Here, the exclamation point is not part of the title, and so it is not italicized.)

6. Exclamation points are placed inside quotation marks only if they are part of the quotation. If they are not part of the quotation, they are placed outside of the quotation marks:
   - The woman screamed, "Get out of my way!"
   - I can't believe that my friend Jonas has been described as the "class clown"!

Everyday Punctuation Activity: Exclamation Point

In the following sentences, insert exclamation points in the appropriate places.

1. This is wonderful
2. Don't touch that beautiful vase
3. Who knows what is "right"
4. The man shouted out to his neighbor, "Good morning"
5. What a peaceful place
6. That is so strange
7. I don't believe it
8. "Run fast" the coach shouted out to the players
9. Thank goodness
10. This is scary

MyWritingLab™ For support in meeting this chapter's objectives, log in to www.mywritinglab.com and select **Final Punctuation**.

Commas

LO1
Use commas correctly

The **comma** (,) is typically used to separate the different parts of a sentence. There are some rules relating to the use of the comma that you should be familiar with:

1. Commas are used to separate words in a series:
   - Aunt Olga, Uncle Henry, Cousin Marie, and our neighbor Frank are all coming over for dinner tonight.
   - Paris, Marseilles, and Lyons are all cities in France.

2. Commas are used to separate adjectives when the word *and* can be inserted between them:
   - Sara tries to stay away from hot, greasy food.
   - Jonas enjoys cool, temperate climates.

3. Commas are used to separate independent clauses when they are joined by any of the seven coordinating conjunctions: *and, but, for, or, nor, so, yet*:
   - It was getting dark, but the children continued to play outside.
   - He canceled his trip to Jamaica, for he had run out of money.

4. Commas are used before clauses, phrases, or words that come before the main clause. Introductory clauses beginning with *after, although, as, because, if, since, when,* and *while* are usually followed by a comma:
   - Although the weather is poor, the game will continue.
   - Because it is so beautiful, Barbados is a favorite vacation spot.
   Note: A comma is not used after a main clause if the dependent clause follows the main clause:
   - Barbados is a favorite vacation spot, because it is so beautiful. (incorrect)

- Barbados is a favorite vacation spot because it is so beautiful. (correct)
- You should clean your room, when you have the time. (incorrect)
- You should clean your room when you have the time. (correct)

5. Commas are used after some introductory words such as *however, at the same time, well, yes,* and the like:
   - However, it is true that some animal species are already extinct.
   - Well, I am not sure about that.

6. Commas are used before, or surrounding the name or title of a person who is being addressed directly:
   - How are you, Tom?
   - Yes, Coach, I will play according to your instructions.

7. Commas are used to separate dates from years:
   - November 9, 1953, is Cambodia's independence day.
   - July 25, 2010, is when the accident occurred.

   Note: If any part of the date is omitted, the comma is left out:
   - December, 2013 is when Jacques will graduate. (incorrect)
   - December 2013 is when Jacques will graduate. (correct)

8. Commas are used to separate the name of a city from the name of a state or country; a comma is also placed after the state:
   - Harvard University was established in Cambridge, Massachusetts, in 1636.
   - Jane began kindergarten in Stuttgart, Germany, in 1999.

9. Commas are used to set off clauses, phrases, and sentences in the middle of a sentence that are not necessary to the meaning of a sentence:
   - January, which is the month in which I was born, marks the beginning of the calendar year.
   - Mongolia, which is a huge and sparsely populated land, is the 19th largest country in the world.

   Note: Commas are not used to set off clauses beginning with *that* or *who*:
   - The black car, that is parked in the garage, was recently in an accident. (incorrect)
   - The black car that is parked in the garage was recently in an accident. (correct)
   - The student, who studied the least, failed the class. (incorrect)
   - The student who studied the least failed the class. (correct)

10. Commas are used between a regular text and a quotation:
    - Adolfo asked his roommate, "What's for dinner?"
    - The manager asked the employee, "How many days vacation do you want?"

11. Commas are used to separate a statement from a question:
    - It is late, isn't it?
    - You are surprised, aren't you?

12. Commas are used to separate contrasting parts of sentences:
    - The cover of the book is white, not gray.
    - Colleen is the oldest child, not the youngest.

Everyday Punctuation Activity: Commas

In the following sentences, insert commas in the appropriate places.

1. The scientist took a long hard look at the specimen.
2. Mr. Ortiz is tired but he is not ready to go to bed yet.
3. The student has signed up for Composition Chemistry Religion and World History classes this semester.
4. At the same time they need to follow the rules.
5. Because the economy is so bad people are saving more.
6. The Republic of Kazakhstan declared independence on December 16 1991.
7. Nooshin's parents who are close to retirement live in Turkey.
8. Nooshin's parents moved to Istanbul Turkey in 1995.
9. The doctor asked the patient "How are you feeling today?"
10. They are all leaving aren't they?

MyWritingLab™ For support in meeting this chapter's objectives, log in to www.mywritinglab.com and select **Commas**.

Chapter 30

Other Punctuation Marks

Learning Objectives

In this chapter, you will learn to:

LO1 Use semicolons correctly

LO2 Use colons correctly

LO3 Use apostrophes correctly

LO4 Use hyphens and dashes correctly

LO5 Use quotation marks correctly

LO6 Use parentheses correctly

LO7 Use ellipses correctly

LO1

Use semicolons correctly

Semicolon

A **semicolon** (;) is a punctuation mark indicated by a period on top and a comma below the period. As in a period, a semicolon usually indicates the completion of a thought, though it doesn't bring a sentence to a complete close as a period does. There are some common rules related to the use of the semicolon that you should be familiar with.

1. A semicolon is used instead of a period to separate two independent sentences, or to join two independent sentences in a manner that indicates a relationship exists between the two sentences without using connecting words such as *and*, *but*, *or*, and so on:
   - The store owner closed shop for the day; his things were already in the car.
   - Niagara Falls is an amazing sight; it attracts thousands of visitors each year.
2. A semicolon commonly joins two independent clauses using transitions such as *however*, *in addition*, *on the other hand*, and *therefore* (see pages 445–448 for a discussion of transitions):

- Benita loves reading mystery stories; in addition, she reads a lot of romance novels too.
- Buying a house is expensive; however, Esther has decided that is exactly what she is going to do in the next few months.

3. A semicolon often separates units of a series, but only if there is one or more commas within the series (as there are with the Toyota models in this sentence):

- The vehicles that Uncle Martin would like to own over his lifetime include the Toyota Camry, Prius, or Rav4; the Honda CR-V; and the Jeep Grand Cherokee.

If there is not a comma in the series, then use a comma to separate the items in the sentence, rather than a semicolon:

- The top five things that I would like to see include the Grand Canyon, Niagara Falls, Buckingham Palace, the Dead Sea, and the Great Wall of China.

Everyday Punctuation Activity: Semicolons

In the following sentences, insert semicolons in the appropriate places.

1. Udiya is a Hebrew name for a girl it means God's fire.
2. Lars had a family emergency as a result, he left for Germany.
3. In the last four years, the meeting has been held in Tulsa, Oklahoma, Omaha, Nebraska, Wichita, Kansas and Des Moines, Iowa.
4. The volcano is not spewing as much lava as we had feared however we should remain careful.
5. Ming loves eating strawberries she makes smoothies from them too.
6. Street violence has escalated the police cannot control the crowds.
7. Food allergies can be very distressing however, we should not overlook their financial impact either.
8. There has been little growth in the number of voice minutes being used by cell phone users on the other hand, the number of text messages has soared.
9. Sales at the local hardware store have gone up however, it is because of more money being spent on advertisements.
10. Shakirah needs to return her library book she has kept it past the due date.

LO2

Use colons
correctly

Colon

A colon is a punctuation mark that consists of two dots along the same vertical line (:). It is a way of continuing a sentence rather than bringing it to a close. There are some common rules relating to the use of colons.

1. The colon is frequently used to introduce a list of items, especially when introductory words such as *for example*, *namely*, and the like are not used. The colon usually comes after a complete sentence and signifies that something more (a word, a phrase, a clause) will follow:
   - Susan needs to pick up the following items from the store: milk, eggs, bread, peanut butter, and chicken wings.
   - These are the errands Nusrat needs to run today: go to the post office, go to the bank, take his grandmother to the doctor, and pick up some household items from the hardware store.

2. A colon is often used before items introduced by words such as *the following*, *as follows*, *these*, *Hint*, and *Note*:
   - Please remember to do the following: prepare lunch, pick up the dry cleaning, and mail the letters.
   - Remember these: don't lie, don't steal, be nice.
   - Note: be sure to be on time for the meeting.

3. A colon is often used to signal that a second independent clause will explain the first independent clause:
   - Attending college is important for many reasons: it makes us more knowledgeable, it sharpens our critical thinking and analyzing skills, and it opens doors to higher-income jobs.
   - Making college more accessible has many benefits: it allows more students to get a higher education, it serves the local communities better, and it brings in more tuition revenue for the college.

4. A colon is used to introduce a direct quotation that is more than three lines in length:
   - The following is an excerpt from *The Diary of Anne Frank*, written on October 9, 1942:

   Our many Jewish friends and acquaintances are being taken away in droves. The Gestapo is treating them very roughly and transporting them in cattle cars to Westerbork, the big camp in Drenthe to which they're sending all the Jews....If it's that bad in Holland, what must it be like in those faraway and uncivilized places where the Germans are sending them? We assume that most of them are being murdered. The English radio says they're being gassed.

5. Colons are used in a formal letter when addressing someone:
   - Dear Miss Chang:

6. Colons are often used to separate an independent clause from a quotation. Usually, the independent clause that comes after the colon begins with a capital letter:
   - Our English teacher in high school often reminded us of her favorite proverb: "Slow and steady wins the race."
   - The boy's father often said: "Waste not, want not."

7. Colons are not used unless the sentence preceding it is an independent clause:
   - Ken's favorite music bands are: Bon Jovi and Metallica. (incorrect)
   - Ken's favorite music bands are Bon Jovi and Metallica. (correct: no colon used after "are")
   - Margo wants to visit: Greece, Bulgaria, and Israel. (incorrect)
   - Margo wants to visit Greece, Bulgaria, and Israel. (correct: no colon used after "visit")

8. Colons are often used to separate titles and subtitles:
   - *Matterhorn: A Novel of the Vietnam War*
   - *Daria: The Complete Animated Series*

9. Colons are used to express time:
   - The show starts at 6:15 p.m.
   - The plumber started work at exactly 8:00 a.m.

10. Colons are used to mark separation between place of publication and publisher in a bibliography:
    - Rose, Mike. *Lives on the Boundary*. New York: Penguin, 1989.

Everyday Punctuation Activity: Colons

In the following sentences, insert colons in the appropriate places.

1. Dear Sir

2. Lying in bed, he thought of several things that remained undone his unfinished homework, the laundry and paying his utility bills.

3. In his inaugural address, President Kennedy said "...ask not what your country can do for you—ask what you can do for your country."

4. My favorite places to write are at my dining table and at the desk in my bedroom.

(continued)

5. Zahra needs to take care of these things get the oil in her car changed, sign up for yoga class, and call her friend Lanai to see how she is doing.

6. The first class starts at 730 a.m., while the last class ends at 930 p.m.

7. Grandpa often repeated his favorite proverb over and over again "Better late than never."

8. Two things that an engineer is usually good at are mathematics and logical thinking.

9. Mr. President and Madame First Lady

10. The name of the book is *Two Fundamentals of Building Construction Materials and Methods.*

Apostrophe

LO3

Use apostrophes correctly

An **apostrophe** is a common punctuation mark ('). It has several functions:

1. An apostrophe indicates that one or more letters in a word are missing. The apostrophe is placed in the spot where the omission occurs:
   - You're (for *you are*) always early.

2. An apostrophe is also used to indicate the omission of numbers:
   - The United Nations was founded in '45.

3. An apostrophe indicates the possessive, both singular and plural:
   - Laura's book (singular possessive)
   - two doctors' cars (plural possessive)

   Note: Names and words ending with –s are not required to have the second "s" added to indicate possession. However, it is often done:
   - Mrs. Jones's mother
   - the Joneses' new TV

4. An apostrophe indicates plurals of abbreviations:
   - Mind your p's and q's.
   - Cross your t's and dot your i's.

5. The apostrophe is used where a noun is implied:
   - That is Sunday's, not today's, dinner. (for That is Sunday's dinner, not today's dinner)

There are some common rules related to the use of the apostrophe that you should be familiar with:

1. When an apostrophe is used with a singular compound noun, the apostrophe comes at the end of the compound word:
   - my father-in-law's property
   - her sister-in-law's music recital

2. With a plural compound noun, the apostrophe also comes at the end of the compound word:
   - their cousins-in-law's visits
   - the two daughters-in-law's wedding dresses

3. The apostrophe is used after the second name if two people possess the same thing:
   - Emily and Jake's grandparents

   Note: The apostrophe is never used with possessive pronouns (*ours, yours, his, hers, its, theirs*) because these words already show possession.
   - his's class schedule; yours' dinner (incorrect)
   - their clothes; that is ours (correct)

Everyday Punctuation Activity: Apostrophes

In the following sentences, insert apostrophes and possessive forms where appropriate:

1. Mrs. Xao and Mr. Jackson teaching schedule did not leave them with enough time to attend department meetings.
2. The Apollo 11 mission to the moon was launched in 69.
3. The commander-in-chief orders cannot be disobeyed.
4. Im going over to my friend Jennifers house for dinner tonight.
5. Mr Jones dry cleaning business had to be shut down.
6. It is theirs; leave it on the table.
7. The two sisters-in-law houses were on opposite sides of the street.
8. That is Mary, not Django jacket.
9. It was in the late 80s that Uncle Bill moved to Canada.
10. The child toy fell into the bathtub.

LO4

Use hyphens and dashes correctly

Hyphen and Dash

Hyphens and dashes are both commonly used punctuation marks. However, they are not exactly the same thing; there is a difference between the two.

A **hyphen** is usually a single line connecting the different parts of the same word. It is also used to divide words that split at the end of a line.

- up-to-date
- brother-in-law

There are some common rules relating to the use of hyphens that you should be familiar with:

1. Some words are always hyphenated:
   - ex-wife
   - mid-July
2. Hyphens are sometimes used to form compound words:
   - Teddy was unhappy with his low-paying job.
   - The Serbo-Croatian language has 31 Roman letters.
3. Hyphens are used when a prefix is added to a proper noun:
   - pro-Quebec protestors
4. Hyphens are used when prefixes are attached to a word:
   - self-promoting
   - quasi-experimental study
5. Hyphens are used when the same letter ends the prefix and begins the main word:
   - self-funded
6. Hyphens are used between two-word numbers:
   - twenty-two

Everyday Punctuation Activity: Hyphens

In the following sentences, insert hyphens in the appropriate places.

1. My step father in law is a very generous person.
2. Employers like to hire those who appear self assured.
3. Co ownership means two or more people share legal rights to a property.
4. Next year, Bernardo's grandmother will be ninety six years old.
5. Tom felt disturbed by the anti English sentiment he noticed around him.

A **dash** usually is made of two typed lines (--). (*Note:* Word processing software will often automatically convert two typed hyphens to a long dash. All but our first example show the use of the long dash.) Unlike the hyphen, it introduces extra material into the text. It also indicates a break or interruption in thought. There are some common rules relating to the use of dashes that you should be familiar with:

1. Dashes emphasize parts of a sentence or text:
   - Sri Lanka—also known as the Pearl of the Indian Ocean—is an island nation in South Asia.

- Bedouins—traditionally nomadic Arabs—are divided into five related tribes.

2. Dashes allow for a related thought to be intermixed with the main idea:
   - Mountain bikes—which are becoming more and more popular—can cost up to $800.
   - Falafel—a Middle Eastern food recognized worldwide—is made from chickpeas and/or fava beans.

3. Dashes are used after a list or series that introduces a sentence:
   - Measles, mumps, chicken pox—Sam has had them all in his childhood.
   - iPod, MP3 player, iPhone—Brandon has all the gadgets one can name.

4. Spaces are not used on either side of a dash:
   - The ice cream maker — gifted to Alicia by her great-aunt — broke. (incorrect)
   - The ice-cream maker—gifted to Alicia by her great-aunt—broke. (correct)
   - Gold prices — which have fallen from record highs — are still pretty steep. (incorrect)
   - Gold prices—which have fallen from record highs—are still pretty steep. (correct)

5. Commas are not used with dashes:
   - Bulgaria,—which shares a border with five other countries,—is located in southeastern Europe. (incorrect)
   - Bulgaria—which shares a border with five other countries—is located in southeastern Europe. (correct)

Everyday Punctuation Activity: Dashes

In the following sentences, insert dashes in the appropriate places:

1. Mr. Verghese whose house is the last one on the street gets up very early each morning.
2. The school drama club which has 35 members is presenting Shakespeare's Hamlet this weekend.
3. Sicily the largest island in the Mediterranean Sea has a sunny, dry climate.

(continued)

4. Salmon caught in Alaska the largest state in the United States are usually low in contaminants.

5. Parking on campus never very easy has gotten worse in the last year.

Quotation Marks

Quotation marks are punctuation marks indicated by a pair of raised double commas (" "), with the left pair inverted, while the right is not. They are usually used to set off, or emphasize, a particular word, or phrase, or a quotation or a piece of text, either by itself, or within a larger text. They are very helpful in avoiding plagiarism when writing research papers. Remember to both open and close quotation marks; do not open but not close quotation marks, or vice versa!

- "There is Mount Everest," the tour guide said to the tourists.
- "When did the flight take off?" the passenger asked the customer service agent.

There are some common rules related to the use of quotation marks that you should be familiar with:

1. Quotation marks are usually placed outside commas, periods, and question marks:
   - "It is late," said Mr. Peterson.
   - Mr. Peterson said, "It is late."
   - Mr. Peterson said, "It is late, isn't it?" (*Note*: a comma is placed before a quotation mark)

2. Quotation marks are placed inside the question mark if the question mark applies to the whole sentence:
   - Does the weatherman always say, "Today is going to be a great day"?
   - Does the patient still say, "I hate hospital food"?

3. Quotation marks are placed inside a period if there is a parenthetical reference at the end of a sentence:
   - Mike Rose wrote, "The Middle Ages envisioned the goddess of grammar, Grammatica, as an old woman " (1).
   - Jules Verne wrote, "The accident happened about five o'clock in the morning, as the day was breaking" (4).

4. Colons and semicolons are placed outside quotation marks:
   - Mr. Wong and Mr. Sharma proposed setting up a "neighborhood watch committee"; other neighbors agreed.
   - The entrepreneur emphasized "purposeful work ethic": sincerity, dedication, and hard work.

5. Quotation marks are used for direct quotations (but not for indirect ones):
   - I remember Rodrigo saying, "All's well that ends well."
   - I remember that Rodrigo said that all's well that ends well.

6. Quotations are used to represent exact language from well-known personalities:
   - "Writing is an exploration. You start from nothing and learn as you go," said American author and editor E. L. Doctorow.
   - "Give me a museum and I'll fill it," said Pablo Picasso.

7. If a quote is placed inside a sentence, and the quote is a complete one, the first letter of the quote is always capitalized:
   - The politician told the crowd, "Vote for anti-corruption, pro-people policies."
   - The writer urged his readers: "Read my book and follow its ideas."

8. If only a part of the original quotation is used, the first letter of the quote is not capitalized:
   - The politician told the crowd to vote for "anti-corruption, pro-people policies."
   - The writer urged his readers to read his book and "follow its ideas."

9. If a quote is broken up mid-sentence, the second part of the quote does not begin with a capital letter, and quotation marks go around both parts of the quotation:
   - "Before school starts next semester," Maya said, "my friend from Spain, Juan Carlos, will visit me."
   - "The water leaking from the faucet," said the plumber, "can be easily stopped by replacing the gasket."

10. If a direct quote has a spelling or grammar error, write that error exactly as it is, but then use the word "sic" after the error to indicate that the error belongs to the original quote and is not an error on your part:
    - "Sicily? I was born their (sic)." (should be "Sicily? I was born there")
    - "Come hear (sic)." (should be "Come here")

11. Quotation marks are not used around quotations that are more than five typed lines. The following quote from famous heart surgeon Christian Barnard demonstrates this:

    I had bought two male chimps from a primate colony in Holland. They lived next to each other in separate cages for several months before I used one as a [heart] donor. When we put him to sleep in his cage in preparation for the operation, he chattered and cried incessantly. We attached no significance to this, but it must have made a great impression on his companion, for when we removed the body to the operating room, the other chimp wept bitterly and was

inconsolable for days. The incident made a deep impression on me.
I vowed never again to experiment with such sensitive creatures.

12. Quotation marks are often used to enclose names of essays and short stories:
    - "A Modest Proposal" (essay)
    - "Araby" (short story)

13. Quotation marks can also be single quotation marks. They are used for quotes within quotes:
    - "Have you read the essay 'The Ancestral Bond'?" Karla asked Vladimir.
    - "Where can I get a copy of the short story 'The Necklace'?" the young man asked the person at the bookstore.

Everyday Punctuation Activity: Quotation Marks

In the following sentences, insert quotation marks in the appropriate places.

1. Finish your homework first, Mrs. Ericsson told her son Tony, and then make sure to do your laundry.
2. Have you read the article Mauritius Dreaming in today's *New York Times*? Lisa asked her Mauritian friend Carlsen.
3. The coach encouraged the players to dribble fast and furious.
4. We need the following items: Band-Aids, duct tape, and a wrench.
5. My father always said wastage is a crime.
6. Is the article titled Writing for College Students, he asked.
7. Carol complained, It is late, and I wish I could go home.
8. A lie cannot live said Martin Luther King, civil rights activist.
9. Kindergarten teacher Mrs. Wu wondered if it would start to rain during recess.
10. What do you wish to order the waitress asked the dinner guests.

Parentheses

LO6
Use parentheses correctly

Parentheses (singular "parenthesis") are indicated by the sign ( ), and they are helpful in offsetting text. There are some common rules related to the use of the parentheses that you should be familiar with:

1. Parentheses are used around words and/or numbers that clarify something, add additional information to the text, or that are used as an aside:

- The flight from New York to London is around five hundred dollars ($500). (The information in parentheses clarifies the amount.)
- The book on learning a second language (which Constantin bought yesterday) offers a lot of strategies for language learning. (The information in parentheses adds additional information.)
- Uncle Jason is a good cook (which, by the way, I will never be!). (The information in parentheses here is used around a phrase that is an aside and uses a punctuation mark, the exclamation point.)

2. Parentheses are used around numbers or letters in a list:
- Some of the songs recorded and/or written by the Beatles include (1) "A Hard Day's Night," (2) "All You Need Is Love," and (3) "Cry Baby Cry."

3. Periods or other punctuation marks are usually placed outside the parentheses. Punctuation marks are not used before parentheses:
- The receptionist asked the caller to remain on the line. (and she has been holding for the last 10 minutes) (incorrect)
- The receptionist asked the caller to remain on the line (and she has been holding for the last 10 minutes). (correct)
- They returned at the end of the day. (having lost their way in the forest) (incorrect)
- They returned at the end of the day (having lost their way in the forest). (correct)

4. If an entire sentence is placed within parentheses, then the final punctuation mark is placed within the parentheses:
- High blood pressure symptoms include headache, dizziness, blood pressure, and nausea. (Of course, not everybody gets all of these symptoms.)
- There are several things to know before buying a home. (Unfortunately, not everybody educates themselves about the home-buying process.)

5. Leave a space before the parentheses:
- It is cold(but not too windy). (incorrect)
- It is cold (but not too windy). (correct)

6. Parentheses are used around dates or citations:
- Kurosawa Akira (1910–1998) was a Japanese film director, producer, editor, and screenwriter.
- I'm not a very good writer, but I am excellent rewriter (James Michener).

Note: Do not overuse parentheses; doing so can take away from the content of the actual text.

Everyday Punctuation Activity: Parentheses

In the following sentences, insert parentheses in the appropriate places.

1. Perez is a good plumber though he did fail to repair the first leak.
2. The following countries are on Deniz's to-visit list: Australia, Indonesia, Norway, Sweden and Nigeria.
3. William Shakespeare 1564–1616 was a famous English playwright.
4. Two thousand dollars $2000 is a lot of money.
5. May you live all the days of your life Jonathan Swift.
6. Holly's late grandfather 1920–2005 ran a sporting goods business.
7. The following items will be important on your hiking trip: cell phone, flashlight, water, first-aid kit.
8. The true sign of intelligence is not knowledge but imagination Albert Einstein.
9. It is a beautiful summer day today though there are some clouds in the sky.
10. Michael Jackson 1958–2009 was an American recording artist and entertainer.

LO7

Use ellipses correctly

Ellipsis

An **ellipsis** is a punctuation mark comprising of three evenly spaced dots (**...**) with spaces between the dots and the letters or other marks preceding it or following it. The plural of ellipsis is *ellipses*. There are some common rules related to the use of ellipses that you should be familiar with:

1. The ellipsis is typically used to indicate that some words have been omitted from a sentence:
   - <u>Original sentence</u>: Russian athletes, who did not do very well during the 2010 Winter Olympics in Vancouver, have been asked to improve before the 2014 Olympics in Sochi, Russia.
   - <u>Sentence with an ellipsis</u>: Russian athletes...have been asked to improve before the 2014 Olympics in Sochi, Russia.
   - <u>Original sentence</u>: In 2004, biologists discovered four drowned polar bears in the Beaufort Sea, and suspect the actual number of drowned bears may have been considerably greater. Never before observed, biologists attributed the drowning to a combination of retreating ice and rougher seas.
   - <u>Sentence with an ellipsis</u>: In 2004, biologists discovered four drowned polar bears in the Beaufort Sea...biologists attributed the drowning to a combination of retreating ice and rougher seas.

Note: When you use an ellipsis, you may leave out punctuation such as commas that were in the original sentence.

2. If the omission in a sentence comes at the end of the sentence, the ellipsis is followed by the period, which means that there will be four dots:

- The judge thought hard about his decision regarding the prisoner ....
- The protestors marched through the streets of downtown Mexico City ....

MyWritingLab™ For support in meeting this chapter's objectives, log in to www.mywritinglab.com and select **Apostrophes, Quotation Marks, and Semicolons, Colons, Dashes, and Parentheses.**

Chapter **31**

Abbreviations and Numbers

Learning **O**bjectives

In this chapter, you will learn to:

LO1 Use abbreviations correctly

LO2 Use numbers correctly when writing

LO1

Use abbreviations correctly

Abbreviations

An **abbreviation** is a shortened form of a word or phrase. The shortened form is usually made up of letters from the original word or phrase.

- The word "information" is often abbreviated to "info."
- The word "automobile" is often abbreviated to "auto."

Formal academic writing generally does not encourage using abbreviations. Thus writing "thru" (for "through"), "nite" (for "night"), "C U" (for "see you"), "Sun" (for Sunday) are discouraged. However, some common abbreviations are usually well accepted. These include:

1. Titles:
   - Mr. (Mister)
   - Mrs. (Misssus)
   - Rev. (Reverend)
   - Dr. (Doctor)
   - St. (Saint)

   Other title abbreviations are not so commonly accepted. It is better to say "Professor Glau" than "Prof. Glau, " and "Senator Williams" instead of "Sen. Williams."

2. Some titles after names are standard abbreviations, and are accepted in academic writing:
   - Ph.D. (Arturo Wong, Ph.D.)
   - M.D. (Jenna Wilson, M.D.)
   - Jr. (Harry Connick Jr.)
   - Sr. (Farooq Abdus Sr.)

3. Other commonly accepted abbreviations include:
   a. Names of countries:
      - USA (United States of America)
      - UK (United Kingdom)
   b. Names of people:
      - MLK (Martin Luther King)
      - JFK (John F. Kennedy)

4. Initials of people's names:
   - W. H. Auden
   - T. S. Eliot
   - J. K. Rowling

5. Names of familiar institutions/corporations/organizations:
   - NYU (New York University)
   - HP (Hewlett-Packard)
   - IBM (International Business Machines)
   - EU (European Union)
   - OAU (Organization of African Unity)

6. Common but long phrases:
   - B.C. (before Christ)
   - mpg (miles per gallon)
   - mph (miles per hour)
   - a.m. (ante meridiem—morning)
   - p.m. (post meridiem—afternoon and evening)

   Note: The examples given in items 5 and 6 are *acronyms*, that is, words that are abbreviated using the first letters in a name or phrase. Some other examples of acronyms include:
   - FBI (Federal Bureau of Investigation)
   - CEO (chief executive officer)
   - CIA (Central Intelligence Agency)
   - NATO (North Atlantic Treaty Organization)
   - HTML (HyperText Markup Language)

7. Names of mathematical units:
   - in. (inches)
   - ft (feet)
   - lb (pounds)

8. Common terms:
   - e.g. (for example)
   - etc. (et cetera)
   - i.e. (id est—that is)
   - vol. (volume)
   - ed. (edition)

Grammar Spotlight: Abbreviations in College Writing

1. If you are not sure whether the abbreviation you are considering using in your college writing is acceptable, always write it out completely rather than risk writing an abbreviation that is considered improper.
2. Be consistent in your use of abbreviations. Do not use an abbreviation for a word in your writing, and then in the same piece of writing, write out the word in full.
3. Check with your professor which abbreviations are acceptable and which are not. Remember, people have different preferences.

LO2

Use numbers correctly when writing

Numbers

Using numbers in your writing can confuse you: should you write out the number as a figure, or should you write it out in words? There are some common rules associated with the use of numbers in writing that you should be familiar with.

1. If a sentence begins with a number, spell out the number:
   - Two thousand people attended last week's concert on the beach.
2. When a number consists of one or two words, it is spelled out:
   - There are only seven more days left till school begins.
3. A two-word number below one hundred is hyphenated:
   - Ninety-eight people applied for the position of lab assistant at the university laboratory.
4. Simple fractions that are written out are hyphenated:
   - One-third of the test-tube was filled with oxygen and two-thirds with carbon dioxide.
5. Figures are used for numbers that consist of more than two words:
   - Our photography club has 219 members.
6. Numbers in addresses are written out as figures:
   - We live at 1905 East University Drive.
7. Decades are spelled out:
   - Maggie's parents bought the house in the nineties.

8. Decades can also be written using figures, complete as well as incomplete:
   - Maggie's parents bought the house in the 1990s. / Maggie's parents bought the house in the '90s. (Note use of apostrophe before the incomplete numeral.)

9. Centuries are spelled out:
   - England produced many great novelists in the nineteenth century.

10. Figures are used for dates:
    - Joran's birthday is on January 31, 1990.

11. Figures are used for specific times of the day:
    - It is now 3:15 p.m.

12. The number is spelled out if you use the words "o clock":
    - Dinner will be served at six o'clock.

13. Figures are used for specific amounts of money:
    - The dress cost $40.25.

14. Figures are used for specific measurements:
    - The car raced across the freeway at 85 mph.

15. Figures are used for mixed fractions, decimals, and percentages:
    - 5 ¼; 2.9; 90 percent

16. Figures are used for volume, chapter, and page numbers:
    - Volume 4; Chapter 5; page 119

17. Figures are used for phone numbers:
    - The phone number for the airport is 1-800-123-4567.

18. Figures are used when creating lists:
    - We need the following items:
      1. A hammer
      2. A wrench
      3. A screwdriver

19. If there are two numbers beside each other, write one of them as a figure, and spell out the other one:
    - There were eight 14-year-olds in the room.

20. Be consistent; don't spell out numbers and use figures in the same sentence:
    - I deposited $500 in my checking account and two hundred and fifty dollars in my savings account. (incorrect)
    - I deposited $500 in my checking account and $250 in my savings account. (correct)

Everyday Writing Activity: Using Numbers in Writing

Each of the following sentences contains numbers. Indicate if the numbers are written correctly or not. Indicate the correct ones with a C, and the incorrect ones with an I. Then correct the incorrect ones.

1. The Svend family lives at eight hundred West Drive.
2. The twins were born on September 10, 2000.
3. The professor asked the class to read chapter five for the test.
4. 2 employees have left the company in the last week.
5. The game starts at two o'clock.
6. Technology is expected to make great strides in the 21st century.
7. There are 115 days left till the end of the year.
8. There was a three percent growth in the economy last year.
9. There are 5 10-pound crates of apples in the farmhouse.
10. One-fourth of the class was unprepared for the test.

MyWritingLab™   For support in meeting this chapter's objectives, log in to **www.mywritinglab.com** and select **Abbreviations and Numbers**.

Spelling

Using spelling correctly is very important for accuracy in writing. Misspelled words are annoying to read, and they can even distort the meaning of your communication. Spelling errors should be corrected during the editing process, not during the invention or drafting process (see Chapters 6–8 for more on the writing process). If you are unsure of how to spell a word, use any standard English dictionary, or use the spell-check program offered by your computer. Incorrect words will be flagged by your spell-checker, probably through underlining of the word. Once the error is corrected (the spell-checker will help you correct the word), the spell-checker will remove the flag from the word, and you will know that the word is now correctly spelled. Note, though, that computer spell-checkers will not indicate if you use the wrong word if that word is spelled correctly (*too* instead of *two*, for example, or *half* instead of *have*).

Some of the most common spelling errors in English are caused by:

- Homonyms
- Confusing word pairs
- Unfamiliarity with rules of capitalization in English

In this chapter, we will discuss these errors one by one.

LO1 Homonyms

LO1
Recognize and spell words that sound alike (homonyms)

Homonyms, sometimes known as **homophones,** are groups of words that often share the same spelling and same pronunciation, but have different meanings. For instance, *right* (correct) and *right* (opposite of left) are homonyms. Sometimes homonyms don't share the same spelling, but share the same pronunciation. More examples of homonyms are included here:

1. Homonyms that share the same spelling and pronunciation:
   - Bark (the sound made by a dog) and bark (the trunk of a tree)
   - Bed (place to sleep) and bed (flower bed, truck bed)
   - Mine (belonging to me) and mine (an underground excavation pit)
   - Shed (discard) and shed (shack, hut)
   - Watch (wristwatch) and watch (look at, observe)

2. Homonyms that share the same pronunciation but not the same spelling:
   - New (novel) and knew (past tense of *know*)
   - No (rejection) and know (to be familiar with/acquainted with)
   - One (the number) and won (to be victorious)
   - Sight (view) and site (place, location)
   - Would (past tense of the verb *to be*) and wood (lumber)

Everyday Writing Activity: Homonyms

Write down the homonyms for the following words, and indicate what kind of homonyms they are (share the same spelling and pronunciation or share the same pronunciation but not the same spelling):

1. Aloud
2. Arm
3. Be
4. Bored
5. Case
6. Crews
7. Die
8. Dew
9. Eye
10. Ewe
11. Fair
12. Flea
13. Fly
14. Grate
15. Hamper
16. Hare
17. Heard
18. In
19. It's
20. Jean

21. Know
22. Last
23. Led
24. Left
25. Lone
26. Male
27. Meat
28. Not
29. Nun
30. Pair
31. Pause
32. Rain
33. Right
34. Sail
35. Seen
36. Threw
37. To
38. Waist
39. Wave

After you have finished this activity, choose eight to ten of these homonym pairs and write sentences of your own using both pairs of words. Then respond to the following questions:

1. What (if any) differences did you notice as you wrote sentences using the homonyms?
2. Did one word in a pair work better than the other? If so, why do you think that happened?

Confusing Word Pairs

LO2

Identify commonly confused words and spell them correctly

When writing, you may sometimes feel confused about which word to use when two words sound alike, and look almost (but not quite) alike, and even though they mean different things, you may not be familiar with their meanings. It is when faced with such **confusing word pairs** that you may make the wrong word choice, which, in turn, negatively affects the quality of your writing by making your communication less effective. It is important, therefore, to be familiar with such confusing word pairs. Sometimes such words can come in groups of three. Here is a list of some commonly confused words:

- Assure/ensure (to comfort, promise etc./make sure, make certain)
- Accept/except (to admit, acknowledge, recognize etc./excluding)
- Advice/advise (guidance, recommendation etc. [noun]/guide, recommend [verb])
- Affect/effect (influence, shape/result, consequence, etc.)

- Allusion/illusion (reference, mention/false impression, fantasy)
- Altar/alter (place where certain rites are performed/change, transform)
- Apart/a part (separate, not together/belonging to)
- Ascent/assent (climb/agree)
- Beside/besides (next to, adjacent to, overcome by/in addition, moreover)
- Brake/break (pedal, slow down/split, crack open)
- Breath/breathe (air that is inhaled or exhaled/inhale or exhale)
- Buy/by/bye (purchase/beside, through/bid farewell)
- Cite/site/sight (refer to/location/see, spectacle, etc.)
- Coarse/course (rough, crude etc./route, path, etc.)
- Compliment/complement (praise/balance)
- Conscious/conscience (aware of, mindful of/principles, awareness of right and wrong)
- Council/counsel (board, committee/advice, lawyer)
- Decent/descent (polite, well-mannered/climb down, drop)
- Desert/dessert (arid land/final course of a meal, usually a sweet dish)
- Discreet/discrete (careful, tactful/separate, distinct)
- Eminent/imminent (famous, well-known/at any moment, about to happen)
- Envelop/envelope (to cover, wrap/a paper container for a letter or document)
- Forth/fourth (forward/from the number four)
- Hear/here (listen to, pay attention to/now, in this location)
- Hole/whole (gap, opening/entire, complete)
- Insure/ensure (to guarantee against loss/make certain, guarantee)
- Its/it's (possessive form of it/shortened form of "it is" or "it has")
- Knew/new (had knowledge of, was familiar with/original)
- Know/no (have knowledge of, be familiar with/the negative, to refuse, etc.)
- Later/latter (afterward/the next)
- Led/lead/lead (take to, direct to/to go first, show the way/bluish-gray metal)
- Lie/lay (to stretch out/to stretch out, to put down)
- Lie/lie (to stretch out/to tell an untruth)
- Lose/loose (to misplace something/not fastened tightly)
- Marital/martial (related to marriage/military, warlike)
- Past/passed (earlier/went by, approved)
- Peace/piece (calm, tranquility/part, portion)
- Plane/plain (airplane/simple, basic)
- Principal/principle (chief, main/code, set of beliefs)
- Quiet/quite (without sound, to certain extent)
- Rain/rein/reign (rainfall/harness/rule over, period in office)

- Sea/see (ocean/sight, catch sight of, observe)
- Stationary/stationery (not moving, at a standstill/writing material such as paper, letterheads, envelopes)
- Supposed to/suppose (intended to, expected to/assume)
- Than/then (in relation to, except/next, followed by)
- Their/there/they're (possessive form of "they"/indicates location/contraction of "they are")
- Threw/through (to hurl something/from beginning to end, to penetrate)
- To/too/two (direction to place, person, time/also/the number two)
- Vain/in vain (proud, arrogant/without success)
- Vain/vein (proud, arrogant/an element, a streak, blood vessel in body)
- Weak/week (feeble, fragile/time period of seven days)
- Wear/were (dress/past tense of the verb "to be")
- Weather/weather (climate/endure, withstand)
- Weather/whether (climate/used for alternatives)
- Who/whom (of a person/objective case of "who")
- Your/you're (possessive of "you"/contraction of "you are")

Everyday Writing Activity: Confusing Word Pairs

Choose eight to ten of the word pairs/word groups from the preceding list, and write sentences of your own using all the words in a pair/group. Then respond to the following questions:

1. What (if any) differences did you notice as you wrote sentences using the different words in the same pair/group?
2. Did one word in a pair/group work better than the other? If so, why do you think that happened?

LO3
Use proper capitalization

Capitalization

Capitalization refers to writing a word or letter or phrase in uppercase letters.

Capitalization is important to good writing; if you do not capitalize in the right places, your writing will be considered error-ridden. It is important, though, unless it is a special circumstance, to not capitalize throughout; that is considered the equivalent of "shouting" at the reader, and thus, very rude. There are some common rules related to the use of capitalization that you should be familiar with:

1. The first letter of the first word of a new sentence is always capitalized:
   - it was a bright, sunny morning. (incorrect)
   - It was a bright, sunny morning. (correct)

2. Names of people are always capitalized:
   - Mary
   - Suneel

3. "I" is always capitalized, even if used in mid-sentence:
   - I wish she would hurry up.
   - It wasn't clear whether I was invited to the soccer game or not.

4. Names of buildings, schools, parks, statues, and the like are always capitalized:
   - the GE Building
   - Maryville High School
   - Sugarhouse Park
   - the Statue of Liberty

5. Names of countries, continents, cities, towns, and the like are always capitalized:
   - Botswana (country)
   - Africa (continent)
   - Sydney (city)
   - Gotsiz (small town in Austria)

6. Compass directions, when they indicate specific parts of a country or region, are sometimes, though not always, capitalized:
   - Southeast Asia
   - western United States
   - eastern Europe

   Note: Do not capitalize directions when they are not used as names:
   - The log cabin was built on the south side of the mountains.

7. Days of the week, months, and holidays are capitalized:
   - Sunday (day)
   - July (month)
   - New Year's Day (holiday)

8. Seasons are capitalized only when used in a title:
   - the Summer 2013 class schedule

   Note: do not capitalize seasons when they are used generally:
   - Every summer, Raima and her friends go camping.

9. Races, nationalities, and names of languages are capitalized:
   - Polynesian (race)
   - Polish (nationality)
   - Swahili (language)

10. Academic and professional degrees are capitalized:
    - MS (Master of Science)
    - MBA (Master of Business Administration)
    - P.E. (Professional Engineer)

11. Names of historical periods and events are capitalized:
    - the Qing Dynasty (historical period)
    - the Great Depression (historical period)
    - the Second World War (event)

12. Names of government departments, offices, and the like are always capitalized:
    - Internal Revenue Service
    - Social Security Office
    - Immigration and Naturalization Service
    - the Supreme Court

13. Names of sacred books and names of religions are always capitalized:
    - the Bible (sacred book)
    - the Quran (sacred book)
    - the Bhagavad Gita (sacred book)
    - Islam (religion)
    - Judaism (religion)

14. Names of all forms of God are always capitalized:
    - God
    - the Almighty
    - Allah

15. Names of all branches of the military are always capitalized:
    - the U.S. Army
    - the Royal Air Force
    - the Marine Corps

16. Names of organizations, organized bodies, associations, societies, corporations etc. are always capitalized:
    - Organization of Petroleum Exporting Countries
    - Federalists
    - Association of Professional Genealogists
    - Society of Professional Journalists
    - Microsoft Corporation

17. Academic, religious, and government titles are always capitalized when it is part of their name:
    - Professor Patel (academic title)
    - Reverend Perry (religious title)
    - President Kennedy (government title)
    - Congressman Shapiro (government title)

    Note: Titles are not capitalized when it is not part of a proper name:
    - The professor reminded the class about the upcoming mid-term exam.

18. Book titles, journal titles, TV shows, movie names, musical composition names, radio program names and document and report titles are always capitalized:
    - *College Calculus* (book title)
    - *College English* (journal title)
    - CNN *Headline News* (television show)
    - *The Blind Side* (movie title)
    - "Banquet Celeste" (musical composition)
    - "Agriculture Report" (radio program)
    - "Childcare in Kentucky: Current Status and Future Improvements" (report title)

19. Names of courses are always capitalized:
    - HIS 101 (History 101)
    - NUR 215 (Nursing 215)

    Note: Names of subjects are not capitalized, unless they refer to languages or unless they begin a sentence:
    - English, Latin, psychology, biology, physics
    - Physics was Gene's favorite subject in high school.

20. Names of brands are always capitalized:
    - Honda
    - Sony
    - Adidas

21. Acronyms are always capitalized:
    - TESOL (teaching English to speakers of other languages)
    - UN (United Nations)
    - AIDS (acquired immune deficiency syndrome)

Everyday Writing Activity: Capitalization

Each of the following sentences contains words that should be capitalized. Capitalize those words.

1. it was not clear to me whether i should deliver the package meant for hiram.
2. the word mri stands for magnetic resonance imaging.
3. in the fall, we will make a trip to the american southwest to see the grand canyon national park in arizona and zion national park in utah.
4. I am wondering if professor hafez will teach art 100 next fall. If not, I will take the class with another professor in spring 2013.

5. judith would like to buy a samsung 50-inch television set before next christmas.

6. have you seen the movie *julie and julia?* no, but i read a review in the local newspaper, the daily herald.

7. the president is due to speak tomorrow to the american red cross workers. After that, he will address both republicans and democrats in new york.

8. roshan is planning a trip down the nile river in egypt before starting his mba degree at the university of bonn in germany.

9. after dinner, mika usually watches her favorite television show, *the Simpsons*, reads a few pages from the bible, and then goes to bed.

10. on Sunday, the us coast guard held practice exercises off the coast of louisiana that drew a big crowd of spectators.

MyWritingLab™ For support in meeting this chapter's objectives, log in to www.mywritinglab.com and select **Spelling** and **Easily Confused Words**.

Chapter 33

Word Choice

Learning Objectives

In this chapter, you will learn to:

LO1 Use synonyms properly

LO2 Identify antonyms

LO3 Identify prefixes and suffixes

LO4 Use contractions properly

LO5 Avoid colloquialisms

LO6 Avoid sexist language

LO7 Avoid wordiness

Vocabulary refers to the body of words that exist in any language to identify things, ideas, events, and so on. Writers, readers, speakers, and listeners draw on this database for words they need to communicate and to understand what is being communicated. Having a good vocabulary helps a person be a good writer, a good reader, a good speaker, and also a good listener.

However, the vocabulary a person has must be used in a particular way for it to make sense. As a writer, misusing vocabulary rules will interfere with writing accuracy. Not knowing some of the complexities related to vocabulary in English will also interfere with reading, speaking, and listening accuracy. This chapter of the handbook will help you understand some of the common vocabulary problems and help you become stronger writers, readers, speakers, and listeners.

In the next few pages, we will discuss some of the most common vocabulary-related issues that you need to be aware of. We will be looking at the following:

- Synonyms
- Antonyms

- Prefixes and suffixes
- Contractions
- Avoiding colloquialisms
- Avoiding sexist language
- Avoiding wordiness

LO1

Use synonyms properly

Synonyms

Synonyms are words that are different, but that have similar or identical meanings. Synonyms can be nouns, verbs, adjectives, adverbs, or prepositions, provided that both words of a pair belong to the same part of speech. Thus, *create* and *make* (both verbs) are synonyms. The similar/identical words are said to be **synonymous** with each other. More examples of synonyms are included here:

- died   expired
- begin   start
- cinema   movie
- car   automobile
- enormous   huge

- accomplish   achieve
- teacher   instructor
- class   course
- lecture   speech
- fortunate   lucky

Everyday Writing Activity: Synonyms

Write synonyms for the following words. Please note that many of these words may have more than one synonym. Use a dictionary or thesaurus to help you if necessary.

1. To accumulate
2. Apparent
3. Attractive
4. To begin
5. Belly
6. To chop
7. Conflict
8. Correct
9. Defective
10. To disappear
11. Eager
12. Explode
13. Fantastic

14. Fool
15. Garbage
16. To glitter
17. Handsome
18. Hunger
19. Impolite
20. Isolated
21. Jealous
22. Lucid
23. Maybe
24. Miserable
25. Necessary
26. Nonstop
27. To object
28. Outside
29. Possibility
30. Praise
31. To receive
32. To remark
33. Select
34. Significant
35. To transform
36. Uncared for
37. Uncooked
38. Vague
39. In vain
40. Warranty

After you have finished this activity, choose eight to ten of these synonymous pairs and write sentences of your own using both pairs of words. Then respond to the following questions:

1. What (if any) differences did you notice as you wrote sentences using the word pairs?
2. Did one word in a pair work better than the other? If so, why do you think that happened?

LO2

Identify antonyms

Antonyms

Whereas synonyms are words that have more or less the same meaning, **antonyms** are pairs of words that have a meaning opposite to one another. Thus, *hot* and *cold* are antonyms. More examples of antonyms are included here:

- alcoholic   nonalcoholic
- child   adult
- clever   dull
- happy   sad
- hungry   full

- sleepy   awake
- peace   war
- slow   fast
- vegetarian   nonvegetarian
- wet   dry

Everyday Writing Activity: Antonyms

Write antonyms for the following words. Please note that many of these words may have more than one antonym. Use a dictionary or thesaurus to help you if necessary.

1. Accept
2. Advantage
3. Beautiful
4. Bless
5. Capable
6. Cheap
7. Decrease
8. Discourage
9. Easy
10. East
11. False
12. Found
13. Gloomy
14. Guest
15. Happy
16. Healthy
17. Increase
18. Inside
19. Junior
20. Justice
21. Knowledge
22. Laugh
23. Landlord
24. Maximum
25. Minority
26. Near
27. North
28. Out
29. Open
30. Past

31. Permanent
32. Rich
33. Rough
34. Slow
35. Sense
36. Tall
37. Top
38. Under
39. Victory
40. Within

After you have finished this activity, choose eight to ten of these pairs and write sentences of your own using both pairs of words. Then respond to the following questions:

1. What (if any) differences did you notice as you wrote sentences using the word pairs?
2. Did one word in a pair work better than the other? If so, why do you think that happened?

Prefixes and Suffixes

LO3

Identify prefixes and suffixes

A **prefix** is an attachment to a word that is placed in *front* of the word. This attachment usually changes or modifies the meaning of the word. Understanding the meaning of some common prefixes can help readers understand the meaning of a word. For example, the prefix "ex" is added to the word "wife" to indicate that a particular woman is no longer the wife of a particular man. We can understand this if we understand that "ex" refers to "former" or "something or someone in the past." The following table shows some common prefixes:

At a Glance: Prefixes		
Prefix	**Meaning**	**Examples**
an-	without	anemic, anarchy
ante-	before	anterior, antecedent
anti-	against	anti-war, anti-religion
auto-	self	automatic, autobiography

Prefix	Meaning	Examples
circum-	around	circumference, circumnavigate
co-	with	co-author, co-conspirator
de-	away from	deflate, decrease
en-	put into	encircle, enclose
ex-	former	ex-landlord, ex-tenant
extra-	more than	extracurricular, extraordinary
hetero-	different	heterogeneous, heterosexual
homo-	same	homogeneous, homosexual
hyper-	more	hyperactive, hypertension
il-, im-, in-, ir-	without	illegitimate, immature, insensitive, irresponsible
in-	into	inject, insert
inter-	between	interval, international
macro-	large	macroeconomics, macromolecules
micro-	small	microorganism, microscope
mono-	one	monologue, monotheistic
non-	without	nonstick, nonsense
post-	after	postscript, postmortem
pre-	before	premeditate, prejudge
sub-	under, below	subway, substandard
tri-	three	trimester, triangle
vit-, viv-	life	vitality, vivacity

Unlike a prefix, a **suffix** is an attachment to a word that is placed at the *end* of a word. Like a prefix, it can alter the form and meaning of the word to which it is attached. For instance, the suffix "er" added to the word "teach" results in the word "teacher" which means somebody who teaches. We can understand this if we understand that "er" refers to "the one who." The following table shows some common suffixes:

At a Glance: Suffixes

Suffix	Meaning	Examples
-able, -ible	capable of	doable, legible
-ac, -ic	pertaining to	maniac, aquatic
-ate	to make	dedicate, consecrate
-cide	kill	suicide, genocide
-cy	state of being	democracy, theocracy
-er, -or	person who	trekker, mentor
-fy	to make	liquefy, solidify
-ics	having to do with	mathematics, physics
-ism	belief in	capitalism, socialism
-ist	believer in, doer	communist, physicist
-ity	state of being	audacity, paucity
-logy	study of	geology, biology
-oid	resembling	meteoroid, asteroid
-ose	full of	morose, glucose
-osis	condition	tuberculosis, osteoporosis
-ous	full of	advantageous, dangerous
-phobia	fear of	claustrophobia, homophobia
-sis	condition of	emphasis, paralysis
-tude	state of	altitude, multitude
-ty	state of	loyalty, enmity
-ulent	nature of	fraudulent, corpulent
-ward	in the direction of	backward, forward
-wise	in the direction of	clockwise, otherwise
-wright	one who is	cartwright, playwright
-y	state of	cloudy, sunny

Everyday Writing Activity: Prefixes

Choose any five of the words created by prefixes and write sentences of your own using the words.

Everyday Writing Activity: Suffixes

Choose any five of the words created by suffixes and write sentences of your own using the words.

LO4

Use contractions properly

Contractions

A **contraction** is a shortened form of a word or group of words, achieved through the omission of certain letters. The omission is usually indicated by the use of apostrophes in the place of the missing letters. Though contractions are more common in spoken English, they are also used in written English.

At a Glance: Contractions			
Original Word	**Contraction**	**Original Word**	**Contraction**
cannot	can't	he is	he's
has not	hasn't	she is	she's
was not	wasn't	we are	we're
will not	won't	you are	you're
could not	couldn't	they are	they're
should not	shouldn't	is not	isn't
did not	didn't	was not	wasn't
are not	aren't	were not	weren't
is not	isn't	that is	that's
here is	here's	what is	what's
where is	where's	I would	I'd
it is	it's	you would	you'd

Original Word	Contraction	Original Word	Contraction
I have	I've	he would	he'd
you have	you've	she would	she'd
they have	they've	they would	they'd
has not	hasn't	would have	would've
I will	I'll	should have	should've
you will	you'll	could have	could've
they will	they'll	we have	we've
that is	that's	had not	hadn't
what is	what's	have not	haven't
I am	I'm	does not	doesn't
you are	you're	did not	didn't
must not	mustn't	what is	what's
how is	how's	of the clock	o'clock
how are	how're	madam	ma'am

Everyday Writing Activity: Contractions

Please write contractions for the underlined words.

1. <u>Who is</u> going to pick up Juan Carlos from the airport?
2. <u>Do not</u> do that!
3. <u>She had</u> already left the party by the time I got there.
4. <u>Is it not</u> too early to go to bed?
5. The car <u>was not</u> in the parking lot.
6. Africa <u>is not</u> the dark continent it has sometimes been thought to be.
7. The neighbors <u>should have</u> helped Mr. Thomas when he was sick.
8. <u>It is</u> easier to take things day-by-day.
9. <u>I am</u> prepared to declare that <u>that is</u> the truth.
10. <u>He is</u> the star athlete on the team.

Colloquialisms

LO5
Avoid
colloquialisms

Colloquial style refers to a pattern of speech or writing that is very informal in tone. It is not typically used in formal speech or writing, and it is often considered inappropriate if used in academic prose, even though it is standard conversational language for many.

- Where are y'all going?
- Where are you all/all of you going? (better)
- I gonna do what I wanna do.
- I am going to do what I want to do. (better)
- How are you, dude?
- How are you? (better)

Everyday Writing Activity: Colloquialisms

Each of the following sentences is a colloquial expression. Underline the colloquialisms and then rewrite the sentences so that they are more appropriate for academic writing.

1. Dominique ain't nothing if not a miser.
2. He is the spitting image of his maternal uncle.
3. Romero's great-grandfather kicked the bucket yesterday.
4. Jake often wished he was as strong as that guy down the street.
5. You bought a new car? That is so cool!
6. This job is the real deal.
7. Unfortunately, Mohsin was involved in a fender bender yesterday.
8. Howdy!
9. We traveled to Niagara Falls, and whoa! were we amazed!
10. Be careful what you say to him; he is a big enchilada.

Sexist Language

LO6
Avoid sexist
language

Sexist language is language that excludes a particular gender when that gender should not be excluded. In the past, masculine nouns and pronouns have been used in cases where the gender was unknown or when the instance included both male and female genders. Today, however, such language is usually considered biased, and, therefore, offensive, even though it may have occurred unintentionally as a result of perpetuation of gender-role stereotypes. A writer who uses sexist language may not command respect from the audience. You should, therefore, guard against using sexist language in your writing.

- Mankind (sexist, because it refers to both men and women)
- Humankind (nonsexist)
- Chairman (sexist, if it refers to a woman holding the position)
- Chairperson/chair (nonsexist)

Solving the Problem of Sexism in Language

There are several ways to solve the problem of sexism in language that you should be familiar with:

1. Rewrite the entire sentence so that the sexist language is erased without changing the meaning. Often, this is done by changing the singular subject to the plural:
   - A store owner needs to make sure he has adequate insurance. (sexist)
   - Store owners need to make sure their stores are adequately insured. (nonsexist)
   - A person alone at home should make sure his front door is locked. (sexist)
   - Persons alone at home should make sure their front door is always locked. (nonsexist)

2. Change the pronoun subject to a noun subject (unless the pronoun subject refers to a specific individual):
   - Give her the directions to the canyon. (sexist)
   - Give the driver the directions to the canyon. (nonsexist)
   - Make sure he finds the shopping experience comfortable. (sexist)
   - Make sure the shopper finds the shopping experience comfortable. (nonsexist)

3. Substitute the gender-specific pronoun with an article (unless the pronoun refers to a specific individual):
   - Who left his book here? (sexist)
   - Who left the book here? (nonsexist)
   - Who left her car in the no-parking zone? (sexist)
   - Who left the car in the no-parking zone? (nonsexist)

4. Replace the gender-specific pronoun with "you":
   - If a student works hard, she can maintain a good GPA. (sexist)
   - If you work hard, you can maintain a good GPA. (nonsexist)
   - If a patient takes his medications daily, he will get better. (sexist)
   - If you take your medications daily, you will get better. (nonsexist)

5. Avoid sexist salutations with non-gender-specific salutations:
   - Dear Sir, Dear Madam (sexist)
   - To Whom It May Concern/The Hiring Manager (nonsexist)

6. Write out both pronoun options (he/she, his/her, him/her):
   - Each writer needs to check with his editor when his manuscript is due. (sexist)
   - Each writer needs to check with his/her editor when his/her manuscript is due. (nonsexist)
   - Each skier needs to bring his own ski equipment. (sexist)
   - Each skier needs to bring his/her own ski equipment. (nonsexist)

Note: Be careful about over-using pronouns in this way; it can make your writing clumsy.

Some common alternatives to sexist terms are provided in the following table.

At a Glance: Avoiding Sexist Terms	
Sexist Term	**Nonsexist Term**
businessman/businesswoman	businessperson
caveman/cavewoman	cave dweller
common man	average person
congressman	congress person/congressional representative
fireman	firefighter
freshmen	first year students
housewife	homemaker
manpower	workers, employees, staff
old wives' tale	myth
policeman	police officer
sportsman/sportswoman	athlete
waiter/waitress	food server
you guys	everyone, everybody

Everyday Writing Activity: Avoiding Sexist Language

Each of the following sentences contains language that is considered sexist. Underline the problem word or phrase and write out a nonsexist version of the sentence.

1. The mailman delivers letters in all kinds of weather.
2. A lawyer should learn all the finer points of law at his law school.
3. A college student should never spend his money unwisely.
4. Air hostesses work hard to please the passengers.
5. Who is at the door? I hope it's not a salesman.
6. Firemen are often considered heroes for the work that they do.
7. Who left his library books here?
8. Corporate wives are also invited.
9. Each hiker needs to bring with him a blanket, a flashlight, bottled water, and a cell phone.
10. Drawings by cavemen indicate what life was like in prehistoric times.

LO7
Avoid wordiness

Wordiness

Wordiness means using unnecessary words. In writing, it means using unnecessary words while writing, and it should be avoided. It is one of the most common problems faced by writers. However, the problem is easily corrected through careful editing and proofreading. This will eliminate the unnecessary words that obscure ideas, distract readers, and serve no purpose other than to fill up space. Just as we trim the fat from the meat, in the same way you need to make your writing concise and to the point by eliminating words and phrases that don't contribute meaning to your writing. Do not stuff your writing with empty phrases so you can meet the required page length or word limit set by your professor. Some common patterns of wordiness are included here so you can make yourselves familiar with them and avoid them in your own writing:

1. Using words with the same meaning twice:
   - Please <u>reconsider again</u> your decision to not hire Mr. Stevens. (wordy)
   - Please reconsider your decision to not hire Mr. Stevens. (better)
   - A <u>consensus of opinion</u> has been reached. (wordy)
   - A consensus has been reached. (better)
   - The squirrel ran <u>fast and swift</u>. (wordy)
   - The squirrel ran fast. (better)

- Aunt Lubna is <u>sleepy and drowsy</u> from all the pain medications. (wordy)
- Aunt Lubna is sleepy from all the pain medications. (better)

2. Using phrases instead of a single word:
   - <u>At this point in time</u>, there are no plans to raise taxes. (wordy)
   - There are no plans now to raise taxes. (better)
   - <u>Due to the fact that</u> it was late, we took a cab. (wordy)
   - Because it was late, we took a cab. (better)
   - <u>In the view of the fact</u> that tuition has been raised, students will have to pay more. (wordy)
   - Because tuition has been raised, students will have to pay more. (better)
   - <u>To come to a conclusion, therefore,</u> we need to pass a resolution. (wordy)
   - Therefore, we need to pass a resolution. (better)

3. Using "catch-all" phrases:
   - <u>The fact of the matter is</u> the city has run out of money. (wordy)
   - The fact is the city has run out of money. (better)
   - <u>One aspect of this is</u> that more people read online newspapers. (wordy)
   - One point is that more people read online newspapers. (better)
   - <u>In today's world,</u> almost everybody carries a mobile device. (wordy)
   - Today almost everybody carries a mobile device. (better)
   - <u>The youth of today</u> are often more ambitious than their parents were. (wordy)
   - The youth are often more ambitious than their parents were. (better)

4. Using wordy verbs:
   - <u>To have an expectation</u> of gifts can mean being disappointed. (wordy)
   - To expect gifts can mean being disappointed. (better)
   - <u>To make an acquisition</u> of property is Uncle Lambert's goal. (wordy)
   - To acquire property is Uncle Lambert's goal. (better)
   - <u>To have an intention of</u> contributing to charity is a worthy goal. (wordy)
   - To intend to contribute to charity is a worthy goal. (better)
   - The board members need <u>to make a decision</u> as quickly as possible. (wordy)
   - The board members need to decide as quickly as possible. (better)

5. Unnecessary use of the verbs "to be" and "being":
   - Writing is considered <u>to be</u> a necessary skill for success in college. (wordy)
   - Writing is considered a necessary skill for success in college. (better)
   - The mountaineers canceled their expedition for the day because of the climate <u>being</u> very snowy. (wordy)
   - The mountaineers canceled their expedition for the day because of the very snowy climate. (better)

6. Using passive instead of active verbs:
   - The train was missed by the tourists because they were late. (wordy)
   - The tourists missed the train because they were late. (better)
   - The musical performance at the Opera House was much appreciated by Liang-Yu and Deng. (wordy)
   - Liang-Yu and Deng appreciated greatly the musical performance at the Opera House. (better)
   - The unpopular politician was much maligned by the crowd. (wordy)
   - The crowd maligned the unpopular politician. (better)
   - The shopping mall was visited by Neeta and three of her cousins. (wordy)
   - Neeta and three of her cousins visited the shopping mall. (better)
   Note: Active verbs make the sentences more clear and concise.

7. Overusing relative pronouns such as *who, whose, which, that*:
   - It was the nurse who said the patient must get more rest. (wordy)
   - The nurse said the patient must get more rest. (better)
   - The Introduction to Dance course, which is called DAN 100, is Julia's favorite. (wordy)
   - The Introduction to Dance course, DAN 100, is Julia's favorite. (better)
   - The book that you must buy for this class is *Introduction to Sociology*. (wordy)
   - The book you must buy for this class is *Introduction to Sociology*. (better)

8. Overusing *there is/are* or *it is*:
   - There is an idea that Phyllis has. (wordy)
   - Phyllis has an idea. (better)
   - There are three employees who will be recognized for their service today. (wordy)
   - Three employees will be recognized for their service today. (better)

- It is certain that it will rain tomorrow. (wordy)
- It will rain tomorrow. (better)

9. Using phrases that really mean nothing:
   - <u>All in all</u>, it was a good experience. (wordy)
   - It was a good experience. (better)
   - <u>At the present time</u>, the business is out of money. (wordy)
   - The business is out of money. (better)
   - Leshina, my friend from Zambia, did well in school <u>by virtue of the fact</u> that she studied hard. (wordy)
   - Leshina, my friend from Zambia, did well in school because she studied hard. (better)
   - <u>Due to the fact that</u> Sania's passport was stolen, she needs a new one. (wordy)
   - Sania's passport was stolen, so she needs a new one. (better)
   - Ms. Dubois had, <u>for all intents and purposes</u>, made France her new home. (wordy)
   - Ms. Dubois had made France her new home. (better)
   - Mathieu called his uncle last evening <u>for the purpose of</u> asking his advice about handling money. (wordy)
   - Mathieu called his uncle last evening to ask his advice about handling money. (better)
   - Zora <u>came to the realization that</u> she needed more practice. (wordy)
   - Zora realized that she needed more practice. (better)
   - <u>In all cases</u>, there is a solution. (wordy)
   - There is always a solution. (better)
   - <u>In my opinion</u>, water conservation measures are absolutely necessary. (wordy)
   - Water conservation measures are absolutely necessary. (better)
   - <u>In the event that</u> the teacher does not show up, class will be canceled. (wordy)
   - If the teacher does not show up, class will be canceled. (better)
   - <u>In today's world</u>, we need to be careful about computer viruses. (wordy)
   - We need to be careful about computer viruses. (better)
   - <u>In conclusion</u>, drought conditions are spreading around the world. (wordy)
   - Drought conditions are spreading around the world. (better)
   - <u>The reason that</u> the vehicles have been recalled is because there is a safety concern. (wordy)
   - The vehicles have been recalled because there is a safety concern. (better)

10. Repeating abbreviations:
- ATM machine (correct form: ATM) (ATM stands for automated teller machine)
- ACT test (correct form: ACT) (ACT stands for American College Test)
- HIV virus (correct form: HIV) (HIV stands for human immunodeficiency virus)
- PIN number (correct form: PIN) (PIN stands for personal identification number)

Everyday Writing Activity: Avoiding Wordiness

Remove the unnecessary words/phrases in the following sentences and write the improved sentence.

1. The Lee family generally sits down for dinner at 6:30 p.m. in the evening.
2. The plumber was called to the house for the purpose of fixing the faucet that was leaking.
3. Hawaii, which is the 50th state of the United States, is home to many varieties of vegetation.
4. Have you seen Bradley's CD disk anywhere?
5. Green tea is considered to be a remedy for many illnesses and ailments.
6. A deal between the two corporations has, for all intents and purposes, been negotiated.
7. At this point in time, there are no more trips planned for South America.
8. In today's world, traveling to different countries has become very common.
9. Many high school students hoping for admission to American colleges and universities have to take the SAT test.
10. They decided to have ice cream because of it being so hot.

MyWritingLab™ For support in meeting this chapter's objectives, log in to **www.mywritinglab.com** and select **Standard and Non-Standard English**.

English Idioms

LO1
Recognize and
define common
English idioms

An **idiom** is an expression consisting of words that together mean something different from the literal meaning of the individual words that make up the phrase. English idioms can, therefore, sometimes be difficult for some students—especially multilingual students—to understand.

- *A OK*—this idiom means that everything is fine. However, the two words "A" and "OK" don't provide any clues to the actual meaning of this idiom.
- *Castles in the air*—this idiom means to be very unrealistic and daydream. However, the two primary words "castles" and "air" don't provide any clues to the actual meaning of this idiom.

There are several thousand idioms in English. The following list includes some of the more common idioms.

LO2
Use idioms
correctly

At a Glance: English Idioms	
Idiom	**Idiom in Sentence**
A little bird told me (the person does not want to reveal the source of his/her information)	A little bird told me that you are moving to Kenya next year to study African wildlife.
A penny for your thoughts (a way of asking someone what they are thinking)	You look like you are thinking deeply; a penny for your thoughts!

Idiom	Idiom in Sentence
A pretty penny (something is very expensive)	Sports cars can cost a pretty penny.
A steal (something costs much less than it is really worth)	At $200, that cashmere coat is a steal.
About face (to change your mind completely)	Mary Lou did a complete about face when she decided on who she wanted her roommates to be.
Add fuel to the fire (to make a bad situation worse)	The landlord added fuel to the fire by accusing the tenants of not having paid their rent.
Back down (to fail to carry through on something that was promised)	Because she was ill, Grandma backed down on her promise to bake us a chocolate mousse cake.
Back on one's feet (to return to good physical, financial, or social health)	Shahzad is back on his feet after a rough few months following his back surgery.
Call a spade a spade (to speak bluntly)	The Spanish professor called a spade a spade when he described certain students in the class as being lazy.
Call it a day (to finish work for that day)	After 10 hours of steady work, Josephine decided to call it a day.
Call the shots (to be in charge)	In our family, my elder brother has always called the shots.
Daily grind (everyday work routine)	Yuki's daily grind includes a 25-mile commute to work and back.
Dance with death (to do something that is very risky)	Brett and Han-Yu were dancing with death when they decided to race their cars against each other.
Dawn on (to become clear or to occur to someone)	It finally dawned on the store owner what the customer was looking for.
Eager beaver (a person who is eager to do hard work or extra work)	Hye-Joon is an eager beaver, always ready to help out where needed.

Idiom	Idiom in Sentence
Early bird catches the worm (one who arrives early has the greatest chance of success)	Mr. Franz has been waiting outside the electronics store since 4 a.m. because he knows that the early bird catches the worm.
Eat humble pie (to admit one's error and apologize)	The twin brothers had to eat humble pie when their friends caught them cheating while playing poker.
Face the music (to face the consequences of something)	The criminals broke the law. Now they have to face the music.
Fair and square (fairly and honestly)	The debate team from St. John's University won the competition fair and square.
Far cry from (very different from something)	The incident as narrated by Ruben is a far cry from the details his cousin Michael offered the family.
Gear up for (to prepare for something)	The students are gearing up for their final exams this week.
Get a break (to get an opportunity or a good deal on something)	The homeless person got a break when a local shelter offered him free housing for the winter.
Get a clean bill of health (to be pronounced healthy by the doctor)	Mrs. Moreno was happy to get a clean bill of health from her doctor during her post-surgery checkup.
Half-baked (ideas or plans not thought out carefully)	Sandra always comes up with half-baked ideas that land her in trouble.
Half the battle (a large part of the work is done)	Getting the bill passed is half the battle. We can worry about implementing it later.
Hammer away at (to be persistent in doing something)	Amira intends to hammer away at her art project this weekend.
Idiot box (the television)	Don't sit in front of the idiot box all day!
Ill at ease (to be nervous or uncomfortable)	The new student looked ill at ease on the first day of class.

Idiom	Idiom in Sentence
Ill-will (hostile feelings)	There is a lot of ill-will between the two political parties on the matter of tax increases.
Jack-of-all-trades (a person who can do many things)	Call Ben when you need something; he is truly a jack-of-all-trades.
Jam-packed (crowded)	The stadium was jam-packed with football fans.
Johnny-come-lately (a newcomer)	Mark is a Johnny-come-lately and doesn't really understand company policies and procedures yet.
Keep a close watch (on someone/something) (to monitor someone/something)	The nanny kept a close watch on the children as they were playing.
Keep a stiff upper lip (to be brave in the face of challenges)	The army general advised his soldiers to keep a stiff upper lip in the face of new challenges from the enemy.
Keep abreast (of something) (to keep up with something)	Everyone should regularly follow the news so that they can keep abreast of current events.
Laid-back (to have a relaxed, casual attitude about something)	Even in the face of many personal crises, Uncle Alfonso always had a very laid-back attitude.
Lame duck (a government servant who has only a few days left in office and, therefore, has less power)	Because President X was a lame duck, he failed to persuade his political opponents of the need to pass a new tax law.
Last straw (the last insult/mistake one can take and, therefore, there is a reaction)	Penelope's dropping out of college was the last straw for her parents, and they disowned her.
Made for each other (two people are romantically well-suited)	Roy and Mikasi look so happy together that they seem made for each other.
Maiden voyage (the first voyage of a ship or boat)	My parents were on the maiden voyage of the ship "Queen Elizabeth."

Idiom	Idiom in Sentence
Make a beeline for (to hurry toward someone or something)	As soon as the plane landed, the passengers made a beeline for the airport terminal.
Naked eye (the human eye without binoculars, microscope etc.)	It was impossible for anyone to see the bacteria in the petri dish with the naked eye.
Near at hand (to be close or handy)	Josef used the calculator that was near at hand to make some quick calculations.
Neck and neck (to be almost equal in a contest)	The runners ran neck and neck to the finish line.
Odd man out (to be out of place somewhere or among some people)	Nikolai felt as if he was the odd man out at his company's annual picnic.
Oddball (a person who acts differently from the others)	The Petrosky family always kept their distance from their cousin Anton because he was such an oddball.
Of late (recently)	The old man has been having nightmares of late, and needs a medical checkup.
Pack of lies (a series of lies)	The pack of lies the accused told the judge was very troublesome.
Packed in like sardines (to be packed very tightly)	The travelers were packed in like sardines in the overcrowded bus.
Pan out (to work out favorably)	Hopefully your plans to find employment soon will pan out.
Quick and dirty (fast and cheap)	Because Harry had not prepared very well, he did a quick and dirty for his presentation.
Quick as a flash (very quickly)	I opened the door and, quick as a flash, the puppy ran outside.
Quiet as a mouse (very silent)	The child sat as quiet as a mouse at the back of the classroom.

Idiom	Idiom in Sentence
Race against time (to rush to beat a deadline)	Students are often in a race against time as they rush to meet project deadlines.
Rain cats and dogs (to rain very hard)	It was raining cats and dogs, so they had to cancel their plans for the evening.
Raise eyebrows (to cause surprise or disapproval)	Mr. Roberts' lawn, overrun with weeds, began to raise eyes in the neighborhood.
Safe and sound (to be safe and/or healthy)	Chinua's parents were relieved when she returned home safe and sound from the camping trip.
To be on the safe side (to take no chances)	Anita decided to remain on the safe side and both call and e-mail her boss about her absence from work.
Sail right through something (to finish something very easily)	Math has never been a problem for me; I have always sailed through all my math homework and tests.
Tag along with (to follow someone somewhere)	The children tagged along with their parents to the food festival.
Take a beating (to lose money)	The stock market took a beating last Thursday.
Take a chance (to take a risk even though failure is possible)	Mansoor decided to take a chance and invest in the stock market.
Under a cloud (to feel sad or depressed)	The class members have been under a cloud since one of their classmates passed away.
Under one's breath (in a low voice)	The parents spoke under their breath so that the sleeping child would not wake up.
Under one's thumb (to be controlled by someone)	Ben resents that he is under his stepfather's thumb at home.
Vanish into thin air (to disappear without leaving a trace)	The two men who were standing at the street corner seemed to have vanished into thin air.

Idiom	Idiom in Sentence
Vicious circle (an unbroken sequence of cause and effect that has bad results)	The student was caught in a vicious circle of not studying, failing his classes, becoming depressed, not studying, and failing his classes once again.
Vote of confidence (a vote to see if a person/political party has majority support)	The boss received a vote of confidence from his employees when they nominated him for the award.
Wait on someone hand and foot (to serve someone by doing everything possible for him/her)	Mrs. Garrison waited hand and foot on her dying mother during the last few months of her life.
Wait tables (to serve food at a restaurant)	A lot of high school and college students like to get a job waiting tables because the tips are usually very good.
Walk a tightrope (to be in a situation that requires a lot of caution)	Jin-Chao is under a lot of stress because he is walking a financial tightrope.
Yakety-yak (to talk a lot)	As expected, there was a lot of yakety-yak at the high school reunion.
Year in and year out (every year)	We have to spend a lot of money year in and year out to maintain the old family property.
A yes-man (someone who agrees with everything that is being said or done in order to be liked)	Friedrich has adopted a yes-man attitude because he likes to keep everyone happy.
Zero hour (the exact moment when an important decision or action will take place)	The enemy waited until zero hour to begin bombing the villages across the border.
Zero in on (to give full attention to something)	The technician tried to zero in on the problem in the computer's hard drive.
Zoom in on (to get a closer view of something or someone)	The photographer zoomed in on the infant's face, trying to catch the details of the lovely smile.

Everyday Writing Activity: English Idioms

Research the meaning of the following English idioms from the Internet. Then use these idioms in sentences of your own.

1. Act as a guinea pig
2. As busy as a beaver
3. Across the board
4. Bad blood
5. Beat around the bush
6. Dressed to kill
7. Face value
8. Fit like a glove
9. Game plan
10. Hard-nosed

MyWritingLab™ For support in meeting this chapter's objectives, log in to **www.mywritinglab.com** and select **Standard and Non-Standard English**.

Credits

Text

Chapter 2

Page 19: The Myth of Jade. International Colored Gemstone Association.

Page 20 (top): Whale Watching: What an amazing fluke!, Joseph Kula. *National Post*, March 20, 2009.

Page 20 (bottom): Facebook, Businessinsider.com

Page 21: The Melting Pot Continues: International Students in America. Reproduced by permission. www.collegeview.com

Page 22: What Is Yoga?, The American Yoga Association.

Page 24: The Basics of Global Warming, Reprinted by permission of the Environmental Defense Fund.

Page 26 (top): Middle Eastern Cuisine, Beth Hrusch, Article Insider.

Page 26 (bottom): Class Mammalia, Matthew Wind & Phil Myers, Animal Diversity Web, Accessed February 2, 2011.

Page 27 (top): New Zealand Cities and Towns, Virtual New Zealand.

Page 27 (bottom): How Much Do Ski Helmets Help? Denis Cummings, March 21, 2009, *Finding Dulcinea*. Reprinted with permission.

Page 29 (top): African Mask Symbolism, Essortment.com

Page 29 (bottom): Benefits of Learning a Foreign Language, Frances Simon, March 15, 2009, Helium.com

Page 30: Acai Berries and Acai Berry Juice—What Are the Health Benefits? Reprinted with permission from Web MD.

Page 32: Special Olympics: Who We Are. Used with permission of Special Olympics, Inc.

Chapter 3

Page 39: U.S. Fish and Wildlife Service.

Page 43: *Occupational Outlook Handbook*, 2010–11 Edition.

Chapter 5

Page 58: Bushman Rabbit, Global Oneness.

Page 59: *Gandhi, An Autobiography*, Mohandas Gandhi, Beacon Press, 1993.

Page 61: How MP3 players work, Explainthatstuff.com

Page 62: Types of Shoppers, Mike Sullivan, English 120 at Montana State University.

Page 64: Nontraditional Students' Library Satisfaction, *Library Philosophy and Practice* vol. 5 no. 1 Fall 2002.

Page 65: Give a cheer to the experimental AIDS vaccine and then get back to work—an editorial by The Cleveland Plain Dealer Editorial Board. Published Wednesday, September 30, 2009. http://www.cleveland.com/opinion/index.ssf/2009/09/give_a_cheer_to_the_experiment.html. Reproduced by permission.

Page 67: Professor gives reasons why students fail, Shamekila Quarles, *The Gramblinite*, 4/23/06.

Page 69: Why British students are opting for American universities, *The Independent*, 30 Nov. 2006.

Chapter 9

Page 126: 7 ways to be worth following on Twitter, Twitip.com

Page 128: Excerpts from Graffiti Wall, www.ricksteves.com. Reprinted with permission.

Page 141: "The Myth of the Latin Woman: I Just Met a Girl Named Maria" by Judith Ortiz Cofer. From *The Latin Deli: Prose and Poetry*. Copyright University of Georgia Press. Reproduced by permission.

Page 143: My Global Study Experience in Dubai: Strong Self-Image Key to Negotiating in Distant Cultures, Brittney Huntley, THE BLACK COLLEGIAN Magazine, First Semester 2006 Super Issue.

Page 147: Excerpt from "The Good Immigrant Student" by Bich Minh Nguyen reproduced with permission.

Chapter 10

Page 150: Jacket Design from *We wish to inform you that tomorrow we will be killed with our families* by Philip Gourevitch. Copyright © 1998 by Philip Gourevitch. Reprinted by permission of Farrar, Straus and Giroux, LLC. CAUTION: Users are warned that this work is protected under copyright laws and downloading is strictly prohibited. The right to reproduce or transfer the work via any medium must be secured with Farrar, Straus and Giroux, LLC.

Page 151: First paragraph from *We wish to inform you that tomorrow we will be killed with our families*, Philip Gourevitch, Farrar, Straus and Giroux, LLC, 1998.

Page 153: Press Release: Software Creates Privacy Mode to Help Secure Android Smartphones. Reprinted with permission of North Carolina State University News Service.

Page 168: Reprinted by permission from Gregorio Billikopf.

Page 170: Reproduced by permission of Debra Behrens.

Chapter 11

Page 196: Women less likely than men to fake soccer injuries, study finds, by Thomas Maugh. *Los Angeles Times*, July 7, 2011. http://www.latimes.com/health/boostershots/la-heb-women-soccer-injuries-07072011,0,5272841.story. Reproduced by permission.

Page 200: "The Truth About Lying." Copyright © 1981 by Judith Viorst. Originally appeared in *Redbook*. Reprinted by permission of Lescher & Lescher, Ltd. All rights reserved.

Chapter 12

Page 211: Reprinted with permission from Medscape 2011.

Page 227: From "The Surprising Causes of Those College Tuition Hikes" by Kim Clark. *US News and World Report*. Reproduced by permission of Wright's Media.

Page 229: MSNBC.COM Copyright 2004 by MSNBC INTERACTIVE NEWS, LLC. Reproduced with permission of MSNBC INTERACTIVE NEWS, LLC in the format Textbook via Copyright Clearance Center.

Page 231: Illegal Immigration to the United States: Causes and Policy Solutions reproduced with permission by Udall Center for Studies in Public Policy, University of Arizona.

Page 232 (Figure): Arrivals of unauthorized immigrants by time period, 1980–2004, by Jeffrey Passel, in *The Size and Characteristics of the Unauthorized Migrant Population in the U.S.: Estimates Based on the March 2005 Current Population Survey*, March 7, 2006. Washington, DC: Pew Hispanic Center. p. 2. http://pewhispanic.org/reports/report.php?ReportID=61.

Chapter 13

Page 239: Reproduced by permission.

Page 258: Excerpt from Best places to work 2010 by Christina Antoniades reprinted by permission of Baltimore Magazine, Feb., 2010.

513

Page 261: Reprinted by permission of the Red and Black.

Page 265: "Community College vs. University" by Jeren Canning. *The Globe Online*, Monday, July 18, 2005. http://www.slccglobelink.com/2.16039/community-college-vs-university-1.2299136. Reproduced by permission.

Chapter 14

Page 271: "In praise of the F word" by Mary Sherry. Reproduced by permission.

Page 288: "Early education pays off," James Fish, *Pittsburgh Post-Gazette*, 02/02/10. Reprinted with permission.

Page 291: Reprinted by permission of the Asia Society.

Chapter 15

Page 318: Patient Education Survey, Stanford University School of Medicine.

Page 323: Inside the Knock-off Tennis Shoe Factory, Nicholas Schmidle, *New York Times* August 19, 2010.

Photos

Chapter 1

Page 2: Andresr/Shutterstock; p. 14 (top): Jupiterimages/Thinkstock; p. 14 (bottom): Photos.com/Thinkstock

Chapter 2

Page 16: Andresr/Shutterstock; p. 21: Brocreative/Shutterstock; p. 24: artiomp/Shutterstock; p. 30: FoodCollection/PhotoLibrary; p. 32: UPI/Newscom

Chapter 3

Page 26: alexskopje/Shutterstock; p. 39: John.59/Dreamstime.com

Chapter 4

Page 45: © 2011 Photos.com, a division of Getty Images. All rights reserved. 50: © 2011 Photos.com, a division of Getty Images. All rights reserved. p. 52 (top left): © 2011 Photos.com, a division of Getty Images. All rights reserved. p. 52 (top right): © 2011 Photos.com, a division of Getty Images. All rights reserved. p. 52 (bottom left): claudio zaccherini/Shutterstock; p. 52 (bottom right): © 2011 Photos.com, a division of Getty Images. All rights reserved.

Chapter 5

Page 56: © 2011 Photos.com, a division of Getty Images. All rights reserved. p. 58: Marek Patzer/Anka Agency/Photoshot; p. 59: Dinodia Photos/Alamy; p. 61: Hugh Threlfall/Alamy; p. 62: Jack Hollingsworth/Photodisc/Thinkstock

Chapter 6

Page 78: © 2011 Photos.com, a division of Getty Images. All rights reserved. p. 81: Sunny_baby/Shutterstock

Chapter 7

Page 89: Vladimir Wrangel/Shutterstock

Chapter 8

Page 108: PEANUTS © 1974 Peanuts Worldwide LLC. Dist. by Universal UClick. Reprinted with permission. All rights reserved.

Chapter 9

Page 124: Gregory Glau; p. 141: © Heinemann 2011, Photograph by Melissa Cooperman; p. 147: Bich Minh Nguyen

Chapter 10

Page 150: Jacket Design from *We wish to inform you that tomorrow we will be killed with our families* by Philip Gourevitch. Copyright © 1998 by Philip Gourevitch. Reprinted by permission of Farrar, Straus and Giroux, LLC. CAUTION: Users are warned that this work is protected under copyright laws and downloading is strictly prohibited. The right to reproduce or transfer the work via any medium must be secured with Farrar, Straus and Giroux, LLC. p. 153: Xuxian Jiang; p. 168: Gregorio Billikopf; p. 170: Debra Behrens.

Chapter 11

Page 176: Claudia Dewald/iStockphoto; p. 192: Terry Morris/iStockphoto; p. 193: asiana/Shutterstock; p. 199 (left): Dan Bannister/Shutterstock; p. 199 (center): manzrussali/Shutterstock; p. 199 (right): Tyler Olson/Shutterstock; p. 200: AP Photos/Richard Drew

Chapter 12

Page 206: AP Photos/The Anchorage Daily News, Erik Hill; p. 211: WebMD www.webmd.com; p. 229: Claudio Lavanga

Chapter 13

Page 236: Copyright *U.S. News & World Report*, August 2010. Reproduced by permission. p. 239: PHOTOlink/Newscom; p. 240: Andia/Alamy; pp. 251, 254: ARENA Creative/Shutterstock; p. 261: Eva Vasquez; p. 262: robjudgesstudying/Alamy; p. 265: Jeren Canning

Chapter 14

Page 268: Steve Benson/Creators Syndicate; p. 285: Kiselev Andrey Valerevich/Shutterstock

Chapter 15

Page 298: Layland Masuda/Shutterstock; pp. 308, 309: The Encyclopedia of Earth; p. 313: Google; p. 321: CBS News

Chapter 16

Page 325: The Photo Works/Alamy; p. 339: Thomas J. Abercrombie/National Geographic Stock; p. 342: Farzana Wahidy

Chapter 17

Page 361: Laurence Gough/Shutterstock

Chapter 18

Page 371: thumb/Shutterstock

Part 4

Page 386: lhoop/iStockphoto

Index

A

AAA Style Guide, 328
a/an, 411–413
Abbreviations, 474–475
Academic reading and writing, 4
"Acai Berries and Acai Berry
         Juice - What Are the
         Health Benefits?"
         (WebMD), 30–31
Active voice, 424–425
Addison, Joseph, 7
Adjectives, 402–403
Adverbs, 403–404
Agreement
    pronoun-antecedent, 433–436
    subject-verb, 431–432
Alta Vista, 311
American Anthropological
         Association, 328
American Psychological
         Association (APA), 327,
         346. *See also* APA docu-
         mentation format
Analysis, definition by, 63
Annotation, 30–31
Antecedents
    agreement between pronoun and,
         433–436
    explanation of, 433
Antoniades, Christina Breda, 258–260
Antonyms, 490–491
APA documentation format
    explanation of, 327, 346
    for in-text citations, 346–347
    for references, 347–351
    sample research paper in, 352–357
Apostrophes, 464–465
Application résumés, 378
Argument. *See also* Persuasion
    explanation of, 64–66, 71, 269
    strategies for, 90, 270
"Art Education" (Burba), 293–295
Aristotle, 72, 279–280
Articles
    definite, 411
    explanation of, 411

guidelines for use of, 412–416
    indefinite, 411–412
Assumptions, 33
Audience
    addressing your, 136–137
    for cause and effect, 206–207
    for comparison and contrast, 238
    critical thinking about, 51
    for division and classification, 178
    explanation of, 50
    genre and, 90–91
    for informative writing, 152
    for shared experience, 125, 126
    for writing, 4, 50–52, 113

B

"The Basics of Global Warming"
         (Fightglobalwarming.com),
         24–25
"Best Places to Work 2010"
         (Antoniades), 258–260
Bias, 33–34. *See also* Sexist language
Billikopf, Gregorio, 168–169
Bing, 312
BioMedCentral, 306
Body
    of essays, 104, 105
    of timed or in-class essay exams,
         362
Body language, 177, 178
Bolden, Charles Frank, Jr.,
         173–174
Books, in libraries, 303–305
Brainstorming
    explanation of, 80, 157
    for informative writing, 158
    for timed or in-class essay exams,
         363–365
Bullet points, 189–190

C

Canning, Jeren W., 264–266
Capitalization rules, 483–486
Carter, John, 21–22
Causal chain, 209

Cause and effect
    audience for, 208–209
    cluster diagrams for, 216–217
    critical thinking about, 216,
         222–223
    drafts of, 220–221, 223–226
    explanation of, 66–67, 71,
         207–208
    introduction to, 219–220
    organization of, 218–219
    professional examples of,
         211–212, 227–235
    purpose of, 208
    relationships in, 209–210
    revision of, 220–223
    thesis for, 217–218
    transitional words for, 102
    used for persuasion, 270
    used for persuasion, 270
Centers for Disease Control, "Parent's
         Guide to Childhood
         Immunization," 293–295
The Chicago Manual of Style, 328
Chronological, transitional words
         for, 102
Claims, 269. *See also* Thesis/thesis
         statements
Clark, Kim, 227–229
Classification, 62–63, 71, 177.
         See also Division and
         classification
Clauses, 422–423
"Climate Change Impact"
         (Environmental Protection
         Agency), 179
Clustering, 84, 85
Cofer, Judith Ortiz, 141–143
Colloquial style, 497
Colons, 462–463
.com, 315
Commas, 457–459
Comma splices, 438–439
Common nouns, 388
"Community College vs.
         University" (Canning),
         264–266

Comparative approach to
    organization, 134
Comparison, 68
Comparison and contrast. *See also*
    Evaluation
    example of, 239–241
    explanation of, 68–69, 71
    function of, 238, 239
    used for persuasion, 270
Complex sentences, 428
Compound sentences, 427–428
Conclusion
    to essays, 105
    in timed or in-class essay exams, 362
    transitional words for, 102
Confusing word pairs, 481–483
Conjunctions, 408–409
Context
    explanation of, 53
    of reader, 53
    of writer, 53–54
    for writing, 4
Contractions, 495–496
Contrast, 68
Coordinating conjunctions, 408, 409
Correlative conjunctions, 408
Council of Science Editors, 328
Countable nouns, 389, 412
CQ Researcher, 306
Credibility, appeal to, 73–74
Criteria
    for evaluations, 237, 245–246
    explanation of, 48
Critical reading
    applied to visual text, 13
    explanation of, 6, 7
    questions for, 7–8
Critical thinking
    about audience, 51
    about cause and effect, 216,
        222–223
    about division and classification,
        183, 194–195
    about evaluation, 245, 252–253,
        256–257
    about informative writing, 157, 167
    about job application letters, 374
    about persuasion, 275–276, 287
    about reader's context, 53
    about research, 91
    about revision, 114, 116, 137,
        163–164, 190–191

about shared experiences, 131
about writing, 6, 131
about writing purpose, 47
applied to visual text, 13
explanation of, 6
for reflection, 140, 167, 195, 226,
    256, 287
Critical thinking skills, 5–6
Critical writing
    applied to visual text, 13
    explanation of, 6, 11, 12
    questions for, 11–12
CSE documentation format, 328
Cubing, 86
"Cultural Differences? Or, Are We
    Really that Different?"
    (Billikopf), 168–169
Cummings, Denis, 27–28

D

Dangling modifiers, 441–442
Dashes, 466–467
Databases
    library, 303–305
    periodical, 305–307
Declarative sentences, 429
Definite articles, 411
Definition writing
    explanation of, 63–64, 71
    used for persuasion, 270
Demonstrative pronouns, 398, 399
Dependent clauses, 422–423
Dependent marker words,
    422, 423
Description
    explanation of, 58–59, 70
    to share experience, 126–129
    strategies for, 90
    used for persuasion, 270
"Developing Global Skills for an
    International Career"
    (Peters-Behrens),
    170–172
The Diary of Anne Frank (Frank), 4
Dictionaries, 308–310
Difference, transitional words
    for, 102
Directions, 151–152
Direct object, 419–420
Discovery activities. *See* Invention
    strategies
Division, 177

Division and classification.
    See also Classification
analyzing through, 179
audience for, 178
critical thinking about, 183,
    194–195
drafts of, 185–189, 192–194
explanation of, 177
introduction in, 187
listing in, 184–185
organization of, 185–187
professional examples of,
    196–204
purpose of, 178
revision of, 188–194
thesis statement in, 185
Documentation. *See also* Research
    papers; Sources
    APA format for, 346–357
    explanation of, 320, 327–328
    MLA format for, 328–345
    plagiarism and, 326–327
DogPile, 312
Domain, Internet, 314–315
"Don't Call Me a Hot Tamale"
    (Cofer), 141–143
Double negatives, 444
Drafts. *See also* Revision
    of body, 104–105
    of cause and effect, 220–221,
        223–226
    of conclusion, 105
    of division and classification,
        185–189, 192–194
    of evaluation, 250–251, 253–256
    examples of, 119–121, 134–136,
        138–139
    explanation of, 94–95
    of informative writing, 159–161,
        165–167
    of introduction, 104
    organizational approaches for,
        133–135
    of paragraphs, 98–99
    of persuasion, 282–283, 285–287
    of shared experiences, 134–135,
        138–139
    of thesis statement, 95–97
    for timed or in-class essay exams,
        366–367
    of topic sentences, 99–100
    of transitions, 101–103

E

"Early Education Pays Off: High-quality Programs Are Good for Kids, for Society and for Business" (Fish), 288–289

Ebert, Roger, 239–241

EBSCO Host's ERIC, 306

Editing. *See also* Drafts; Revision
explanation of, 117
of timed or in-class essay exams, 367

.edu, 315

The Elements of Style (Strunk & White), 109

Ellipsis, 472–473

E-mail, 372–373

Emotional appeal, 74–76

Emphasis, transitional words for, 102

Encyclopedias, 308–310

Environmental Protection Agency, 179

EPSCO Host's Academic Search Complete, 305

Essay exams, 362–367

Essays
body of, 104, 105
conclusion of, 105
format for, 100
introduction to, 104

Ethical appeal, 73–74, 76. *See also Ethos*

Ethos, 72–74, 76, 270

Evaluation
audience for, 238–239
critical thinking about, 245, 252–253, 256–257
drafts of, 250–251, 253–256
explanation of, 48, 237–238
introduction to, 250
invention activities for, 245–246
organization of, 247–249
professional examples of, 239–241, 258–266
purpose of, 238
revision of, 250–253
thesis for, 247
use of comparison and contrast for, 239–242

every/many, 436

Evidence, 33, 269

Example, transitional words for, 102

F

Feelings, appeal to, 74–76. *See also Pathos*

Field research
explanation of, 316
methods for, 316–318

Fish, James, 288–289

"Five Surprising Reasons You're Gaining Weight" (Zelman), 211–212

Fox, Raychelle, 9–10

Fragments, 441

Fragments, sentence, 441

Frank, Anne, 4

Freewriting
for evaluation, 246
explanation of, 83–84
for shared experience, 132

Function, definition by, 63

Fused sentences, 440–441

Future tense, 392, 393

G

Genre
explanation of, 79, 90
selection of, 90–91

"Give a Cheer to the Experimental AIDS Vaccine and Then Get Back to Work - An Editorial" (The Plain Dealer Editorial Board), 65–66

"The Good Immigrant Student" (Nguyen), 147–148

Google, 311–313

Gourevitch, Philip, 150, 151

.gov, 315

"Graffiti Wall" (Rick Steves' Europe), 128–129

H

Headings, 24–25

Hemingway, Ernest, 126

Higher-level reading strategies
analysis of text as, 33–34
annotation as, 30–33
explanation of, 29–30

Homonyms, 479–480

Homophones, 479

"How Much Do Ski Helmets Help?" (Cummings), 27–28

"How to Excel in Your College Classes" (Fox), 9–10

Huntley, Brittney, 143–146

Hyphens, 465–466

I

Idioms, 505–511

"Illegal Immigration to the United States" (Udall Center for Studies in Public Policy), 231–235

Imperative sentences, 429

In-class essay exam
checklist for, 363–364
determining purpose of, 363–364
organization for, 362–363
student example of, 365–367
time management for, 364

Indefinite articles, 411–412

Indefinite pronouns, 399

Independent clauses, 422–423

Indirect object, 419–420

Infinitives, 395

Informative writing
audience for, 152
brainstorming for, 157–158
critical thinking about, 157, 167
drafts for, 159–161, 165–167
example of, 153–154
explanation of, 47–48, 60–61, 70, 151
organizational approaches to, 159–161
professional examples of, 168–174
purpose of, 152
revision of, 161–167
thesis statement for, 158, 159

"In Praise of the F Word" (Sherry), 271–273

Interjections, 409–410

Internet
e-mail and, 372–373
evaluating information on, 314–316

Internet (*continued*)
  keyword searches on, 312–314
  overview of, 311
  search engines for, 311–312
Internet Corporation for Assigned
    Names and Numbers
    (Icann), 316
Internet domain, 314–315
Interrogative pronouns,
    398, 399
Interrogative sentences, 429
Interviews
  requests for job, 375
  research, 317
In-text citations, 328
Intransitive verbs, 421
Introductions
  for cause and effect, 219–220
  for division and classification, 187
  for essays, 104
  for evaluation, 250
  for informative writing, 161
  for persuasion, 282
  for shared experience, 134–135
  for timed or in-class essay exams,
    362
Invention strategies
  brainstorming as, 80, 157, 158,
    276, 277
  clustering as, 84–85, 216–217
  cubing as, 86–87
  explanation of, 79–81
  freewriting as, 83–84, 132, 246
  listing as, 81–83, 184–185
  use of, 87–88
Irregular verbs, 394

J

Job advertisement, 376
Job application letters
  critical thinking about, 374
  example of, 377
  explanation of, 373–374
  information included in,
    374–375
Journals, 4–5
JStor, 305

K

Keyword searches, 312–314

L

"Language Change" (National
    Science Foundation),
    196–197
Lavanga, Claudio, 229–231
LexisNexis Academic, 305
Librarians, 302
Libraries
  books in, 303–305
  databases in, 303, 304
  encyclopedias and dictionaries in,
    308–310
  periodicals and specialized in-
    dexes in, 305–307
  tips for using, 302
  Web sites for, 303
Linguistic Society of America, 328
Listing
  bullets for, 189–190
  in division and classification,
    184–185
  explanation of, 81–82
Livaccari, Chris, 291–292
Logical appeal, 75–76. *See also Logos*
Logos, 72, 73, 75–76, 270
LSA Style Sheet, 328

M

Main idea strategies
  explanation of, 18–19
  focus on headings and subhead-
    ings as, 24—25
  outlining as, 27–28
  reading and understanding indi-
    vidual paragraphs as, 25–26
  reading introduction and conclu-
    sion first as, 19
  skimming as, 20–24
Maugh, Thomas H., 196–197
"The Melting Pot Continues:
    International Students in
    America" (Carter), 21–22
MERB, 306
Metaphor, 58
Michener, James A., 110
MLA documentation format
  explanation of, 327
  in-text citations in, 328–333
  sample research paper in,
    338–345

Works Cited entries in, 328,
    333–337, 345
Modern Language Association,
    109, 327. *See also MLA
    documentation format*
Modes, 578
Modifiers
  dangling, 441–442
  misplaced, 443–444
"MP3 Players" (Explainthatstuff.com),
    60–61
MSN, 311
"My Global Study Experience
    in Dubai: Strong Self-
    Image Key to Negotiating
    in Distant Cultures"
    (Huntley), 143–146

N

Narrative writing
  explanation of, 59–60, 70
  to share experience,
    128–129
  strategies for, 90
Negatives, double, 444
.net, 315
Nguyen, Bich Minh, 147–148
Notes
  example of source, 321
  strategies for source, 319–320
Nouns
  common, 388
  countable, 389, 412
  explanation of, 387
  proper, 388
  uncountable, 389, 412
Numbers, 476–477

O

Object, of sentence, 419–420
Object complements, 421
Object pronouns, 400
Observations, 316–317
Oral presentations, 368–369
.org, 315
Organization
  for cause and effect, 218–220
  comparative approach to, 134
  for division and classification,
    185–187

for evaluation, 247–249
for informative writing, 159–161
for persuasion, 279–282
reflective approach to, 133–134
sequential approach to, 133
for shared experiences, 133–135
or/nor, 435
Outlines
creating simple, 27
explanation of, 92
scratch, 92–93

P

Paragraphs
explanation of, 98–99
reading and understanding individual, 25–26
topic sentence in, 25–26, 98–100
transitions between, 445–446
Paraphrase, 320, 322–323
Parentheses, 470–471
"Parent's Guide to Childhood Immunization" (Centers for Disease Control), 293–295
Passive voice, 424, 425
Past tense, 391, 393
Pathos, 72–76, 270
Peer review
benefits of, 116
explanation of, 111–112
guidelines for, 112–114
questions for, 114, 115
revision based on, 135–136, 181–182, 188–189, 220–221, 250–252, 282–283
Perfect form of verb, 392, 393
Perfect progressive form of verb, 393
Periodical databases, 305–307
Periodicals, in libraries, 305–307
Periods, 450–451
Personal pronouns, 398, 399
Persuasion. *See also* Argument
brainstorming for, 276–277
critical thinking about, 275–276, 287
drafts of, 282–283, 285–287
emotional appeal as, 74–75, 270
ethical appeal as, 72–74, 76, 270
explanation of, 48–49, 64–66, 269
introduction for, 282

logical appeal as, 72, 73, 75–76, 270
organization of, 279–282
problem-solving and, 274
professional examples of, 271–273, 288–295
revision of, 282–285
rhetorical strategies for, 72–73, 270, 274
thesis statement for, 277–278
Peters-Behrens, Debra, 170–172
Plural pronouns, 400, 434
Possessive pronouns, 399
Post-reading strategies, 34–35
Predicate, 418, 419
Prefixes, 35, 492–493
Prepositions
explanation of, 405
functions of, 405–407
Prereading strategies, 17–18
Present tense, 391–393
Prewriting strategies. *See* Invention strategies
"Privacy Mode Helps Secure Android Smartphones" (ScienceDaily), 153–154
Problem-solving, in persuasive writing, 274
"Professor Gives Reasons Why Students Fail" (Quarles), 67
Progressive form of verb, 392, 393
Pronoun-antecedent agreement
explanation of, 433–434
problems related to, 434–436
Pronouns
clear references to, 283–284
demonstrative, 398, 399
explanation of, 397, 433
indefinite, 399
interrogative, 398, 399
object, 400
personal, 398, 399
plural, 400, 434
possessive, 399
reflexive, 398, 399
relative, 398–399
singular, 400, 434
subject, 400
Proofreading, 118
Proper nouns, 388

PsycINFO, 306
Publishing, 119–121
Punctuation
apostrophe, 464–465
colon, 462–463
comma, 457–459
dash, 466–467
ellipsis, 472–473
exclamation point, 455
explanation of, 449
hyphen, 465–466
parentheses, 470–471
period, 450–451
question mark, 452–454
quotation mark, 468–470
semicolon, 460–461
Purpose
of cause and effect, 206
of comparison and contrast, 238
of division and classification, 178
of evaluation, 238
genre and, 90–91
of informative writing, 152
to share experience, 125–126
of writing, 4, 46–47, 113, 125–126

Q

Quarles, Shamekila, 67
Question marks, 452–454
Questionnaires, 317–318
Quotation marks, 468–470
Quotations, 320–322

R

Reader-centered writing, 50
Readers. *See* Audience
Reader's context, 53
Reading
academic, 4
critical, 6, 7, 13
types of precollege, 3
Reading strategies
higher-level, 29–34
main idea, 18–28
post-reading, 34–35
prereading, 17–18
supporting details, 28–29
Reason, appeal to, 75–76. *See also* *Logos*

Reflective approach to organization, 133–134

Reflexive pronouns, 398, 399

Refutation, 362

Relative pronouns, 398–399

Research. *See also* Sources
determining need for, 91
field, 316–318
Internet, 311–316
library, 302–310
planning for, 319

Research papers. *See also*
Documentation; Sources
avoiding plagiarism in, 326–327
choosing topic for, 299–300
finding and evaluating sources for, 302–319
incorporating sources in, 321–324
in MLA style, 338–345
narrowing topic for, 300–301
note taking for, 319–321

Responses, 37, 38

Résumés
application, 378
elements of, 379–380
example of, 382
format for, 380–381
working, 378

Revision. *See also* Drafts
of cause and effect, 220–223
of division and classification, 188–194
editing and, 117
of evaluation, 250–253
example of, 116–117
explanation of, 109
function of, 110–111, 114
importance of, 109, 110
of informative writing, 161–167
peer review for, 111–116,
135–136, 181–182,
188–189, 220–221,
250–252, 282–283
of persuasion, 282–285
proofreading and, 118–119
of shared experience, 135–140
strategies for, 111–113
of timed or in-class essay exams, 367

Revision checklist, 138, 164, 191,
223, 253, 284–285

Rhetorical appeals
ethos as, 72–74, 76, 270
logos as, 72, 73, 75–76, 270
pathos as, 72–76, 270
for persuasion, 72–73, 270, 274

Rhetorical situation, 54

Run-on sentences, 440

S

ScienceDirect, 306

Scratch outlines, 92–93

Search engines, 311–312

Semicolons, 460–461

Sensory details, 58

Sentence complements, 421

Sentence errors
comma splice as, 438–439
dangling modifiers as, 441–442
double negatives as, 444
misplaced modifiers as, 443–444
run-on sentences as, 440
sentence fragments as, 441

Sentence fragments, 441

Sentences
clauses in, 422–423
combining, 252
complex, 428
compound, 427–428
declarative, 429
explanation of, 418
imperative, 429
interrogative, 429
object of, 419–422
revision of awkward, 221–222
simple, 427
subjects and predicates of, 418–419
topic, 25–26
transitions between, 445
transitions in, 445–447
voice in, 424–425

Sequential approach to
organization, 133

"7 Ways to Be Worth Following on
Twitter" (JoLynne), 126–127

Sexist language, 497–499

Shared experiences. *See also*
Description; Narrative
writing

audience and purpose for, 125,
126
critical thinking about, 131
drafts for, 134–135, 138–139
examples of, 126–129
for informative writing, 159–161
organizational approaches for,
133–135
professional examples of, 141–148
revision of, 135–140
writing thesis statement for,
132–133

Sherry, Mary, 271–273

"Shutter Island" (Ebert), 239–241

Similarity, transitional words for,
102

Simile, 58

Simple form of verb, 392, 393

Simple sentences, 427

Singular pronouns, 400, 434

Sources. *See also* Research
analysis of, 33
documentation of, 320, 327–328
(*See also* Documentation)
field research, 316–318
incorporated into research papers,
321–324
Internet, 311–316
library, 302–310
method to quote, 163, 321–322

"Special Olympics: Who We Are"
(Special Olympics), 32–33

Spelling errors
for confusing word pairs,
481–483
for homonyms, 479–480
resulting from unfamiliarity with
rules of capitalization,
483–486

Split infinitives, 395

Structure, definition by, 63

Strunk, William, 109

Subheadings, 24–25

Subject pronouns, 400

Subject (sentence)
compound, 435
explanation of, 418, 419
identification of, 419

Subject-verb agreement, 431–432

Subordinating conjunctions, 408, 409

Suffixes, 35, 493–494

Summaries
  examples of, 39–40, 42
  explanation of, 37, 38, 320
  job application, 42
  job description, 43–44
  of source material, 322
  uses for, 41–42
Supporting details, 28–29
"The Surprising Causes of Those
    College Tuition Hikes"
    (Clark), 227–229
Surveys, 317–318
Synonyms, 489

T

Text, 33–34
the, 411, 413–414
Thesis/thesis statements
  for cause and effect, 218
  characteristics of, 95–96
  for division and classification, 185
  for evaluation, 247
  explanation of, 65, 133, 159
  for informative writing, 59, 158
  for persuasion, 277–278
  for shared experience, 132–133
  strong and weak, 96
  writing purpose and, 96–97
Thinking. *See* Critical thinking
Timed-essay exams
  checklist for, 363–364
  determining purpose of, 363–364
  organization for, 362–363
  student example of, 365–367
  time management for, 364
Time management, 364
Topics
  decisions related to, 79
  explanation of, 133, 159, 218
  for research papers, 299–301
  rhetorical situation and, 54
  strategies to narrow, 300–301
Topic sentences
  explanation of, 25–26, 98–100
  thesis vs., 133
Transitional expressions, 446–447
Transitions
  explanation of, 101–102, 445
  list of common, 446–447
  between paragraphs, 445–446

  between sentences, 445
  types of, 102
Transitive verbs, 420–421
"Travel for Distinction: UGA
    Study Abroad Offers
    Many Options" (Vasquez),
    261–264
"The Truth About Lying" (Viorst),
    200–204

U

Uncountable nouns, 389, 412
URL extensions, 314, 315
URLs (Uniform Resource Locators),
    311, 312
"U.S. Fish and Wildlife Service
    Releases Annual List of
    Foreign Candidates under
    Endangered Species Act,"
    39–40

V

Vasquez, Eva, 261–264
Verbs
  agreement between subject and,
    431–432
  explanation of, 391
  infinitives of, 395
  intransitive, 421
  irregular, 394
  perfect form of, 392
  perfect progressive form of, 393
  progressive form of, 392
  simple form of, 392
  transitive, 420–421
Verb tenses, 391–393
Viorst, Judith, 200–204
Visuals
  analysis of body language in, 177,
    178
  critical thinking reading and
    writing about, 13
  questions about, 13
Vocabulary, 34–35, 488. *See also*
    Words
Voice, 424–425

W

Web browsers, 311
Web sites. *See also* Internet

  evaluation of, 314–316
  for libraries, 303
"We wish to inform you that tomor-
    row we will be killed with
    our families" (Gourevitch),
    150, 151
"What Is Keeping Italian Men at
    Home?" (Lavanga), 229–231
"What Is Yoga?" (American Yoga
    Association), 22–23
"What's Next for NASA?"
    (Bolden), 173–174
White, E. B., 109
"Why British Students Are Opting
    for American Universities"
    (Independent Web site), 69
"Women Less Likely Than Men to
    Fake Soccer Injuries, Study
    Finds" (Maugh), 196–197
Wordiness, 500–504
Word pairs, confusing, 481–483
Words
  analysis of use of, 35
  antonyms, 490–491
  colloquial, 497
  contractions for, 495–496
  dependent marker, 422, 423
  prefixes for, 492–493
  sexist, 497–499
  suffixes for, 493–494
  synonyms, 489
  transitional, 102
  use of unnecessary, 500–504
Working résumés, 378
Workplace, e-mail in, 372–373
Writer-centered writing, 50
Writer's block, 79
Writer's context, 53–54
Writing
  academic, 4
  audience and, 50–52, 113
  context of, 53–54
  critical, 6, 11–13
  to evaluate, 48, 237–266 (*See also*
    Evaluation)
  to explain why, 207–235 (*See also*
    Cause and effect)
  getting started with, 79–80
  to inform, 47–48, 151–174
    (*See also* Informative
    writing)

Writing (*continued*)
  to persuade, 48–49, 64–65,
      268–295 (*See also*
      Persuasion)
  purpose for, 4, 46–49, 113,
      125–126
  reader-centered, 50
  rhetorical situation of, 54
  to share experiences, 125–148
      (*See also* Shared
      experiences)
  types of precollege, 3
  writer-centered, 50
Writing process
  drafting step in, 90–107

editing step in, 117
invention step in, 80–88
proofreading step in, 118
publishing step in, 119–121
revision step in, 109–122
thesis statement and, 96–97
Writing strategies. *See also specific*
      writing strategies
argument and, 48–49, 64–66,
      72–77
cause and effect, 66–68
classification, 62–63
comparison and contrast, 68–70
definition, 63–64
description, 58–59

explanation of, 57–58
as influence on writing,
      90–91
information and, 47–48, 60–61
narration, 59–60
summary of, 70–71

Y

Yahoo, 311
"Your Brain on Languages"
      (Livaccari), 291–292

Z

Zelman, Kathleen, 211–212